Othello
New Perspectives

Othello in his jealous phrenzy. preparing to smother Desdemona
Page

The frontispiece illustration from *Dramatic Tales from Shakespeare* (London: J. Duncombe, n.d.) from the early nineteenth century; the caption underneath reads: "Othello in his jealous phrenzy, preparing to smother Desdemona" (Act V, scene ii). Reproduced courtesy of the Art Collection of the Folger Shakespeare Library.

Othello

New Perspectives

EDITED BY
Virginia Mason Vaughan
and Kent Cartwright

Madison ● Teaneck
Fairleigh Dickinson University Press
London: Associated University Presses

Associated University Presses
440 Forsgate Drive
Cranbury, NJ 08512

Associated University Presses
16 Barter Street
London WC1A 2AH, England

Associated University Presses
P.O. Box 338, Port Credit
Mississauga, Ontario
Canada L5G 4L8

The paper used in this publication meets the requirements of the American National Standard for Permanence of Paper for Printed Library Materials Z39.48–1984.

Library of Congress Cataloging-in-Publication Data

Othello : new perspectives / edited by Virginia Mason Vaughan and Kent Cartwright.
    p.   cm.
  Includes bibliographical references.
  ISBN 0-8386-3398-6 (alk. paper) (cloth)
  ISBN 0-8386-3708-6 (alk. paper) (paperback)
  1. Shakespeare, William, 1564–1616. Othello. I. Vaughan,
Virginia Mason. II. Cartwright, Kent, 1943–   .
PR2829.O87 1991
822.3'3—dc20   89-46413
                                                                    CIP

PRINTED IN THE UNITED STATES OF AMERICA

Editors' Note: With the exception of Thomas L. Berger's essay, all textual references to Shakespeare are made to G. Blakemore Evans, ed., *The Riverside Shakespeare* (Boston: Houghton Mifflin Company, 1974). To avoid some confusions, brackets used by *The Riverside Shakespeare* to indicate textual variants have been eliminated.

Contents

List of Contributors

THOMAS L. BERGER, well known bibliographer, teaches at St. Lawrence University and serves as U.S. Secretary-Treasurer of the Malone Society.

KENT CARTWRIGHT teaches at the University of Maryland and is the author of *Shakespearean Tragedy and Its Double: The Structure of Audience Response* (forthcoming).

EVELYN GAJOWSKI, author of *The Art of Loving: An Inquiry into the Nature of Love in Shakespeare's Tragedies* (forthcoming), specializes in gender and genre theory as well as gender issues in Shakespeare's texts; she teaches Shakespeare, Renaissance drama, and literary interpretation at the University of California, Santa Cruz.

JAMES HIRSH, an associate professor of English at Georgia State University, is the author of *The Structure of Shakespearean Scenes*, as well as articles on Shakespeare in *Modern Language Quarterly, Essays in Theatre, Shakespeare Quarterly* and elsewhere.

BARBARA HODGDON is National Endowment for the Humanities Professor of English at Drake University and the author of *The End Crowns All: Closure and Contradiction in Shakespeare's History* (forthcoming).

B. A. KACHUR, Director of Theatre at the University of Missouri–St. Louis, is author of essays on Tree's Shakespearean career and modern American drama, including the forthcoming "Women Playwrights on Broadway: Henley, Howe, Norman and Wasserstein" in *Contemporary American Theatre,* and is preparing a book-length study of Beerbohm Tree's Shakespearean revivals.

THOMAS MOISAN is chair of the Department of English at St. Louis University and has published work on Shakespeare and, among others, Chaucer and Robert Herrick.

MICHAEL E. MOONEY, associate professor of English at the University of New Orleans, has published essays on Renaissance drama and Samuel Beckett in *The Journal of Beckett Studies, Comparative Drama, SEL, ELR, ELH,* and *Shakespeare Survey;* he has essays forthcoming in *Rethinking Beckett, JEGP, Colby Library Quarterly,* and *Michigan Quarterly Review,* and a book, *Shakespeare's Dramatic Transactions.*

DAVID L. POLLARD, professor at Nazareth College, is a specialist in Renaissance and comparative literature and has published widely on Shakespeare and George Herbert.

JOSEPH A. PORTER, author of books and articles about Shakespeare, pragmatics, and characterology, teaches at Duke.

MARTHA TUCK ROZETT, associate professor of English at the State University of New York at Albany, is the author of *The Doctrine of Election and the Emergence of Elizabethan Tragedy* and various articles on Shakespeare.

FRANCES TEAGUE teaches at the University of Georgia.

VIRGINIA MASON VAUGHAN teaches at Clark University and is proud to have survived her part in *"Othello": An Annotated Bibliography, 1940–1985.*

Othello
New Perspectives

Introduction
Perspectives on *Othello*: Old and New

VIRGINIA MASON VAUGHAN

Until the mid-1980s *Othello* criticism remained, for the most part, a bastion of formalism and psychological analysis. No other Shakespearean tragedy seemed to generate such prolonged and repetitive discussions of characters and their motives. No other Shakespearean tragedy seemed so little affected by the critical theories emanating from France and England. Feminist critics in the early 1980s provided new perspectives on the women characters, and in 1980 Stephen Greenblatt chose to discuss *Othello* in the book that began New Historicism, *Renaissance Self-Fashioning*.[1] While Greenblatt's approach and material were startlingly new, he dealt with the same problem that obsessed his predecessors: the assessment of Othello's character, particularly his sexual nature. But aside from these efforts, the countless books and articles that had been written about *Othello* seemed—to me and to my collaborator on *"Othello": An Annotated Bibliography, 1940–1985*—like endless rehashes of Coleridge, Bradley, Stoll, Leavis, and Eliot.[2]

As the 1980s progressed, however, there was evidence of increasing interest in *Othello*. The 1987 *Shakespeare Quarterly,* for example, included three major articles devoted to the play, more than to any other.[3] That same year, the Trustees of the Shakespeare Association of America asked me to organize a seminar for the 1988 annual convention: "*Othello:* New Perspectives." Then I discovered what hot property *Othello* had become. So great was the demand for the seminar that two sessions were formed. When we finally met, auditors packed the room at both sessions and could barely refrain from interrupting the formal part of our meeting.

Those eager auditors—not to mention my enthusiastic seminar participants—convinced me that there was a wide audience for new perspectives on *Othello*. I asked Kent Cartwright to co-edit a volume of essays selected from the papers I had received. The essays included here have been carefully revised since then, with an eye to a larger audience and, I believe, to larger contexts. They represent a new wave of critical interpretation of Shakespeare's tragedy. They employ a variety of theories and methodologies characteristic of the poststructuralist literary climate of the late 1980s.

Our anthology begins with the foundation of Shakespeare studies—the text. *Othello* has a particularly complicated textual history because it has come down to us in three versions: the First Quarto, printed by Nicholas Oakes in 1622, the First Folio of 1623, and a Second Quarto in 1630. For decades the Second Quarto has been ignored. Believing that close examination of the text could reveal authorial intentions as well as a definitive reading for each line, traditional editors such as W. W. Greg and Alice Walker privileged the First Folio, occasionally making emendations from the First Quarto. M. R. Ridley's 1958 edition accordingly differed appreciably from traditional conflated texts, which used the Folio as copytext. Though Ridley inserted the 160 Folio lines missing from the First Quarto into his edition, he relied for the most part on the First Quarto and adopted its readings. Despite ensuing controversy, the central issue remained the same: which version was better, i.e., closer to Shakespeare's original text.

Then, as Thomas L. Berger emphasizes in the essay that opens our anthology, came a revolution in textual editing. With the publication of Gary Taylor and Michael Warren's *The Division of the Kingdoms: Shakespeare's Two Versions of "King Lear,"*[4] the notion of a conflated text, the editor's reconstruction of the author's intentions from careful comparison of variant readings, was out. The notion that variant readings might represent authorial revisions was in. The new approach to *King Lear* necessarily affected *Othello*. Following the Warren-Taylor reasoning, John Hazel Smith, editor of the New Variorum Edition of *Othello* until his death in 1986, argued that any definitive edition of the play must place the First Quarto and Folio versions on parallel pages. But the Second Quarto still remained in limbo. Berger corrects that oversight in a reconsideration of the entire textual question: what should we do when we have multiple texts with significant variations? In his reexamination of the Second Quarto, Berger suggests that its editor is a useful mediator of differences between Q1 and F in the person of someone contemporaneous with them. And, as Berger further reminds us, the Second Quarto was based upon theatrical practice close to that of Shakespeare's lifetime.

Texts are words, words make language, and language constructs character. Ever since G. Wilson Knight characterized the "Othello music" in 1930, critics have been fascinated by the play's language.[5] Knight described Othello's grand speeches, full of fine vocabulary and exotic proper names, as "highly coloured, rich in sound and phrase, stately. Each word solidifies as it takes its place in the pattern."[6] In Othello's moments of agony, his rhetoric is exaggerated and false, but when he is in control, he speaks in "an architectural stateliness of quarried speech."[7] Knight's interpretation was overtly essentialist; the character's true nature—his essence—could be discovered through close study of his language. Knight concluded that "Othello is essential man in all his prowess and protective strength; Desdemona essential woman, gentle, loving, brave in her trust of her warrior husband."[8] Iago, in turn, is "pure cynicism."[9]

Four years later, Caroline Spurgeon took a formalistic view of Shakespeare's patterns of imagery. She discovered in *Othello* a dominating pattern of animals in action, preying on one another. They are mischievous, lascivious, cruel, or suffering. The play is also animated, she argued, by repeating patterns of black/white, light/dark imagery, perhaps not very surprising in a play about a black man who marries a white woman.[10]

In 1956 Robert B. Heilman continued the New Critical framework pioneered by Spurgeon in his close scrutiny of *Othello's* language in his *Magic in the Web*. Heilman caught the resonant verbal irony inherent in repetitions of "honest, honest Iago," as well as the discrepancies between "seeing" and "seeming" that reverberate through the play. He explicated the use of magic as a prevailing motif and images of poison and disease as they characterize Iago. Heilman concluded that Othello's language determines his character; it reveals his tendency toward posturing and self-deception.[11]

Verbal patterns and the repetition of images—these were the raw material for language study of *Othello* until the mid-1980s. That *Othello* was ripe for a deconstructive reading was made brilliantly clear in Patricia Parker's essay, "Shakespeare and Rhetoric: 'dilation' and 'delation' in *Othello*," published in 1985.[12] Parker unfolded the multiple meanings of "dilation," a pun on "delation" that incorporates suggestions of amplification (dilating on a narrative, filling in the gaps), accusation, and delay (dilatoriness). During the temptation scene, Iago describes his thoughts as "close dilations, working from the heart, / That passion cannot rule" (3.3.123–24). The many meanings of "dilation," Parker demonstrated, resonate through the text and reinforce its self-reflexive qualities. Parker concluded with a warning against editorial practices that choose one meaning over another, "a process of elimination which so often presupposes a singularity of either definitive text or authoritative meaning."[13] Critics must be aware of language as a multivalent force because, as Parker noted, "Rhetoric in the Renaissance is inextricably embedded in other discourse—of logic and politics, of theology and the ideology of sexual difference."[14]

Parker's pleas for further investigation of Shakespeare's discourse did not fall on deaf ears. But her deconstructive approach was completely ignored in a recent book-length study of *Othello,* Martin Elliott's *Shakespeare's Invention of Othello.*[15] Like his predecessors in the 1930s and 1940s, Elliott combed Othello's speeches for signs of his character. He used the *Oxford English Dictionary* and Alexander Schmidt's *Shakespeare Lexicon*[16] to gloss the protagonist's vocabulary, and concluded that the Moor is prone to "self-publication." Othello, argued Elliott, consistently denies Desdemona's right to information and, instead of listening to those around him, luxuriates in publishing his own emotions. For Elliott, Othello is not a noble hero, but a primitive obsessed with his own identity.

Parker's desire for a recognition of language's multivalent qualities—though ignored by Elliott—is amply met by two essays included in this anthology. Thomas Moisan's "Repetition and Interrogation in *Othello*" starts where Parker left off. Like Parker, Moisan recognizes the instability of words, the multivalent quality of Shakespeare's text. The rhetoric of *Othello* is at once reflexive and subversive, he argues; it is a self-aware discourse that comments on its own inability to comment. Repetitions and interrogations echo through the play, subverting language and its relations to clear referents. Moisan notes linguistic inflections of Iago's double character in his speech duplications.

Joseph A. Porter also examines Iago's speech patterns in light of contemporary philosophy's speech act theory. Iago's lines abound with performatives, speech acts intended to induce some action or behavior. Moreover, his discourse about vision forces the audience to comply by directing its attention to the action. In Iago's speech we see language used to manifest contradictions in the process of self-fashioning.

Both Moisan and Porter suggest—as Elliott did in 1988—how easily the study of discourse leads to observations about character. The play's hero is constructed in many respects through his speech; and, as Stephen Greenblatt demonstrated in 1980, the hero himself constructs or "fashions" a self largely through rhetoric. For generations, however, concepts of *Othello*'s major characters have been shaped by the observations made by A. C. Bradley at the turn of the century. To Bradley, Othello was the noble Moor: "his whole nature was indisposed to jealousy, and yet was such that he was unusually open to deception, and, if once wrought to passion, likely to act with little reflection, with no delay, and in the most decisive manner conceivable." As the most romantic of Shakespeare's heroes, he is a simple man with a big heart. He is therefore no match for a villain whose creed "is that absolute egoism is the only rational and proper attitude and that conscience or honor or any kind of regard for others is an absurdity." Still, Bradley's Iago is not exactly motiveless; he is driven by his craving for power.[17]

As early as 1927 T. S. Eliot took issue with Bradley in his essay on "Shakespeare and the Stoicism of Seneca."[18] To Eliot, Othello's last speech seemed a terrible exposure of human weakness. Before he dies, the Moor, contended Eliot, endeavors to escape reality, to "cheer himself up" by creating an aesthetic attitude.[19] We see him more clearly than he sees himself—a pathetically weak man. In 1952 F. R. Leavis echoed Eliot's theme, arguing that Othello's vulnerability arises from a "noble egotism" and a penchant for "self-dramatizing." He argues that Bradley erred in making Iago into a diabolic villain who manipulates a noble man to evil. Leavis contended that Iago's success comes not from his own Machiavellian skill, but from Othello's inner tendencies, "the essential traitor within the gates." Instead of a noble hero, Leavis portrayed Othello as egotistical, blind, and incredibly stupid. The hero's final speech is not a recognition at all, but the sentimentalist's final act of self-dramatization.[20]

The culmination of character study may be found in Jane Adamson's *"Othello" as Tragedy,* published in the same year as Greenblatt's *Renaissance Self-Fashioning.* Adamson focused primarily on Othello, suggesting that his insecurity is apparent in his reliance on external measures of worth and his need to justify himself. The entire play offers a "radical inquiry" into people's propensity to judge others in accord with their own needs. Adamson rejected both Leavis and Bradley because they attempted to assess Othello morally. She concluded that the play evokes a complex response that transcends the Bradley/Leavis dichotomy and demonstrates the difficulties of trust and uncertainty in human relationships.[21]

Whether critics saw Othello as Bradley's noble Moor, or Leavis's and Eliot's simple-minded egoist, or somewhere in between, they implicitly analyzed him as if he were a real person.[22] Not surprisingly, the 1960s spawned many psychoanalytic interpretations of *Othello.* Psychologists dubbed chronic, pathological jealousy "the Othello syndrome." In turn, literary critics identified strawberries on the handkerchief as penis symbols or virginal blood. Iago, and at times Cassio, could be motivated by homoerotic attraction to their General, an interpretation that influenced Olivier's 1964–65 enactment for the National Theatre. At its best, this tradition has led to sensitive and significant readings. Lynda Boose's discussion of the handkerchief's symbolic relation to the wedding sheets is a good example,[23] as is Edward Snow's discussion of male anxiety at the discovery of Desdemona's sexuality.[24] David Pollard continues in this mode with "Iago's Wound," a look at Shakespeare's Ensign in the sadomasochistic topos later perfected by Baudelaire. For Pollard, Iago is Baudelaire's "l'homme ennuyé"; he is a human gargoyle who reveals horrific designs of self-conscious deviance. The play's conclusion, moreover, invites us to join this erotomania by indulging in sadomasochistic fantasies as we gaze on the prone Desdemona horribly murdered in her bed.

Feminist readings of *Othello* during the early 1980s also drew upon a psychoanalytic tradition to reexamine Desdemona. Coppélia Kahn's 1981 study of masculine identity outlined the force of male bonding between Iago and Othello.[25] Madelon Gohlke also noted Iago's desire to recover lost intimacy with Othello.[26] Both Iago and Othello, she suggested, demonstrate marked sexual anxiety that shapes their behavior toward women.

In 1988 Richard Levin attacked most feminist criticism of the tragedies (including *Othello*), charging that its concern with thematic concepts of masculinity and patriarchy was inherently reductive.[27] Such criticism, he charged, treats the characters as exemplars of a general theme and homogenizes them to the lowest moral level. In *Othello,* for example, all the male characters are identified with Iago's misogynistic view of women; because no distinctions are made, all the male characters become equally culpable. This leads, in turn, to denigration of the tragic hero and dilutes the generic properties of the tragic action.

Evelyn Gajowski examines issues of gender and genre less through psychology than by explanation of patriarchal marriage, whose credo has always been that men, fathers and husbands, possess women. Her concern is not so much thematic as structural. Desdemona's display of the wifely virtues of obedience and humility—virtues that should guarantee her marriage's success—ironically confirm rather than deny Othello's suspicions. The play, Gajowski contends, shows the degradation of those who would presume to possess another. This degradation she finds in Iago's misogyny, Othello's jealousy, and Cassio's treatment of Bianca. An opposing view is briefly asserted in Emilia's analysis of marriage in the Willow Song scene, but this vision is powerless against the dominant discourse of patriarchy.

Gajowski's and Pollard's essays consider psychological and institutional constraints that necessarily shape Shakespeare's characters. If he were living, E. E. Stoll would probably be as harsh with them as he was with Bradley. Stoll decried any attempt to psychologize Shakespeare's characters. Iago's villain is a mechanical device that moves the plot, claimed Stoll. No internal motive is needed. In fact, throughout the play Shakespeare successfully creates "the illusion of delusion." In the theatre, according to Stoll, we never notice inconsistencies or worry about sudden changes.[28]

Recent performance criticism has recognized *Othello*'s superb dramatic properties. Michael Goldman noted the play's peculiar theatrical quality in *Acting and Action in Shakespearean Tragedy,* describing the audience's repeated desire to stop the action.[29] The audience, Goldman observed, enters into Othello's imagination and recoils from his destruction, a response it does not share with respect to Shakespeare's other tragic heroes. Critics like Goldman, concerned with the interaction of audience and actor, have greater respect than Stoll ever expressed for the observational powers of an audience and its ability to respond in complex ways to difficult representations. The performance essays in this volume use the facts of performance—that a play is a series of impressions changing through time—to reevaluate criticism's longstanding binary opposition between Bradley's noble Moor and Leavis's sentimentalist.

Michael Mooney is a prime example. Drawing upon the work of German theatre historian Robert Weimann, he finds this traditional opposition embedded in the play's symbolic locus. *Othello*'s language offers two distinct idioms: (1) that of Desdemona and Othello, whose daring courtship reflects the *Liebestod* tradition combined with discourse from the sonneteers; and (2) Iago's alehouse diction. Iago's *Figurenposition* is downstage, as was the Medieval Vice's. Iago invites other characters and the audience to share his locus, to see from the alehouse's perspective. The opposition of these two worlds, and Othello's movement between them, means that he must be viewed from two complementary perspectives, both of them supported by the play.

James Hirsh is also concerned with perceptions. He sees a parallel between Othello's changing perceptions of Desdemona and the audience's changing perceptions of Othello. Each playgoer must draw conclusions—as Othello must—from inconsistent and equivocal evidence. Othello is both noble and contemptible; a playgoer absorbs evidence for both viewpoints and oscillates between them, but, at any time, the viewer may commit to one or the other. The drama thus depicts our daily struggle to piece together fragmentary and contradictory experience to fashion a coherent viewpoint. As Othello fashions his self-image, we fashion the play to accord with our own.

Kent Cartwright returns to the noble Moor/sentimentalist opposition, particularly as it informs the play's final scene. He focuses even more forcefully on the viewer, who experiences repeated assaults, repeated failures, and whose appetite for satisfaction is repeatedly thwarted. We accept, on the one hand, Emilia's outrage and judgment that Othello is a fool, as ignorant as dirt. Yet we also respect his effort to self-fashion a heroic image in his final speech. Both reactions are true to the sequential experience of the play. In short, Bradley and Leavis were both partly right. But in their desire to formulate their experience, to end their discomfort and nail down an interpretation, they minimized or ignored elements deeply embedded in the play that contradict the viewpoint they were most comfortable with.

I use "performance criticism" here to describe essays concerned with the text(s)' theatricality and with audience reactions that specific actions and language elicit. Such criticism sees the play as a process, meant to be performed through time, conveying an ever-changing range of emotions and thoughts within the spectators. But words and action are not the only cues that elicit audience response. So, too, do objects. Frances Teague's essay provides a complete list of all stage properties needed in *Othello*'s text(s). She argues that these properties help establish the double world of Venice and Cyprus and simultaneously reinforce the double time scheme. Letters, for example, suggest to the audience a change in the play's direction. The most important prop, the handkerchief, and its movement from Desdemona to Emilia to Iago to Cassio, is a key symbol, but the Senate table and Desdemona's bed also signify a range of meanings associated with power and authority on the one hand, and sexuality on the other.

Teague distinguishes performance criticism from performance history, the analysis of specific productions. The most influential study of *Othello*'s performance history, published in 1961, set the tone for subsequent discussions. Like the literary criticism of its time, Marvin Rosenberg's *The Masks of Othello* was overtly essentialist. His aim, he declared in the Preface, was to "search particularly for the look and sound of Othello, Iago, and Desdemona; and for the inner shapes, the character essences, that the look and sound express."[30] To this end he surveyed the history of great Othellos—Betterton, Barry, Quinn, Garrick, Kean, Macready, Irving, Booth, Salvini, Robeson, and Olivier—and measured their performance against his conception of Othello's essence. For Rosenberg, productions succeeded or failed depending on whether the lead actor conveyed Othello's noble stage presence, spoke with a magnificent voice, and projected the depth of his passions. Garrick and Irving failed because they were, respectively, too small in physique and too intellectual.

A new direction in theatre-history interpretations of *Othello* was apparent in James R. Siemon's pathbreaking article, " 'Nay, that's not next': *Othello,* V.ii in Performance, 1760–1900."[31] Siemon used extant promptbooks to show how the actual staging of the murder scene—the use of a dagger or a pillow, the placement of the bed, cuts, and so forth—reflected changing attitudes toward the violent act being represented. Siemon recognized the multivalent quality of Shakespeare's text and showed how the same action could be portrayed in a variety of ways. B. A. Kachur's study of Herbert Beerbohm Tree's 1912 *Othello* continues this new direction. Instead of judging Tree's performance in comparison to an idealized notion of the perfect Othello, she locates the production within its cultural and historical context. This approach foregrounds the audience and asks what values, beliefs, and expectations it brought to the theatre. To satisfy Edwardian appetites for display and decorum, Tree reshaped *Othello* into a romantic and sentimental tragedy about an aging, gentlemanly, light-skinned Moor whose devotion to his wife ensured his downfall. Tree, as Kachur shows, privileged the private husband over the public general; he appealed to Edwardian tastes for luxury, beauty, and refinement. Even so, his production was sufficiently powerful to enthrall some members of the audience, while outraging others.

What directors, performers, and screenwriters do to *Othello* is the focus of Barbara Hodgdon's essay, "Kiss Me Deadly." Hodgdon draws upon feminist film criticism, particularly the work of Laura Mulvey,[32] to examine male treatment of Desdemona in a series of appropriations of *Othello:* Verdi's opera, Orson Welles's film, and adaptations by August Blom, George Cukor, Charles Marowitz, and Basil Dearden. This essay combines a feminist perspective with performance criticism in a penetrating analysis of the male gaze during the murder scene. It also is a performance history that de-privileges the original text(s) to consider seriously adaptations in media other than theatre. As Hodgdon observes, what we do to Shakespeare may indicate not simply changes in taste and fashion but what Shakespeare does to us—how his play makes us uncomfortable and how we dissipate the discomfort. Hodgdon thus directly addresses issues of sexism and racism that too often have been ignored or downplayed in *Othello* criticism.

Lest we rest too comfortably in the rarefied air of poststructuralist discourse, our final essay returns to the chief marketplace for Shakespeare in today's United States and Britain—the classroom. Martha Rozett's candid summation of her students' responses to reading and seeing *Othello*, strange as it may seem, takes us back to where modern criticism began, A. C. Bradley. For whatever dismay we feel about Bradley's attempts to psychologize Shakespeare's characters as real people, in the classroom our students respond in much the same way. We should perhaps ask ourselves whether it is necessarily bad that they judge the characters' actions in light of contemporary moral issues and, thereby, feel intense pity or anger. After all is said and done, I think we must recognize that something about *Othello* invites everyone to make such judgments, that the intensity of our response to Othello's, Desdemona's, and even Iago's humanity is a mark of Shakespeare's achievement. Moreover, when we question the characters of *Othello*, we also raise concerns about the nature of dramatic causation and motivation, about whether any analysis of motives actually explains the ensuing action.

That our students do not readily recognize racism as an issue within *Othello* says something frightening about the United States in the early 1990s. Perhaps they feel that the civil rights movement settled the problem once and for all, and that it should no longer be an issue. If so, we need to make them aware of the realities of racism in 1990, not to mention 1604. That our students use pop psychology and the language of Dear Abby and Dr. Ruth also tells us much about the culture in which we live. But that they see the play in light of their own needs and values is neither surprising nor appalling, for each generation, including ours, has crafted its own *Othello*.

The perspectives gathered here remain fragmented, for unlike our students, we realize that no single person or critical voice can capture or fix the prismatic signifiers of Shakespeare's text(s). There remains room for other approaches. Building on the work of Stephen Greenblatt, new historicists might provide further contextualization for *Othello* by examining Cyprus and Venice as symbolic locations, by analyzing Europe's exploitation of mercenary armies, and by considering Renaissance military protocols. To the eighteenth and nineteenth centuries *Othello* was basically a domestic tragedy between husband and wife. Betterton and Irving would probably have denied that *Othello* was political at all. But our definitions of "political" have changed; we now see that culture and art can reinforce dominant ideologies as well as allow controlled transgression against those ideologies. Although several of the essays collected here do address political questions, much more could be learned from further analysis of the ideologies embedded in *Othello*.

The issue of race also needs reconsideration. We still often rely on works like Winthrop Jordan's discussion of *Othello* in *White over Black* or G. K. Hunter's essay on "*Othello* and Colour Prejudice."[33] Written during the civil rights movement of the 1960s, these works provided useful historical contexts for *Othello*. Now we should examine more carefully how racism informs the play and affects our responses. We must go beyond the old debate over Othello's blackness and trace the symbolic action of white and black that Shakespeare deliberately emphasizes through his language. We must consider the entire issue of miscegenation, including cultural attitudes toward it and its effect upon audience reaction.

One thing is also evident from this volume: *Othello* remains a profoundly theatrical text. Nearly all the essays gathered here have something to say about audience response, effects, or performance. The old war between theatre historians and literary critics is over, at least when it comes to *Othello*. Our understanding of what Bradley called Shakespeare's best-made play is much richer as a result.

Feminism, New Historicism, Cultural Materialism, Deconstructionism—the "isms" of our time—offer new perspectives on old texts. The essays gathered here speak for themselves; they show what can be done with a much-discussed play like *Othello* if one looks at it afresh. At the same time, they do not pretend to be the last word. As impressive as they are in their own right, they nonetheless call for further exploration of this wonderfully rich dramatic text.

It remains for me to acknowledge those who helped Kent Cartwright and me assemble this anthology. First, I thank the Shakespeare Association of America for inviting me to chair the *Othello* seminar at the 1988 convention. I am thankful as well to all who participated; all in their own ways contributed to this volume. We are also grateful to the University of Maryland College of Arts and Humanities Computing Center for assistance in preparation of the manuscript, to Pamela Cartwright for reprocessing much of the material, and to Alden T. Vaughan for his support and criticism. A

Faculty Development Grant from Clark University enabled graduate student Elaine Brousseau to check all citations and quotations. Finally, we acknowledge assistance from the staff of the Folger Shakespeare Library, home base for our initial acquaintance and ensuing deliberations.

NOTES

1. Stephen Greenblatt, "The Improvisation of Power," *Renaissance Self-Fashioning from More to Shakespeare* (Chicago: University of Chicago Press, 1980), pp. 222–54.

2. See Margaret Lael Mikesell's survey of *Othello* criticism from 1940 to 1985 in "Introduction, Part I," *"Othello": An Annotated Bibliography, 1940–1985* (New York: Garland Publishing, 1990) pp. xi–xxv.

3. They are Martin Orkin, *"Othello* and the 'plain face' of Racism," *Shakespeare Quarterly* 38 (1987): 166–88; Eamon Grennan, "The Women's Voices in *Othello:* Speech, Song, Silence": 275–92; and James L. Calderwood, "Speech and Self in *Othello*": 293–303.

4. Gary Taylor and Michael Warren, *The Division of the Kingdoms: Shakespeare's Two Versions of "King Lear"* (Oxford: Clarendon Press, 1983).

5. G. Wilson Knight, "The *Othello* Music," in *The Wheel of Fire: Interpretations of Shakespearian Tragedy* (Oxford: Oxford University Press, 1930), pp. 97–119.

6. Ibid., p. 104.

7. Ibid., p. 103.

8. Ibid., p. 117.

9. Ibid., p. 117.

10. See Caroline F. E. Spurgeon, *Shakespeare's Imagery and What It Tells Us* (Cambridge: Cambridge University Press, 1935), pp. 335–36, 64, 159–62.

11. Robert B. Heilman, *Magic in the Web: Action and Language in "Othello"* (Lexington: University Press of Kentucky, 1956).

12. Patricia Parker, "Shakespeare and Rhetoric: 'dilation' and 'delation' in *Othello,*" in *Shakespeare and the Question of Theory,* ed. Patricia Parker and Geoffrey Hartman (New York: Methuen, 1985), pp. 54–74.

13. Ibid., p. 56.

14. Ibid., p. 70.

15. Martin Elliot, *Shakespeare's Invention of Othello: A Study in Early Modern English* (New York: St. Martin's Press, 1988).

16. Alexander Schmidt, *Shakespeare Lexicon* (Berlin, 1902).

17. A. C. Bradley, *Shakespearean Tragedy* (1904: repr., London: Macmillan, 1971), pp. 142–98.

18. T. S. Eliot, "Shakespeare and the Stoicism of Seneca," in *Selected Essays* (New York: Harcourt, Brace and World, 1932), pp. 107–20.

19. Ibid., p. 111.

20. F. R. Leavis, "Diabolic Intellect and the Noble Hero: or the Sentimentalist's Othello," in *The Common Pursuit* (New York: George R. Stewart, 1952; repr., New York: New York University Press, 1964), pp. 136–59.

21. Jane Adamson, *Othello as Tragedy: Some Problems in Judgment and Feeling* (Cambridge: Cambridge University Press, 1980).

22. A notable exception is E. E. Stoll, discussed below.

23. Lynda E. Boose, "Othello's Handkerchief: 'The Recognizance and Pledge of Love,'" *English Literary Renaissance* 5 (1975): 360–74.

24. Edward A. Snow, "Sexual Anxiety and the Male Order of Things in *Othello*," *English Literary Renaissance* 10 (1980): 384–412.

25. Coppélia Kahn, *Man's Estate: Masculine Identity in Shakespeare* (Berkeley: University of California Press, 1981), pp. 140–46.

26. Madelon Gohlke, "'All that is spoke is marr'd': Language and Consciousness in *Othello*," *Women's Studies* 9 (1982): 157–76.

27. Richard Levin, "Feminist Thematics and Shakespearean Tragedy," *PMLA* 103 (1988): 125–38.

28. E. E. Stoll, *"Othello,"* in *Art and Artifice in Shakespeare: A Study in Dramatic Contrast and Illusion* (Cambridge: Cambridge University Press, 1933), pp. 6–55.

29. Michael Goldman, "Othello's Cause," in *Acting and Action in Shakespearean Tragedy* (Princeton: Princeton University Press, 1985), pp. 46–70.

30. Marvin Rosenberg, *The Masks of "Othello"* (Berkeley: University of California Press, 1961), p. vii. For other surveys of *Othello*'s performance history, see Gino J. Matteo, *Shakespeare's "Othello": The Study and the Stage, 1604–1904* (Salzburg: Institut für Englisch Sprach und Literatur, 1974) and Carol Jones Carlisle, *Shakespeare from the Greenroom: Actors' Criticisms of Four Major Tragedies* (Chapel Hill: University of North Carolina Press, 1969), pp. 172–263.

31. James R. Siemon, "'Nay, that's not next': *Othello*, V.ii in Performance, 1760–1900," *Shakespeare Quarterly* 37 (1986): 38–51.

32. See Laura Mulvey, "Visual Pleasure and Narrative Cinema" (1975); in *Feminism and Film Theory,* ed. Constance Penley (New York: Routledge, Chapman and Hall, 1988), pp. 57–68.

33. Winthrop D. Jordan, *White over Black: American Attitudes toward the Negro, 1150–1812* (Chapel Hill: University of North Carolina Press, 1968), pp. 37–39; G. K. Hunter, "*Othello* and Colour Prejudice" (Annual Shakespeare Lecture), *Proceedings of the Bibliographical Association* 53 (1967): 139–63; repr. in *Dramatic Identities and Cultural Tradition: Studies in Shakespeare and His Contemporaries* (Liverpool: Liverpool University Press, 1978), pp. 31–59.

1

The Second Quarto of *Othello* and the Question of Textual "Authority"

THOMAS L. BERGER

I

The text of *Othello* presents countless problems. To begin, there are problems of number, for we cannot talk about "the text of Othello," as if some sort of "perfect" text existed to be assembled by editors of Shakespeare and criticized by readers of the play.[1] What we must talk about are the *texts* of *Othello,* and when we talk about those texts, we refer most often to two texts. The first to appear was the quarto text of 1622, hereinafter Q1.[2] The first folio text, hereinafter F1, considerably different from that of Q1, appeared a year later in 1623.[3]

About the origins of both texts there has been much debate. The copy behind Q1 may be a private transcript of foul papers.[4] Or it may derive from a bookkeeper-prompter.[5] I think good evidence exists for traces of Shakespeare's foul papers in such indefinite stage directions as *"Exit two or three."* (C3, 1.2; 2.3.121 s.d.)[6] and *"Enter* Desdemona, Iago, *and the rest"* (C3ᵛ, 1.6; 1.3.169 s.d.). Whatever its precise origins, Q1 is in every sense a "substantive" and "authoritative" document.

Behind F1 lies a revised text. Some fifty-two of Q1's oaths have been removed, perhaps in deference to the 27 May 1606 "Acte to Restraine Abuses of Players." To the text of Q1 much has been added, but by whom? The additions may be "authoritative," "Shakespearean," and Q1 may represent a "deformed" text, mangled by scribes and compositors and shorn of its F1 beauties.

The above two paragraphs represent what could be called the "received" truth(s) about *Othello* and its texts until the mid-1960s. There was "a" text of *Othello,* a single text that could be gotten at by conflating Q1 and F1, and by deleting or emending those words, phrases, and passages that compositors and scribes behind Q1 and F1 (may have) corrupted. The year 1964 saw *Shakespeare's Professional Skills,* where Nevill Coghill demonstrated that Q1 was not a shortened version of F1 but an independent version of the play. The F1 text was a later sophistication of the Q1 text (pp. 145–53, 164–202). In the following year E. A. J. Honigmann presented evidence that in Q1 and F1 there were "indifferent" variants, variants that someone, perhaps Shakespeare, might have introduced into a revision of the play behind the F1 text or into an earlier version that came to be represented in print in Q1.[7]

And then came the deluge, the two texts of *King Lear.*[8] After numerous books and articles, reviews and rebuttals, counter-reviews and rebuttals of rebuttals, it is difficult, if not impossible, to think of "a" text of *King Lear* again. In 1982 Honigmann linked *Othello* with *King Lear* in his essay "Shakespeare's Revised Plays: *King Lear* and *Othello.*"[9] Here Honigmann reviewed the arguments advanced for the two versions of *King Lear,* concluding, "Who, other than the author, when a monumental master-piece has been completed, would still think about improving it and would re-touch it at so many points, and so delicately? Who, other than Shakespeare, was capable of dramatic thinking at this level?"[10] In the second "half" of his article Honigmann investigates the two texts of *Othello,* combining his own earlier work and that of Coghill with the findings of the proponents of a two-text *King Lear.* Honigmann's critical conclusion is optimistic and excited: "A strong case can be made for the 'revision' of *Othello* and of *King Lear;* the fact that Shakespeare is thought to have re-touched not one but two of his greatest tragedies, and to have strengthened both in similar (and unusual) ways, makes the 'revision-theory' more compelling—and more exciting."[11] Honigmann's article, however, does not end on the same exciting note as the paragraph just quoted. Rather, it continues and considers the editorial implications of two-text plays. Are we to proceed with a two-text theory for *Othello,* following the lead of the Oxford Shakespeare, which prints two texts of *King Lear?*[12] If that is the case, what are we to make of Shakespeare the reviser? Must we omit from the F1 text all the oaths that were deleted because of (possible) censorship? If F1 represents a text that has been revised first with an eye toward the censor and, at the same time or at a later time, with an eye toward more clearly defining character and situation, how much of that text was altered in the course of passing through copyists and compositors? In short, how many of the Q1 readings are more "Shakespearean" than their "revised" F1 counterparts? Then too, however, the manuscript behind Q1, Shakespeare's foul papers, may well have been changed when it was copied and was most likely changed when it came to be printed in 1622.[13] Both Q1 and F1 are "superior" and "inferior" in different ways. Honigmann's editorial conclusion is a good deal less exciting and more depressing than his critical one: "Those who wish to disentangle the second from the first version of *Othello* are bound to return to a more general consideration of authorial 'instability', and will find traditional editorial principles as unsatisfactory as the traditional conflated texts."[14]

A review of editorial practice reveals if not certain prejudices then certain predispositions. Let me start in 1957 with the old New Cambridge edition of Alice Walker and John Dover Wilson:

> In view of what the readings of Q. and F. suggest about their transmission and the manifest superiority of F., our principle has been to give precedence to what is, in general, the better text (F.) whenever the merits of variants seem evenly matched and whenever we have failed to agree over the choice of variant; but whenever Q. appears to have preserved a reading more consonant with Shakespeare's style and dramatic intentions we have not hesitated to adopt it.[15]

One year later appeared M. R. Ridley's new Arden edition:

> In conclusion, then, I think that in Q1, amplified by the reinstatement of the cuts, we have as near an approximation as we are likely to get to the play as Shakespeare first wrote it, with nothing between us and him but the blunders of honest but not always skilful transcriber and compositor. On the other hand, I think that in F we have probably a good deal of Shakespeare's second thoughts, but also, almost certainly, a good deal of divergence from the original for which he was not responsible. And with each individual instance of divergence we are left to guess-work selection of the source, Shakespeare, the actors, memorial contamination, editorial sophistication.[16]

Kenneth Muir's New Penguin edition seeks a middle path:

> The present edition . . . is based mainly on F. It adds passages omitted from F; it deviates from F in about 250 readings, and in nearly 200 of these Q has been followed. In other words it accepts more Q readings than the New Cambridge . . . but fewer than the new Arden.[17]

In *The Riverside Shakespeare* G. B. Evans relies on editorial tradition:

The present edition, therefore, accepts F1 as the basic copy-text, since it is considered by the majority of earlier editors as generally superior, but it also admits, either from necessity or by editorial choice, roughly 190 readings from Q1.[18]

More complex, but still eclectic, is Lawrence Ross's procedure in his Bobbs-Merrill edition:

The Quarto's text is adjudged on the whole more reliably to represent a less authoritative manuscript of the play, and the Folio's less reliably to represent a more authoritative one. On this theory, then, an editor is obliged to follow the Folio, but only where his analysis of its various probable kinds of corruption does not lead him to distrust it. Wherever he has cause to suspect its readings, and he cannot plausibly recover those of the underlying authoritative manuscript, he must attempt to reconstruct those of the original draft through the printed evidence of the transcript used as copy for the Quarto.[19]

The first edition to appear after the "discovery" of *King Lear*'s two texts and Honigmann's piece on *King Lear* and *Othello* was the new New Cambridge edition of Norman Sanders. Again, the text is eclectic, but Sanders displays less confidence (if that is possible) in his eclecticism than earlier editors:

The practice adopted in the present edition is based on the belief that Q1 and F are derived from two distinct manuscripts of equal authority, both of which have been variously corrupted in transmission, by scribes and compositors in Q1 and by editorial intervention and compositors in F. In fact, my strong impression is that what we are dealing with is Shakespeare's first version of the play (behind Q1) and his own transcription of it (behind F), during the process of making which he not only created additions for dramatic clarification or imaginative amplification but was also enticed into changes in words and phrases which appeared to him at the time as improvements on his first thoughts. This means that the [new New Cambridge] text is, like its predecessors, an eclectic one; but one which has been arrived at by treating each pair of variants as a separate entity.[20]

Sanders's final comments reflect his frustration:

The procedure outlined above is only slightly different in result, if not in theory, from that adopted by previous editors of the play. It is when we come to think about the treatment of those hundreds of variants between Q1 and F, encompassing variations in number, alternative verb forms, and numerous different words and phrases equally appropriate and equally 'Shakespearean', that the difficulties arise. Previous editors have attempted to establish one text or the other as the primary authority by arguing that one text is based upon the other or that both have behind them a common original Shakespearean copy. But no one who has studied Q1 and F variants can fail at least to suspect that, when all possible allowance has been made for scribal and compositorial sophistication or memorial contamination, the two texts reflect two stages of composition for both of which Shakespeare himself was responsible.[21]

Such frustration is less evident in the recently published Oxford Shakespeare and its *Textual Companion*. After reviewing the origins of Q1 and F1, the editors conclude that

Q1 represents a scribal copy of foul papers.
F represents a scribal copy of Shakespeare's own revised
manuscript of the play.
F therefore brings us closer to Shakespeare's final text than Q1.
[Yet] Q1 obliterated fewer authorial characteristics than F.[22]

Accordingly, Wells and Taylor proceed "to take Q1 as the copy-text, to graft onto it passages found only in F, and to observe Shakespeare's substitutions and alterations at other points."[23] They "nevertheless follow F in all readings which make acceptable sense, whether or not [they] prefer them to Q1's, unless [they] suspect them of corruption."[24]

We are left to make a number of decisions. We can choose Q1 over F1, F1 over Q1, or we can conflate. Ideally, but frighteningly, exists the prospect of a parallel-text *Othello,* with each reader preparing his/her own conflated text. One emends Don John's line in *Much Ado* to "Leonato's *Othello,* your *Othello,* every man's *Othello.*" Such conflation has the virtue, if it can be called that, of being democratic. Everyreader will need to determine what the censor has cut and make restorations. Everyreader will need to determine when Q1 has been corrupted by the process of textual transmission and prefer F1 readings. Everyreader will have to do the same thing for F1 readings, duly preferring Q1. This is tricky business, as a vexed Norman Sanders has made clear.

II

What I should like to propose is that as we conflate, as conflate we will, we pay special attention to the text of the second quarto

(Q2) of *Othello,* published eight years after Q1 (seven after F1). This text represents the first "conflated" text of *Othello,* probably the first consistently conflated text of any Shakespearean play.[25] Thomas Walkley, owner of the "copyright" to *Othello,* transferred his rights to the play to Richard Hawkins on 1 March 1628. In 1630 Augustine Mathewes printed a quarto of *Othello* for Hawkins.[26]

The text Mathewes printed for Hawkins was based on Q1. Indeed, it used an "edited" copy of Q1 with F1 additions included. That Q2 has no textual "authority" Charlton Hinman has brilliantly (and characteristically) demonstrated.[27] Hinman cites scholars of the late nineteenth and early twentieth centuries who tacitly accepted Q2 as having authority, a "deference . . . in practice if not in theory."[28] Using evidence from uncorrected copies of both Q1 and F1, Hinman shows how the Q2 text was assembled without any reference to an independent manuscript; he demonstrates from mislineation how the shorter additions from F1 must have been written into the margins of a copy of Q1, the longer additions with correct lineation on separate slips of paper.[29] Hinman concludes that "the 1630 quarto of *Othello* is of no textual authority and of little textual value. Modern editors may well be interested, when neither Q1 nor F presents an acceptable reading, in the emendations made by an early Caroline editor; and in all four of the instances where F is definitely wrong in a passage unrepresented by Q1 the Q2 reading should probably be accepted into the *Othello* text—not as authoritative, but only as probably right. For it seems virtually certain that Q2 is nowhere based upon any manuscript version of the play."[30]

But Hinman's idea of what "authority" in a text represents was determined by a school of criticism, textual and otherwise, that sought (and believed it could find) the single, authoritative text. Looking at Q2 in the light of the two-text theory, one which sees Shakespeare as reviser, makes Q2 if not an "authority" (an "eyewitness") then an "expert witness."[31] Hinman suggests as much when he says that "modern editors may well be interested, when neither Q1 nor F presents an acceptable reading, in the emendations made by an early Caroline editor."[32] Not only should we be interested in the emendations of a Caroline editor, we should be interested in his editorial choices as well. For each of "those hundreds of variants between Q1 and F, encompassing variations in number, alternative verb forms, and numerous different words and phrases equally appropriate and equally 'Shakespearean,'"[33] that Caroline editor made a choice. The quality of his choices is an aesthetic question, open to debate. But the proximity of that editor in 1630 to Shakespeare's language is neither aesthetically questionable nor debatable. In 1630 he was much closer to Shakespeare's language than we are in the last decades of the twentieth century.

Of the several modern editions mentioned above, only Ridley's new Arden takes care to include Q2 readings throughout its collations. But Ridley was virtually alone in preferring Q1 to F1. Ridley concludes of the Q2 text:

> In the upshot Q2 is an eclectic text, and for the determination of the 'true' text it has just this amount of importance. It is not in the least authoritative, since the editor cannot be proved, nor I think, even reasonably supposed, to have had access to any MS. But, for what it is worth, its editor clearly did not regard Q1 as an inferior text, since, in spite of the minuteness with which he sometimes corrects it by F, he still adheres to it, against F, nearly twice as often as he deserts it. When, therefore, in the more critical divergences he adheres to Q1, it means at least this, that a careful contemporary, who was ready enough to alter Q1 when he saw fit, did not feel that in these instances any alteration was called for.[34]

III

Turning specifically to the Q2 text, I would like to examine fifteen examples of Q2 readings as they help (or hinder) a determination of the "text" of *Othello*.[35] To indicate how recent editors treat the lines in question, I indicate their readings as follows: **OC** = Old Cambridge (Alice Walker and John Dover Wilson), **NA** = New Arden (M. R. Ridley), **NP** = New Penguin (Kenneth Muir), **R** = Riverside (G. B. Evans), **BM** = Bobbs-Merrill (Lawrence J. Ross), **NC** = New Cambridge (Norman Sanders), and **OX** = Oxford (Stanley Wells and Gary Taylor). **OC–OX** means that all the editions agree with a particular reading.

My first five examples are those Hinman pointed to in Q2 that are "almost universally accepted."[36] All five deal with passages missing from Q1.[37]

1. 3.3.387–88 (TLN 2032–2033):

> F1: Ile haue some proofe. My name that was as fresh / As *Dians* Visage
>
> Q2: Ile haue some proofe: her name that was as fresh / As *Dians* visage

Q2/her   **OC, NP, R, NC**   F1/My   **NA, OX, BM**

Neither the Old Cambridge, the Riverside, nor the New Cambridge feels compelled to justify its choice of Q2, whereas the new Arden and Bobbs-Merrill go to some length to explain the F1 reading, whose best defense seems to have been written by Charles Knight in his edition of 1841.[38]

2. 4.3.38 (TLN 3011):

> F1: *The poore Soule sat singing by a Sicamour tree*
> Q2: *The poore soule sate sighing by a sicamour tree*

Q2/*sighing* **OC–OX**   F1/*singing*
Hinman observes that the manuscript behind Q2 may have referred to a copy of F1 that had the uncorrected reading "sining," "an error much more in need of correction than 'singing.' "[39]

3. 1.3.364 (TLN 728):

> F1: Ile sell all my Land
> Q2: Ile goe sell all my land

Q2/goe sell   F1/sell **OC–OX**
The new Arden rejects both F1 and Q2 additions, reading with Q1 (and omitting the line). Hinman notes (in 1948, nine years before the Old Cambridge) that he "is in disagreement with almost all modern editors in finding the Folio reading perfectly acceptable here."[40]

4. 3.3.456 (TLN 2105):

> F1: Neu'r keepes retyring ebbe, but keepes due on
> Q2: Ne'r feels retiring ebbe, but keepes due on

Q2/feels **OC, NA, NP, R, BM, NC**   F1/keepes   White/knows **OX**
F1's "keepes" is an anticipation of the word's later appearance in the same line.

5. 4.2.154 (TLN 2869):

> F1: Delighted them: or any other Forme
> Q2: Delighted them in any other forme

Q2/them in **OC–OX**   F1/them: or
Hinman's cast of mind here is interesting to note, insofar as it is in

his interest to establish that Q2 has no "authority": "Again F is clearly in need of correction; but again Q2's reading is not one that requires us to suppose ms authority, and Rowe's 'Delighted them on any other form' may conceivably be right."[41]

While it may well be true that "not one of Q2's five generally accepted unique readings lends any real support to the 'independent manuscript' hypothesis,"[42] the readings demonstrate an active, alert editorial intelligence at work. Q2's emendations of F1 reveal an editorial intelligence of some variety. In the third example, the Q2 editor appears to be as meddling as some of his eighteenth-century counterparts will be, adding that unnecessary "goe." In the first and fifth examples, he demonstrates good judgment and a perfectly fine sense of language. In the second and fourth examples he makes those kinds of leaps on which the best emendations depend.

In the following ten examples, the same three characteristics appear.

1. 1.1.181 (TLN 200):

> Q1: And raise some speciall Officers of night **OC–OX**
> F1: And raise some speciall Officers of might
> Q2: And raise some speciall Officers of might

Furness's defense of F1-Q2 "might" is the fullest, deriding Malone's note on Shakespeare's use of Lewes Lewkenor's translation of Gaspar Contareno's *The Commonwealth and Government of Venice* (1599), and pointing out that the customary officers of the night, described by Contareno, are hardly "special."[43] I suspect the suggestion of mightiness in "get Weapons (hoa)" of the preceding line helped the Folio compositor misread "n" for "m." The Q2 editor, unlearned in matters Venetian, followed F1.

2. 1.3.273–74 (TLN 627–628):

> Q1: And speede must answer, you must hence to night.
>   *Desd.* To night my Lord?
>   *Du.* This night. **NA, NP, NC**
> *F1:* And speed must answer it.
>   *Sen.* You must away to night. **OC, BM**
> *Q2:* And speed must answere, you must hence to night.
>   *Des.* To night my Lord?
>   *Du.* This night.

Riverside and Oxford conflate:

> And speed must answer it.
> *Sen.* You must away to night.
> *Desd.* To night my Lord?
> *Du.* This night.

F1's deletion of Desdemona's line seems "to present a more mature Desdemona,"[44] which may be what Shakespeare decided he needed for the latter parts of his tragedy, but it eliminates her impulsive expression of her desire to consummate her marriage. What is of real importance here is the Q2 editor's refusal to conflate Q1 and F1, as Riverside and Oxford have done. Such a conflation is a distortion of both texts, both Desdemonas.[45] The Q2 editor is not averse to accepting F1's "nine" over Q1's "ten" ("At nine i'th' morning, here wee'l meet againe") a mere two lines later, a change further stressing the urgency of the Venetian cause.[46]

3. 2.1.70 (TLN 832):

> Q1: Traitors enscerped; to clog the guiltlesse Keele **NP, NC**
> F1: Traitors ensteep'd, to enclogge the guiltlesse Keele **R, OX**
> Q2: Traitors ensteep'd, to clog the guiltlesse Keele **OC, NA, BM**

It would appear the Q2 editor conflated accurately. Only the New Penguin and the New Cambridge editors read with Q1, seeing (as the Q2 editor did not) "enscerped" as a variant of "enscarped" (drawn up into ridges). The "en" of F1's "enclogge" appears to be a dittographic error caused by the attraction of the earlier "ensteep'd." It renders the line hypercatalectic, whereas Q2's line is regular blank verse.

4. 2.1.284 (TLN 1086):

> Q1: If this poore trash of *Venice,* whom I crush
> F1: If this poore Trash of Venice, whom I trace **R, NC, OX**
> Q2: If this poore trash of *Venice,* whom I trace

New Arden and Bobbs-Merrill adopt Steevens's "trash," though with regret, Ridley making a case, characteristically, for Q1's "crush" and Ross adopting the emendation because "[he does] not have anything else to propose."[47] The Old Cambridge and New Penguin adopt Bailey's conjecture in the Cambridge edition, "leash," since it is "a recurring image in Shakespeare" and some of its variant spellings "would explain the divergent errors of Q. and F."[48] In a supplementary note the New Cambridge editor defends the F1-Q2 reading and points out that Steevens's "trash" (check by weights or a cord) is entirely inappropriate to the action at this point in the play.[49]

5. 3.3.451 (TLN 2099–2100):

> Q1: For tis of Aspecks tongues.
> *Iag.* Pray be content.   *he kneeles.*
> F1: For 'tis of Aspickes tongues.
> *Iago.* Yet be content.   **OC, NP, R, BM, NC, OX**
> Q2: For tis of Aspicks tongues.   *he kneeles.*
> *Iag.* Pray be content.   **NA**

The Q1-Q2 "Pray" is surely the livelier reading, especially in a scene that will eventually find both protagonist and antagonist on their knees. F1's "Yet" may well derive from the hand of the "censor" who removed so many of the oaths found in Q1. Q2's retaining the Q1 reading may be the result of laziness, or it may suggest that the editor, who was assiduous in following the censor behind F1's copy, at this point did not regard "Pray" as scurrilous.[50] To be noted as well is the correct positioning of the stage direction in Q2, one adopted by new Arden and New Cambridge.

6. 4.2.3 (TLN 2690):

Q1: *Oth.* Yes, and you haue seene *Cassio* and she together. **NA**
F1: *Othe.* Yes, you haue seene *Cassio,* and she together. **OC, NP, R, BM, NC, OX**
Q2: *Oth.* Yes, and you haue seene *Cassio* and she together.

F1's line occurs in a cramped section of type on Sig. vv2, where one line is turned under. Having cast off copy, Folio Compositor B may well have omitted the "and" from this line in order to avoid having to use another line, a turnover (either up or down) being impossible because of the length of the preceding and following lines. In F1, Othello virtually accuses Emilia of lying. As the scene opens, he asks her if she has seen anything. She says that she has not, nor has she heard or suspected anything. In Q1, supported by Q2, the "and" means "if." Othello is saying "If you have seen Cassio and Desdemona together, then you have seen something, the very something I suspect." Their being together damns them in Q1–Q2.

7. 4.3.22 (TLN 2992):

Q1: *Des.* All's one good faith: how foolish are our minds? **OC, NA, NP, R, NC, OX**
F1: *Des.* All's one: good Father, how foolish are our minds? **BM**
Q2: *De.* All's one, good father; how foolish are our minds;

The Bobbs-Merrill editor defends the F1-Q2 reading by citing Scripture:

> The reason the heroine recognizes before her "Good Father" that her superstitious foreboding is *foolish* can be found in Romans 8:15–16, "For ye have not received the Spirit of bondage, to fear again: but ye have received the Spirit of adoption, whereby we cry, Abba, Father. / The same Spirit beareth witness with our spirit, that we are the children of God."[51]

The Old Cambridge editors call the F1-Q2 reading a "curious error, suggesting the collator's misreading" and citing the same error in Q2 *Romeo and Juliet,* 4.4.20 (p. 207).[52] Rejecting Q2, the New Arden *Romeo and Juliet* reports that "the oath good father does not occur elsewhere in Shakespeare."[53] None of the foregoing inspires much confidence in either reading.

8. 5.1.104–8 (TLN 3209–3213):

> 104-Q1 *Iag.* What, looke you pale? O beare him out o'th aire. **A-OX**
> 104-F1 *Iago.* What? looke you pale? Oh beare him o'th'Ayre.
> 104-Q2 *Iag.* What, looke you pale? O beare him out o'the aire.

105–8 Q1 Stay you good Gentlewoman, looke you pale mistrisse?
          Doe you perceiue the ieastures of her eye,
          Nay, an you stirre, we shall haue more anon:
          Behold her well I pray you, looke vpon her, **NA**
105–8 F1 Stay you good Gentlemen. Looke you pale, Mistris?
          Do you perceiue the gastnesse of her eye?
          Nay, if you stare, we shall heare more anon.
          Behold her well: I pray you looke vpon her: **OC, NP, R, BM, NC, OX**
105–8 Q2 Stay you good Gentlewoman, looke you pale mistrisse?
          Doe you perceiue the ieastures of her eye?
          Nay, an you stirre, we shall haue more anon:
          Behold her well I pray you, looke vpon her,

Again, I defend the Q1 reading with Q2. The action at this point in the play is quite complex. Roderigo has been killed, Cassio has been wounded, and if Iago doesn't play his cards right, he may lose all. In the first half of line 105 it makes more sense for Bianca to be exiting with the wounded Cassio than Gratiano and Lodovico, who ostensibly should be trying to get to the bottom of the misdeeds. Iago needs someone on whom to focus blame and picks Bianca, the only one available. Iago cites as evidence the sexuality of her eye, its "ieastures." While there may well be reasons for Bianca to exhibit "gastnesse" (her lover is bleeding and barely conscious), that is not as damning as her sexuality. Sanders (**NC**), choosing F1 at 107, allows that "it is not clear what exactly Iago means here."[54] With Q1-Q2's "stirre" there can be little difficulty: "Iago has a hold on Bianca, who starts to struggle and is threatened by him."[55] Indeed, in lines 107–8 Iago uses the "stirre" of line 107 to prove that Bianca is guilty. Guilty of what is of little importance. In little, the action of the play is here recapitulated. Iago works on Lodovico and Gratiano in the same way he worked on Othello. Indeed, need Bianca stir or struggle at all?[56] With "Gastnesse" and "stare," the F1 readings, the second follows from the first. Once the compositor has misread "gestures" as "gastness," "stare" makes far better sense than "stirre."

9. 5.2.251 (TLN 3552):

Q1: It is a sword of Spaine, the Isebrookes temper **BM**
F1: It was a Sword of Spaine, the Ice brookes temper **OC, NA, NP, R, NC, OX**
Q2: It is a sword of *Spaine,* the Isebrookes temper

There is less here than meets the eye. It may be true that Q1-Q2's "Isebrookes" may be a variant seventeenth-century spelling for "Innsbruck," a city that produced notably fine steel. But so too is "Ise" a common variant of "Ice." Pistol's "prickeard cur of Iseland" in Q1 *Henry V* becomes "prickeard cur of Island" in F1. Theseus's "That is hot Ise, / And wondrous strange snow" of Q1 *A Midsummer Night's Dream* gives way to "That is, hot ice, and wondrous strange snow" in F1.[57] The "Isebrookes" of Q1-Q2 are the same "Ice brookes" of F1.

10. 5.2.343 (TLN 3658):

Q1: Like the base *Indian,* threw a pearle away **OC, NA, NP, R, NC, OX**
F1: (Like the base Iudean) threw a Pearle away **BM**
Q2: Like the base *Indian,* threw a pearle away

I shall spill no more ink on Othello's most famous crux than the amount it takes to observe that Q2 follows Q1 in reading *"Indian."*

Q2 *Othello* in no way resembles a flawless text. Its editor, like all editors, probably nodded from time to time, and its compositor(s) may well have found the marginal notations in Q1 impossible to follow and returned to the printed Q1 text. But as an early witness to the text of *Othello,* Q2 merits attention and repays scrutiny.

IV

The fortunes of that second quarto combine with several currents in recent criticism to give this "expert witness" more "authority" than previous schools of criticism have bestowed upon it. The 1630 quarto was reprinted four times in the seventeenth century and once in the early years of the eighteenth century.[58] In the first reprint, published by William Leake in 1655, the title page advertises the play "*As it hath beene divers times Acted at the* Globe, and at the Black-Friers, by his Majesties Servants."[59] The same puff appears on Q4, published in 1681 by W. Weak [*sic*? for *Leake*?] and are to be sold by Richard Bentley and M. Magnes. In this reprint of Q2 the puff continues: "And now at the THEATER ROYAL BY HIS MAJESTIES SERVANTS."[60] Another quarto of the play, Q5, appeared in 1687 (Wing, STC S2941), its title-page puff and text derived from Q4. By now Bentley appears to have the copyright. Still another quarto, Q6, was printed in 1695 (Wing STC S2942), again for Richard Bentley. It was printed from Q5. Thus a quarto tradition of *Othello* extends through the Commonwealth and into the Restoration, a feat matched only by *King Lear*'s one Commonwealth quarto (1655) and three Restoration quartos (1681, 1689, and 1699).[61] The quarto tradition continued into the eighteenth century with another quarto, the final derivation of Q2, appearing in 1705.[62]

What the foregoing illustrates is that Q2 *Othello* pursued an active textual and theatrical life of its own in the seventeenth and early eighteenth centuries, one independent of the folios of 1623, 1632, 1663, and 1685. "As it hath beene diuerse times acted" may have been a publisher's puff for Q2 and Q3, as no records of performances in and around 1630 and 1655 exist. But it certainly appears that Q2, providing the copy for Q4, which led in sequence to Q5, Q6, and 1705, was very much the quarto on which theatrical performance was based. If that is the case, then it provides further reasons for studying the "editorial" choices Q2 made and for broadening our definition of "authority" in printed texts.

But the history of Q2 *Othello* does not end when its string of quartos runs out in 1705. In his dedication to the Duke of Somerset, Nicholas Rowe begins his edition of the *Works* by saying that

> I have taken some Care to redeem him [Shakespeare] from the Injuries of former Impressions. I must not pretend to have restor'd this work to the Exactness of the Author's Original Manuscripts: Those are lost, or, at least, are gone beyond any Inquiry I could make; so that there was nothing left, but to compare the several Editions, and to give the true Reading as well as I could from thence.[63]

From Capell's edition of 1768 on, Rowe has been thought to have corrected a text of F4 and used it as copy for his edition. Capell says that Rowe "went no further than the edition nearest to him in time, which was the folio of 1685, the last and worst of these impressions."[64] Alfred Jackson's study of "Rowe's Edition of Shakespeare" gives the impression that beyond F4 Rowe consulted only a quarto edition of *Romeo and Juliet* for the Prologue and the 1676 quarto of *Hamlet* for act 4, scene 2.[65] As late as 1985 Philip Brockbank would say that "Rowe followed the usual practice of basing his text upon the most recent edition (Fourth Folio), and his use of the earlier folios is casual and unsystematic. He made some use of quarto readings in *Henry V* and *King Lear,* but for the most part his interventions were, like those of earlier scribes and press editors, modernizations and clarifications meant for the convenience of the modern reader."[66] In the even more recent *Textual Companion* to the Oxford *Complete Works,* Gary Taylor continues what seems to have become a tradition: "Textually, the 1709 edition was a reprint of the 1685 folio, transferred to a more manageable multi-volume quarto format. Rowe made almost no use of the 1623 Folio, or the early substantive quartos, though he was aware of the existence of at least some of them."[67]

That Rowe was telling the truth, rare enough in humans, much less eighteenth-century editors of Shakespeare, has been amply demonstrated by Barbara Mowat, whose essay on "The Form of *Hamlet*'s Fortunes" demonstrates that Rowe used the 1676 quarto of *Hamlet* if not to conflate fully then to consider consciously and conscientiously two very different texts.[68] It appears evident from the most casual of collations that Rowe consulted Q2 *Othello* (or one of five descendants) as he was preparing his edition of the play, using F4 as his control text.[69] From changes in lineation to more verbally substantive alterations, Rowe conscientiously makes use of the quarto text. Let me illustrate with three of the play's shorter scenes: 1.2, 3.4, and 5.1.

1. Act 1, scene 2 (TLN 202–322):
   00 s.d. *Enter* Othello, Iago, *and Attendants with torches.* Q2 and Rowe read *"and"*, which is omitted in F1/F4.
   34 "The servants of the duke and my lieutenant!" This is one line in Q2 and Rowe, two in F1/F4, divided after "Duke."
   34 "Duke" in Q2 and Rowe, "Dukes" in F1/F4.
   59 "the dew will rust them"; "em" in Q2 and Rowe, "them" in F1/F4.
   62 "O thou foul thief! Where hast thou stowed my daughter?" This is one line in Q2 and Rowe, two in F1/F4, divided after "thief!"
   81 "Hold your hands"; this is "hands" in Q2, F1, and Rowe, "hand" in F4.

2. Act 3, scene 4 (TLN 2136–2368):
   32 "Give me your hand. This hand is moist, my lady." One line in Q2 and Rowe, two lines in F1/F4, divided after "your hand."
   44 "I cannot speak of this. Come now, your promise." One line in Q2 and Rowe, two lines in F1/F4, divided after "this."
   75 "Why do you speak so startingly and rash?" "Startingly" in Q1, F1, Q2, and Rowe, "staringly" in F4.
   82 "Why so I can sir; but I will not now." "Sir" in Q2 and Rowe, omitted in F1/F4.
   85 "Fetch me that handkerchief. My mind misgives." One line in Q2 and Rowe, two lines divided after "handkerchief" in F1/F4.
   182 "I know not neither; I found it in my chamber." One line in Q2 and Rowe, two lines in F4, divided after "neither," which F4 and F1 read instead of the "sweet" of Q1, Q2, and Rowe.

3. Act 5, scene 1 (TLN 3080–3237):
   1 "Here, stand behind this bulk, straight will he come." One line in Q2 and Rowe, two lines in F1/F4, divided after "bark," the F1/F4 reading of "bulk," which Rowe accepted.
   37 "What ho! No watch? No passage? Murder, murder!" One line in Q2 and Rowe, two lines in F1/F4, divided after "passage."
   61 s.d. *"He stabs Roderigo."* Rowe's *"Jago stabs him"* may derive from Q2's *"Thrusts him in,"* a stage direction omitted in F1/F4.
   63 "Kill men i'the dark? Where be those bloody thieves?" One line in Q2 and Rowe, two lines in F1/F4, divided after "dark."
   98 "He, he, tis he. O, that's well said, the chair." One line in Q2 and Rowe, two lines in F1/F4, divided after "tis he."
   100 "I'll fetch the general's surgeon." "General's" in F1, Q2, and Rowe, "general" in F4.

110 s.d. "*Enter* Emilia." Q2 and Rowe, omitted in F1/F4.

124 "Kind gentlemen, let's go see poor Cassio dressed." One line in Q2 and Rowe, two lines in F1/F4, divided after "gentlemen."

These three scenes sample Rowe's use of Q2. Most of the variations between Rowe and his F4 control text have to do with lineation. Rowe's inclusion of Q2 stage directions confirms his concern for an acting text. And his preference for Q2 reading over F4 readings shows a respect for a continuing theatrical textual tradition.[70]

V

In addition to causing minor and major irritations to a generation of Shakespeareans, the Wells-Taylor Oxford Shakespeare has had the effect of making us review, rethink, and in many cases modify our ideas about what should constitute the text of an edition of any particular play. In an earlier time the goal of textual critics would be to establish a text as close to the author's "final intention" as possible. Editors purged misreadings due to scribal errors and compositorial bungling, and readers were presented with as "pure" a text as was possible in our "scientific" age.

With the revolution brought about by a two-text *King Lear,* though, the purity of a final text went out the window. Dramatic texts were recognized for what they were, documents that, like the plays they represented, were subject to the whims of revision and alteration. The text of a dramatic document for the theatre has become at least as valuable as the text of a dramatic document from the author's pen. Acting on this principle, Wells and Taylor have produced the Oxford Shakespeare:

> Theatre is an endlessly fluid medium. Each performance of a play is unique, differing from others in pace, movement, gesture, audience response, and even—because of the fallibility of human memory—in the words spoken. It is likely too that in Shakespeare's time, as in ours, changes in the text of plays were consciously made to suit varying circumstances: the characteristics of particular actors, the place in which the play was performed, the anticipated reactions of his audience, and so on. The circumstances by which Shakespeare's plays have been transmitted to us mean that it is impossible to recover exactly the form in which they stood either in his own original manuscripts or in those manuscripts, or transcripts of them, after they had been prepared for use in the theatre. Still less can we hope to pinpoint the words spoken in any particular performance. Nevertheless, it is in performance that the

plays lived and had their being. Performance is the end to which they were created, and in this edition we have devoted our efforts to recovering and presenting texts of Shakespeare's plays as they were acted in the London playhouses which stood at the centre of his professional life.[71]

At least two problems appear. Given two documents, one derived from the stage, the other from the author's papers, how sure can editors be that the theatrical document before them had any touch of the author, something the less theatrical but more authorial document possesses? What are the circumstances surrounding that theatrical document on which editors are basing their text, and do these circumstances affect the text before them and the text they will present to a reader? With such two-text plays as *Othello,* editors cannot present the multiplicity of "texts." What editors can do, though, is attend to those texts which reflect definitively their actual theatrical existence, while at the same time attending to an authorial presence. I have spent too much time making exaggerated claims for Q2 *Othello,* so I'll recapitulate with one last claim. I believe that quarto to be a document that in its history reflects a definitive theatrical existence and in its adherence to Q1 readings, attendance to an authorial presence. I would not make Q2 into a control-text or a copy-text for an edition of *Othello,* but I would grant, indeed I have granted it, an "authority" it has previously and undeservedly been denied.

NOTES

    1. This essay appeared in a slightly different form in *Analytical and Enumerative Bibliography,* new series, vol. 2, no. 4 (1988): pp. 141–59. It appears here with permission of the editor of that journal.

    2. W. W. Greg, *A Bibliography of the English Printed Drama to the Restoration,* vol. 2 (London: Bibliographical Society, 1951), #379a; STC 22305. Thomas Walkley entered the play in the Stationers' Register on 6 October 1621. It was licensed by George Buc.

    3. Ibid., #379b; STC 22273.

    4. M. R. Ridley's New Arden edition of *Othello* argues for such a transcript (London: Methuen, 1958), p. xliii, as do W. W. Greg, *The Shakespeare First Folio* (Oxford: Clarendon, 1955), p. 362, and J. K. Walton, *The Quarto Copy for the First Folio of Shakespeare* (Dublin: Dublin University Press, 1971), p. 281.

    5. This theory has been put forward by Alice Walker, *Textual Problems of the First Folio* (Cambridge: Cambridge University Press, 1953), p. 138; Hardin Craig, *A New Look at Shakespeare's Quartos* (Stanford, Calif.: Stanford University Press, 1961), pp. 37, 40, 43; and Nevill Coghill, *Shakespeare's Professional Skills* (Cambridge: Cambridge University Press, 1964), p. 167.

    6. I cite Norman Sanders's New Cambridge text of *Othello* (Cambridge: Cambridge University Press, 1984) throughout.

7. E. A. J. Honigman, *The Stability of Shakespeare's Text* (Lincoln: University of Nebraska Press, 1965), pp. 37–39, 100–111.

8. For a summary, see Gary Taylor and Michael Warren, eds., *The Division of the Kingdoms: Shakespeare's Two Versions of "King Lear"* (Oxford: Clarendon, 1983).

9. E. A. J. Honigman, "Shakespeare's Revised Plays: *King Lear* and *Othello,"* *The Library,* ser. 6, 4, no. 2 (1982): 142–73.

10. Ibid., 155.

11. Ibid., 171.

12. Stanley Wells and Gary Taylor, gen. eds., *William Shakespeare: The Complete Works* (Oxford: Clarendon, 1986). In this modern-spelling edition, the quarto text of *King Lear,* distinguishing itself as *The History of King Lear,* occupies pp. 1025–61. The folio text, *The Tragedy of King Lear,* occupies pp. 1063–98.

13. Editors have been reluctant to read 3.4.42–43 ("A liberal hand! the hearts of old gave hands, / But our new heraldry is hands; not hearts") topically. A topical reading would place the line in 1612, after James I had created a new baronetage, the coat of arms of which had the addition of a hand gules. Admitting such a topical reading would require some redating of the play as well as transform Shakespeare into a critic of his monarch. See the New Variorum edition of *Othello,* ed. H. H. Furness (Philadelphia: Lippincott, 1886), pp. 219, 346–57. But all that would need redating are those lines, not the entire play. The occurrence of the lines in both Q1 and F1 suggests that Shakespeare's "original" (Q1) and "revised" (F1) manuscripts date from then. Such problems offer little comfort to tidy theories of the origins of texts and encourage general, nonspecific, and topically free readings.

14. Honigmann, "Shakespeare's Revised Plays," 173.

15. Alice Walker and J. Dover Wilson, eds., *Othello* (Cambridge: Cambridge University Press, 1957), p. 133.

16. Ridley, *Othello,* p. xliii.

17. Kenneth Muir, ed., *Othello* (Harmondsworth: Penguin Books, 1968), p. 220.

18. G. Blakemore Evans, ed., *The Riverside Shakespeare* (Boston: Houghton Mifflin, 1974), p. 1241.

19. Lawrence J. Ross, ed., *The Tragedy of Othello, Moor of Venice* (Indianapolis: Bobbs-Merrill, 1974), p. xxxvi.

20. Sanders, *Othello,* p. 206.

21. Ibid.

22. Stanley Wells and Gary Taylor, *William Shakespeare: A Textual Companion* (Oxford: Clarendon, 1987), pp. 477–78.

23. Ibid., p. 478.

24. Ibid.

25. Technically, the honor of being first should go to the "editor" of Q4 *Romeo and Juliet* (1622?), who consulted the "bad" first quarto (1597) even as he used Q3 (1609) as his control text. See Brian Gibbons's New Arden edition of the play, *Romeo and Juliet* (London: Methuen, 1980), pp. 2 and 24. G. Blakemore Evans concurs in his New Cambridge edition, *Othello* (Cambridge: Cambridge University Press, 1984), p. 212.

26. Greg, *Bibliography,* #379 (c); STC 22306.

27. Charlton Hinman, "The 'Copy' for the Second Quarto of *Othello,"* in *Joseph Quincy Adams Memorial Studies,* ed. James G. McManaway, Giles E. Dawson, and Edwin E. Willoughby (Washington, D.C.: The Folger Shakespeare Library, 1948), pp. 373–89.

28. Ibid., p. 375.

29. Ibid., pp. 377–81.

30. Ibid., p. 388.

31. Thus Dares Phrygius and Dictys Cretensis are eyewitnesses to the Trojan War, Homer an expert witness.

32. Hinman, "The 'Copy' for the Second Quarto of *Othello,*" p. 388.

33. Sanders, *Othello,* p. 206.

34. Ridley, *Othello,* p. 232.

35. If I have not already made it apparent, it will soon become so. In order to pursue my argument, my sympathies and my prejudices lie with the Q2 text.

36. Hinman, "The 'Copy' for the Second Quarto of *Othello,*" p. 384.

37. The act/scene/line numbers refer to Sanders's New Cambridge text; the TLN numbers refer to the Through Line Numbers of *The Norton Facsimile of the First Folio of Shakespeare,* prepared by Charlton Hinman (New York: W. W. Norton, 1968).

38. "It is is his intense feeling of *honour* that makes his wife's supposed fault so terrific to him. It is not that *Desdemona*'s name is begrimed and black, but that *his own name* is degraded. This one thought, here for the first time exhibited, pervades all the rest of the play; and when we understand how the poison operates upon Othello's mind, we are quite prepared fully to believe him when he says, in conclusion,—'For naught I did in hate, but all in honour' " (New Variorum, p. 205). The Oxford *Textual Companion* says that Q2's reading is "purely interpretive" (p. 480).

39. Hinman, "The 'Copy' for the Second Quarto of *Othello,*" p. 386.

40. Ibid.

41. Ibid., pp. 386–87.

42. Ibid., p. 387.

43. Furness, Variorum, pp. 28–29.

44. Ridley, *Othello,* p. 38.

45. See Paul Werstine, "The Textual Mystery of *Hamlet,*" *Shakespeare Quarterly* 39 (Spring 1988): 1–26.

46. Edwin Booth sees the change as being metatheatrical (a term hardly in use in Booth's time), nine in the morning being the hour at which the King's Men would rehearse (cited in New Variorum, p. 78).

47. Ross, *Othello,* p. 72.

48. Walker and Wilson, *Othello,* p. 170.

49. Sanders, *Othello,* pp. 189–90.

50. I would argue that in this case it is the F1 reading that needs defending, not the Q1-Q2 reading. The F1 reading needs to be shown to be *not* the work of the censor but the work of Shakespeare the reviser. No one has considered that necessary.

51. Ross, *Othello,* p. 199.

52. Walker and Wilson, *Othello,* p. 207.

53. Gibbons, *Romeo and Juliet,* p. 208.

54. Sanders, *Othello,* p. 171.

55. Ibid.

56. If Iago's greeting to Bianca upon her entry, "O notable strumpet" (1.78; TLN 3179) is an aside, then we can see Iago beginning his plan to place the blame on her.

57. "When Isacles hang by the wall" in Winter's song at the conclusion of Q1 *Love's Labour's Lost* becomes "Isicles" in F1; and the "ysicles" that "*Phaebus* fire scarce thawes" in 2.1 of Q1 *Merchant of Venice* remain "ysicles" in F1.

58. I am indebted to Barbara Mowat of the Folger Shakespeare Library for leading me beyond Q2 *Othello* to its descendants in the remainder of the seventeenth century and the beginning of the eighteenth.

59. London, 1655 (Wing STC S2939), Sig. A1. The play was transferred from Richard Hawkins, the publisher of Q2, to R. Mead and C. Meredith on 29 May 1638; they in turn transferred it to William Leake on 29 January 1639 (Greg, *Bibliography,* vol. 2, p. 524). Leake reissued the 1637 quarto of *The Merchant of Venice* in 1652, a text derived from Q1–2 of that comedy.

60. London, 1681 (Wing STC S2940), Sig. A1.

61. *Hamlet's* two Caroline quartos (1632 and 1637) and its four Restoration quartos (1676, 1676, 1683, and 1695) testify to its popularity. It lacks a Commonwealth printing, however.

62. This quarto was printed for Richard Wellington, who took over Bentley's copyrights in 1697. See Terry Belanger, "Tonson, Wellington and the Shakespeare Copyrights," in *Studies in the Book Trade in Honour of Graham Pollard* (Oxford: The Oxford Bibliographical Society [vol. 18], 1975), p. 202.

63. London, 1709, 1, Sig. A2–A2ᵛ.

64. Capell, *Mr. William Shakespeare his Comedies, Histories, and Tragedies* (London: J. and R. Tonson, 1768), 1: 15–16.

65. *The Library,* ser. 4, 10 (1929–30): 466.

66. "Shakespearean Scholarship: From Rowe to the Present," in *William Shakespeare; His World, His Work, His Influence,* ed. John F. Andrews (New York: Charles Scribner's Sons, 1985), 3: 718.

67. Wells and Taylor, *William Shakespeare: A Textual Companion,* p. 54.

68. Barbara Mowat, "The Form of *Hamlet's* Fortunes," *Renaissance Drama,* n.s. 19 (1988), pp. 97–126.

69. Rowe most likely used the 1681 quarto (Q4) or later, as he conflates the F4 *dramatis personae* with that of the later quartos, Q4, Q5, Q6, and 1705 being identical.

70. Rowe could have relined F4 without consulting Q2, just as he could have created stage directions without using Q2. Q2's influence rests more firmly with its textual contributions, which may not be fully represented in the scenes I chose. Three examples from act 1, scene 3, better demonstrate Q2's influence:

1. 1.3.138–39 (TLN 484–85):

> And with it all my travels' history
> Wherein of antres vast and deserts idle

F1/F4 read "portance in" for Q1-Q2-Rowe "With it all." F1/F4 read "Travellers." Rowe reads "Travels," following Q1-Q2. F4 reads "wild" for Q1-F1-Rowe "idle."

2. 1.3.144 (TLN 490):

> Do grow beneath their shoulders. This to hear

F1/F4 read "Grew" against Q1-Q2 "Do grow," which becomes Rowe's "Did grow." Q1's "This" is replaced by "These Things" F1/F4. Q2 drops "things," and Rowe follows, reading "These to hear."

3. 1.3.256–57 (TLN 610–11):

> Let her have your voice.
> Vouch with me, heaven, I therefore beg it not

The New Cambridge follows the F1/F4 reading. Q1 reads "Your voices, Lords: beseech you, let her will / Have a free way; I therefore beg it not." Rowe follows Q2's conflation: "Your voices, Lords: bessech you let her will / Have a free way. / Vouch with me heaven, I therefore beg it not."

71. Wells and Taylor, *Shakespeare: Complete Works,* p. xxxvii.

2

Repetition and Interrogation in *Othello*
"What needs this Iterance?" or, "Can anything be made of this?"

THOMAS MOISAN

INTRODUCTION

And first of all others your figure that worketh by iteration or repetition of one word or clause doth much alter and affect the eare and also the mynde of the hearer, and therefore is counted a very braue figure both with the Poets and rhetoriciens. . . .

There is a kind of figuratiue speech when we aske many questions and looke for none answere, speaking indeed by interrogation, which we might as well say by affirmation.
—George Puttenham

The ears of men are not only delighted with store and exchange of divers words but feel great delight in repetition of the same. . . .

Interrogation is but a warm proposition, and therefore oftentimes serves more fitly than a bare affirmation, which were but too gentle and harmless a speech. . . . It is very fit for a speech to many and indiscreet hearers . . . and then it may well be frequented and iterated.
—John Hoskins

To the ears of a Puttenham or a Hoskins Shakespeare's *Othello* would not have sounded out of tune. For it is a play that has been frequently cited, and celebrated, for, in Bernard Shaw's phrase, "the splendor of its word-music,"[1] for memorable resonances created and impressed, and reimpressed, upon the ear by an opulent array of what Puttenham calls "auricular figures."[2] Conspicuous among these are the figures described above, interrogation and repetition, or what Othello at one point in his most critical and enlightening exchange with Emilia near the end of the play (5.2.150) terms "iterance." Much of what is said in *Othello* seems to get said a number of times and is often repeated in the form of questions, questions not infrequently answered by their own reiterated echoes. Hence, with Othello we may ask, "What needs this iterance?" What purpose is served, what effect achieved by the numerous and recurrent questions uttered in the play? For all that they may contribute to its acoustical architecture, what role do repetition and interrogation in *Othello* play in its definition, and the audience's experience of it, as tragic theater?

Or, rather, what "roles"? For in what is to follow I would propose that the figures of repetition and interrogation in *Othello* "operate" in a diversity of ways and with a polyphony of resonance that complicate our experience of the play and underscore the complexity that its students, at least since the time of Rymer, have found in it. Instrumental in giving formal shape to *Othello* as an argument and fable, underscoring the premises of its plot and the predicates of its actions, the play of repetition and questioning simultaneously evokes a dissonance that challenges our understanding of what the play enacts and, more to the point, challenges our ability to know and make judgments about what we have experienced. This challenge has been most perceptible, perhaps, in the notorious penumbrae that invest the issues of character and motive in the play, in the ever recurrent questions it has inspired concerning character motivelessly malignant and character all too readily corrupted. Yet the workings of repetition and questioning in *Othello* seem to have a deeper and subversively reflexive force as well, giving voice to an ambivalence within the play about the very medium of its expression: exemplifying the manipulative power of rhetoric, they at times suggest a rhetoric that eludes the control of those who would manipulate it; employed ostensibly to underscore a reference and seek elucidation, they often appear to underscore nothing so much as the power of language to obscure or suppress reference, and help to enunciate what Gayle Greene has called the play's "refusal to elucidate."[3]

At the same time, the repetition and questioning we encounter at the verbal surface of *Othello* are but the audible signatures of that deeper recursiveness and "demand for narrative" which, as Patricia Parker has reminded us recently, are central impulses in the play, impulses dramatized in its opening moments and in its closing words.[4] By the same token, however, the dissonances we detect in the operations of repetition and questioning alert us to the tensions which that recursiveness and "demand for narrative" occasion. For in the rhetorical world of *Othello* narration seems ever to entail variation, repetition with a "difference"—or *differance*—while the insistent demand for narrative seems persistently part of an ambivalent response to what has already been narrated, a response in part incredulous and resistant to what has been heard, but ultimately willing to hear more. "Tush, never tell me," Roderigo tells Iago in the opening line of the play, and waits to be told again, and again, how Iago hates the Moor. "She wish'd she had not heard it," Othello recalls Desdemona saying after she had heard his "story," a demurral attended by a request that Othello takes as grounds for a reprise (1.3.162–66).

A central activity of contemporary criticism, Jonathan Culler has observed, has been to dis-cover in a text its appetency for "self-reference," a "self-reference that ultimately brings out the inability of any discourse to account for itself."[5] Culler's remark comes to mind here because to a considerable degree the activity, and preoccupations, to which it alludes are reflected in the issues my essay raises, the strategy it pursues, the vocabulary it employs, and— with some qualification—the argument it constructs. To examine the play of repetition and interrogation in *Othello* is, I would maintain, to encounter a rhetoric at once reflexive and subversive, and suggestive of a discourse commenting upon itself and turning what it says and enacts either literally into questions or into something questionable, something that evades accountability. In the echo chamber *Othello* comes at times to resemble, the action of the play gets distilled into catechetical *examens* of individual phrases and words which in their reverberations ultimately remain unelucidated, leaving unresolved the very issues to which they are instrumental in calling attention. Yet far from expressing an inability "to account for itself," what I believe the operations of "iterance" and interrogation ultimately enable us to experience in *Othello* is theater proclaiming with no little self-assurance its power to create spectacle and hold attention, no matter how inscrutable its protagonist, no matter how fluid—or flimsy—the narrative premises of the main action. Indeed, in that recursiveness and demand for narrative we hear in the play of its repetition and interrogation, *Othello* engages us intertextually in the kinds of narratives, and narrativity, from which it derives its fable, only to underscore its distance and difference from those narratives, only to assert its power to improvise, creating and revising its script as it goes along, a power that it incarnates in, and ultimately arrays against, the arch improviser of the play, Iago.

I

At the verbal surface of *Othello,* the many instances of repetition and interrogation one encounters seem very much the accouterments of mimetic fidelity, with the impression of rhetorical eloquence they impart to the play a measure of its thematic elegance. Investing the play with that "formality" of style G. Wilson Knight so admired,[6] figures of repetition and questioning help to frame it *as* a formal discourse, or, as Marion Trousdale has analyzed it, as a rhetorical *res,* as an illusion to be perpetrated and argument to be mounted and persuasively sustained.[7] To hear Othello, for example, refer again and again to "honest" Iago is, again and again, to hear "amplified"—as Shakespeare's contemporaries understood the term[8]—the deceit of Iago and the credulity of Othello. To gauge the enormity of Iago's duplicity, we need but sense the surprise implicit in Emilia's reiterated question, "My husband?" when Othello insists to her that Iago knew all about Desdomona's alleged infidelity: "Thy husband knew it all" (5.2.136–52). And to be reminded of how widely Othello's suspicion of Desdemona misses the mark, we need but listen to Desdemona ask Emilia repeatedly whether a woman would ever "do such a deed" as Othello has accused her of, "for all the world," only to turn the words of her question into an emphatic denial: "Beshrew me, if I would do such a wrong / For the whole world" (4.3.61–79). Examples abound the cumulative effect of which is to shape and italicize what would appear to be the central premises of the tragedy: the curiously grand yet precarious credulity of Othello, the abused and misprised virtue of Desdemona, the perfidy of "honest, honest" Iago.

In fact, rather than ask what the repetition and interrogation tell us, we might wonder why we need to be told it so often, why we need, to take one of the most blatant examples, to have the magnitude of Iago's duplicity—and others' gullibility—impressed upon us so insistently by the word *honest* and its cognates no fewer than, to go by William Empson's count, fifty-two times.[9] Here, though, we sense something of the reflexive, and subversive, force in the play of repetition and interrogation in *Othello.* For, as has often been remarked, the proliferation of references to "honesty" in *Othello*—as a term for the bluntness with which Iago colors his speech, or for the moral probity he is erroneously perceived to possess, or for the sexual fidelity Desdemona is erroneously perceived to lack, or for any of the fifty-seven varieties of the word Empson has so finely sifted—brings nothing to our attention as much as it does the multivalency, and semantic slipperiness, both in the word *honest* itself and in the language of the play as a whole. Parker has addressed this multivalency with especial acuteness by exploring the sundry and complementary significations of the word "dilations," in the phrase, "close dilations" (3.3.123). Enumerating the meanings attached to the word, *dilate,* in Shakespeare's time, "to unfold" or "amplify," "to delay," and "to accuse," Parker argues that to understand the "close dilations" of *Othello* is not to choose any one preferred connotation of *dilation,* but to read the term for its totality of reference and as "a kind of semantic crossroads or freighted term suggestive of all three of those resonances—amplification, accusation, delay—which are so much a part of the unfolding of this particular tragedy."[10] Still, the more appreciative we grow of the "multivalency" of the language in *Othello* in general, the more keenly we may feel the "ambiguity" of that language in particular instances, a feeling that the operations of repetition and interrogation greatly help to intensify. There is irony in hearing Iago referred to as "honest," an irony that increases with the reiteration of the reference. Yet the irony lies in our repeated recognition, not simply of a discrepancy between what Iago is and how he is perceived and described, but of a dissonance between the word and the reality it has failed to represent. To hear Iago repeatedly called "honest" is to hear the language of the play repeatedly advertise its own unreliability and the tenuousness of its relationship to "truth."

At the same time, however, in the echoing refrains of "honest, honest Iago" the language of Othello may be signaling, not only its unreliability—literally, its irresponsibility—but its rhetorical power as well, its power to shape illusions and theatrical facsimiles of reality. Trousdale, for one, has argued that through Iago in particular Shakespeare shows "not how evil rhetorical method is, but how effective in the most unpromising of situations such rhetorical method can be."[11] Implicit in this comment is the suggestion that Shakespeare's challenge in *Othello* is but one remove from Iago's. If Iago's is to bring about, in almost no time at all, the subversion of the noble Othello's love for the virtuous Desdemona through nothing more substantial than the power of language, so Shakespeare's is to bring all of this off *and* to remind us that he is bringing it off by employing a rhetoric that calls attention to its own power by repeatedly insisting upon what it has contrived.

We hear this rhetorical self-advertisement in the reiteration that highlights, as we have noted, the central premises of the play: the credulity of Othello, the virtue of Desdemona, their love, his jealousy, and ever, of course, the "marvelous" malignancy and skill of Iago.[12] We also hear it, though, in the repetition of a number of rhetorical questions that punctuate the play as so many pieces of ecphrasis. "Is he not jealous?" asks Emilia about Othello (3.4.29), only to answer her question by repeating it when Othello gives Desdemona her first hint that he might, indeed, be subject to that emotion (3.4.99). "Is this the noble Moor whom our full Senate / Call all in all sufficient? Is this the nature / Whom passion could not shake?" asks Lodovico after one of Othello's least "sufficient," most passionate displays, "whose solid virtue / The shot of accident nor dart of chance / Could neither graze nor pierce?" (4.1.264–68). "I will catechize the world for him," the Clown remarks in response to Desdemona's request that he find Cassio, "that is, / make questions, and by them answer" (3.4.16–17).

In no instance does interrogation in *Othello* seem more rhetorical and more self-referential than in the recurrence of the seemingly inconsequential and exclamatory question, "Is't possible?," a "question" to be taken, one presumes, not as a genuine solicitation for information or clarification, but as a rhetorical interjection—an interrogative translation, perhaps, of *mirabile dictu!,* or forerunner of "That's incredible!" Expressive of incredulity in varying degrees of sincerity, the question "Is't possible?" challenges the plausibility of the proceedings to which it responds only to underscore their marvelousness and their dramatic truth, only to call attention to the dramatic pass to which matters have been brought by Iago's machinations. Yes, it is possible that Cassio was drawn into an extremely compromising brawl with someone and for some reason entirely unknown to him (2.3.284–87); and that Othello's suspicions move so far so fast that the mere thought of them convinces him that his "occupation's gone" (3.3.347–58); and that Othello's obsession with his jealousy is such that he endows that errant handkerchief with magical powers—"weaving" various stories about its history—the more significant to make its disappearance (3.4.55–75); and that, Othello's disbelief notwithstanding, Desdemona is neither a "strumpet" nor a "whore" (4.2.70–87). In its reiteration the question, "Is't possible?" functions as a commentary on the action of the play, and, as much as it asks anything of anyone onstage, it demands the audience's acknowledgment that these "incredible" developments have really come off. "Is't possible?" we hear ourselves being asked, to which we feel expected to answer yes.

Do "we," though? Or do the very configurations of language that ask the audience to ratify the experience of the play permit it to question that experience at the same time? Some years ago John Shaw charted the recurrence in *Othello* of yet another seemingly inconsequential question, "What is the matter?" To listen repeatedly to this altogether ordinary query, Shaw argued, is ultimately to grow more aware of how little most characters at most points of the play know, but also to grow less assured that we in the audience know at a given moment "what the matter is," or, even, what "matter" may mean.[13] Similarly, however "rhetorical" we may take a question to be, its very formulation as a question entails the conversion of a statement or assertion of fact into something hypothetical. The more we are asked, "Is't possible?" the more we may feel invited, not only to affirm the possibility of what has happened onstage, but to affirm it as mere possibility. Reiterated in the repetition of "Is't possible?" are both the insistent appeal the play is making for our credence, but also the insistent reminder that in *Othello* we find a fictional enterprise where what "is" is only as certain as what "may be," and where what "may be" demands our continued assent for its validation. "I have told thee often, and I retell thee again and again," Iago admonishes his not entirely credulous dupe, Roderigo, "I hate the Moor" (1.3.364–66). Even as Iago's reiterated appeals to Roderigo's trust elicit repeated doubts, so the credence the play repeatedly seeks from the audience may have the effect of engendering the very disbelief it would have the audience suspend. In short, the more we are asked, "Is't possible?" the more we may wonder whether we must or can say yes.

II

In its fullest resonance, the question, "Is't possible?" echoes the action of *Othello* as a whole. For *Othello* is very much a drama of and *about* hypothetical shreds and patches, of surmises and questions concerning character and conduct which in being voiced and rehearsed yield further surmises and questions that turn unexamined assumptions about character and conduct into threatening nebulae. At no point does the question of what is possible reverberate more destructively, of course, than in the celebrated "seduction" scene of act 3, in which the insinuations of Iago turn the loving and trusting Othello into the "green-ey'd monster" of hateful jealousy. To comment on a scene that has been so frequently discussed is to risk a redundancy especially embarrassing in an essay on repetition, but I turn to it here because it demonstrates so richly the doubleness, the impulses mimetic and subversive, embodied in the play of repetition and interrogation throughout *Othello*. Instrumental, on the one hand, in the rhetorical procedure through which Iago "poisons" the character of Othello, the tropes of repetition and questioning in the "seduction" scene have the underlying effect of reducing Othello's character, and character itself, to enigmas, to things inscrutable; exemplifying a language cunningly manipulated and misused, the reflexive pulsations of question and repetition in the scene suggest a discourse calling attention to its own power, its power to elude the control of those who would manipulate it and to confuse "what is real" with "what is possible."

In the unfolding of the "seduction" scene, figures of repetition and interrogation are most immediately conspicuous for the contribution they make to that syntax of indirection in which Iago ensnares Othello. A half-completed, half-retracted remark here and question there seem all that Iago requires to arouse Othello's curiosity and direct his attention to the possibility of Desdemona's infidelity and Cassio's dishonesty, a possibility Iago makes appear all the more luridly real by conveying the impression that he would rather drop the matter, so that, as Trousdale has put it, "Othello must literally drag the facts out of him."[14] For a choice reprise of Iago's method, we need but consider that proto-Pinteresque exchange that ensues when Othello, prompted by Iago's leading questions, recalls that, yes, Cassio did know of Othello's love for Desdemona before they were married, "and," in fact, "went between us very oft":

> *Iago.* Indeed?
> *Oth.* Indeed? ay, indeed! Discern'st thou aught in that?
> Is he not honest?
> *Iago.*　　　　　Honest, my lord?
> *Oth.* Honest? ay, honest.
> *Iago.*　　　　　My lord, for aught I know.
> *Oth.* What dost thou think?
> *Iago.*　　　　　Think, my lord?
> *Oth.* Think, my lord? By heaven, thou echo'st me,
> As if there were some monster in thy thought
> Too hideous to be shown. Thou dost mean something.
>
> (3.3.101–8)

It is a measure of Iago's rhetorical acumen that in what Puttenham calls "redoubling" the last word of Othello's question, "honest,"[15] Iago turns the question back upon Othello and compels him to ponder its multiple significations. Again, as with the reiterated question, "Is't possible?", the mere reference to Cassio's honesty *as* a question—whatever answer Othello thought he was eliciting—

makes Cassio's honesty something questionable and turns Othello's likely supposition that Cassio is honest into the possibility that he *may* be, from which cannot be excluded the possibility that he may *not* be, a possibility that Iago's interrogative echoing of "honest" enhances simply by not dispelling it.

The ease with which Iago triumphs in the "seduction" scene, and the rapidity with which Othello succumbs, have been crucial to the distinctions critics have drawn between the characters of Othello and Iago, distinctions which, in turn, have often been associated with the ostensible differences in the ways in which the two characters use and conceive of language, differences in their elocutionary styles, in the degrees of self-consciousness they bring to their speech, indeed, in the relationship they see between their words and their "selves." As Greene has noted, for example, perceptions of Othello have consistently fused, or confused, grandiloquence and inner grandeur, as Othello's "splendid, mouth-filling phrases win our allegiance and admiration" and lead us to take his eloquence as the "expression of that character's nobility."[16] More important, Othello's eloquence and attitude toward language have been taken as metaphors of his integrity and what might genuinely be called his self-possession, a sense of self predicated in Othello's belief in an absolute correspondence between the outer and the inner man, between what he says and does and what he is, a sense of wholeness reflected in the conviction he confides to Iago that "My parts, my title, and my perfect soul / Shall manifest me rightly" (1.2.31–32).[17] A character so deeply convinced of the correspondence between his own words and the truth may well be especially vulnerable to the rhetoric of an Iago, whose sense of self, inscribed in that frequently cited negation, "I am not what I am" (1.1.65), is clearly not burdened by any similar conviction. Madeleine Doran has argued that the poetically graceful, declarative pronouncements we associate with Othello's speech are more than an accident of style; they are the idiom of Othello's self, an idiom inimical and unequal to the conditional syntax with which Iago shapes the dialogue of the "seduction" scene. "Othello cannot entertain *ifs,*" Doran observes; unable to cope with the uncertainty of "what is possible," Othello can only replace the certitude of his unquestioning trust of Desdemona with the certitude of her infidelity.[18]

Such distinctions, and the essentialist reading of character in which they are rooted, would very much seem to be challenged by the operations of repetition and interrogation both in the "seduction" scene and in the play as a whole. The often stichomythic and catechetical exchanges through which Iago "works" upon Othello turn the two into rhetorical mirrors of each other in which distinctions of character are effaced, with the result, not so much of transforming the "noble" Othello into a clone of the "ignoble" Iago—though Othello's ultimate behavior might suggest that—but of revealing the character of Othello to be as much of an enigma, his motivations as far beyond accountability, as are the character and motivations of his adversary.

For one thing, Iago's ability to lead Othello on in the "seduction" scene depends heavily upon Othello's ability to follow, upon, not Othello's rhetorical innocence, but his sophistication, his ability to "read" the cues transmitted by Iago's repetition and questioning as a Puttenham or Hoskins would have them read, that is, as cues, as signifiers of some deeper, perhaps darker, meaning.[19] One senses that Othello and Iago may be communicants in the same rhetorical idiom in that exchange I cited just above, where, from Iago's first "indeed?" Othello's "victimization" is triggered by Othello's ability to read Iago's words closely, scrutinizing them rather as if he were interpreting a text, offering a commentary on both the verbal and nonverbal inflections of Iago's remarks:

> And when I told thee he was of my counsel
> In my whole course of wooing, thou criedst,
> "Indeed!"
> And didst contract and purse thy brow together,
> As if thou then hadst shut up in thy brain
> Some horrible conceit. If thou dost love me,
> Show me thy thought.
>
> (3.3.111–16)

As Portia remarks of her unfortunate suitors in *The Merchant of Venice* (2.9.81), Othello displays just enough rhetorical wisdom here by his wit to lose: he takes Iago's "Indeed" to be very much what Puttenham calls the figure of *"Synechdoche"* or *"Quicke conceit,"* a "single word" in which a "quicke wit" will discern some "intendment or large meaning . . . as by the halfe to vnderstand the whole," and he construes Iago's behavior in general as, in Puttenham's terminology, a figure of *Noema* or *"close conceit,"* "whereof," Puttenham explains, "we do not so easily conceiue the meaning, but as it were by coniecture, because it is wittie and subtle or darke,"[20] in Othello's words, "[s]ome horrible conceit."

Nor, it must be recalled, is that "horrible conceit" the exclusive property of Iago. Indeed, it can be argued that what Othello "drags out" of Iago, what he seeks to hear from Iago, are not "the facts"

Iago has invented, but the voiced confirmation of Othello's own "exsufflicate and blown surmises." "[T]hou echo'st me," Othello complains, "As if there were some monster in thy thought / Too hideous to be shown," an echoing that at once conceals the monster in Iago's thought only to reveal the monster Othello himself has conceived. "Give thy worst of thoughts / The worst of words" (132–33), Othello will subsequently demand of Iago, to which might be appended the translation, "give *my* worst of thoughts *thy* worst of words."

"Characters," Jonathan Goldberg has insisted, "exist within texts; their interiors are texts,"[21] an argument brought forcibly to mind by the rebounding words and echoing questions of the "seduction" scene, which seem less to reflect, or represent, the motivations, the "interiors" of character than to prescribe and conscribe them. Othello becomes suspicious of Cassio and Desdemona, it can be argued, because it is rhetorically possible to conceive of such a suspicion; the rhetorical canniness Othello displays in "reading" Iago's words enables him to make the case, or "cause," of this suspicion, and the formulation of the "cause" suffices for its substance. In the process, what might have appeared to be the *données* of Othello's character are effaced: the "free and open" nature Iago had ascribed to him (1.3.399), indeed, even his love for Desdemona. That Othello loves Desdemona initially would seem unquestionable; he proclaims that love quite unequivocally, after all, during a lull in the "seduction" scene, just before Iago renews his attack. Yet he expresses his love for Desdemona by casting it as part of an antithesis, as a condition coexistent with its negation:

> Excellent wretch! Perdition catch my soul
> But I do love thee! and when I love thee not,
> Chaos is come again.
>
> (3.3.90–92)

The reiterated sonorities of "love thee" and "love thee not" testify to the felicitous sound of Othello's speech, but one consequence of Othello's penchant for euphony here is, once again, the eradication of the distinction between fact and possibility, with what we might have taken to be the fact that Othello loves his "[e]xcellent wretch" sharing equal rhetorical billing with the chance that he may come not to love her, a chance worded very much as if it were an eventuality. When Chaos is imaginable in this way, Chaos can most surely be come again.

Here it might be objected that the analysis to this point both wrongly ignores the instrumental role accorded Iago in hastening Chaos's arrival and blurs a critical distinction between Iago's designs and their effects upon Othello. Put simply, Iago is in control and Othello is not; Iago knows what he is doing with language; Othello appears not to know what language is doing to him. Still, to scrutinze the "inner workings" of Iago's character, to assay, with many others, what Coleridge dubbed Iago's "motiveless malignity," and to note what Stephen Greenblatt has described as the improvisational properties of Iago's machinations[22] is to grow increasingly dubious of the nature or degree of that control. "I know not if't be true," Iago observes, in private, of the rumor about Othello that "twixt my sheets / H'as done my office; But I, for mere suspicion in that kind, / Will do as if for surety" (1.3.387-90). Scan Iago's notoriously unhelpful autobiographical pronouncements, or as Alessandro Serpieri terms them, his *énonciations,*[23] and one will find an ego-centrifugal "self" whose "deepest" impulses are sublimated and conscribed within reiterative formulas: the tautologous stipulation that "Were I the Moor, I would not be Iago" (1.1.57), the self-denying assertion that "I am not what I am" (1.1.65). In Iago's speech duplication is the linguistic inflection of the duplicity that is his character, a "doubleness" self-canceling rather than self-affirming, concealing his real self from others only to reveal that self to be, in Greenblatt's words, "absolute vacancy" (p. 236). Doubly corrosive, then, is the echoing that leads Othello to hear himself in Iago's words, which even as it renders questionable the inherent nobility of Othello's self, makes it conceivable that at the core of that self lies a vacancy no less absolute than Iago's.[24]

III

So far, at least, it might be argued that what has been observed about the effects of repetition and interrogation in *Othello* is simply consistent with the rhetorical dicta of a Puttenham or Hoskins or other commentators of the period, who envisioned such figures as instruments of an orator's or poet's intentions and extensions of his control.[25] That Shakespeare has Iago make use of repetition and interrogation to mirror Othello's thoughts in such a way as to render questionable what had been presumed would seem nothing more than an exemplary demonstration of the adroit indirection and manipulation that Puttenham describes above in that "kinde of figuratiue speach when we aske many questions and looke for none answere, speaking indeed by interrogation, which we might as well say by affirmation,"[26] or that the rhetorically astute Falstaff has in mind when he upbraids Hal for employing "damnable iteration" to twist Falstaff's words into jokes at Falstaff's expense. Yet, as the dynamics of the "seduction" scene suggest, the self-referential play of questioning and repetition in *Othello* simultaneously evokes as a possibility the power of language to elude control and divorce itself from clear and clearly retrievable referents, rendering motives ever ulterior or elliptical and turning emotions and convictions of identity into mere traces of feeling and hypotheses of self-definition.[27]

Such is the effect of the repetition and questioning through much of the interaction of Iago and Othello, and one finds an especially vivid example in the piece of *catechesis* one happens upon in the opening moments of act 4:

> *Iago.* Will you think so?
> *Oth.*   Think so, Iago?
> *Iago.*   What,
> To kiss in private?
> *Oth.*   An unauthorized kiss.
> *Iago.* Or to be naked with her friend in bed,
> An hour, or more, not meaning any harm?
> *Oth.* Naked in bed, Iago, and not mean harm?

In his analysis of the "seduction" scene, Serpieri has commented on the use Iago makes of such deictic remarks as "I like not that" (3.3.35) to leave "the precise sense suspended" and excite a "demand" in Othello for "explication of the meaning, that is for a semantic disambiguation" (p. 141). In the opening of act 4 we find both an echo and an elaboration of this pattern, with Iago once again making use of deixis, though not so much to suspend the "precise sense" of something Othello has said, as to render it dubious, questioning it to turn it into something warranting justification and, shortly thereafter, rejection. Here, however, dramatic form and Iago are in clear collusion. For the assertion literally in question is submerged in the interval between Othello's peremptory exit from the previous scene and the start of this one, submerged only to be refracted and metonymized at the verbal surface in the bits and pieces of Iago's—and Othello's—prurient exempla: "To kiss in private," "An unauthorized kiss," "to be naked with her friend in bed, / An hour, or more." Moreover, in repeating Iago's opening question in elliptical, subjectless form, "Think so, Iago?", Othello implicitly dissociates himself from whatever it was to which Iago—and the trace word "so"—had been referring. When, as the exchange develops, we surmise that what has been questioned and undermined here is the possibility that had been raised—presumably, but not "unquestionably," by Othello—that Desdemona did "not mean harm," we can appreciate how erosive the force of language has been in this instance. For in effacing the original statement in which the possibility of Desdemona's innocence had been advanced, the play of repetition and questioning in the exchange also suppresses the connective tissue of emotion and thought that had made that possibility at least conceivable. To be sure, the exchange can be read as still more evidence of Iago's rhetorical agility; yet the suppressive and reflexive force of interrogation and reiteration here effectively asserts the power of language to create and re-create its own contexts of reference even as it obliterates the contexts from which it had proceeded.

Nor is it only in the interaction of Iago and Othello that this power is trumpeted. One hears it as well in the recurrent transformation of persons and propositions into metonyms, in words or labels which in being echoed in reiterative and interrogative configurations might seem intended to divert attention from what they ostensibly represent.[28] Nowhere is this more dramatically evident than at the moment in act 5 in which Othello contemplates the sleeping Desdemona and weighs the action he is about to take against her:

> It is the cause, it is the cause, my soul!
> Let me not name it to you, you chaste stars,
> It is the cause.
>
> (5.2.1–3)

It is one of the speeches Bradley cites as evidence of Othello's "poetic" nature,[29] and at least a part of its poetic and emotional resonance lies in the eloquent reiteration of the "cause." What has been called in passing Othello's "logically needless" insistence upon the "cause"[30] might well be explained as evidence of a conflict within Othello between his love for Desdemona and the "cause" which has been ordained, and to which he is impelled, by Justice. Yet to offer this hypothesis is to overlook how much the sense, or reference, here is elliptical, and how much the effect of the reiterated "cause" is to divert the audience, and Othello himself, from identifying what "it" is. In fact, far from attesting to Othello's love for Desdemona, the repetition of "cause" might just as readily inscribe an attempt by Othello to absolve himself from having to acknowledge and reexamine the conviction that has determined her

fate, the more assuredly to pass on to her execution. That "it" refers
to the issue of Desdemona's infidelity one might infer from Othello's
reluctance to mention "it" to the "chaste stars" who happen to be
present in the bedroom, though, again, their very presence provides
a convenient pretext for Othello not to name, or, perhaps, think, of
the "it" for which Desdemona is shortly to be dispatched. Instead,
the antecedent of "it" gets subsumed within the multiple and un-
discriminated significations of "cause"—as "agency," "principle,"
and "argument"—in a passage that reads like an odd variation on
praeterition, one in which the matter to be passed over actually gets
passed over!

In turn, the same metonymic process that suppresses the antecedent of "it" and "cause" in this speech works upon the presence
and very identity of Desdemona as well. "Put out the light," Othello
instructs himself, "and then put out the light"(7). In repeating the
words, Othello turns the self-instruction into a self-referential trope,
and what begins as the preparative to the killing of Desdemona
turns into a brief exercise in explication and a process of trans-
figuration, with Desdemona undergoing a depersonification to become "Thou cunning'st pattern of excelling nature" (11), even as
the candle, whose light put out can be "relumed," is personified as
"thou flaming minister" (8). With Desdemona at once raised and
reduced to an image, to but an exquisite "pattern" of perfection,
Othello effectively suppresses Desdemona's identity, acknowledging that suppression only after he has smothered her, when Emilia's
knock at the door brings back to him the word and with it the wife
he has extinguished:

> If she come in, she'll sure speak to my wife.
> My wife, my wife! what wife? I have no wife.
>
> (96–97)

Indeed, the recognition into which Othello is jolted here serves
not only to alert us to what has transpired in this scene, but to
underscore the connubial disfigurement Desdemona has sustained
throughout the play by being represented either as Othello's "wife-
about-to-be" or his "wife-about-to-be-destroyed." Epitomized in
Othello's repetition and questioning and final negation of the word
wife is an effect produced by iteration and interrogation throughout
the play, and that is, not simply to leave the complexities of
character and relationships shadowy, but to illuminate them as
shadows.

At the same time, the divorce of language and reference evoked by the subversive and suppressive play of repetition and questioning in Desdemona's murder scene is allegorized in the various tautological configurations and allusions to "words" that recur throughout *Othello*. The frequent use of reiterative devices, such as the *diaphora* and *ploce* that Iago employs in his self-nondefinitions, creates an aural image of language as some self-contained, self-referential system, powerful and destructive, not in spite of its literal "irresponsibility," but because of it. "[W]ords are words," the aggrieved Brabantio replies to the Duke's platitudinous *sententiae* of consolation. "I never yet did hear / That the bruis'd heart was pierced through the ear" (1.3.218–19), a proposition which, as Greene has commented, much of what actually happens in the play would seem to refute (p. 270). In turn, *paranomasia*, the pun, emerges as the figurative emblem of this studied insistence of language upon its "disconnectedness." If this disconnectedness is at first comically underscored in the exchange between Desdemona and the Clown in which the latter "answers" Desdemona's question, "Do you know, sirrah, where Lieutenant Cassio lies?," by teasing out of thought the divers significations of the word "lie" (3.4.1–13), its destructive force is more lugubriously reaffirmed in that reprise on "lie" in the very next scene, where, amid the echoing possibilities of lying "with," lying "on," and belying her, Othello falls from sense to, as James Calderwood has put it, "the edges of the sublinguistic" (p. 297): "Pish!" (4.1.35–43). "Can anything be made of this?," Desdemona asks (3.4.10); "Is't possible?," Othello demands (4.1.42): questions to which the rhetoric of the moment seems to impel the successive answers, "No," and "Yes."

Again, answers to such questions in *Othello* seem never to be quite as univocal as might at first be supposed, and here one must be careful not to confuse what the language of the play proclaims and what it actually achieves. For the recurrent imbrication of words in doubling, self-referential tropes serves not so much to secure the divorce of language from a referential function as to create the sense that everything in the play is to be heard and seen through a tension created by dual and dissonant foci of reference, the one encased in rhetorical discourse, the other in a veritably shadowy realm that lies beyond the world of rhetoric and that rhetoric cannot reach, and of which the words themselves that rhetoric employs *may* be but chimeras. Such is the tension Othello at once acknowledges and challenges en route to his verbal and physical collapse when he protests that "Nature / would not invest herself in such shadowing passion / without some instruction. It is not words that shakes / me thus" (4.1.39–42), with what Kittredge calls Othello's "incoherent madness"[31] but a theatrical reflex of his inability to locate coherence, to ascertain if there is a coherence between the "shadowy passion" of his words and some ulterior "instruction." Such is the tension Desdemona feels when she tells Othello that "I understand a fury in your words, / But not the words," when Othello's rhetorical power subsumes both his rage at her infidelity and the need to confront her in an elaborate parody of a brothel transaction (4.2.23–33). And finally, it is the tension born of this dual perspective that is metonymically underscored through the interaction of figures of repetition and interrogation calling into question the meaning, identity, and very being of the words designating the fundamental relationships in the play. Even as Othello formally voids his "wife" some moments after destroying the person who bore that title, so Desdemona must ask Emilia, "Who is thy lord?" only to conclude, "I have none" (4.2.101–2), and even as Emilia herself, in that exquisitely protracted moment of *anagnorisis,*[32] will repeatedly incarnate everything she cannot understand, or accept, in Othello's account of Desdemona's infidelity in just two words: "My husband?" "I say thy husband," Othello reiteratively insists. "[D]ost understand the word?" (5.2.141–153).

IV

Even as Emilia's repeated question, "My husband?", very much vexes Othello in his attempt to give an account and justification of his "cause," so it also brings emphatically into juxtaposition, or collision, two significant elements of our experience of *Othello,* on the one hand, the dissonances and instability of the "word" that we encounter on the verbal surface of the play, and on the other, the underlying recursiveness and demand for narrative that inform the structure of the play. The most audible registers of this recursiveness and narrativity, figures of reiteration and interrogation, alert us in their subversive and self-referential play to the narrative discontinuities *Othello* embodies, redefining the play for us as a set of revisionary texts and enabling us to hear in its repeated calls for narrative a repeated questioning, as in Emilia's interrogation of Othello, of the narratives it presents. Indeed, that the call for and the questioning of narrative are inseparable is underscored in the opening line of the play, where Roderigo's rejection of whatever it was that Iago had most recently said, "Tush, never tell me!", ensures its being resaid, though clearly resaid with a difference calculated to gain its acceptance and Roderigo's credence. Opening as it does, *Othello* casts itself from the start in a rhetorical posture curiously identical to that of its designated villain, while establishing an equally curious—and somewhat demeaning—mutuality of interests between its audience and one of its villain's designated dupes. If unlike Roderigo "we" as audience do not enter the play on a note of hostility and outright rejection, we are quickly associated with him in our need to hear rehearsed the grounds for whatever it is that Iago is contriving. Trousdale has made the Renaissance rhetorical predilection for *copia* through variation central to her discussion of Shakespeare's dramaturgical strategies in *Othello* and other plays,[33] and the use to which Iago puts "varying" in reessaying, or reassailing, Roderigo well exemplifies the power of this method when skillfully applied. In Iago's practice, however, "varying," repetition with a difference, comes so much to resemble Derridean *differance* in the violence of its revisions and displacement of antecedents as to seem a travesty and transgression of the very method it exemplifies.[34] If Iago's singular variation on varying is most conspicuously on display in his repeated voicings of his motives, it is epitomized in his hortatory remarks to Roderigo near the end of act 1, where the forcible reiteration of "put money in thy purse" ironically italicizes the disparate character of the particulars Iago has forcibly yoked together to make the case for the imminent dissolution of Othello's and Desdemona's relationship (1.3.339–72). Again, the audience may find its own response personified in Roderigo, who, repeatedly questioning Iago's account of things, is repeatedly a witness to and participant in the ever more elaborate spectacle of Iago's rhetorical improvisation.

Nor, of course, is it in the language of Iago alone that this spectacle is to be beheld. It takes no more than the first twenty lines of Othello's first appearance in the play, after all, to sense the degree to which Othello equates himself with the telling of the story of himself, with the narrative voicing of his deeds: alerted by the solicitous Iago that Brabantio is likely to take action because of the elopement of Desdemona, Othello is confident both that the "services which I have done the signiory / Shall out-tongue his complaints" (1.2.18–19), and that his own "demerits / May speak, unbonneted, to as proud a fortune / As this that I have reach'd" (22–24). So too, because for Othello one's self and one's résumé are so closely linked, there are a recursiveness and reflexivity intrinsic to Othello's very sense of being, so that, as Calderwood has remarked, Othello's "self-defense" before the Venetian Senate parses as "a voice telling about himself telling about himself" (p. 294).

Yet as storytelling is inherently rhetorical, so the story that Othello equates with his life is indissociable from a rhetorical agenda. Well aware of the curiosity the recitation of his story repeatedly arouses in both Desdemona *and* Brabantio, Othello recalls taking that curiosity as the "hint" to relate his story again and again (1.3.142, 166). At the same time one would expect Othello, rhetorically attuned to the interests of his auditors, to be rhetorically sensitive to the strategies required to shape and re-shape his narrative to keep its reiteration "still" (i.e., repeatedly) interesting, repeatedly responsive to the questions that his account repeatedly engenders (1.3.128–29) and that call for further narration. So it is that one finds evidence of "varying" in Othello's story—varying which, given the identification of Othello's story with his "self," amounts to a genuine self-differentiation. One hears such varying in the discrepancies of Othello's successive descriptions of that errant handkerchief, which Othello will ultimately say was "an antique token" given to his mother by his father (5.2.216–17), but which he earlier had "woven" into a talisman given his mother by an Egyptian charmer (3.4.55–68), as if in an attempt, not only to intimidate Desdemona with its importance but, again, to invest it with a significance that would exacerbate his suspicion that Desdemona had given it away. And, to be sure, one finds evidence of "varying" in the surprise one feels at Desdemona's recollection of the role Cassio had played in Othello's courtship (3.2.70–73), a detail that had managed not to find its way into the account of his wooing that Othello had earlier given to the Senators.[35] To the degree, then, to which Othello's "story" draws our attention to the narrativity of the play, it also helps to inscribe the play as a discourse ever revising itself and improvising its own text, and calls to mind G. Wilson Knight's intuitive perception of *Othello* as a work of "outstanding differences."[36]

To the degree, however, to which *Othello* calls attention to itself as a narrative, it also, and literally, contextualizes itself among the narrative sources that provide the nutrients of its fable and the models for its characters. One vein of the writings to which *Othello* is heir has, of course, been well explored by Geoffrey Bullough, who has gone far in compiling the many details of plot and characterization that connect *Othello,* not only to its likely immediate source in Cinthio's *Gli Hecatommithi,* but to the store of Italian *novelle* so popular in the latter decades of the sixteenth century— those stories of domestic tragedy and sensationialist love cum violence so excoriated by Ascham as the "merry books" and "enchantments of Circe brought out of Italy to mar men's manners in England."[37] Yet another vein, however, has been discussed in recent studies by Rosalind Johnson and Karen Newman, and comprises the various travel accounts of Africa that at once appealed to and stimulated Shakespeare's contemporaries' sense of the exotic, among them *The History and Descryption of Africa* (1526, trans. 1600) by Al-Hassan Ibn-Mohammed Al-Wezaz Al-Fasi, or, as he was more often called in the West, Leo Africanus.[38]

To situate *Othello* among these writings is to sharpen and complicate one's sense of its recursiveness. Reprising and affiliating itself with scenarios and characters already and often rehearsed for its audience in other works, *Othello* also proves recursive in the degree to which the incidence of reiteration we encounter in its language and structure is but an echo of and allusion to the recursiveness to be heard in its sources and analogues. In listening to Othello tell about telling about the story of himself, one may, for example, be reminded both of the repeated accounts Leo Africanus delivered about himself as he made his way, sometimes captive, through the numerous cultures of the Mediterranean region, and of the many marvels and strange travails which Leo, like Othello, endured and re-presents as the record of his life. Yet what most audibly connects Othello and Leo is the frequentative, reiterative character of their accounts and exploits. "I maruell much how euer he should haue escaped so manie thousands of imminent dangers," Leo's English translator, John Pory, remarks, recording his admiration at—if not for—his subject's repeated feats of survival in a set of interrogative variations on "Is't possible?". "I maruel much more, how euer he escaped them. For how many desolate cold mountaines, and huge, drie, and barren deserts passed he? How often was he in hazard to haue beene captiued, or to haue had his throte cut by the prouling Arabians, and wilde Mores? And how hardly manie times escaped he the Lyons greedie mouth, and the deuouring iawes of the Crocodile?" (p. 6).

So too, the ecphrastic, exclamatory questions that punctuate *Othello*, such as Emilia's "Is he not jealous?", would seem to have their antecedents in the recurrent efforts of the *novella* writers and translators to fit the often lurid spectacles they are presenting into at least a facsimile of a moral frame. So it is that the narrator in Geoffrey Fenton's translation of Bandello's story of "The Albanian Captain" opens the tale by asking "how he can be acquitted from an humour of a frantic man, who, without any cause of offence in the world, commits cruel execution upon his innocent wife, no less fair and furnished in all perfections than chaste and virtuous without comparison?"[39] Later, just in case the answer to that question may have eluded his reader, Fenton asks an easier "follow-up": "What life were like to the married man's state, or pleasures semblable to the joys of the bed, if either the one or the other might be dispensed withal from the fury of frantic jealousy?"[40] "Is not this man jealous?"

Yet even as *Othello* offers a repetition of the details and conventions of its narrative sources, its repetition is, again, one with a "difference." At the outset of "The Albanian Captain" Fenton promises to "expose" to his readers "a miserable accident, happening in our time, which shall serve as a bloody scaffold or theatre, wherein are presented such as play no parts but in mortal and furious tragedies."[41] *Othello* enacts the "accident" and provides the "Scaffold or theatre," but, as has been seen, it undermines the very sort of questions that a Fenton would use as moral framing devices, eschews narrative continuity, and in doing so asserts its self-sufficiency as a theatrical spectacle. Indeed, the tension we encounter at the verbal surface of *Othello,* the sense the play of repetition and interrogation conveys of a duality of focus, is a signature of a dissonance the play orchestrates between the particularity of its action, its "accident," and the paradigms and revisions inscribed in the stories and discourses that have nurtured it. The most conspicuous—and most frequently noted—trace of this dissonance is the dual time scheme, through which the play makes just enough reference to actions that demand a frequentative and extensive duration of time to recall, on the one hand, the temporal spaciousness and illusion of temporal verisimilitude inhabiting the fictional world of its sources, and on the other, the temporal economy of the world of the stage.[42] In the juxtaposition of the two temporal orders, the audience is confronted with an incongruity that cannot be explained, or explained away, and with a vivid image of the right claimed by theater to improvise the unfolding of its spectacle by its own laws.

The uneasy antiphony the play negotiates between its narrativity and its theatricality receives its final and fullest voicing in the play of repetition and interrogation with which *Othello* concludes. Like the final moments in other Shakespearean tragedies the ending of *Othello* invites its audience to empathize with those onstage seeking to make sense of the spectacle they have witnessed, even as it ultimately leaves the effort unrewarded, or, at least, incomplete. The audience may, at any rate, hear its own desire for clarification articulated in Lodovico's question:

> O thou Othello, that was once so good,
> Fall'n in the practice of a damned slave,
> What shall be said to thee?
>
> (5.2.291–93)

At once ecphrastic and censorious, Lodovico's question in its very framing would appear to prescribe its answer and obviate further questions. For once the premise is accepted that Othello was "once so good" but had "Fall'n in the practice of a damned slave," what more need or can be said? Here one detects an attempt on the part of the play to circumscribe and finalize itself in morally lucid and reassuring terms, with Othello the culpable dupe whose "fault" must "be known / To the Venetian state" (336–37). When Othello subsequently stabs himself Lodovico punctuates the act as a "bloody period" (356), at once a tribute to the periodic eloquence— and length—of Othello's closing "word or two" (338–56), but also a compensatory attempt to declare the case resolved, with no further adjudication required than to dole out suitably grim punishment to the insolently silent Iago, to whom now falls the sole responsibility for "the tragic loading of this bed; / This is thy work" (363–64). When Lodovico then closes the play with the declaration that he "will straight abroad, and to the state / This heavy act with heavy heart relate" (370–71), one fully expects that his account will include a reiteration of the moralistic and self-answering question he had moments before uttered, a question bound to do little to elucidate the tragedy of Othello, but just the sort of reassuring question that one could imagine oneself encountering in the kinds of sensationalized fiction that provide the sources for plays like *Othello.*

Contributing to the sense that all has not been resolved, and leaving an impression of dissonance in what it does not say, is the silence of Iago, a silence that, among other things, suggests a resistance of the play as theater to being inscribed in the kind of account Lodovico will "relate."[43] In the articulation of his will to remain silent, however, Iago offers a recapitulation and epitome of the subversive roles repetition and interrogation have performed throughout the play:

> Demand me nothing; what you know, you know:
> From this time forth I never will speak word.
>
> (303–4)

So familiarly tautological in style, Iago's nonresponse to a question that had not yet been directly posed ensures the questioning it ostensibly would preempt. Denying Othello's question, it turns back upon and locates in Othello himself the literal responsibility for its answer. Italicizing what "we" know, it intensifies our sense of not knowing and our sense of language in the play as a domain impervious to the demands of reference.

Above all, the silence that ensues offers itself as the improvisationally resourceful Iago's ultimate *coup de théâtre,* a gesture which asserts the distinction between what theater enacts and what others may say about what has been enacted, and which, coupled with Othello's act of suicide, transforms the theatrical action into something self-consuming, self-immolating. At the same time, a gesture that asserts the particularity of what has been transacted onstage, Iago's very silence is an articulate repetition of the silence that envelops the tragic stage throughout Shakespeare's time. In the silence assumed by Iago and Othello, a silence assumed against the background noise of Lodovico's final words and promised report, one hears the self-enforced silence of the tongueless Hieronimo and the "silence" that for Hamlet was all "the rest."

NOTES

Sources for the epigraphs are as follows:
George Puttenham, *The Arte of English Poesie,* ed. Edward Arber (Westminster: A. Constable and Co., 1895), pp. 208, 220; John Hoskins, *Directions for Speech and Style,* ed. Hoyt H. Hudson (Princeton: Princeton University Press, 1935), pp. 32–33.

1. George Bernard Shaw, "*Othello:* Pure Melodrama," in *A Casebook on "Othello,"* ed. Leonard F. Dean (New York: Thomas Y. Crowell Co., 1961), p. 135. Shaw's sense of the musicality of *Othello* had already found expression, of course, in the collaboration of Verdi and his librettist, Boito, and would receive fuller elaboration in G. Wilson Knight, "The Othello Music," in *The Wheel of Fire: Interpretations of Shakespearean Tragedy, with Three New Essays* (London: Methuen, 1949), pp. 97–119.

2. Puttenham, *Arte of English Poesie,* p. 173.

3. Gayle Greene, " 'But Words Are Words': Shakespeare's Sense of Language in *Othello,*" *Etudes Anglaises* 34 (1981): 281.

4. Patricia Parker, "Shakespeare and Rhetoric: 'dilation' and 'delation' in *Othello,*" in *Shakespeare and the Question of Theory,* ed. Parker and Geoffrey Hartman (New York: Methuen, 1985), pp. 55ff.

5. Jonathan Culler, *On Deconstruction: Theory and Criticism after Structuralism* (London: Routledge and Kegan Paul, 1983), p. 201.

6. Knight, *Wheel of Fire,* pp. 97–98.

7. Marion Trousdale, *Shakespeare and the Rhetoricians* (London: Scolar Press, 1982), pp. 162–68.

8. See Hoskins, *Directions for Speech,* pp. 17, 29, and Puttenham, *Arte of English Poesie,* pp. 230–31; see also the discussions in Parker, "Shakespeare and

Rhetoric," pp. 54–59, and Rosemond Tuve, *Elizabethan and Metaphysical Imagery: Renaissance Poetic and Twentieth Century Critics* (Chicago: University of Chicago Press, 1947), pp. 146–54.

9. William Empson, *The Structure of Complex Words* (Norfolk, Conn.: James Laughlin, 1951), p. 218.

10. Parker, "Shakespeare and Rhetoric," p. 56.

11. Trousdale, *Shakespeare and the Rhetoricians,* pp. 162–63.

12. One is reminded of the reaction of the audience to the machinations of the Ensign against the Moor and Disdemona in the principal source of *Othello,* the story of the Moorish Captain and his Venetian wife in Giraldi Cinthio's *Gli Hecatommithi,* translated by Geoffrey Bullough in his *Narrative and Dramatic Sources of Shakespeare,* vol. 7 (London: Routledge and Kegan Paul, 1973). At the conclusion of the tale the narrator observes that "It appeared marvellous to everybody that such malignity could have been discovered in a human heart," p. 252.

13. John Shaw, " 'What Is the Matter?' in *Othello,*" *Shakespeare Quarterly* 17 (1966): 157–61.

14. Trousdale, *Shakespeare and the Rhetoricians,* p. 165.

15. Puttenham, *Arte of English Poesie,* p. 210.

16. Greene, " 'But Words Are Words,' " p. 271.

17. See Knight, *Wheel of Fire,* p. 105; D. A. Traversi, "Othello," in *Shakespeare: The Tragedies,* ed. Clifford Leech (Chicago: University of Chicago Press, 1965), p. 171; and James L. Calderwood, "Speech and Self in *Othello,*" *Shakespeare Quarterly* 38 (1987): 294–95.

18. Madeleine Doran, "Iago's 'if': An Essay on the Syntax of *Othello,*" in *The Drama of the Renaissance: Essays for Leicester Bradner,* ed. Elmer M. Blistein (Providence: Brown University Press, 1970), pp. 69–72. See also Wolfgang Clemen, *The Development of Shakespeare's Imagery* (London: Methuen & Co., 1977), pp. 119–32; Norman Rabkin, *Shakespeare and the Common Understanding* (New York: Free Press, 1967), pp. 67–73; and Greene, pp. 270–82.

19. Othello's sensitivity to rhetorical cues is evident from the account he gives the Senators of how Desdemona came to be in love with him, or, rather, how she came to love him "for the dangers I had passed." Twice in his speech he uses the word "hint" in a rhetorically suggestive context, saying first that it was his "hint" and his "process" to talk to Brabantio of his exotic exploits and travails (1.3.142), while adding later that when he perceived Desdemona's interest in his story he took that as his "hint" to speak (166). Indeed, Othello prefaces his address to the Senators with what, given his eloquence, sounds suspiciously like a rhetorically canny "modesty topos," when he announces, "Rude am I in my speech, / And little bless'd with the soft phrase of peace." Interestingly, one finds a similar disclaimer in the prefatory remarks of a figure who has at times been thought of as the inspiration for Othello, Leo Africanus, who appeals to his reader to accept his account of Africa "albeit not adorned with fine words, and artificiall eloquence," a rhetorically prudent but not overwhelmingly sincere note to be struck by someone described by his translator as having been "euen from his tender yeeres trained up at the Vniuersitie of Fez, in Grammar, Poetrie, Rhetorick, Historie, Cabala, Astronomie, and other ingenuous sciences. . . ." See John Pory's translation of Leo Africanus, *The History and Description of Africa* (1600), ed. Robert Brown (London: Hakluyt Society, 1896), vol. 1, pp. 5, 188.

20. Puttenham, *Arte of English Poesie,* p. 238.

21. Jonathan Goldberg, *Voice Terminal Echo: Postmodernism and English Renaissance Texts* (New York: Methuen, 1986), p. 3.

22. Stephan Greenblatt, *Renaissance Self-Fashioning from More to Shakespeare* (Chicago: University of Chicago Press, 1980), pp. 232–34.

23. Alessandro Serpieri, "Reading the Signs: Towards a Semiotics of Shakespearean Drama," trans. Keir Elam, in *Alternative Shakespeares,* ed. John Drakakis (London: Methuen, 1985), p. 139.

24. Serpieri (ibid., p. 142) has suggested an underlying equivalence between Othello and Iago in the degree to which both are "imprisoned" in the antithetical "rhetorical modes" that Serpieri takes to be the defining idioms of their beings, Iago in "negation," Othello in "hyperbolic affirmation." In *Shakespeare: Seven Tragedies: The Dramatist's Manipulation of Response* (London: Macmillan, 1976), pp. 77–100, E. A. J. Honigmann has established a bond between Othello and Iago in the degree to which the personalities and behavior of both are shaped by "secret motives" that are kept inaccessible to the audience throughout the play.

25. Puttenham, for example (*Art of English Poesie,* p. 207), commends the use of auricular figures as a strategy enabling the author to manipulate and capture the mind of his reader by appealing to the reader's ear: "Therefore the well tuning of your words and clauses to the delight of the eare, maketh your information no lesse plausible to the minde than to the eare: no though you filled them with never so much sence and sententiousnese."

26. Puttenham, *Arte of English Poesie,* p. 220.

27. It is this power that is implicated in Plato's suspicion that the use of rhetoric was indissociable from its abuse, a suspicion voiced most stridently, perhaps, in Socrates' analysis of the "art" of rhetoric in Plato's *Gorgias,* trans. W. R. M. Lamb (London: William Heinemann, 1925), pp. 313–21. And it is this power that Shakespeare most memorably italicizes in that scene in *Julius Caesar* in which the Plebeians, incensed by the rhetorical "mischief" of Marc Anthony's rhetoric (3.2.259), mistake Cinna the poet for Cinna the conspirator and demand that he be torn apart because "his name's Cinna. Pluck / but his name out of his heart, and turn him going" (3.3.33–34).

28. Tuve (*Elizabethan and Metaphysical Imagery,* pp. 129–30) has argued that figures of metonymy and synecdoche work by reducing what they represent and name, giving delight in the degree to which we as readers acknowledge the aptness of their designations. For Renaissance rhetoricians, Tuve observes, "Metonymy is . . . praised for serving to variety, brevity, and signification." As Tuve's discussion would suggest, then, for the writer of the Renaissance metonyms are a kind of rhetorical shorthand that permits us to acknowledge and admire their "aptness" without having to articulate the lines of connection between the figures themselves and whatever it is for which they are designations.

29. A. C. Bradley, *Shakespearean Tragedy: Lectures on "Hamlet," "Othello," "King Lear," "Macbeth"* (London: Macmillan and Co., 1904), p. 188.

30. Albert Cook, "Milton's Abstract Music," in *Milton: Modern Essays in Criticism,* ed. Arthur E. Barker (London: Oxford University Press, 1965), p. 398.

31. See Kittredge's note to 4.1.35–43, in *The Kittredge Shakespeare: Othello,* rev. Irving Ribner (New York: John Wiley & Sons, 1966), p. 94.

32. Harley Granville-Barker, *Prefaces to Shakespeare* (Princeton: Princeton University Press, 1947), 2:130, likened each of the replies Emilia's reiterated question fetches from Othello to "the tearing of a screen from before that closed mind." Doubtless it was Emilia's mind to which Granville-Barker was referring, but the effect of the exchange is to give us a glimpse of two minds locked into two very different illusions of reality.

33. Trousdale, *Shakespeare and the Rhetoricians,* pp. 38–64.

34. In his notorious coinage, *differance,* Jacques Derrida deliberately conflates the notions of "difference" and "deferral" in order to underscore the full dynamics of the "differentiation" he sees inherent in the play of language. For Derrida an utterance always bears the suggestion, not only of "nonidentity," of "distinction" or "inequality," but also of temporal "deferral," "the possible that is presently impossible." See Derrida's delineation of the term in *"Difference,"* in *Speech and Phenomena And Other Essays on Husserl's Theory of Signs,* trans. David B. Allison (Evanston, Ill.: Northwestern University Press, 1973), pp. 129–30.

35. Empson (*Structure of Complex Words,* p. 222) feels that the disclosure of Cassio's role in the courtship serves the dramatic purpose of giving Iago yet one more pretext for his jealousy of Cassio and his hatred of Othello: "Iago feels he has been snubbed, as too coarse to be trusted in such a matter, and he takes immediate advantage of his discomposure."

36. Knight, *Wheel of Fire,* p. 104.

37. Bullough, *Narrative and Dramatic Sources,* pp. 193ff; Roger Ascham, *The Schoolmaster,* ed. Lawrence V. Ryan (Charlottesville: University Press of Virginia, 1967), pp. 67–68.

38. Rosalind Johnson, "African Presence in Shakespearean Drama: parallels between *Othello* and the Historical Leo Africanus," in *African Presence in Early Europe, Journal of African Civilizations* 7 (1985): 267–87; Karen Newman, " 'And wash the Ethiop white": Femininity and the Monstrous in *Othello,*" in *Shakespeare Reproduced: The Text in History and Ideology,* ed. Jean E. Howard and Marion F. O'Connor (London: Methuen, 1987), pp. 143–62.

39. *Bandello: Tragical Tales,* trans. Geoffrey Fenton (1567), introd. Robert Langston Douglas (London: George Routledge and Sons, 1923), p. 187.

40. Ibid., p. 200.

41. Ibid., p. 188.

42. To take but one example, the reference by Desdemona to the fact that Cassio has known of Othello and Desdemona's courtship and had even spoken on behalf of Othello bears an intrusive force in the play, not only because it complicates the audience's perception of the relationship of the three characters and creates the possibility of a triangle where none had existed before, but also because it disrupts the audience's sense of time, creating the illusion of a frequent activity extending over some nebulously long duration of time either before the play begins or even, and more unsettlingly, after the play has begun. The allusion to Cassio's implication in the relationship of Othello and Desdemona is, however, an echo of a detail from Cinthio that fits much more naturally into the capacious temporality of prose fiction. "In the same company there was also a Corporal who was very dear to the Moor. This man went frequently to the Moor's house and often dined with him and his wife. The Lady, knowing him so well liked by her husband, gave him proofs of the greatest kindness, and this was much appreciated by the Moor," in Bullough, *Narrative and Dramatic Sources,* 7:243.

43. It is, perhaps, the moment in the play at which one feels most keenly the coincidence of Derrida's contention in "Border Lines: Living On," trans. James Hulbert, in *Deconstruction and Criticism,* ed. Harold Bloom et al. (New York: Seabury Press, 1979), pp. 104–5, that "all organized narration is 'a matter for the police,' even before its genre (mystery novel, cop story) has been determined." See Parker's reference to Derrida's remark, "Shakespeare and Rhetoric," p. 69.

3

Complement Extern
Iago's Speech Acts

JOSEPH A. PORTER

A mere sixty lines into *Othello* Iago with characteristic certainty, decisiveness, assurance, generality, and absoluteness, and a characteristically abrupt, concrete, and unsettling image, says that he will wear his heart on his sleeve for daws to peck at

> . . . when my outward action doth demonstrate
> The native act and figure of my heart
> In complement extern . . .
>
> (1.1.61–63)

He thereby brings into play a complex of metadramatic truth and paradox at which Shakespeare himself has been pecking for a good decade. For whereas with nondramatic works such as the sonnets and the narrative poems, a reader may have as direct access to a character's heart as to the character's action, drama is more like life. With dramatic characters as with real people other than ourselves, all we ever have is outward action, complement extern. Performance of a play compounds the inaccessibility of the characters' hearts: the actor playing Iago is no Amoret in thrall to Busirane, this is Venice, and Brabantio's house is not a *grand guignol*.

Even with this most superficial range of metadramatic paradox *Othello* gives us its own peculiar wrinkles, such as the fact that when the King's Men perform it, of the three leads only the actor playing Iago, who says he is not what he is, actually is what he seems in terms of both the play's major sociological variables, gender and race. And more deeply, too, the play turns around and around the radical undecidability of what its characters' outward action can demonstrate, and the absence of direct access to the

native acts and figures of their hearts. Because convention pre-
cludes conscious falsehood in soliloquy, we may loosely think of
soliloquy as providing a direct line of access to a character's heart.
All the same, words are not thoughts, and words spoken in soliloquy constitute one particular sort of outward action.

I mention soliloquy here because Iago has a near-monopoly on
this sort of verbal action in the play and his soliloquies have proved
variously troublesome—to actors inclined to twirl moustaches and
rub hands, and to commentators who, even if they recognize the
seeming psychological verisimilitude of the stages of the hatching
of the plot, still may feel a gnawing wish for something more
resonant, more Hamlet-like in Iago's soliloquies.[1] Coleridge's
"motive-hunting" seems to be officially rejected more often than
not nowadays, but it is surely on target in locating much of what is
most troublingly unforthcoming about Iago in his soliloquies and
asides. After all, while in the first scene we see Iago open up to
Roderigo and tell him a good bit of what he later reveals in soliloquy
to us, at the same time we know, or learn, that Roderigo is "this
young quat" (5.1.11) to Iago. We might thereby be led to a slight
shadow of doubt about Iago's good faith toward his major confidant,
us. Such an effect could be enhanced by distinctive qualities of the
soliloquies such as their comparative freedom from the emotional
self-characterizations that make Hamlet's soliloquies seem almost
involuntary. The effect of deliberateness could also be enhanced by
the bunching of the soliloquies and asides. None appears before the
end of Iago's third scene, 1.3, and after the last soliloquy, the
"young quat" speech ending at 5.1.22, and the last brief aside some
hundred lines later, we have the entire 370-line final scene, in which
Iago plays a major role and has a certain amount to say before he
vows never more to speak word. This placement of Iago's soliloquies may suggest that he has the power to grant or withhold
speech, and therefore truth, from us as from the other characters of
his play.

All this is by way of saying that with Iago more than with any
other character in *Othello,* and perhaps more than with any
character from the preceding canon, Shakespeare seems concerned
to problematize potentially comforting distinctions between speech
directed to other onstage characters on the one hand and soliloquy
and aside on the other. Therefore I shall look more or less indis-
criminately here at both kinds of Iago's verbal "outward action,"
even though the problematization of the distinction between them
bears in a general way on most of the points I make and in a
particular way on one.

Before I proceed to the text, let me pause for a thumbnail sketch of my method. The Latin *ago* in Iago's name signals, as is generally recognized, a heightened activeness that contrasts notably with Othello's passion in all its senses. While Iago's activity includes a fair amount of going and coming onstage, as well as two murders (counting his stabbing of Roderigo as fatal), his most memorable actions, and those most directly consequential for Othello and Desdemona, are verbal. In the commentary on Iago one finds, of course, a good many observations about the things he does with words.[2] Nevertheless, these observations, however useful, remain basically impressionistic inasmuch as they make no use of the only method we have for the thoroughly systematic description of verbal action, namely speech act theory.

Speech act theory and analysis begins, in the work of such philosophers as J. L. Austin, John Searle, and H. P. Grice, by keeping to the fore the traditionally obscured fact that saying is a kind of doing, and indeed that to say something is as a rule to do several things at once. To say something is to utter a string of words, or to perform what Austin calls a locutionary act, which itself of course may be described at several levels of analysis, from the mechanics of vocal sound production to the grammar of sentences. At the same time, a speaker may, with words or sentences, perform such verbal acts as promising, denying, thanking, or naming. Austin calls such acts illocutions, since they are performed in the locution, and they are what he and other authorities almost always mean by "speech acts."[3] Speech acts have properties not shared by nonverbal acts. For instance, they are either explicit or inexplicit. I may perform the action of denial explicitly with "I deny being Hamlet" or inexplicitly with "No! I am not Prince Hamlet." Austin called explicit speech acts performatives, and I follow his usage here below. Speech acts may also be variously divided into families, by virtue of such linguistic properties as direction of address, reference, and meaning, and such other factors as the relative status of speaker and hearer. In Austin's taxonomy based on "illocutionary force," for instance, one of the families of acts consists of those that commit the speaker to a certain course of action, such as promising, vowing, swearing, and betting.

First-generation speech act theory has proved useful in discussions of a number of literary texts, including works of Shakespeare.[4] Meanwhile, in the hands of philosophers and especially linguists, speech act analysis, also termed "pragmatics," has grown and developed. Speech act theory currently is reaching such levels of richness and precision as to render a complete pragmatic de-

scription of Iago's speech no more feasible than a complete phonetic description. Therefore some idealization and impressionism
must remain even in the fullest speech act account.

Still, speech act theory makes possible a comparatively rigorous
description and analysis of Iago's verbal action. With the acknowledgment, then, that more could be said at every turn in what
follows, let me now consider Iago from the vantage of speech act
theory.

The Opening Scene. Here before Othello and Desdemona appear, Iago establishes his vigorous directive presence, in conversation with Roderigo and Brabantio. The "outward action" lines
previously quoted are from the opening interchange with Roderigo.
During it, in Iago's sixty-nine lines (to Roderigo's eight), he not only
provides considerable background information about himself and
Othello, but he also exhibits some of the features that will characterize his later verbal action. The "official" hierarchy between the
two men shows in their respective pronouns of address, Roderigo
calling Iago "thou" and Iago calling him "you," and also in the fact
that the opening, unusual as it is for cutting into a conversation
whose subject is never quite clear, still gives the first words to
Roderigo. Immediately, however, Iago demonstrates that the real
hierarchy of control in the verbal action is the reverse of the official
one. In his first speech he answers Roderigo's "Tush" with an oath
that outdoes it, "Sblood," stakes a claim for a more obedient
hearing (a claim Roderigo all too readily grants in this scene and
through the play), and then performs a particularly deft maneuver in
"If ever I did dream of such a matter, / Abhor me" (5–6). The
utterance masquerades as a kind of bluff offering up of Iago's
friendship in pawn, but the more we look at it the more strangely
vacuous it becomes, the "ever" wobbling between past and future
in an expanded version that would read something like "If ever you
do learn that I have ever dreamed of such a matter, abhor me." But
this is almost as much as to say, quite without any superflux of
soldierly liberality, "If you find me guilty, hold me guilty."

The imperative grammatical mood of this "offer" characterizes
Iago too. His next speech begins similarly—"Despise me if I do
not" (8)—and then after lecturing Roderigo about preferment, self-
interest, and duplicity, Iago shifts back into the imperative mood
with a vengeance at "Call up her father" (67), delivering six imperatives in his first two and a half lines to Roderigo and ten more in his
following sixteen lines to Roderigo and Brabantio. All these imperatives have the general illocutionary force of exhortation but with

Roderigo, despite Iago's maintenance of the polite "you" and his repeated polite "sir," the exhortation has an undertone of directive.

Iago in this scene of course also displays that breathtakingly sudden, vivid, and brutal coarseness he later springs on Othello, as well as the racism he shares here notably with Roderigo, the sexism he shares with most of the characters in the play, and other features of his verbal action that have received attention in the criticism. From the standpoint of pragmatic theory the most interesting moment may be

> *Bra.* Thou art a villain.
> *Iago.*   You are a senator.
>
> (118)

Brabantio is straightforwardly contemptuous in both his pronoun and his noun, but Iago's reply is more mysterious, as varying editorial and directorial treatment of it indicates.[5] We seem here to have a textbook example of the flouting of the principle of conversational cooperation that Grice calls conversational implicature,[6] since what Iago says is hardly news to Brabantio. One possible point or force of the remark might be that with it Iago means to suggest to Brabantio that the "disgrace" of Desdemona's marriage may bear on Brabantio's own public political career.[7]

Performatives. Since particular kinds of speech acts may be characteristic of a given speaker, and since in a performative the speaker makes explicit the kind of act being done with the utterance, Iago's performatives compromise a natural subject of inquiry. Surveying them is useful even though we find nothing so immediately interesting as Mercutio's conjurings or Hal's promises in Iago's blander performatives.

By my count Iago has around thirty performatives.[8] In a number of them he uses "I say" not for testimony but rather for exhortation, as when he tells Roderigo, "Away, I say" (2.3.381), or Othello, "I say, but mark his gesture" (4.1.87). Another of Iago's hortatory groups consists of forms of "I pray you." Add to these the more insidiously deferential exhortations to Othello in 3.3—"I do beseech you" three times—and the sharper "I charge you" to Bianca and then Emilia, and we have the majority of Iago's performatives falling into the family of speech acts intended to induce some action or behavior in the speaker. So far nothing surprising, for the notion of Iago as director is familiar. What is most unusual and charac-

teristic about the revealed hortatoriness may be its persistent unobtrusiveness.

Iago's remaining performatives share some of the same unobtrusiveness, which may be read or played as barely hiding a smile,
as when with Othello in 3.3 Iago obediently takes his leave at line
241, only to linger for a bit more working on Othello before "I once
more take my leave" (257). In the same scene, whatever the degree
and kind of truth in Iago's

> . . . I confess it is my nature's plague
> To spy into abuses
>
> (146–47)

we may read a subliminal smile into the performative, knowing that
Iago in important respects is not drawn to confession.

Imperatives. Throughout the play, what seems to be an excep-
tionally high proportion of Iago's utterances are in the imperative
mood. Throughout, as in the first scene, Iago directs an especially
large number of imperatives to Roderigo, in the form of general
advice as in the sequence "Put money in thy purse . . . provide thy
money" (1.3.339–71) or such specific instructions as "Here,
stand. . . . Wear thy good rapier bare, and put it home. . . . fear
nothing. . . . think on that, / And fix . . . thy resolution" (5.1.1–5),
with six imperatives in five lines in which, incidentally, Iago has
assumed the familiar pronoun of address with his young quat.
Furthermore we have a reprise of Iago's 1.1 doubled hypothetical-
imperative combination in "If thou [more pronominal familiarity]
. . . enjoy not Desdemona, take me from this world . . . and devise
engines for my life" (4.2.214–17). With Roderigo throughout, Iago
tends to imperatives, as earlier in the similar flurry of five at
2.3.378–82, where he also uses the intimate contemptuous "thou."

Iago generally, as in the examples just quoted, keeps the force of
his imperatives explicit, and when he does make illocutionary force
explicit in performatives—

> [to Cassio] I pray you call them in.
>
> (2.3.46)
>
> [to Roderigo] I pray you, after the lieutenant, go.
>
> (2.3.137)
>
> [to Desdemona] I pray you be content . . . Go in,
> and weep not. . . .
>
> (4.2.165–71)

—the express force of entreaty seems to disguise something more like an order. With Emilia Iago lets the genuine imperative force of his commands show more clearly. While in private he may mollify an order with a touch of soldierly endearment—"A good wench, give it me" (3.3.313)—and in public he may add a token abbreviation of expressed supplication with his imperatives to her—"Prithee, Emilia, / Go know of Cassio" (5.1.116–17)—any failure of prompt compliance on Emilia's part increases not Iago's supplication but rather his imperative demanding, in private—"Be not acknown on't . . . / Go, leave me" (3.3.319–20)—and most memorably in public in the last scene with his series of orders—"Go to, charm your tongue," "hold your peace," "Be wise, and get you home" (5.2.183–223)—and the performative "I charge you get you home" (194), which lays bare the intended force of the command and Iago's sense of his right to exert it.

With Othello in the great "temptation" scene (3.3),[9] Iago's first imperatives, such as "pardon me" (133), have a courtly solicitousness, and he also employs a sort of would-be imperative, "Would take no notice, nor build yourself a trouble" (150), buried under the too-much-protesting performatives "I do beseech" and "I confess" (144–46). From these Iago modulates, through the loaded term "slave" (158), to his first unadorned imperative to Othello in the scene, "O, beware, my lord, of jealousy" (165). It is only his third such in the play and it falls in a telling series with "be assur'd" (1.2.11) and "be advis'd" (1.2.55). The foot in the door is shortly followed by a characteristic flurry of imperatives—"Receive it," "Look to your wife, observe her well," "Wear your eyes thus," "look to't" (196–200)—which are followed with an intricate series of imperatives in this scene and the next, culminating in "Do it not with poison; strangle her in her bed" (4.1.207).

All of Iago's other imperatives deserve notice, and many are memorable, as with two of the "aside addresses" treated below, "Look where he comes," (3.3.330), and "Work on, / My medicine" (4.1.44–45). Perhaps the most discussed of Iago's imperatives occurs in the beginning of his last two lines, "Demand me nothing" (5.2.303). It is memorable because, since it forestalls the question Othello has asked Lodovico to ask ("demand that demi-devil / Why he hath thus ensnar'd my soul and body"), it may be taken as addressed either to Othello or Lodovico or to both, and because at the same time the unmarked direction of address seems to widen to include not only everybody else onstage, but also us. The remark is memorable also because what shortly follows and elaborates it, "From this time forth I never will speak word" (304), could in fact be the metadramatically accurate final words of every dramatic character.

"Look where he comes." In 3.4 after the clown has left to summon Cassio, Desdemona and Emilia have some ten lines of conversation ended by

> *Emil.* Look, where he comes.
> *Enter* Othello.
>
> (31 s.d.)

While Emilia's line is a familiar sort of throwaway serving to direct audience attention to a character just entering, we may suspect involuntary spousal resemblance in her repetition of the words Iago has used, also about Othello, in the preceding scene. Iago's own use of the sentence might seem a throwaway were it not for the emphasis on the active eye and ocular proof in the first letter of his name and in his speech throughout,[10] as with

> I have look's upon the world for four times seven years . . .
>
> (1.3.311–12)
>
> Look to your wife, observe her well . . .
>
> (3.3.197)
>
> Wear your eyes thus . . .
> look to't.
>
> 3.3.198–200)
>
> Would you, the supervisor, grossly gape on?
> Behold her topp'd?
>
> (3.3.395–96)
>
> Look, he stirs.
>
> (4.1.55)
>
> mark the fleers . . . mark his gesture.
>
> (4.1.82–87)
>
> Behold her well; I pray you look upon her.
> Do you see, gentlemen?
>
> (5.1.108–9)

This context raises to special prominence those moments when Iago is concerned to direct eyes to someone approaching—Cassio in "Here he comes" (4.1.99), Bianca in "Look where she comes" (4.1.145), and Othello in "Look where he comes!" (3.3.330). Since the first and third of these appear in asides, the imperatives may be directed straight out of the fiction to us in the audience, so that we are made formally complicit with Iago, by Iago, in his designs against Othello. Even in terms of spatial location, these speech acts create a certain unity between Iago and us since we, like Iago, occupy an immobile point to which other characters come.

"I see." In the "temptation" scene Iago exhibits his command of the discourse of vision with a separate group of four remarks whose power derives partly from their unobtrusiveness:

> I see this hath a little dash'd your spirits.
>
> (3.3.214)
>
> But I do see y' are mov'd.
>
> (217)
>
> My lord, I see y' are mov'd.
>
> (224)
>
> I see, sir, you are eaten up with passion. . . .
>
> (391)

The mounting embedded clauses at once describe and create what they purport merely to describe, as Othello denies the first categorically (and perhaps a jot more vigorously than is necessary), ignores the second, replies to the third with a denial, "No," followed by a qualified denial, "not much mov'd," that is also a qualified admission, and ignores the fourth in a way that seems to amount to complete acceptance of its truth. But why does Iago not simply say, "This hath a little dash'd your spirits"? What is the function of the single frame clause that governs the series? While a full answer to the question would take us quickly afield into the logic and psychology of seeing and being seen, a consideration of the respective sorts of speech act reveals some of Iago's rationale. For one thing, the clause embedded may be thereby partly insulated from denial. "You are mov'd," is open to an unambiguous "No [I am not]," but the same reply to "I see your are mov'd" is ambiguous, as it stands, between "I am not mov'd" and "you do not see." For a sense of some of the further pragmatic complexities of the matter, complexities treated by numerous speech-act theorists and philosophers of language,[11] one need only consider the difference between Iago's "I see you are mov'd" said to Othello, and the same sentence uttered to an optometrist during an eye examination.

Aside address. In 2.1, while Desdemona, Iago, Cassio, Montano, Roderigo, and Emilia await the arrival of Othello's ship, Iago in his long aside as he watches Desdemona and Cassio (167–77) shifts interestingly between third- and second-person reference to Cassio. From a third-person account of what he sees ("He takes her by the palm"), Iago shifts to a second-person imperative ("ay . . . whisper"), and then back to an implied third person for a prediction ("With as little a web as this will I ensnare as great a fly as Cassio") and finally back again to the second person for a long address, still in aside, to Cassio, with more imperatives and with numerous uses of the "you" of address, ending "Yet again, your fingers at your lips? Would they were clyster-pipes for your sake!" The final image has a characteristic abrupt unsavoriness,[12] and as for the wish itself, the more one considers its point the more characteristically cryptic it looks.

Quite as distinctively characteristic of Iago, not only in the play but also, I believe, in the whole canon, is his address in aside to a person present onstage. The aside about Cassio and also "to" him is the first such moment of Iago's and at the beginning of it, as he shifts by degrees from soliloquy-like aside description and prediction to what may be termed the aside address, we watch him move beyond the speech-situation he has already established for himself in earlier soliloquy into a kind of alarming superdialogue, formally like apostrophe except that the addressee is present before him, problematizing the conventional distinctions that separate dialogue from soliloquy and aside.

As if having found his way into this kind of speech at 2.1.167–77, Iago moves into it promptly when Othello appears and rejoins Desdemona: "[Aside] O, you are well tun'd now!" (199). In the "temptation" scene he returns to it in

> Look where he comes! Not poppy, nor mandragora,
> Nor all the drowsy syrups of the world
> Shall ever medicine thee to that sweet sleep
> Which thou ow'dst yesterday.
>
> (3.3.330–33)

Here Iago makes full use of the privilege of his aside address, to describe Othello coming to him, and then to address him for the only time in the play with the contemptuous and/or intimate form of the second person pronoun. A kind of residue or after-image linked by the word *medicine* as well as by the situation of aside address, and also occasioned by Othello, appears in "Work on, / My medicine, work!" (4.1.44–45).

The heart and the sleeve. Martin Orkin, discussing "the opacity of deliberately deceptive discourse" such as Iago's, writes that

> Othello's only protection against his ensign would be extra-human powers of perception—an X-ray vision granted to no person.[13]

Here, during remarks about Iago in a fine essay, figures of seeing or failing to see come naturally to hand. I wish, however, to conclude my survey of Iago's verbal action by suggesting that Orkin may have let Iago hoodwink him a bit with talk of native acts versus outward actions, and that Shakespeare in 1604 may have been accomplishing stranger negotiations with Iago than Orkin allows. As my use of a key term of Stephen Greenblatt's will suggest, my speculation here derives not only from the foregoing pragmatic analyses but also from recent currents in Shakespeare study and other criticism and theory.[14] Promptings from the body of *Othello* study have come in particular from Jane Adamson and above all from James L. Calderwood.[15]

Iago's

> For when my outward action doth demonstrate
> The native act and figure of my heart
> In complement extern, 'tis not long after
> But I will wear my heart upon my sleeve
> For daws to peck at. . . .
>
>   (1.1.61–65)

at once assents to and violently problematizes a traditional way of talking about inside and outside. The assent comes in the opposition between native act and outward action, and in the phrase "complement extern." The violent problematizing comes in the repeated "heart." The "heart" of line 62, itself partly a figure, being the seat (as we say) of emotions and intentions, becomes in lines 64–65 the physical organ that, if Iago could wear it as he envisages, might feed daws but would hardly give viewers complete access to its owner's emotions and intentions, any more than would X-rays.[16] A moment later Iago further problematizes the traditional opposition when he tells Brabantio "Your heart is burst, you have lost half your soul" (87), making the heart itself a kind of container.

This bind resembles some of the predicaments Iago puts Othello in, of course, and one may wish to call Iago's practice fully intentional if often improvised. With the "complement extern" speech, though, the bind I have described does not seem intended by Iago for Roderigo so much as intended by Shakespeare for his audience or himself, or simply allowed to happen by Shakespeare, through Iago. Iago's characteristic speech acts produce similar effects. His discourse of vision both sensitizes and paralyzes the audience, enforcing its complicity with him by directing its attention to the tragedy unfolding beyond the fourth wall his discourse erects. Similar effects are produced by ambiguities in Iago's speech, and by his way of blandly saying things that sound conventional but that prove strangely empty upon inspection. And similar effects are produced in Iago's soliloquies and asides—by their flatness, by the distribution that may make them seem deliberate, by the fact that they seem possibly to violate conventional truth-conditions of soliloquy, and by those moments in them when Iago turns away from the very possibility of addressing the audience, to speak in what I have called aside address "to" another onstage character.

This in not the place to attempt any extended account of reasons for Shakespeare's thus letting Iago do things with words that make notions of inner and outer, of seeing and being seen, and indeed of self itself less easily tenable than Iago himself takes them to be. I will, however, suggest a couple of directions that such an account might usefully explore. First, the initial letter of "Iago" as a first-person pronoun, together with Iago's status as playwright within the play, makes me wonder whether he might in some ways and at some moments serve as a simulacrum of Shakespeare himself, or whether Shakespeare uses Iago to manifest contradictions in the notion of self, or in the process of self-fashioning, that were not apparent to him only a few years before. Whereas the speaker of *Sonnet 121*, confident of the immediacy of the self, could boldly echo *Exodus* with "I am that I am," now Iago ends his "complement extern" speech with "I am not what I am." If one sees some of the Jacobean Shakespeare in Iago one might also be tempted to speculate about a degree or kind of his own leave-taking in "From this time forth I never will speak word." And then my collocation of "Iago" and "Jacobean" may suggest another direction of inquiry, for Iago's name is of course a version of that of the new monarch, with whom Shakespeare seems already to have had some negotiation in the character of the Duke of *Measure for Measure*. Here the inquiry might begin with a comparison of Iago's speech acts with those of James that were known to Shakespeare.

Finally, I would mention that speech act theory offers a way out of some of the dilemmas Iago poses. It does so by giving the lie to oppositions like Iago's "native" and "outward," and this not with Iago's violence, but rather with seeming ease. In a consideration of speech acts the traditional opposition between inner and outer is somewhat beside the point. Such is the case not only if we have in view the mere physiology of speech, but also if we consider speech from a pragmatic standpont as an inherently social activity.

NOTES

1. In M. R. Ridley's Arden edition of *Othello* (London: Methuen, 1958), the account of Iago's hatching the plot in the "Introduction," pp. lxi–lxiv, and textual notes passim, still seems astute and useful. The sense of a missing resonance in Iago's speech appears widely, as again passim in Ridley's notes, or in Jane Adamson, *"Othello" as Tragedy: Some Problems of Judgment and Feeling* (Cambridge: Cambridge University Press, 1980): "Iago's *tone* varies hardly at all throughout the play" (p. 79). Adequate account remains to be taken, I believe, of the imaginative reach evident in the transit from Hamlet's soliloquies to Iago's in the next tragedy.

2. Observations like Coleridge's "motive-hunting" characterize Iago's verbal action in a summary way. Robert B. Heilman, *Magic in the Web: Action and Language in "Othello"* (Lexington: University Press of Kentucky, 1956), as his title suggests, directs attention somewhat as here, and three of his seven chapters are about Iago. It is all the more regrettable, then, that Heilman apparently had no access to the first stirrings of speech act theory, for, as his title also suggests, he falls prey to a traditional, obfuscatory, and erroneous dichotomizing of "actional" vs. "verbal," to use his terms. Almost from the beginning it is clear how useful speech act theory might have been to him, as when he writes that " 'doing' and 'saying' are not always properly distinguishable; saying is often a very important way of doing" (p. 6). However important, saying is always a kind of doing. More recent commentators writing after the dissemination of classic first-generation speech act theory sometimes to their detriment fail to take advantage of the kinds of discriminations the theory allows. For instance, some of the remarks of Iago's in which, according to Adamson, he "tries to justify himself and to insist on his own worth, reasonableness and rectitude" (p. 21) fit her description easily, but others, such as "Despise me if I do not [hate Othello]," seem to me not to fit easily or naturally.

3. J. L. Austin, *How to Do Things with Words* (Oxford: Clarendon, 1962), originates speech act theory. Two other essential first-generation texts are H. P. Grice, "Logic and Conversation," in *Speech Acts,* ed. Peter Cole and Jerry L. Morgan (New York: Seminar, 1975), and John R. Searle, *Speech Acts: An Essay in the Philosophy of Language* (London: Cambridge University Press, 1969). Pragmatics has developed through other publications by these three and by very many others. See my "Pragmatics for Criticism: Two Generations of Speech Act Theory," *Poetics* 15 (1986): 243–57.

4. Pragmatic analysis has by now been applied to many literary texts. Discussions of speech acts in Shakespeare include those in Heather Dubrow, *Captive Victors: Shakespeare's Narrative Poems and Sonnets* (Ithaca: Cornell University Press, 1987), Keir Elam, *Shakespeare's Universe of Discourse: Language-games in the Comedies* (London: Cambridge University Press, 1984), Stanley Fish, "How to Do Things with Austin and Searle: Speech Act Theory and Literary Criticism," *Modern Language Notes* 91 (1976): 983–1025, Eamon Grennan, "The Women's Voices in *Othello*: Speech, Song, Silence," *Shakespeare Quarterly* 38 (1987): 275–92, and Mary Louise Pratt, *Toward a Speech Act Theory of Literary Discourse* (Bloomington: Indiana University Press, 1977), and in my own *The Drama of Speech Acts: Shakespeare's Lancastrian Tetralogy* (Berkeley: University of California Press, 1979), *Shakespeare's Mercutio: His History and Drama* (Chapel Hill: University of North Carolina Press, 1988), and "Fraternal Pragmatics: Speech Acts of John and the Bastard" in *King John: New Perspectives,* ed. Deborah Curren-Aquino (Newark: University of Delaware Press, 1989).

5. Constantin Stanislavsky, *Stanislavsky Produces Othello,* trans. Helen Nowak (London: Geoffrey Bles, 1948), has a general pause after Iago's "You are a senator" because "Everybody is indignant at the impertinence and wit of the reply" (p. 30). I find Stanislavsky's rationale mysterious since I see no obvious wit in Iago's reply, and only the impertinence of its seemingly not pertaining to the subject at hand. Discomfort with the moment dates back at least to John Upton, *Critical Observations on Shakespeare* (1747, p. 176), who suggested pointing the line as "You are—a senator," to indicate Iago's having checked himself from replying to Brabantio's "Thou art a villain" with some equivalent insult. Authority for Upton's pointing can be found in similar behavior of Iago elsewhere, as at "Nothing, my lord; or if—I know not what" (3.3.36), and Upton's suggestion is followed generally in the nineteenth century and in many twentieth-century editions including some in current use such as that edited by G. E. Bentley in *The Complete Pelican Shakespeare* (1969; repr., New York: Viking, 1977). Ridley, however, like G. Blakemore Evans in the *Riverside Shakespeare,* restores the line to its original form. Barbara Hodgdon writes in an unpublished account of the 1986 Royal Shakespeare Company *Othello* directed by Terry Hands with David Suchet as Iago, "There's real venom (class envy, rather) in Iago's 'You are—a senator.'" Venom and class envy could of course show in an Iago using the sentence to perform the sort of act I hypothesize, namely a reminder that is ostensibly superfluous and thus cautionary, and thus racist.

6. Grice, "Logic and Conversation," p. 49.

7. Brabantio's office was not hereditary. See Frederic C. Lane, *Venice: A Marine Republic* (Baltimore: Johns Hopkins University Press, 1973), pp. 95–96, 263. Even were the office hereditary its exercise could conceivably have been affected by disgrace. In Shakespeare's source, Cinthio, we hear nothing of Brabantio.

8. The precise total depends on whether we include what may be called protoperformatives like "I'll [instead of 'I'] warrant her" (2.3.19). There are five of them, and twenty-five full-dress performatives.

9. It might better be called a persuasion scene. The traditional designation seems to me to prejudice the case against Othello by implying that mistrust of Desdemona is in itself somehow already attractive or desirable to him. Granted, the scene's traditional designation accords with the diabolical in Iago. Even the title of Tempter, though, begs a question about human proclivity to evil.

10. Many editors and commentators remark on the thematic importance of seeing in the play, and Heilman, pp. 58–64, discusses "seeing is believing" as a theme associated with Iago. Joel Fineman, *Shakespeare's Perjured Eye: The Invention of Poetic Subjectivity in the Sonnets* (Berkeley: University of California Press, 1986), treats the eye-I correspondence at length and in depth. As he and others demonstrate, that correspondence works so powerfully and pervasively in Shakespeare that it would seem potentially effective even with eye-Iago, where there is no phonetic identity.

11. A typically rich philosophical investigation of statements of the form "I see . . ." can be found in the posthumous lecture notes of J. L. Austin, *Sense and Sensibilia,* edited by G. J. Warnock (New York: Oxford University Press, 1962).

12. Ridley in his note, p. 59, seems at pains to misrepresent Iago's image by glossing "clyster-pipes" as "syringe for a (vaginal) douche." The discrepancy of number may be a simple oversight, but such can hardly be the case with Ridley's careful parenthesis "(vaginal)." It runs counter to all relevant *OED* entries, which make it clear that clyster-pipes were for administering medicines, enemas, or

suppositories anally. We may have here the censoring of a potentially sodomic image similar to the censoring of Mercutio's "open-arse" in *Romeo and Juliet* 2.1. See my *Shakespeare's Mercutio,* pp. 161–62, and my "Marlowe, Shakespeare, and the Canonization of Heterosexuality," *South Atlantic Quarterly* 88 (1989): 127–46.

13. "Othello and the 'plain face' of Racism," *Shakespeare Quarterly* 38 (1987): 166–88, 177.

14. See Stephen Greenblatt, *Shakespearean Negotiations: The Circulation of Social Energy in Renaissance England* (Berkeley: University of California Press, 1988). It will be apparent that this portion of my essay is indebted to too large a host of commentators for easy acknowledgment.

15. I have found Adamson, *"Othello" as Tragedy,* especially useful in her account of the audience's "forced complicity" (p. 66) with Iago. Calderwood's characteristically brilliant "Speech and Self in *Othello,*" *Shakespeare Quarterly* 38 (1987): 293–303, really stakes out the territory for my observations.

16. Calderwood seems to assent to the inner-outer division but to couch it in safer—tellingly safer—figures than Orkin's X-ray vision when he writes that Othello

> would understand Iago's mind not as mortal men are obliged to do, by reason and discourse, but as angels do, simply by knowing. Unfortunately . . . Othello lacks clairvoyance.
>
> (p. 296)

Iago's "demonstrate," with the second syllable accented, carries with it the monster-monstrous that soon becomes explicit in the play, and that here grounds the violence of the image of the heart on the sleeve. With Iago one naturally also wonders about a subliminal demon in the word even so accented. The demon peeps out more in Desdemona's

> some unhatch'd practice
> Made demonstrable here in Cyprus to him,
> Hath puddled his clear spirit . . .
>
> (3.4.141–43)

The same demon may work mischief with Desdemona's name, and with the "hell" in Othello. See *OED,* s.vv. "demonstrate," "contemplate," for the historical shifting forward of stress, which seems to be reversed with "demonstrate" in Shakespeare, with *Othello* possibly the precise moment at which the reversal happens. I agree with Adamson, p. 88, that this speech of Iago's is "highly revealing," although not with her claim that the speech "makes it clear that Shakespeare knew exactly what he was about right from the very beginning," if she means that the knowledge was fully conscious.

4

Iago's Wound

DAVID POLLARD

Charles Baudelaire felt certain that the world was destined to be swallowed up by the "delicate monster" boredom. Boredom ("ennui"), for the French poet, meant a complex state of soul: its victim is deprived of interest in life as he finds it and turning inward surveys a vast emptiness. This "encounter with nothingness"[1] is oppressive. Agitated and restless, the bored person recoils with horror from the blank and void and thereafter is fretted by the mental anguish which Baudelaire calls "spleen"—the peevish sense that he is "le roi d'un pays pluvieux . . . impuissant, jeune et pourtant très-vieux." Such a state can arise out of little or no commensurate pressure from external forces, for it is essentially endogenous. The splenetic person suddenly discovers in himself feelings of estrangement and world hatred. His response is one of lassitude or edgy hostility attended by a conviction of metaphysical absurdity—in short, the helpless apprehension that there may be final truth in such a statement as August von Platen's chillingly succinct line: "Denn jeder sucht ein All zu sein, und jeder ist im Grunde nichts."[2]

In *Les Fleurs du Mal* many poems address the description of this spiritual affliction; many more record strategies of aesthetic escape. Baudelaire fashions flights to imaginary paradises ("Invitation au voyage"); he explores the delights of voyeuristic sex ("Les Bijoux"); and in several impressive poems, he engages in meditative people watching on the streets of Paris. One liberation from boredom, however, takes a more disturbing turn. "L'Héautontimorouménos," as the title reveals, derives its inspiration from a play by Terence, and treats of self-activation by recourse to deliberate self-torment. Its subtext is that pain can supply meaning when it is otherwise lacking. The poem's speaker feels that he must first abuse someone else. Thus he threatens to thrash his lover and make her weep in order that, like Moses striking the rock, he can turn his spiritual desert ("mon Sahara") into an ocean on which he can set sail to new experiences. The woman's sobs promise to be like a drum that will sound the speaker's rush into the excitement of battle. Partly, the speaker wants to force the woman to recognize herself as tormentor by beholding in him a reflection of her own identity ("Je suis le miroir / Où la mégère se regarde!") More importantly, however, he longs to see himself in her agony as a way of filling the inner blank with a self-image of some kind, albeit loathsome and painful. The torture works. The speaker has his releasing epiphany:

> Je suis la plaie et le couteau!
> Je suis le soufflet et la joue!
> Je suis les membres et la roue,
> Et la victime et le bourreau![3]

Willfully accepting himself as source and most fitting recipient of clarifying hatred, Baudelaire's speaker asserts with a sense of triumph his morally marginal status as nature's pariah ("Un de ces grands abandonnés").

Leo Bersani has discussed "L'Héautontimorouménos" suggestively in terms of Freud's ideas about sadomasochism. Baudelaire's poem, as Bersani insists, presents one extended sadomasochistic moment during which the erotogenic process of self-location through the abuse of another, self-declaiming theatricalization, and preemptive self-punishment, is enacted. I would add that the poem's startling mimesis connects thoughts that its author had mulled over darkly in his intimate journal: "When I have inspired universal horror and disgust, I shall have conquered solitude. . . . As for torture, it has been devised by the evil half of man's nature, which is thirsty for voluptuous pleasures. Cruelty and sensual pleasure are identical like extreme heat and extreme cold."[4] "L'Héautontimorouménos," poised on these values, riots in an exultant exhibitionism of determined moral ugliness.

Freud, rather more dispassionately, takes up sado-masochism as an anomalous challenge to the overriding supremacy of the "pleasure principle." Freud at first thought that sadism was a primary instinct; later he changed his mind and, in *Beyond the Pleasure Principle,* speculated that masochism was primary, deriving directly from the death instinct.[5] In any case, the sadistic and masochistic impulses are convertible, and when the one is transformed into the other, the process is always accompanied by a sense of guilt. This leads Freud to conclude about masochism that it is in essence a "punishment for [a] forbidden genital relation" with the father and in fact its "pleasurable substitute."[6] Instructively, Freud brackets sadomasochism with scoptophilia-exhibitionism as parallel examples of how instincts may revert into their opposites. In such a reversal, Freud claims, the "passive aim (to be tortured, or looked at) has been substituted for the active aim (to torture and to look at)."[7] Masochism is, then, sadism, only "turned round upon the subject's own ego," fired by an attendant libidinal delight. On the reconvertibility of these instincts, Freud adds an intriguing observation: "Where once the suffering of pain has been experienced as a masochistic aim, it can be carried back into the sadistic situation and result in a sadistic aim of *inflicting pain,* which will then be masochistically enjoyed by the subject while inflicting pain upon others, through his identification of himself with the suffering object."[8] This brilliant formulation, it seems to me, helps to assign the place in the sadomasochistic "loop" where the gargoyled psychodynamics of Baudelaire's poem are located.

Shakespeare's absorption in the psychology of self-torment is virtually coterminous with his art. From Richard III to Leontes, the Shakespearean *Gemäldegalerie* is filled with a variety of tormenting and tormented characters. Certainly, however, Hamlet and Iago stand as excelling hyperboles of the type—siblings, as it were—the former, the glamorous; the latter, the decidedly unglamorous, version. Shakespeare's *Othello,* like *Hamlet,* has yielded fruitful results from characterological considerations along psychoanalytic lines.[9] And the figure of Iago, in particular, strikes me as an apt subject for analysis under the light of Baudelairean example and Freudian precept. Iago challenges us the way Baudelaire's "héautontimorouménos" does, in that he is a human gargoyle too, and with him also we are compelled to experience horrific designs from the emotional perspective of an excitingly intelligent and self-conscious deviance. This character, besides, provokes disturbing speculations with respect to the sexual component in the aesthetics of audience response.

At the outset of *Othello* Iago is indeed splenetic—disillusioned, restive, hostile, young, and yet very old—Baudelaire's *l'homme ennuyé.* Cassio and Desdemona, rivals for Othello's favor, have already received their promotions; she, in fact is the "general's general." Iago, on the other hand, has been consigned (symbolically) at the age of twenty-eight to the role of "ancient," and in this capacity we see him as squire to the ladies and as sage counselor. The practiced soldier has become in effect the real "moth of peace." As with Richard III, however, this deflection offers Iago an opportunity for deep, malevolent disguise.

At the beginning of the temptation scene, watching Cassio withdraw from Desdemona's presence, Iago reacts with concern:

> *Iago.* Hah? I like not that.
> *Oth.*   What dost thou say
> *Iago.* Nothing, my lord; or if—I know not what.
>
> (3.3.35–36)

The concern is of course staged for its auditor; nevertheless, the subtext makes this a critical exchange in the play. "Nothing" is precisely what Iago is looking at. On the other hand, "nothing"— inner emptiness, deprivation, absence, and denied access to a woman's genitals—is what drives Iago to invention. His compulsion becomes the desire to stuff the word "nothing" with materialist fact.

Considered as metaphysics, Iago's riddling announcement, "I am not what I am" (1.1.65), is a worrying of the old paradox of how to be present by means of duplicitous self-cancellation. In Iago's case, the moral program of disguising whatever is real entails the assumption that the "nothing" of others is actually only a competitive version of fraudulence that the discerning eye of imagination can penetrate with the help of projection. To put the matter slightly differently, for Iago, as for Baudelaire (not to mention Schopenhauer), human existence boils down to the view of the world as will and idea. As Iago explains to his dupe Roderigo: " 'Tis in ourselves that we are thus, or thus. Our bodies are our gardens, to the which our wills are gardeners" (1.3.319–21). A gardener can choose what will be present or absent—nettles or lettuce. Likewise, the will is free to guess or even influence the contents of other "gardens." Whatever—in the beginning, there is "nothing."

Iago's concept of the self-fashioning will is radically sexualized. His response to *le néant*, therefore, is to infuse it with libido. Thus, quite in the way of Freud's description, his behavior is sadomasochistic. This is apparent in his paralleled relationships with Cassio, Desdemona, and Othello. In each case, the tormented Iago—a "poisonous mineral" gnawing his innards—identifies with a victim and achieves pleasure from the recognizability of the pain he has caused. In each instance, he could conceivably gloat, "Work on, / My medicine, work!" (4.1.43–44), for the goal of such a self-reflexive and narcissistic identification is to attain that totality of being that von Platen claims is humanity's deep desire.

Iago's interaction with Cassio is paradigmatic of his method. Cassio is one of those "duteous and knee-crooking knaves" whom Iago despises, and yet he has succeeded in filling his space. While he vilifies his rival to Roderigo, inwardly Iago is forced to acknowledge an envious respect. Cassio is a "proper" man, sexually attractive, who "hath a daily beauty in his life" (admits Iago) "That makes me ugly" (5.1.19–20). The villain, therefore, proceeds to deface that beauty and put ugliness in its stead. On the parapet, alcohol is the "medicine" that makes Cassio cease to be himself.

Cassio sustains thereby the disfiguration he most dreads: in reputation he is hurt "past all surgery." Later this is extended to bodily wounding when Cassio is "maim'd for ever" (5.1.28). After his dismissal (act 2), in any event, Cassio has foisted on him a new identity as Desdemona's secret lover. This is entirely a projection of Iago, based on his own fantasies. Iago warms to the excitement of inventing Cassio's dream-life and thus creates a blind for an intense scoptophilic lechery:

> In sleep I heard him say, "Sweet Desdemona,
> Let us be wary, let us hide our loves";
> And then, sir, would he gripe and wring my hand;
> Cry, "O sweet creature!" then kiss me hard,
> As if he pluck'd up kisses by the roots
> That grew upon my lips; then laid his leg
> Over my thigh, and sigh'd, and kiss'd, and then
> Cried, "Cursed fate that gave thee to the Moor!"
>
> (3.3.419-26)

In a curious mixture of projection and identification with Cassio together with a sadistic torment of Othello, Iago enjoys Desdemona while simultaneously managing the provocation which will bring about his delayed installation as lieutenant.

Like Cassio, Desdemona holds a place close to Othello that Iago experiences as personal displacement. Desdemona, however, represents a vastly more complex incitement to sadomasochistic emotions. For one thing, she possesses a reputation for "honesty"—with all of that word's ambiguity—which contends with Iago's own. The task becomes, therefore, for masculine "honesty" to find means to discredit its feminine counterpart. Desdemona's honesty is correlated with her whiteness. As Iago understands, whiteness is a kind of nothing which black Othello invests with moral significa-tion: "that whiter skin of hers than snow" must point to Desde-mona's chaste disposition. For this reason, in his jealousy, Othello becomes desperately perplexed: "Was this fair paper, this most goodly book, / Made to write 'whore' upon?" (4.2.71–72). It is Iago, of course, who has made the false inscription.

In a direct manner, as Terry Eagleton has suggested, the genitals of Othello's heroine stand for a kind of inscrutable "nothing" too.[10] On the one hand, they confirm male power by their need to be filled ("She loved me for the dangers I had passed"). On the other, their vacancy may adumbrate a yawning gulf of appetite that can arouse fears of inner lack and threaten male adequacy. Playing on such fears, Iago torments Othello with his keenest sadism by sharing his imaginings of prodigious female erotomania. For Iago, women "rise to play, and go to bed to work" (2.1.115); Desdemona, therefore, both a "supersubtle Venetian" and "sport for Jove," must really be guided by a changeable appetite and a need to enjoy "stolen hours of lust." One such hour Iago recreated through the fiction of Cassio's dream. What is most interesting about the fiction is its demonstration of Iago's identification with Desdemona. After all, in the supposed encounter, Cassio had mistakenly confused Iago with Othello's wife. The sadomasochistic implications are clear. Thereafter, the inventor of a feminine criminal self who has enjoyed forbidden pleasures—a self with which he has identified—Iago proceeds to devise the appropriate punishment. Throughout the play, Iago has ached to enter Desdemona's bedroom. In the end he succeeds and there receives from Othello the phallic wound ("I bleed, sir, but not killed"), which completes the identification.

Iago's soliloquy of 2.1.286–312 ("That Cassio loves her, I do well believe 't; / That she loves him, 'tis apt and of great credit. . . . Now I do love her too . . . [and] I do suspect the lusty Moor / Hath leap'd into my seat . . .") puts forth a festival of private Baudelairean misery: envy, suspicion, self-justifying vindictiveness, and an oversexed paranoia. It is pivotally placed. The Othello of the first act is, I think, "valiant" Othello of heroic poise and dignified eloquence—the authentic man to whom Desdemona gave away her heart. What invades him gradually on the isle of Cyprus is a second self. This self is the projection of Iago. Here the transaction differs essentially from those involving Cassio and Desdemona, for their effects are extrinsic. As the vengeance oath dramatizes ("I am your own forever"), Iago and Othello achieve an *égoisme à deux;* this enables Iago's identification with his general and in turn opens the way for the absorption of an interfering self on the part of the latter.

Accurately Iago calls Othello's epileptic trance an "ecstasy" (4.1.79), for it signifies the departure of the original ego, leaving the victim "nothing of a man." By the beginning of the fourth act, consequently, Iago has reached the plateau of his success; his scheme—the establishment of fictive versions of Cassio and Desde-

mona and the hypnotic ingress into Othello's mind and language—
all expressive of Iago's sadistic narcissism—is fully realized:

> *Iago.* Will you think so?
> *Oth.*   Think so, Iago?
> *Iago.*   What,
> To kiss in private?
> *Oth.*   An unauthoriz'd kiss?
> *Iago.* Or to be naked with her friend in bed
> An hour, or more, not meaning any harm?
> *Oth.* Naked in bed, Iago, and not mean harm?
>
>   (4.1.1–5)

Again, Iago is occluding "nothing" with a monstrous something,
only now Othello shares fully in the scoptophilic imaginings, as he
does later in the eavesdropping scene (4.1.102–70).

As the play draws toward an end, Othello, still the embodiment of
the Iago self, nevertheless recovers something of his first identity
and we hear in the restoration of his authentic language (5.2.1–22) a
melodramatic grandeur. This is too weak, however, and Othello
becomes the instrument of violence for Iago that Roderigo had
been. In the event Othello achieves some understanding of his
divided self. When asked: "Where is this rash and most unfortunate
man?" Othello responds: "That's he that was Othello; here I am"
(5.2.283–84). Yet Desdemona is not altogether wrong in saying that
"nobody" killed her (5.2.124). It is, after all, the essential act of the
sadomasochistic personality to seek to destroy all that is without
and within. Finally, then, Iago, like Baudelaire's speaker, is both the
wound and the knife that inflicts it: and the sadomasochist who is
attempting to escape "boredom" and vacuity will find (with Iago)
that "Pleasure and action make the hours seem short" (2.3.379).

Plays too—the writing and the viewing of them—make the hours
seem short. One cannot evade, consequently, the reality that, as
with "L'Héautontimorouménos," it is the artist who has slapped
his heroine in *Othello* (4.1); Shakespeare's also are the unseen
hands that strangle her throat. The dramatist is in fact the "nobody" that Desdemona's lie is ultimately meant to conceal. To his
great credit, Baudelaire had the honesty to admit that the artist is
always the primal self-tormentor who creates in his work a means of
exhibitionist escape from isolation at the risk of raising a universal
horror. A play like *Othello* shows Shakespeare in prophetic agree-
ment with the French poet. It too is a flower of evil. We the
audience, on the other hand, share in its exciting pathology. Our
instincts healthily repressed or sublimated under compulsion from
the reality principle, we do not shrink, like the self-tormented and

emotionally violent Dr. Johnson, from the play's finale. Rather we release the libidinal energies of our own scoptophilia as we join vicariously Othello and Iago in Desdemona's bedroom. Thus do we indulge our own sadomasochistic fantasies in the aesthetically pleasing mayhem on the heroine's wedding sheets as it unfolds before our view. *Othello* thereby becomes the focusing instrument for complex and collusive "communal" aggression. The only possible justification for experiencing such a work is whatever clarifying catharsis it might momentarily effectuate. The likehood is, however, that the clarification we attain will induce something like self-loathing—as with Baudelaire and (one fancies) Shakespeare himself.

NOTES

1. Reinhard Kuhn, *The Demon of Noontide: Ennui in Western Literature* (Princeton: Princeton University Press, 1976), p. 13.

2. "For each man tries to be a universal whole, and every man is at bottom nothing at all," *The Penguin Book of German Verse* (New York: Penguin Books, 1980), p. 322.

3. Charles Baudelaire, *Les Fleurs du Mal* (Oxford: Basil Blackwell, 1980), p. 78. "I am the wound and the knife! / I am the buffet and the cheek! / I am the limbs and the rack! / Both the victim and the executioner!" (translation mine).

4. Leo Bersani's book is *Baudelaire and Freud* (Berkeley: University of California Press, 1977), see pp. 92–94 and 100–5. The citation from Baudelaire comes from *Intimate Journals* (San Francisco: City Lights Books, 1983), pp. 37 and 64.

5. Sigmund Freud, *Beyond the Pleasure Principle* (repr., New York: Liveright, 1961), pp. 48–49.

6. Freud, "A Child is Being Beaten," *Sexuality and the Psychology of Love* (New York: Basic Books 1963), p. 117.

7. Freud, "Instincts and Their Vicissitudes," *General Psychological Theory* (New York: Liveright, 1963), p. 91.

8. Freud, "Instincts and Their Vicissitudes," p. 93. See also in the same volume, "The Economic Problem in Masochism," pp. 190–201. Richard Wolheim's exasperating but insightful essay, "Identification and Imagination: The inner Structure of a Psychic Mechanism," is relevant here. See Wollheim, ed., *Freud: A Collection of Critical Essays* (Garden City, N.Y.: Anchor Books, 1974), pp. 172–95.

9. See, for instance, Madelon Gohlke, " 'All that is spoke is marred': Language and Consciousness in *Othello,*" *Women's Studies* 9, no. 2 (1982): 157–76; Carol McGinnis Kay, "Othello's Need for Mirrors," *Shakespeare Quarterly* 34 (1983): 261–70; and Meredith Skura's valuable overview of Shakespeare and psychoanalysis in "Shakespeare's Psychology: Characterization in Shakespeare," in John F. Andrews, ed., *William Shakespeare: His World, His Work, His Influence,* vol. 2 (New York: Charles Scribner's Sons, 1985), pp. 571–87; pp. 581–85 deal exclusively with *Othello.*

10. Terry Eagleton, *William Shakespeare* (Oxford: Basil Blackwell, 1986), pp. 64–70.

5

The Female Perspective in *Othello*

EVELYN GAJOWSKI

Shakespeare represents in *Othello* the reality of women—their wholeness—in high contrast to the fragmented notions of them held by men.[1] Iago's false portrayal of Desdemona comes closest to crumbling when confronted by her plain truth. Her entry into the deception scene breaks—albeit momentarily—his hold over Othello's imagination: "Look where she comes: / If she be false, O then heaven mocks itself! / I'll not believe 't" (3.3.277–79). It is no coincidence, of course, that Shakespeare has the "phantasmagoric questioning, raving, mocking debate go on among the men about their stereotype women," to quote Roger Stilling, "while at the center of it Desdemona sits, [a] . . . denial of a whole tradition of masculine invention and myth." This disparity between delusion and reality is, rather, "the source of one of the play's dominating structural ironies."[2]

Male fantasies prevail in act 3; they stand the test of reality in act 4. Were Shakespeare's focus merely on the male point of view that culminates in the deception scene, he would depict women solely as they are valued by men. But his focus on the female point of view that culminates in the willow song scene places a value on women's affections that is different from their worth in men's eyes. The female characters in *Othello* differ in this way from the female protagonist of *Troilus and Cressida*. Women in the play embody an emotional commitment the men would seem to be incapable of reciprocating. Their attitudes and feelings toward the men in their lives, moreover, sharpen the focus on male treatment of women: Desdemona's absolute devotion to Othello accentuates his cruel treatment of her; Bianca's genuine affection for Cassio highlights his ridicule of her; Emilia's obedience to Iago likewise underscores his hatred of her, and of all women.[3]

Even as the story of women tutoring men in *Love's Labor's Lost* anticipates the dynamics of the love relationship in *Romeo and Juliet,* that of the true woman falsely accused in *Much Ado* anticipates the action of *Othello.* It is a story that may have fascinated Shakespeare, for he returns to it time and again throughout his artistic development, exploring its different generic implications in plays as dissimilar as *Much Ado, Othello, Cymbeline,* and *The Winter's Tale.* In comedy, Hero is pelted with the accusations of Leonatus and Claudio at the wedding altar; in tragedy, Desdemona confronts father and husband in separate crises. And, of course, Beatrice's justifiable anger at the humiliation of the accusation is replaced by that of Emilia. But the female protagonist is dead, not to be resurrected.

Desdemona, like Juliet, enjoys her father's love while she is a compliant, obedient daughter. Each female protagonist confronts real paternal anger rather than the prerogatives of paternal authority of the comedies, however, when she attempts to exercise her will in the choice of a marital partner. The one act Juliet is incapable of—standing up to her father and revealing the secrecy of her marriage—Desdemona disposes of as soon as she walks onstage. Yet Desdemona does not stand up to Brabantio in the sense of challenging him so much as she compassionately, pointedly answers his question. She is honest with him in the same way that Cordelia is honest with Lear; the strength and honesty of her response to her father's challenge, in fact, link her more closely to Cordelia than to Juliet. Juliet faces the threat of banishment from her father's house; Desdemona and Cordelia face the reality of paternal banishment from house and kingdom.

Desdemona and Cordelia confront situations that, although different in dramatic context, are similar in emotional content. In facing specific challenges they face the generalized problem inherent in the female condition, a daughter's "duty" to her father when it must, on her maturity, be "divided" with a wife's "duty" to her husband. Cordelia's response to Lear's question, "Which of you shall we say doth love us most . . .?" (*King Lear,* 1.1.51), condemns her in her father's eyes, of course, because of her plainness on her "bond." But what are we to make of the fact that Desdemona's response to Brabantio's question, "Do you perceive in all this noble company / Where most you owe obedience?" (1.3.179–80), also condemns her, despite her eloquence on her "divided duty?" The problem is neither filial inability to adapt to the new situation nor unwillingness to split emotional commitment, but rather, paternal refusal to relinquish full share of filial attention and commitment. Lear responds to Cordelia with wounded love; Brabantio responds to Desdemona with jealousy.

Desdemona skillfully manages the balancing act of acknowledging her bond to Brabantio, diplomatically elaborating on what he needs to hear—and what she genuinely feels—before insisting on the implications of her new status as Othello's wife:

> My noble father,
> I do perceive here a divided duty:
> To you I am bound for life and education;
> My life and education both do learn me
> How to respect you; you are the lord of duty;
> I am hitherto your daughter.
>
> (1.3.180–85)

Desdemona understands the cyclical nature of human existence, one generation repeating the life events of another in patterns of birth, growth, marriage, maturity, and death. This understanding— one that she reiterates when she greets her husband at Cyprus[4]— would seem to guarantee the success of her plea to her father:

> But here's my husband;
> And so much duty as my mother show'd
> To you, preferring you before her father,
> So much I challenge that I may profess
> Due to the Moor, my lord.
>
> (1.3.185–89)

Her analogy of her situation to that of her mother attempts to gain understanding from Brabantio by drawing him out of his present paternal role and reminding him of his past marital role in his wife's similar dilemma. Her eloquence echoes that of Isabella in *Measure for Measure;* her insistence that would-be judge project himself into the situation of offender reminds us of the comic female protagonist's persuasive appeal for empathy in pleading with Angelo for the life of her brother:

> If he had been as you, and you as he,
> You would have slipp'd like him. . . .
> Go to your bosom,
> Knock there, and ask your heart what it doth know
> That's like my brother's fault.
>
> (*Measure for Measure,* 2.2.64–138)

What emerges from this exchange is an understanding that Desdemona's self-defense depends on her immediate comprehension, even anticipation, of Brabantio's challenge. Her confidence and resilience are based on her new connection with Othello, on her new status as partner in the joint enterprise of marriage. Taking the risk of marrying him is an active choice whose consequences she is capable of anticipating and willing to accept: "That I did love the Moor to live with him, / My downright violence, and storm of fortunes, / May trumpet to the world" (1.3.247–49). The possessiveness of her husband follows as naturally as that of her father from the premise of patriarchal marriage that operates so powerfully in this play. Yet it is difficult to understand the woman who is incapable of standing up to her father, but not her husband.[5]

Desdemona is, of course, unaware of the change in Othello when she declares to Emilia, immediately following the deception scene, that "my noble Moor / Is true of mind, and made of no such baseness / As jealous creatures are. . . . / I think the sun where he was born / Drew all such humors from him" (3.4.26–31). Only in the brothel scene when his explicit epithets, "strumpet" and "whore," assail her consciousness, does understanding dimly set in. Then so great is the shock of comprehension that her near-catatonia reminds us of Hero's swoon at the wedding altar in *Much Ado About Nothing:*

> *Emil.* How do you, madam? how do you, my good lady?
> *Des.* Faith, half asleep.
> *Emil.* Good madam, what's the matter with my lord?
> *Des.* With who?
> *Emil.* Why, with my lord, madam.
> *Des.* Who is thy lord?
> *Emil.*   He that is yours, sweet lady.
> *Des.* I have none.
>
>   (4.2.96–102)

It is in this context, I think, that we are able to understand A. C. Bradley's infamous comparison of the suffering of Desdemona to that of "the most loving of dumb creatures."[6] "She is dazed," S. N. Garner more recently notes; "her mind simply cannot take in what it encounters."[7] The source of Desdemona's loss of confidence and resilience is, of course, the severance of her connection to Othello. She is quite aware of a loss that is no less than the loss of her marital partner: "I have none," that is to say, "I have no lord." Because Othello's history is that of a warrior hero, as A. D. Nuttall reminds us, the state of marriage, even before he succumbs to

Iago's influence, is disorienting to him.[8] Conversely, because marriage is Desdemona's sole adventure in life, its disintegration is disorienting to her. That marriage depends for its existence on a mutuality of feeling of the kind dramatized by both protagonists throughout act 1; despite the constancy of her faith in Othello, the foundation of their relationship is fissured from his loss of faith in her.

Shakespeare understands women such as Mariana in *Measure for Measure* whose lack of a sense of self makes her vulnerable to exploitation. But he does not depict Desdemona in this way. When Othello strikes her, she stoutly responds, "I have not deserv'd this" (4.1.241). She resolutely defends herself, in fact, from the moment she comprehends his accusations in the brothel scene until the moment she dies:

> *Oth.* Impudent strumpet!
> *Des.*   By heaven, you do me wrong.
> *Oth.* Are not you a strumpet?
> *Des.*   No, as I am a Christian.
> If to preserve this vessel for my lord
> From any other foul unlawful touch
> Be not to be a strumpet, I am none.
> *Oth.* What, not a whore?
> *Des.*   No, as I shall be sav'd.
> (4.2.81–86)
>
> *Oth.* That handkerchief which I so lov'd, and gave thee,
> Thou gav'st to Cassio.
> *Des.*   No, by my life and soul!
> Send for the man, and ask him. . . .
>   I never did
> Offend you in my life; never lov'd Cassio
> But with such general warranty of heaven
> As I might love. I never gave him token.
> (5.2.48–61)

Regardless of her intermittent self-defense and loss of confidence, Desdemona's devotion to Othello is unchanging. Indeed, her "active effort to mend and renew the relationship," to quote Carol Thomas Neely, is constant.[9] The closing couplet of the willow song scene quintessentially expresses her optimism concerning reconciliation and healing: "God me such uses send, / Not to pick bad from bad, but by bad mend" (4.3.104–5).

Desdemona's expectation of Brabantio's possessiveness and her ease in responding to it establish her skill in anticipating situations

and her resilience in responding to them. While Brabantio's challenge demands of Desdemona simple responsibility for the consequences of her action—her choice of husband—nothing of the
kind can possibly suffice in responding to Othello's accusations.
Her various suspicions about the reasons for the change in him
reveal a sensibility that is keenly aware of the emotional nuances
and dissonances of which human ties are woven—a sensibility that
is, moreover, occupied with the work of restoring those ties. First,
she suspects the magic spell of the sibyl's handkerchief: "I nev'r
saw this before. / Sure, there's some wonder in this handkerchief; / I
am most unhappy in the loss of it" (3.4.100–2). Next, she guesses at
a political matter as the cause for the change in Othello: "Something sure of state, / Either from Venice, or some unhatch'd practice
/ Made demonstrable here in Cyprus to him, / Hath puddled his
clear spirit" (3.4.140–43). Finally, she speculates that Brabantio is
the reason: "If happily you my father do suspect / An instrument of
this your calling back, / Lay not your blame on me" (4.2.44–46).
But Desdemona is wrong, of course, on all counts. The variety and
number of her suspicions only accentuate the futility of any anticipation of and responsibility for the consequences of her actions in
her new situation.

There can be no anticipation of such a loss of faith as Othello's
because it is rooted not in empirical reality, but in the mind, as
Emilia understands: jealous souls "are not ever jealous for the
cause, / But jealous for they're jealous. It is a monster / Begot upon
itself, born on itself" (3.4.160–62). Nor can there be any defense
against such a loss of faith other than a simple reaffirmation of faith.
The imperatives of reason and justice are irrelevant to the realm of
love and jealousy. "Immunity from jealousy would lie in the con-
tinuance of this simple act of faith," Winifred M. T. Nowottny
maintains. Shakespeare "deliberately forces upon the audience the
question, In what strength could Othello reject Iago? The answer
would seem to be, By an affirmation of faith which is beyond
reason, by the act of choosing to believe in Desdemona."[10]

The tragic action follows from Othello's inability to reaffirm his
faith in Desdemona in this way. But it is precisely a reaffirmation of
faith such as Nowottny describes that characterizes the generosity
of Desdemona's response to the change in him: "I was (un-
handsome warrior as I am) / Arraigning his unkindness with my
soul; / But now I find I had suborn'd the witness, / And he's indicted
falsely" (3.4.151–54).[11] Desdemona kneels alone in an enactment of
her reaffirmation of faith in Othello: "Unkindness may do much, /
And his unkindness may defeat my life, / But never taint my love"

(4.2.159–61). This visual emblem is a powerful reminder of her declaration of weddinglike vows before the Venetian Senate in act 1: "I saw Othello's visage in his mind, / And to his honors and his valiant parts / Did I my soul and fortunes consecrate" (1.3.252–54). But it also throws into high relief the inversion of the wedding ceremony in act 3—Othello kneeling side by side with Iago in an enactment of his loss of faith in her. The effect of these two stage emblems is to emphasize that his spirit erodes, while hers does not.

"Desdemona's love for Othello," Nowottny concludes, "has been made 'unreasonable' in a way which permits discussion of it in the drama."[12] The irony of Desdemona's continued obedience and humility—wifely virtues that should guarantee success within the institution of patriarchal marriage—does not escape us, particularly since Shakespeare visually and orally places such emphasis on them. Her response to Othello's physical blow, "I will not stay to offend you," is amplified, sympathetically, by Lodovico, "Truly, an obedient lady," then, sneeringly, by Othello, "she's obedient, as you say, obedient; / Very obedient" (4.1.247–56). Barbary's self-effacement in the willow song lyric, " 'Let nobody blame him, his scorn I approve' " (4.3.52) is but an echo of Desdemona's: " 'Tis meet I should be us'd so, very meet" (4.2.107); "My love doth so approve him, / That even his stubbornness, his checks, his frowns— / . . . have grace and favor in them" (4.3.19–21). The infinite capacity for giving of herself evident in her obedience and humility is at last concentrated in the generosity of forgiveness. She forgives both the unknown villain who wrongs her—"If any such there be, heaven pardon him!" (4.2.135)—and the husband who murders her: "Nobody; I myself. . . . / Commend me to my kind lord" (5.2.124–25). The depth and totality of her emotional commitment is such that, having deliberately chosen Othello for her husband, she bears the consequences of that choice in a way that reanimates the meaning of the words, "for better, for worse," from the traditional wedding ceremony. Her devotion is as unchanging as her purity and innocence are absolute.

Desdemona's absolute innocence of the act of adultery is all that is necessary to make the point of Othello's mistake—her absolute purity and devotion are not. Shakespeare, I believe, exploits the absoluteness of her purity to accentuate the degree of Othello's mistake. Likewise, he exploits the absoluteness of her devotion to accentuate the contrast between Othello's reaction to his imagined mistreatment by her and her reaction to her real mistreatment by him. Shakespeare thus portrays a love that, like the charity of Cordelia, surpasses understanding in its ability and willingness to subsume individual needs to the demands of a bond with another. If in tragedy as in romantic comedy "self-knowledge is achieved through indirect means: learning how to love," as Edward Quinn contends,[13] then the self-knowledge of Desdemona—like that of Juliet and the female protagonists of the romantic comedies before her, and Cordelia after her—is a donnée of the drama. Whether or not the hero is capable of achieving self-knowledge through learning how to love is the question that reverberates throughout the unfolding dramatic action.

The nature of Desdemona's love for Othello depends in part upon her response to his cruel treatment of her. Either she is self-deceiving or she is as honest with herself as she is with her father and her husband. If she continues to love Othello because she denies his cruelty, her love is not an idealized love. If she continues to love him despite her admission and acceptance of that cruelty, her love is an idealized love, indeed. But there is no greater degree of ambivalence surrounding the nature of her love, I believe, than there is surrounding her characterization. That is not to bring us full circle back to those critics who would simplify her character into an abstraction of Good, vying with an Evil Iago for the soul of Othello in a Jacobean version of a medieval morality play—one that happens to be focused in the bedroom. But it is to take issue with those critics who find fault in her dissembling over the stolen handkerchief: "It is not lost" (3.4.83). To condemn Desdemona for this fearful lie, or for her determination in bringing Cassio's suit, or for her incidental mention of Lodovico in the willow song scene, or indeed, for marrying Othello in the first place,[14] requires, it would seem, a mentality not unlike that of Iago. To find Desdemona "guilty" of these small "crimes" or to seek in them any responsibility for or complicity in the larger crime of her murder is not only to reveal an appetite for red herrings; it is perverse, and reveals the lengths to which critics are prepared to go to avoid the ineluctable truth of the plot—Othello murders an innocent Desdemona.

The problem would seem to be, rather, that the dramatic action exhibits Desdemona's inalterable love in the central situation—Othello's loss of faith—in which she is acted upon rather than acting. It is true that after her choice of husband, her interaction with her father, and her argument for accompanying Othello to Cyprus—in the essentially comic action of the first two acts of the play—she does not appear to originate a series of events by a deliberate choice. The comic action of the first half of the play emphasizes her independence and courage; the tragic action of the last half of the play stresses her purity and innocence. The divided

Desdemona of which I speak—a split between character and construct—is significant because it goes to the heart of the larger question concerning Shakespeare's female protogonists.[15] Female integrity is inflected in the comedies in the autonomy and wit of a Portia, a Beatrice, a Rosalind, a Viola, an Olivia. These traits are mitigated but not eliminated in the tragedies, where female integrity is inflected instead in the moral excellence of a Cordelia or a Desdemona. In both *Lear* and *Othello,* as Madeleine Doran points out, "the characters in whom we feel the greatest moral strength are not the heroes, although they are both good men, but the heroines—the daughter Cordelia and the wife Desdemona." If the female protagonists are silenced and victimized by the tragic action, it is to raise questions about the destructive forces that bring about that silencing and victimizing. Cordelia and Desdemona are both destroyed, Doran concludes, "because the failure to understand their evident goodness by the father and husband who should know them best engulfs them in the deadly scheming malice of ambitious and evil men."[16]

Although act 3 forces us to view Desdemona from Othello's perspective, Shakespeare alters impressions of character when he shifts perspectives in act 4. We no longer look at her and her imagined mistreatment of Othello through his eyes; we look at men and their real mistreatment of women through her eyes, and those of Bianca and Emilia. Our apprehension of Desdemona's characterization as the embodiment of moral excellence deepens into understanding as the tragic action develops, controlling our responses to that action. The locus of moral strength in her character magnifies the masculine impulses of insecurity—Othello's—and misogyny—Iago's—that dominate act 3 and represents the reality of women that Bianca and Emilia mirror in acts 4 and 5. Shakespeare exploits the fiction of Desdemona's betrayal of Othello to accentuate the reality of his betrayal of her. Our final impression is not the innocent Othello victimized by the cruel Iago, but the innocent Desdemona victimized by the cruel Othello.

Shakespeare's invention of the character of Bianca is one of the more significant transmutations of his source material. In Cinthio's *Gli Hecatommithi,* Cassio is a married man who emerges "one dark night from the house of a courtesan with whom he used to amuse himself" when he is attacked by Iago.[17] From this hint Shakespeare omits Cassio's wife and creates Bianca. Obviously her dramatic function is not to provide local color or to give us a flavor of the night life on this military outpost on Cyprus. Her presence expands the theme of men's treatment of women, particularly that which is dramatized in the central relationship—of a husband who believes his wife to be a whore. Both Bianca and Emilia serve as dramatic contrasts to Desdemona, as critics generally recognize, but in their treatment by the men in their lives and in their attitudes toward those men, they serve as parallels as well.[18]

Baldly put, Bianca is Bianca because Iago is Iago. Women in *Othello* are, as the arc of the tragic action emphasizes, what men make them. Initially she seems merely to be a reflection of Othello's mistaken notion of Desdemona—paramour, courtesan, whore. She may be thought "to supply in living form on the stage," to quote Maynard Mack, "the prostitute figure that Desdemona has become in Othello's mind."[19] Her role is transitional in nature: Cassio's mistreatment of Bianca contrasts with Othello's early treatment of Desdemona and parallels his later mistreatment of her. She enters the action immediately following the deception scene, dramatizing the state of mind of a soldier who—either because accustomed to a lifetime of military victory and defeat, or by nature disposed to action and impatient with deliberation—perceives reality in terms of absolute polarities. Whatever the reason, a consciousness such as Othello's has little room for doubt, as the deception scene makes clear. Desdemona falls straight from the status of chaste wife to that of whore. And at the point when, "In Othello's mental imagery, Desdemona becomes the soliciting whore," Mack maintains, "Bianca enters in the flesh."[20]

We might agree that Bianca is no more than a manifestation of Othello's false image of Desdemona were she not completely lacking in sensuality. While Othello's jealousy is focused exclusively in the sexual, Shakespeare has no interest in characterizing women solely by this aspect of human behavior. What is striking, rather, is the disparity between Cassio's view of Bianca and her self-evaluation, the gap between the shallowness of his feeling for her and her genuine affection for him. She reiterates Desdemona's response to Othello in her willingness to "be circumstanc'd" and in her good-natured humor. Cassio's lie, "Not that I love you not," prompts her quick retort: "But that you do not love me" (3.4.196). Her obedience to his wish that she copy the handkerchief parallels Desdemona's and Emilia's obedience to their husbands. Conversely, her change of mind emphasizes the constancy of Desdemona's obedience: "What did you mean by that same handkerchief you gave me even now? I was a fine fool to take it. I must take out the work? . . . I'll take out no work on't" (4.1.148–55). Bianca is consistent, though, in placing a value on her affections and her identity that is different from her worth in men's eyes: "I am no strumpet, but of life as honest / As you that thus abuse me" (5.1.122–23).

Cassio is not Iago's superior, of course, in his ability to distinguish women into two categories—chaste virgins such as Desdemona and "courtesans" such as Bianca—because his distinction depends on Iago's filthy premise. "It is impossible to trust either the adoring or the degrading perspective," as Cook puts it.[21] Cassio's conversation with Iago reveals a man who does not take seriously the woman he beds: he refers to her as "customer," "monkey," "bauble," and "fitchew," echoing in a minor key the obscene epithets Othello hurls at Desdemona. He alternately ridicules Bianca (in her absence) and is embarrassed by her affections (in her presence). The disparity between Cassio's mistreatment of Bianca and her sincere feelings for him broadens the critique on male treatment of females that is focused in the relationship of the protagonists. The contrast between his courtly idealization of Desdemona and his casual denigration of Bianca—particularly in view of Shakespeare's theatrical representation of these women onstage—makes clear the inadequacy of his splintered vision. His split perspective focuses on two separate women; Othello's focuses on Desdemona alone. Cassio "divides women into two types, Desdemona and Bianca," observes Gayle Greene, "but Othello directs his confusions at one woman, his wife."[22] Such reductive, splintered visions as these appear to be simpler alternatives for both men than any recognition of the whole, complex reality presented by the women in ther lives.

Shakespeare further alters *Gli Hecatommithi* when he fills in the outlines of Emilia's character sketched by Cinthio: "this false man had likewise taken to Cyprus his wife, a fair and honest young woman. Being an Italian she was much loved by the Moor's wife, and spent the greater part of the day with her."[23] Although initially her dramatic function, like that of Bianca, would seem to be one of contrast, her characterization grows in significance until her defiance of Iago in the final scene defies his view of women throughout the play.

When we enter the willow song scene, we enter a world of women from which men are excluded. For a brief moment the door of the bedchamber shuts out masculine fantasizing about women—the "phantasmagoric questioning, raving, mocking debate" of which Stilling speaks. Women are represented as neither objects of male demands nor fragments of male delusions. Desdemona's virtues of honesty, kindness, and loyalty "are repeated in a lower key," Doran

notes, "in Emilia."[24] As the two women indulge in quiet, intimate
conversation with one another, the reasons for Emilia's fierce at-
tachment to Desdemona throughout the play become clear. The
emphasis two scenes before her murder on "the alabaster innocence of Desdemona's world," to quote Mack[25]—on her total lack
of preparation for what is happening to her—render it one of the
most poignant scenes in the tragedies. Desdemona's own articulation of the very view that is responsible for her condemnation and
murder heightens its poignancy: "Dost thou in conscience
think . . . / That there be women do *abuse* their husbands / In such
gross kind?" (4.3.61–63, italics mine). The worldly humor of Emilia's response emphasizes her practicality and shrewdness but does
not conceal the generosity of motive that so often characterizes
Shakespeare's female figures: "for all the whole world—'ud's pity,
who would not make her husband a cuckold to make him a monarch? I should venture purgatory for 't" (4.3.75–77).[26] The willow
song scene is one of those scenes of "spiritual cross purposes,"
Mack maintains, which appear toward the close of a Shakespearean
tragedy. In the two opposed voices of Desdemona and Emilia "the
line of tragic speech and feeling generated by commitment" is
crossed by "an alien speech and feeling very much detached."[27]
Like the gritty accents of the Clown echoing between the lines of
Cleopatra's exultation, those of Emilia sound between the lines of
Desdemona's innocence.

Emilia's forthright discussion of human sexuality views it as
neither male "appetite" for females—Iago's credo—nor wives'
"abuse" of husbands—Othello's delusion. It emphasizes instead
the shared traits of both sexes of the human animal:

> Let husbands know
> Their wives have sense like them; they see, and smell,
> And have their palates both for sweet and sour,
> As husbands have. What is it that they do
> When they change us for others? Is it sport?
> I think it is. And doth affection breed it?
> I think it doth. Is't frailty that thus errs?
> It is so too. And have not we affections,
> Desires for sport, and frailty, as men have?
>
> (4.3.93–101)

Her emphasis on the similarity of female and male needs creates an
impression of balance, reciprocity, and equality within relationships
between the sexes. The partnership model for heterosexual relations that emerges from this speech is suggested by the denotations

of the Latin roots of the word *conjugal,* in sharp contrast to the dominator model that is suggested by the Latin roots of the words *marriage* and *marry.*[28] She voices an attitude of moderation that is painfully absent in the play—a middle ground between the extremes of Desdemona's purity and innocence, on the one hand, and Othello's insecurity and Iago's misogyny, on the other. Emilia's articulation of the female point of view echoes another minority view, that of Shylock:

> Hath not a Jew eyes? Hath not a Jew hands, organs, dimensions, senses, affections, passions; fed with the same food, hurt with the same weapons, subject to the same diseases, heal'd by the same means, warm'd and cool'd by the the the same winter and summer, as a Christian is? If you prick us, do we not bleed? If you tickle us, do we not laugh? If you poison us, do we not die?
>
> (*The Merchant of Venice,* 3.1.59–66)

Shylock's self-justification contributes to the exposé of Christian treatment of Jews that is implicit throughout the comic action of *The Merchant of Venice.* Similarly, Emilia's defense of the female sex finally makes explicit the critique of male treatment of females that is implicit throughout the tragic action of *Othello.*

The power of Emilia's argument, like that of Beatrice in *Much Ado,* is allowed utterance, but because Shakespeare's emphasis is on destroyed innocence in this play, its only audience is the female protagonist in the confinement of her bedchamber. It has no impact on the tragic action bearing down on Desdemona from the male realm. Although Emilia voices the precise corrective to Iago's misogyny, the attitude that has the potential to prevent catastrophe, it has no chance of reaching and affecting the deluded hero until it is too late. This is tragedy, not comedy. Unlike Dogberry and the bumbling Watch, who manage against all odds to convey the truth to the point it eventually impinges on the potentially tragic action of *Much Ado,* Emilia simultaneously learns of Iago's villainy and reveals it to Othello. But Desdemona is dead.

Reconciling Emilia's characteristic practicality and shrewdness with her status as Iago's wife presents a problem—one that is mitigated, however, by her utter ignorance of his villainy until the final scene. The disparity between his hatred of her and her desire to please him, like the gap between the feelings of Cassio and Bianca for one another, further broadens the critique on male treatment of females. Her obedience to his wish that she steal the handkerchief, "I nothing but to please his fantasy" (3.3.299), paral-

lels Bianca's obedience to Cassio's wish that she copy it. The
obedience of both women doubly mirrors Desdemona's compliant
devotion to Othello. Emilia's defiance of Iago, conversely, like
Bianca's of Cassio, accentuates the unchanging obedience, humility,
generosity, and forgiveness of Desdemona. Shakespeare's emphasis
on Emilia's defiance of her husband necessarily dispels any doubt
that lingers about her ignorant complicity in his plot:

> *Iago.*   Go to, charm your tongue.
> *Emil.* I will not charm my tongue; I am bound to speak.
> 'Tis proper I obey him; but not now.
> My mistress here lies murthered in her bed— . . .
> And your reports have set the murder on . . .
> *Iago.* What, are you mad? I charge you to get you home.
> *Emil.* Good gentlemen, let me have leave to speak.
> Perchance, Iago, I will ne'er go home . . .
> *Iago.* 'Zounds, hold your peace.
> *Emil.*   'Twill out, 'twill out! I peace?
> No, I will speak as liberal as the north:
> Let heaven and men and devils, let them all,
> All, all, cry shame against me, yet I'll speak.
> *Iago.* Be wise, and get you home.
> *Emil.*   I will not.
>
> (5.2.183–223)

Four times Iago attempts to exercise the prerogatives of patriarchal
marriage and commands his wife to silence or to her house. Four
times, as though exhilarated by the power of language, Emilia defies
him with the truth before she pays the price for that defiance with
her life. Like her beloved mistress, she dies by her husband's hand.

Emilia's instruction of Othello prompts merely a discovery of his
mistake about Desdemona's innocence of adultery rather than any
psychological self-knowledge or moral awakening. He reveals the
attenuated nature of his moment of truth: he would be "an honorable murderer . . . / For nought I did in hate, but all in honor"
(5.2.294–95). The judicial review of the case by all the characters
onstage finally leads, as Robert B. Heilman puts it, to "the hero's
self-recognition in error (discovery of his 'mistake' if not complete
discovery of himself)."[29] Robert Ornstein is less parenthetical in
distinguishing between discovery of error and gain of insight: "it is
not clear that Othello gains a new or greater wisdom from murdering Desdemona. Though he recovers enough of his former stature to
admit that he is an 'honourable murderer,' he learns only the simple

truth which was obvious to the coarse Emilia, to Cassio, and even at last to the foolish Roderigo—that Desdemona was chaste."[30] The reappearance of Paris—the parody of Romeo's early self—at the Capulet vault emphasizes Romeo's ennoblement. The reappearance of Lodovico—the representative of civilized Venice—accentuates the degeneration of Othello's nobility:

> Is this the noble Moor whom our full Senate
> Call all in all sufficient? Is this the nature
> Whom passion could not shake? whose solid virtue
> The shot of accident nor dart of chance
> Could neither gaze nor pierce?
>
> (4.1.264–68)

In *Othello* as in *Hamlet* revenge is consummated, with the difference that Hamlet takes vengeance upon Claudius while Othello takes vengeance upon himself. His final act is not shocking because—despite the influence of Iago—we feel that Othello is guilty. In response to Desdemona's affirmation and reaffirmation of faith that are expressions at once of self-confidence and courage, the best Othello is capable of offering in return is self-assertion in the form of self-destruction.

Shakespeare's comic treatment of the story of the true woman falsely accused in *Much Ado* exposes the inadequacy of male constructions of females; his tragic treatment of the same story in *Othello* plumbs greater psychological depths to emphasize the degradation of those who would presume to possess another human being. To search either *Romeo and Juliet* or *Othello* for evidence that endorses or condemns the hero's nobility or ignobility is to miss the larger commentary on sexual possession. Male concern with possession is inflected in both the Petrarchan and the Ovidian discursive traditions that Shakespeare inherits, as well as the institution of patriarchal marriage that characterizes his culture. It underlies the Petrarchan stance away from which Juliet draws Romeo. It animates the prerogatives of patriarchal marriage and erupts in Iago's misogyny, both of which debase Othello despite the healing influence of Desdemona. Neither Romeo's participation in the Petrarchan discursive tradition nor Othello's participation in the institution of patriarchal marriage, and, under Iago's influence, the Ovidian discursive tradition, allows for the possibility of a mutual relationship between two whole selves. These discourses and institutions are inadequate because they are reductive of both love partners: romantic desire requires a male lover to glorify the physical appearance of a female beloved; patriarchal marriage requires a husband's honor to depend upon a wife's chastity. These gaping inadequacies suggest the viability of another option—a partnership between equals such as that which Emilia articulates—that is freed of the constraints of both.

NOTES

1. An earlier version of this essay was presented at the 1988 Annual Meeting of the Shakespeare Association of America in Boston; a condensed version, "The Female Perspective in *Othello:* The Divided Desdemona," was read at the 1988 Rocky Mountain Modern Language Association Convention in Las Cruces, New Mexico, and won the RMMLA Best Feminist Essay Award for that year.

2. Roger Stilling, *Love and Death in Renaissance Tragedy* (Baton Rouge: Louisiana State University Press, 1976), p. 159.

3. Iago is, I believe, the only misogynist in the play.

4. In response to Othello's absolutes—"If it were now to die, / 'Twere now to be most happy; for I fear / My soul hath her content so absolute / That not another comfort like to this / Succeeds in unknown fate"—Desdemona declares: "The heavens forbid / But that our loves and comforts should increase / Even as our days do grow!" (2.1.189–95).

5. This, I believe, is the central question concerning Desdemona's characterization. My attempt at an answer, incidentally, takes me on a path that is the inverse of the one followed by Ann Jennalie Cook ("The Design of Desdemona," *Shakespeare Studies* 13 [1980]: 187–96). She has profound doubts about Desdemona's actions early in the play—her "disobedience" to her father, for example—which are resolved only as the tragic action develops. I find in those same actions the very traits that we so admire in Shakespeare's comic female protagonists—independence, confidence, the courage to take risks—and I am concerned to understand why these traits diminish as the dramatic action turns from comic to tragic.

6. A. C. Bradley, *Shakespearean Tragedy* (London: Macmillan, 1904; repr., Cleveland: World, 1955), p. 147.

7. S. N. Garner, "Shakespeare's Desdemona," *Shakespeare Studies* 9 (1976): 248.

8. A. D. Nuttall, *A New Mimesis: Shakespeare and the Representation of Reality* (London: Methuen, 1983), p. 139.

9. Carol Thomas Neely, "Women and Men in *Othello:* 'What should such a fool / Do with so good a woman?' *Shakespeare Studies* 10 (1977): 147.

10. Winifred M. T. Nowottny, "Justice and Love in *Othello,*" *University of Toronto Quarterly* 21 (1951–52): 334.

11. This emphasis on active generosity in love is, of course, made explicit throughout the comedies: in Rosalind's "To you I give myself, for I am yours" (*As You Like It,* 5.4.117); in Olivia's "Love sought is good, but given unsought is better" (*Twelfth Night,* 3.1.156); in Helena's "I dare not say I take you, but I give /

Me and my service, ever whilst I live, / Into your guiding power" (*All's Well That Ends Well,* 2.3.102–4).

12. "Justice and Love in *Othello,"* 334.

13. E. Quinn, "Introduction" to *The Shakespeare Hour,* ed. Edward Quinn (New York: New American Library, 1985), pp. xxiii–xxiv. He is discussing *King Lear.*

14. G. Bonnard, I believe, initiates this curious approach ("Are Othello and Desdemona Innocent or Guilty?" *English Studies* 30 [1949]: 175–84), while Robert Dickes epitomizes it ("Desdemona: An Innocent Victim?" *American Imago* 27 [1970]: 279–97).

15. Shakespeare's differing generic representations of women have, of course, absorbed the attention of feminist critics. The variety and the vigor of their responses to the gender/genre question is, I believe, an indication of its complexity.

16. Madeleine Doran, "The Idea of Excellence in Shakespeare," *Shakespeare Quarterly* 27 (1976): 146.

17. G. Cinthio, *Gli Hecatommithi* (1566), trans. Geoffrey Bullough, in *Narrative and Dramatic Sources of Shakespeare* 7 (New York: Columbia University Press, 1973), p. 249.

18. The studies of Garner and Neely are notable for emphasizing the links among the three female characters in the tragedy.

19. Maynard Mack, "The Jacobean Shakespeare," in *Modern Shakespearean Criticism,* ed. Alvin B. Kernan (New York: Harcourt, Brace and World, 1970), p. 340; 1st pub. in *Stratford-upon-Avon Studies: Jacobean Theatre,* no. 1, ed. John Russell Brown and Bernard Harris (London: Edward Arnold, 1960). Kay Stanton reminds us, however, that it was not until Nicholas Rowe's edition that the practice of giving Bianca the designation of "Courtesan" in the dramatis personae began ("Male Gender-Crossing in *Othello,"* paper presented at seminar on "Shakespearean Tragedy and Gender," Annual Meeting of the Shakespeare Association of America, April 1987).

20. Mack, "The Jacobean Shakespeare," p. 340.

21. Cook, "The Design of Desdemona," 191.

22. Gayle Greene, " 'This that you call love': Sexual and Social Tragedy in *Othello,"* *Journal of Women's Studies in Literature* 1 (1979): 21.

23. Bullough, *Narrative and Dramatic Sources* 7, p. 243.

24. Doran, "The Idea of Excellence in Shakespeare," 146.

25. Mack, "The Jacobean Shakespeare," p. 334.

26. See n. 11 above.

27. Mack, "The Jacobean Shakespeare," p. 332.

28. *Oxford English Dictionary,* s.vv. *conjugal, conjugality, marriage,* and *marry.* and *Oxford Latin Dictionary,* combined ed., s.vv. *coniugo,* etc., *maritus,* and *mas: coniugo* "to join in marriage; to form (a friendship)"; *coniunctio* "the act of joining together, uniting; that state of being joined, union; a bond (of association, friendship, etc., between persons); mutual association, friendship, familiarity; an association by marriage or betrothal, connexion; (also) the entering into such an association"; *coniunctus* "closely associated (by friendship, obligation, kinship, etc.), attached; (of relationships, etc.) close"; *coniungo* "to join together, connect; to yoke together; to unite sexually; to bring into close association, unite (by friendship, obligation, kinship, etc.); to bring into alliance; to form an alliance, make common cause; to join in marriage; to be married"; *maritus* "a husband"; *mas* "male, masculine; possessing masculine faculties or characteristics; manly,

virile; the male of the species." I have adopted the terms *partnership model* and *dominator model* from Riane Eisler, *The Chalice and the Blade* (San Francisco: Harper, 1987), p. xvii.

29. Robert B. Heilman, *Magic in the Web: Action and Language in Othello* (Lexington: University Press of Kentucky, 1956), p. 161.

30. Robert Ornstein, *The Moral Vision of Jacobean Tragedy* (Madison: University of Wisconsin Press, 1960), p. 228.

6

Location and Idiom in *Othello*

MICHAEL E. MOONEY

"The special pathos of our urge to intervene"

Since the translation of Robert Weimann's *Shakespeare and the Popular Tradition in the Theater,* scholars have come to realize that there is indeed a correlation between an actor's stage location and "the speech, action, and degree of stylization associated with that position."[1] Weimann's term for this correlation is *Figurenposition,* or "figural positioning"; it promises to provide us, for the first time, with a way to relate our analysis of dramatic language to the flexible dimensions of the platform stage.

In proposing this term, Weimann carefully examines the influence two earlier theatrical modes had on the formation of Elizabethan dramaturgy: the courtly or hall drama, with its illusionistic, "representational," and self-enclosed frame; and the popular drama's illusion-breaking, "presentational," focus. T. S. Eliot, of course, felt that the art of the Elizabethans was an "impure art" because it confused the "realism" of illusionistic representation with the "conventions" of popular staging. But later critics have recognized that the essence of this drama may well lie precisely in the mixture of "naturalism" and "conventionalism" that so often fuses in "complementary perspective."[2] In Weimann's view, this "complementary perspective" may be discerned in the "traditional interplay between *platea* and *locus,* between neutral, undifferentiated 'place' and symbolic location [which] . . . accommodates action that is both nonillusionistic and near the audience (corresponding to the 'place') and a more illusionistic, localized action sometimes taking place in a discovery place, scaffold, tent or other *loci.*"[3] But if, in earlier popular and illusionistic modes of staging, there is a clear distinction between illusionistic and nonillusionistic effects, this is not so clearly the case in the later drama. In earlier drama, a character's delivery of illusion-breaking asides, choric speeches, and other kinds of direct or indirect address is facilitated by a downstage, *platea* position; "realistic" dialogue, on the other hand, is often tied to a specific *locus* and held within the illusionistic frame of the play. In the Elizabethan and Jacobean theater, however, a character's *Figurenposition* may not, finally, be restricted to a particularized *locus* or to a generalized *platea* position. "This *Figurenposition,*" Weimann points out, "should not be understood only in the sense of an actor's physical position on the stage, but also in the more general sense that an actor may generate a unique stage presence that establishes a special relationship between himself and his fellow actors, the play, or the audience, even when direct address has been abandoned."[4] A character's *Figurenposition* may "thus be defined verbally as well as spatially,"[5] and even when he seems fixed within the illusion, an actor may figuratively "step away" from that illusion through an "aside" or other "extradramatic" device.

In this analysis of *Othello* I will examine the relation among the play's language, staging, and effect by applying Weimann's distinctions between *locus* and *platea* staging to the characters' *Figurenpositionen*. In doing so, I will consider the way Shakespeare sets a number of static, upstage "pictures" against the machinations of a downstage Vice and juxtaposes the lyrical blank verse related to upstage locations with a coarse, animalistic idiom associated with the "place." My point of departure will be the well-known premise that, when Othello falls to Iago, he begins to speak in Iago's idiom. In *Othello* the noble Moor and his love, like their sonnet-lover predecessors, Romeo and Juliet, are held within the illusion. It is Iago who speaks to the audience. His *Figurenpositionen* are linked to his presentational parts as presenter and Vice-figure and to his representational role as Othello's "honest" ensign. The emergence of Iago's parts from his representational role provides *Othello* with a shocking revelation and contributes to the play's effect on an audience that "feel[s] the possibility of tears rising through an action" it yearns "in vain to interrupt."[6]

I
"I' TH' ALEHOUSE"

At the end of act 2, scene 1 of *Othello* Iago lets us know that he intends to have Michael Cassio "on the hip" to "Abuse him to the Moor in the rank garb" (305–6). By bringing Cassio down, Iago hopes to take Cassio's place as lieutenant and to set into motion his revenge against Othello. But Cassio proves difficult to bring down. When he enters in 2.3, Iago finds Cassio ready to guard the citadel while Othello and Desdemona enjoy the "fruits" of their union. For his opening gambit, Iago claims that Othello deliberately advanced the watch so he could spend more time making the night "wanton":

> *Iago.* Our general cast us thus early for the love of his Desdemona;
> who let us not therefore blame. He hath not yet made wanton the
> night with her; and she is sport for Jove.
> *Cas.* She's a most exquisite lady.
> *Iago.* And I'll warrant her, full of game.
> *Cas.* Indeed, she's a most fresh and delicate creature.
> *Iago.* What an eye she has! Methinks it sounds a parley to provocation.
> *Cas.* An inviting eye; and yet methinks right modest.
> *Iago.* And when she speaks, is it not an alarum to love?
> *Cas.* She is indeed perfection.
> *Iago.* Well—happiness to their sheets!
>
> (2.3.14–29)

I select this exchange to open my analysis because it allows us to distinguish between the play's idioms. Iago's words invite Cassio to see Desdemona as "sport for Jove" and "full of game," her eye "a parley to provocation." But Cassio matches Iago's images with ones that identify her as "a most exquisite lady," "fresh and delicate," her eye "inviting" but "right modest." Indeed, Cassio so qualifies Iago's every word that Iago gives up trying to persuade Cassio to see things his way: "Well—happiness to their sheets!" Foiled, he takes another tack, isolating Cassio's weakness by making him drink enough wine to be quarrelsome. With Roderigo's help Iago succeeds in disrupting the watch, in raising the town and—after Othello enters to question whether his men have "turn'd Turks" (170)—in getting Cassio dismissed as Othello's officer.

Iago will not bring "happiness" to Othello's and Desdemona's "sheets": he will transform those wedding "sheets" into winding ones, and Othello will "strangle" Desdemona in "her bed, even the bed she hath contaminated" (4.2.105; 4.1.207–8). As we will see, the love-in-death or *Liebestod* theme is as powerful in *Othello* as it is in *Romeo and Juliet*. For the moment, however, I would like to draw attention to the patterning of this exchange. Here, as in Desdemona's questions about being a "whore" in 4.2 (115ff.) and in the patterning of her and Emilia's words about women who might commit adultery "for all the world" in 4.3 (61ff.), Shakespeare sets distinct idioms and oppressed value systems at odds. Here, as in act 1, he dramatizes different ways of perceiving and defining value.

Not believing in "virtue," Iago rationalizes love as "merely a lust of
the blood and a permission of the will" (1.3.334–35). In Desdemona's declaration of love for Othello, on the other hand, love is a
kind of religion. Defending her marriage, she insists that her
"heart's subdu'd / Even to the very quality of my lord" and explains
that "I saw Othello's visage in his mind, / And to his honors and his
valiant parts / Did I my soul and fortunes consecrate" (1.3.250–54).
Readers and scholars have long recognized that *Othello* contains
contrasting idioms, that of the "alehouse" and that of the sacra-
mental world of love. As the exchange between Iago and Cassio
makes clear, the perspectives are diametrically opposed. They provide the play with distinct linguistic "worlds."

The dramaturgical significance of this opposition has not been
fully understood. In *Othello,* one idiom infects the other,
thematically *and* dramaturgically, and the coarse, animalistic,
obscene, relativistic, and prosaic language of the "place" taints the
lyrical, idealized, poetic, and spiritual values found in Othello's and
Desdemona's language. The dramaturgy of *Othello,* like that of
Romeo and Juliet, sets mercantile value against the spiritual absolutes embodied by the lovers, who remain within the illusion. Even
though the language cannot always be tied to an undifferentiated
place or to a specific locus, the relation between idiom and location
recalls the opposition between downstage, prosaic language and
bustling movement and upstage lyricism and stillness in *Romeo and
Juliet*. What most distinguishes *Othello* from *Romeo and Juliet* is of
course the source of this downstage idiom, Shakespeare's finest
Vice, Iago, who controls and envelops the action and whose sheer
number of lines asserts his dominance. Indeed, when Iago's way of
seeing and valuing comes to dominate Othello's, the results are
tragic.

Iago's ability to turn "virtue into pitch" (2.3.360) is apparent
from the start. As readers note,[7] Iago uses economic, light, diabolic, and animal images when he awakens Brabantio to warn him
about the loss of his daughter, to "poison" his "delight" and to
"Plague him with flies" (1.1.68, 71). "Awake! what ho, Brabantio!
thieves, thieves! / Look to your house, your daughter, and your
bags!" (79–80). "An old black ram / Is tupping your white ewe . . .
your daughter [is] cover'd with a Barbary horse," is "making the
beast with two backs . . . ," is in the "gross clasps of a lascivious
Moor" (88–89, 111–12, 116–17, 126). Indeed, Iago will again and
again "begrime" Desdemona's and Othello's "names" with "black"
(3.3.386–87). Typically, he will supply his victims with a kind of

"proof"—in this case Desdemona's absence. Brabantio's call for "light" (144) will not clarify what has been obfuscated.

Iago "poisons" Roderigo's and Brabantio's minds just as he will try to poison Cassio's and will succeed in poisoning Othello's when he convinces the Moor that Desdemona is not "honest" (3.3.325–26). "Exchange me for a goat, / When I shall turn the business of my soul / To such exsufflicate and blown surmises," says Othello when Iago first leads him to question Desdemona (3.3.180–82). The blackening is implicit in Othello's animal reference. "If I do prove her haggard, / Though that her jesses were my dear heart-strings, / I'd whistle her off, and let her down the wind / To prey at fortune," he continues later, "plagued" with thoughts that, like "flies," "quicken" "even with blowing" (3.3.260–63, 273, 276–77; 4.2.66–67). Recalled from his advice to Roderigo in 1.3, Iago's homily on his purse is part of the seduction. Setting the loss of "good name" and "reputation" against the "theft" of his purse, he introduces Othello to that monster, "jealousy." "It were not for your quiet nor your good, / Nor for my manhood, honesty, and wisdom, / To let you know my thoughts," he tells Othello. "Zounds, what dost thou mean?" asks the Moor.

> Good name in man and woman, dear my lord,
> Is the immediate jewel of their souls.
> Who steals my purse steals trash; 'tis something, nothing;
> 'Twas mine, 'tis his, and has been slave to thousands;
> But he that filches from me my good name
> Robs me of that which not enriches him,
> And makes me poor indeed.
> . . . O, beware, my lord, of jealousy!
> It is the green-ey'd monster which doth mock
> The meat it feeds on.
>
> (3.3.152–61, 165–67)

It is Iago, of course, who steals Othello's "soul" and separates him from his "chrysolitic" "jewel," Desdemona; Iago who "robs" Othello and Desdemona of their "good name." Roderigo may bemoan the loss of his "jewels," which, he thinks, have been given to Desdemona (4.2.198); Brabantio may think Othello a "foul thief" who has "stol'n" his "jewel" (1.2.61; 1.3.195). But it is Iago who robs these men, and Othello who most painfully feels the loss of "what is stol'n" (3.3.342).

Desdemona would rather lose her valueless "purse" or her handkerchief than the love of her "noble Moor," so "true of mind"

(3.4.25–27). She can "understand a fury in [his] words, / But not the words" themselves (4.2.32–33). She knows that she never "gave" Othello "cause" to be jealous, but Emilia, a benign inhabitant of the "alehouse," knows that jealousy is "a monster." Desdemona may hope that "heaven keep the monster from Othello's mind!" (3.4.158ff.). But his words are indeed infected, his "tranquil mind," "content," and belief in the nobility of human action utterly "gone"—as his "Farewell" speech makes clear (3.3.345–57). Othello's "occupation" is gone, and with it a belief in a world defined by absolutes. His ideals have lost their meaning, been begrimed black as pitch; and instead of turning back thoughts of infidelity he turns "Turk" (1.3.210; 2.1.114; 2.3.170; 5.2.353), becomes an infidel. Caught in an emotional storm, his grieved soul suffers "mere perdition." "Chaos is come again" (2.2.3; 3.3.90, 92; 3.4.67; 5.2.98–101). "Love" has become carnality, faith is reduced to facts, "ocular proof," "causes," and "satisfying reasons." Othello moves outside a relationship based on faith, reducing his love to the equivocal evidence of things seen. Iago's cruellest line is, predictably, his suggestion that Desdemona's "honor is an essence that's not seen" (4.1.16).

By the end of the third act Othello turns into the figure of darkness his nobility and language so belied in the opening scenes. His eloquent responses to Brabantio and to the Venetian senators thwarted Iago's earlier attempt to make him into a "devilish" Moor. When Iago urged him to "go in" to avoid Brabantio, Othello insisted that he "must be found." "My parts, my title, and my perfect soul / Shall manifest me rightly" (1.2.30–32). His behavior gave the lie to Brabantio's accusations. Othello's powerful words, "Keep up your bright swords, for the dew will rust them" (59), disarmed his enemies and asserted his nobility. Desdemona had indeed fallen in love with "what she fear'd to look on" (1.3.98). But when Iago burdens Othello with an "aspic's tongue" Othello turns into a figure of darkness, invoking "black vengeance, from the hollow hell" (3.3.447).[8] "In the due reverence of a sacred vow" he betroths himself to Iago, engages his "words" to him, promising himself "bloody thoughts" (461–62). He now speaks in Iago's idiom. Once Othello's "fair warrior," Desdemona is now a "fair devil" and a damnable "lewd minx!" (2.1.182; 3.3.479, 475).

Commentators continue to uncover *Othello*'s imagistic riches, but they have not yet recognized the ways these idioms are related to the conventions governing down and up-stage speech. Robert B. Heilman's analysis of action and language in *Othello*—an analysis that dominates readings of the play—hints at the "techniques of infiltration" by which Iago "flows" into the community of the play,[9] and many readers note that Iago often "stages" and provides interpretative commentaries on the events. We have yet to understand the dramaturgical means by which this infiltration occurs or the relation it bears to the play's effect upon the spectators. In this sense it is important to remember that each time Iago invites another character to share his perspective he plays upon the very idea of "overhearing" so fundamental to the nature of dramatic performance, in which the spectators eavesdrop upon the action. In *Othello* the spectators witness an action in which scenes are often staged by Iago, scenes in which what they hear and see is at variance with what the characters appear to perceive and during which the spectators are helpless observers. Indeed, when Othello literally "sees" and "hears" from Iago's perspective he substitutes the equivocal evidence of things seen for a belief in things unseen. In *Othello,* neither eyes nor ears are reliable. The most familiar of these moments occurs in 4.1, when Othello overhears Iago and Cassio talk—apparently about Desdemona but actually about Bianca. When Othello "withdraws," Iago tells us what he intends to do:

> Now will I question Cassio of Bianca,
> A huswife that by selling her desires
> Buys herself bread and clothes. It is a creature
> That dotes on Cassio (as 'tis the strumpet's plague
> To beguile many and be beguil'd by one);
> He, when he hears of her, cannot restrain
> From the excess of laughter. Here he comes.
>   *Enter* Cassio
> As he shall smile, Othello shall go mad;
> And his unbookish jealousy must conster
> Poor Cassio's smiles, gestures, and light behaviors
> Quite in the wrong. How do you now, lieutenant?
>
>   (93–103)

Here we eavesdrop upon a scene of misunderstanding and misperception. Here Iago greets Cassio after he "re-enters" the illusion, just as he appears to "step out" of it after Othello withdraws. He has not actually "moved" at all; but he has, as it were, stepped outside the illusion to address the spectators. And because they have been privileged, the spectators know that Othello will misinterpret the following conversation: he will construe things clean from the meaning of the things themselves, and the spectators will not be able to help him. After mentioning Desdemona's name aloud, Iago speaks "lower" about Bianca, baiting his trap and again pouring "pestilence" into Othello's "ear" (2.2.356). And after Bianca enters, jealous about the handkerchief whose pattern Cassio asked her to copy, matters grow worse. Othello recognizes the handkerchief, realizes Cassio has given it to Bianca, and believes in the evidence of what he sees and hears. Bianca will not "take out the work": "A likely piece of work, that you should find it in your chamber, and know not who left it there!" "This is some minx's token," she says angrily, thereby appearing to confirm Othello's judgment that Desdemona is a "lewd minx" (4.1.151–53; 3.3.476).

In this "staged" scene Iago "blocks" the actors and is helped by a walk-on, Bianca. The scene is typical of the play's dramaturgy. Throughout *Othello* Iago engages the audience and the characters in his soliloquies and private conversations. The spectators and the characters then "withdraw," so to speak, to witness a scene, and are addressed or reengaged in private conversation at its end. Often, these conversations begin in undifferentiated "places" that are localized later in the scene. The first act is exemplary. In 1.1, the spectators overhear Iago and Roderigo in conversation in a Venetian "place" that will be transformed into a location beneath Brabantio's "house," at one "window" of which the aroused Brabantio will enter to respond to Iago's and Rodergio's taunts. At the opening of 1.2, it is Othello who converses with Iago before confronting Brabantio; and at the end of 1.3, localized as the Venetian "council chamber" by use of a table and some lights, we again overhear Iago and Roderigo in conversation before Iago offers his first soliloquy. In 2.3, as we have seen, Iago and Cassio initially engage in private conversation. At the scene's end Iago and Cassio and then Iago and Roderigo speak privately before Iago offers a closing soliloquy. This pattern of separation and reunion recurs in the temptation and fall scene, 3.3, in which, as in 4.1, Iago moves into and out of the illusion, alternately assuming his representational role and speaking to the spectators in his presented self. Indeed, this scene is generally divided into two parts, with Iago's soliloquy (321–29) placed between Othello's temptation and fall. Dialogue, soliloquy, and dialogue map the dramaturgical contours of this scene, one that concludes with Othello's outcry: "Damn her, lewd minx! O, damn her, damn her!" (476).

By 5.1, Othello has only to stand aside and to listen in the dark to believe the "brave Iago, honest and just," has kept "his word" (31, 28) by murdering Cassio. Iago has "taught" Othello, who steels himself for revenge:

> Minion, your dear lies dead,
> And your unblest fate hies. Strumpet, I come.
> Forth of my heart those charms, thine eyes, are blotted;
> Thy bed, lust-stained, shall with lust's blood be spotted.
>
>   [*Exit Othello*]
>
>   (33–36)

Othello is cast into darkness, unable to see or hear accurately. In his concluding couplet he gives his "worst of thoughts / The worst of words" (3.3.132–33).

These scenes seem "staged" because the spectators know Iago's true intentions. They are dramatically possible because Iago establishes his *Figurenpositionen* relative to the illusionistic action early in the play. But there is another reason why his "practices" work so well. He is diabolically effective because his victims, like those of his villainous predecessor, Richard III, are "cast in darkness" and bound within the illusion. Othello and Desdemona simply do not know what is going on. They are "ignorant as dirt!" (5.2.164).

Like Romeo and Juliet, Othello and Desdemona are set within the illusion. There is little need to rehearse the mythological and iconographic backgrounds Shakespeare drew upon in his portrayal of the lovers. They have been examined fully and well.[10] His borrowings from the earlier love tragedy and from the sonnet tradition, however, have not received full credit. Romeo and Juliet first meet at Capulet's feast, where, after the servingmen's banter, the Capulets, Tybalt, the Nurse, and the guests enter, and the masked ball begins amid the whirling measures of the masked dancers. Those fluid movements "stop," however, when Romeo asks the Servingman, "What lady's that which doth enrich the hand / Of yonder knight?" (1.5.42). The Servingman's response ("I know not, sir.") is swept away by Romeo's lyrical and rhapsodic description of Juliet's beauty (44–53). And now Romeo approaches Juliet. "The measure done," he has watched "her place of stand" (50) and advances to her. Here Romeo and Juliet create an on-stage, fixed picture that remains in our minds. Here, in an elegant verbal and visual duet, the lovers "make blessed" their hands; and their kiss appropriately supplies their embedded sonnet (93–106) with its couplet. Juliet's "Saints do not move, though grant for prayers' sake" is embraced and held by Romeo's "Then move not while my prayer's effect I take" (105–6), and their accompanying kiss holds time in suspension. When Romeo and Juliet first intertwine their hands and lips their interlocking words create a moment of suspended action and separate them from the surrounding movement. Juliet recalls Romeo's paradoxes when she finds out his name ("My only love sprung from my only hate!" [138]), and she supplies the play's dominant topos in saying that if Romeo "be married, / My grave is like to be my wedding-bed" (134–35). This still point within a turning circle will be revisualized at the play's end, when Romeo and Juliet lie intertwined in deadly stasis upon the bedlike upstage locus of the tomb while all the others hasten around in confusion.

These elements are recalled at those moments in *Othello* when movement is contrasted with stasis, energy with lyricism, and images of death with feelings of love. These contrasts are linked to the play's staging. Indeed, although the relation they bear to "sonnet figures" may be less noticeable, Othello and Desdemona's story owes a great deal to sonnet narrative and to the *Liebestod*. Both pairs of lovers are "lifted" from literary love-traditions.[11]

Shakespeare establishes these backgrounds in 2.1, a carefully constructed scene that, like 3.3, 4.1, and 5.1, invites us to view the characters from a particular perspective. Cassio is the first of the Venetian force to land at Cyprus after the tempest that separates Othello's ships and destroys the Turkish fleet. His comments prepare for the arrival of the "divine Desdemona" (73). When she appears, Cassio tells all the men of Cyprus to kneel:

> O, behold,
> The riches of the ship is come on shore!
> You men of Cyprus, let her have your knees.
> Hail to thee, lady! and the grace of heaven,
> Before, behind thee, and on every hand,
> Enwheel thee round!
>
> (82–87)

Here the kneeling men encircle her. The action "stops." Desdemona is set apart, held in everyone's eyes, frozen in our view as much as Juliet is. And here Desdemona's mythological and religious iconography as Venus and the virgin is established.[12] She silently stands at the still point of a turning circle of figures. The Neoplatonic, syncretic traditions Shakespeare draws upon to create this "chrysolitic" "jewel" crystallize in her dramatic entry.

Othello's arrival similarly draws upon literary and iconographic backgrounds. "Lo, where he comes," says Cassio (181). "O my fair warrior!" says Othello; "My dear Othello!" answers Desdemona. This is Mars greeting Venus, love and war commingled. The lovers' kiss joins them before our eyes:

Des.   The heavens forbid
            But that our loves and comforts should increase
            Even as our days do grow!
Oth.   Amen to that, sweet powers!
            I cannot speak enough of this content,
            It stops me here; it is too much of joy.
            And this, and this, the greatest discords be
                                They kiss.
            That e'er our hearts shall make!

                                                (193–99)

As we know, Othello will again kiss Desdemona before he murders
her. And when he dies, his final couplet draws from the *Liebestod*
topos underlying the action:

            I kiss'd thee ere I kill'd thee. No way but this,
            Killing myself, to die upon a kiss.

                                                (5.2.358–59)

Like Romeo and Juliet, the lovers reunite when they lie in stasis on
the *locus* of their bridal-and-death bed. As Lodovico says, this
spectacle "poisons sight / Let it be hid" (364–65). Othello's couplet
returns him and Desdemona to the tradition from which they
emerged. Although Othello's "spirit" has been expended in a
"waste of shame," he is able,

            at the last gasp of love's latest breath,
            When, his pulse failing, passion speechless lies,
            When faith is kneeling by his bed of death,
            And innocence is closing up his eyes,[13]

to fall again into "Desdemona's arms" (2.1.80).

II
"HOW AM I THEN A VILLAIN"

There is of course another dramaturgical force and another style
at work throughout the play. Othello and Desdemona are set apart
by their language. Iago is not. His voice and *Figurenpositionen*
provide another perspective. When Cassio takes Desdemona by the
hand in 2.1, Iago offers his own commentary:

[*Aside.*] He takes her by the palm; ay, well said, whisper. With as little a web as this will I ensnare as great a fly as Cassio. Ay, smile upon her, do; I will give thee in thine own courtship. You say true, 'tis so indeed. If such tricks as these strip you out of your lieutenantry, it had been better you had not kiss'd your three fingers so oft, which now again you are most apt to play the sir in. Very good; well kiss'd! an excellent courtesy! 'Tis so indeed. Yet again, your fingers to your lips? Would they were clyster pipes, for your sake!

(167–77)

Galled, perhaps, by Cassio's "bold show of courtesy" in kissing Emilia (99), Iago reinterprets and condemns Cassio's gentlemanly kissing of his hand using his characteristic metaphors of hunting and trapping. Standing on the edge of the illusionistic scene, he alternates comments and nods to Cassio and Desdemona with glosses on their actions. And when Cassio kisses his three fingers once more, Iago adds vulgarity to his description. He will similarly "set down the pegs that make this music" (200) when he sees Othello and Desdemona kiss, striking a discordant note that clashes with Othello's aria of love by commenting on an upstage action from his downstage place.

None of the characters "hears" Iago, of course. His comments are audible only to the spectators, with whom he has developed a privileged relationship. In this sense he recalls Richard III, that other figure of Iniquity who moralizes "two meanings in one word." Like Richard III, Iago is an identifiable symbolic Vice who maintains a realistic facade. But with Iago, as with Richard III, critics seem torn between the poles of psychological analysis and theatrical convention. There is little doubt that Iago is a type figure; it is also clear that Shakespeare conflates his persona as the Vice with his representational role. His motives for behaving as he does so multiply during the play that he seems, finally, to be a figure of "motiveless malignity"—a phrase that suggests his innate depravity. It seems to me, however, that Coleridge's view upholds a psychological approach at the cost of Iago's theatrical lineage and that it flattens out the process by which the spectators are led to recognize that lineage and to condemn Iago for what he is.[14]

It is important to remember, however, that when we first see Iago, he is a "character" set in the world of the play. In the opening dialogue with Roderigo he reveals himself only as a disgruntled, envious subordinate who dislikes the Moor because Othello passed him over by appointing Cassio as his lieutenant. " 'Tis the curse of service; / Preferment goes by letter and affection, / And not by old

gradation, where each second / Stood heir to th' first" (1.1.35–38).
His "reasons" for not loving the Moor are apparently justifiable:
even though he had seniority, practical experience, and the support
of "three great ones of the city" (8), Othello overlooked him in favor
of an "arithmetician" and a Florentine outsider. His grievance
seems legitimate enough, and certainly would have seemed so to
those in the audience who, even today, appreciate his remarks and
side with him, drawn into complicity with his prejudices and complaints. Not until he explains that he follows the Moor "to serve my
turn upon him" do we realize his disappointment is laced with
deep-seated hatred and a desire for revenge. But even now there is
nothing to indicate he is a figure of Iniquity. His code of self-interest
and his hypocrisy are deplorable, but the reasons he provides seem
"satisfying" and seem to grow, naturally enough, from losing a
position he thought should be his.

In the final lines of this well-known speech Iago may suggest
another dimension:

> In following Othello, I follow but myself;
> Heaven is my judge, not I for love and duty,
> But seeming so, for my particular end;
> For when my outward action doth demonstrate
> The native act and figure of my heart
> In complement extern, 'tis not long after
> But I will wear my heart upon my sleeve
> For daws to peck at: I am not what I am.
>
> (58–65)

The last phrase hints at his underlying part as the Vice, but it may
be understood either as a statement confirming his hypocrisy or as
a revelation about "the native act and figure" of his "heart." At the
start of *Othello* Iago possesses the unattractive but identifiable
feelings of jealousy, envy, and hate. His symbolic nature is not
visible, and his morality persona is subordinate to his realistic
portrayal. No wonder analysis of his character follows a psychological path. By giving us "satisfying" reasons, Iago elicits psychological responses. Here is a character who does evil not for its own sake
but because he believes he has been wronged. His egocentricity and
hypocrisy are component parts of his psychological makeup.

Unlike Richard III, who admits that he is "determined to prove a
villain" in his opening soliloquy, Iago does not immediately reveal
himself as a Vice figure. Shakespeare may not have wanted Iago to

identify himself at the start because he wished to play upon an audience's response to the Moor's devilish blackness. He may also have wished to draw the spectators into complicity with Iago, the better to lead them to a revelation about Iago's underlying part and to suggest the dehumanization that occurs when a man steeps himself in sin. Like Richard III, Iago will be a presenter of, a participant in, and a commentator upon the action. But the order in which Iago introduces his personae is different from Richard's. Unlike Richard, Iago is not granted a play-opening soliloquy in which to delineate these personae, and he does not conclude scene 1 or 2 with asides, soliloquies, or scene-ending couplets.

When scene 2 begins, Iago is again set within the illusion, again a character in a play engaged in conversation with another character:

> *Iago.* Though in the trade of war I have slain men,
> Yet do I hold it very stuff o' th' conscience
> To do no contriv'd murder. I lack iniquity
> Sometime to do me service. Nine or ten times
> I had thought t' have yerked him here under the ribs.
> *Oth.* 'Tis better as it is.
>
> (1–6)

His hypocrisy is obvious, and there may be another suggestion that a part lies beneath his surface characterization ("I lack iniquity"). But there is no clear indication, there or in the scene-ending conversation with Roderigo in 1.3, that Iago will be anything more than a "naturalistic" character. Act 1 concludes as it began, with Iago duping Roderigo and articulating his code of self-interest. Not until the end of his soliloquy, after he gives another reason for hating the Moor ("it is thought abroad that 'twixt my sheets / H'as done my office [387–88]) and after we hear him "thinking aloud," does Iago's natural complexion truly begin to emerge:

> Let me see now;
> To get [Cassio's] place and to plume up my will
> In double knavery—How? how?—Let's see—
> After some time, to abuse Othello's ear
> That [Cassio] is too familiar with his wife.
> He hath a person and a smooth dispose
> To be suspected—fram'd to make women false.
> The Moor is of a free and open nature,
> That thinks men honest that but seem to be so,
> And will as tenderly be led by th' nose
> As asses are.

I have't. It is engend'red. Hell and night
Must bring this monstrous birth to the world's light.
(1.3.392–404)

This soliloquy closes act 1, asserts Iago's dominance, and establishes his unique relationship with the spectators. In it Iago "thinks aloud" in a psychologically realistic way, offers his plans to the spectators as a presenter might, and then, in his final couplet, hints at the presentational, satanic figure lurking beneath his representational role.

Here Iago establishes "a rapport with the audience" that, like Richard III's, privileges their knowledge. At times, it will be like the "rapport . . . established by the comedian in the music-hall."[15] Full of "an unholy jocularity and a blasphemous wit,"[16] Iago will taunt and torture his victims with glee. "How do you now, *lieutenant*?" (4.1.103; emphasis mine), he greets Cassio, never missing an opportunity. "I see this hath a little dash'd your spirits," he comments after reminding Othello that Desdemona deceived "her father, marrying you" (3.3.214, 206). "How is it, general? Have you not hurt your head?" he asks after the Moor *"Falls in a trance."* "Dost thou mock me?" answers Othello (4.1.43, 59-60). Iago is indeed a devilishly witty thrill-seeker who skirts close to revealing himself.[17] At times his stratagems are so successful that he cannot believe it. When Othello declares that his "occupation's gone," Iago questions, "Is't possible, my lord?"; this refrain is also heard when Cassio laments the loss of his "good name" and "reputation" (2.3.287). A savage comedian, he clearly enjoys telling Othello about Cassio's dream and about Desdemona's being "naked with her friend in bed / An hour, or more, not meaning any harm" (4.1.3-4). He equally delights in awakening people in the night (1.1; 2.3; 5.1).

Much of his humor may be seen in his exchanges with Emilia. This "alehouse" pair go at it a number of times. After Cassio kisses Emilia, Iago tells him, "Sir, would she give you so much of her lips / As of her tongue she oft bestows on me, / You would have enough"; Emilia has tongue enough to chide Iago when he "list[s] to sleep" (2.1.100-2, 104). And when Emilia tries to give him the handkerchief, Iago is obscene:

> *Iago.* How now? what do you do here alone?
> *Emil.* Do not you chide; I have a thing for you.
> *Iago.* You have a thing for me? It is a common thing—

Emil. Hah?
Iago. To have a foolish wife.

(3.3.300–304)

Quick-witted, Iago can sidestep any danger. But when Emilia suggests that some "villainous knave" "abus'd" the Moor, Iago
cautions her, "Speak within door" (4.2.144). Emilia's outspoken-
ness prepares for her actions in 5.2, when she will not "charm" her
"tongue" or hold her "peace," and will upbraid Iago for his "lies,"
revealing that she gave the handkerchief to him (183–84, 219, 230–
31). On each of these occasions Iago entertains the spectators, who
simultaneously delight in and are repulsed by his fascinating dev-
ilry.

Iago also provides a running commentary on the action in the
manner of a chorus. From 1.3 to 5.1 he speaks at least one soliloquy
or aside in each of the scenes in which he appears. These soliloquies and asides make him the play's presenter and underscore his
dominant role in the action. At times, they seem to deepen his
psychological makeup, since in them he often adds reasons for his
actions and formulates his plans by "thinking aloud." They are
psychological and expository. In one important soliloquy, however,
Iago sheds his personae as presenter and character to reveal his
underlying symbolic nature, and this soliloquy best indicates the
relation between him and the spectators. At the end of 2.3, Iago
convinces Cassio to enlist Desdemona's "help to put" him "in [his]
place again" (319). After Cassio exits, Iago turns to the audience:

> And what's he then that says I play the villain
> When this advice is free I give, and honest,
> Probal to thinking, and indeed the course
> To win the Moor again? For 'tis most easy
> Th' inclining Desdemona to subdue
> In any honest suit; she's fram'd as fruitful
> As the free elements. And then for her
> To win the Moor, were 't to renounce his baptism,
> All seals and symbols of redeemed sin,
> His soul is so enfetter'd to her love,
> That she may make, unmake, do what she list,
> Even as her appetite shall play the god
> With his weak function. How am I then a villain,
> To counsel Cassio to this parallel course,
> Directly to his good? Divinity of hell!
> When devils will the blackest sins put on,
> They do suggest at first with heavenly shows,
> As I do now; for whiles this honest fool

Plies Desdemona to repair his fortune,
And she for him pleads strongly to the Moor,
I'll pour this pestilence into his ear—
That she repeals him for her body's lust,
And by how much she strives to do him good,
She shall undo her credit with the Moor.
So will I turn her virtue into pitch,
And out of her own goodness make the net
That shall enmesh them all.

(335–62)

Iago's advice to Cassio is "honest," and he here plays, ironically and self-consciously, with the adjective so often associated with him. And with "As I do now," Iago admits that he is like the devil, turning good into evil. The terrible pathos of acts 3, 4, and 5 is anticipated, and the utter helplessness of the audience is made plain. It might even be said that Iago teases and taunts the spectators, who are powerless to prevent what will occur. As records of performance indicate,[18] spectators have often felt compelled to rise from their seats to shout warnings to Othello and Desdemona. Here, at the threshold of the great temptation and fall scene, Iago not only tells us what he intends to do but also reveals his kinship with other stage Vices by echoing Richard III's words. Appearing to deny it, he consciously acknowledges his histrionic part, and he toys with the audience's knowledge about the part ("what's he then that says I play the villain"; "How am I then a villain"). This theatrically self-conscious soliloquy is revelatory, not of his character, but of his underlying "part" as the Vice. He *is* a "villain" who "puts on" the "blackest sins" with "heavenly shows." This "zestful malice" is spoken by a "lover of footlights,"[19] an actor the spectators " 'Curst for Acting an Ill part' " so well.[20]

In this soliloquy Iago provokes the spectators and creates the "special pathos of our urge to intervene" in the action.[21] "Knavery's plain face" is seen at last (2.1.312). Iago's surface psychology conceals a deeper symbolic nature. A "diabolical personality" emerges "from the multiple folds of humane seeming,"[22] and his hypocritical "seeming" becomes his "being." It is not a question of acknowledging that we have known what Iago truly is all along, but of discovering what he is. In keeping with his hypocritical ways, Iago has even duped the spectators. But when we discover that Iago is the Vice, his reasons for behaving as he does turn into rationalizations, and as Iago adds more and more reasons he becomes less and less believable. As those reasons multiplied, they strained credulity and undercut their claim for truth. After this soliloquy, however, he stops giving us reasons and becomes more like a dehumanized Vice. Only his dupes, Roderigo, Cassio, and Othello, continue to receive "satisfying reasons" (4.2.244–45; 5.1.9). Othello's "It is the cause" soliloquy, with its illogical and ambiguous referent, "it," betrays his faulty reasoning. There are no "causes," in fact, and Cassio's words to Othello, "I never gave you cause" (5.2.299), only remind us how superficial are all the reasons given in the play.

Iago never sheds his representational and recognizably human role, as his aside in 5.1 makes clear: "This is the night / That either makes me, or foredoes me quite" (128–29). And he reinforces the psychologocal sense of self-contempt by condemning Cassio as one who "hath a daily beauty in his life / That makes me ugly" (19–20). But that representational role is laminated upon a presentational part, and it is Iago's lineage as the Vice that determines his stage movements and devilish machinations. We see flesh and blood figures, and not abstractions, even in morality plays. From this soliloquy forward, however, Iago is as much the play's Vice as one of its representational characters, and he becomes increasingly viperous, more and more like a tempting, uncoiling snake, whose

> Dangerous conceits are in their natures poisons,
> Which at the first are scarce found to distaste,
> But with a little act upon the blood
> Burn like the mines of sulphur.
>
> (3.3.326–29)

When Othello reenters here, Iago greets his victim's arrival with relish: "Look where he comes!" (330).

Envenomed, Othello knows that he will "roast . . . in sulphur" for murdering Desdemona and that when they meet "at compt" Desdemona's look "will hurl" his "soul from heaven, / And fiends will snatch at it" (5.2.279, 273–75). But "heaven" will also requite Iago's actions "with the serpent's curse" (4.2.16). Emilia's words to Othello here, and her later advice to Desdemona that some "eternal villain, / Some busy insinuating rogue, / Some cogging, cozening, slave" has "devis'd this slander" (130–33), are insights, teasing revelations about Iago's true nature as one who "proves" himself a "villain" and whose "plots" and "inductions" set characters "in deadly hate the one against the other" (*Richard III,* 1.1.30ff.). They raise the hope that the characters will realize Iago is the source of evil in time to save Desdemona, and they increase the pathos of our urge to intervene. Only at the end, however, is Iago's symbolic dimension apparent to all. "Where is that viper? Bring the villain forth," Lodovico orders (5.2.285). Othello looks "down towards" Iago's feet to see if they are cloven, and then wounds him, saying,

> If that thou be'st a devil, I cannot kill thee.
> > *Wounds Iago*
> *Lod.* Wrench his sword from him.
> *Iago.* I bleed, sir, but not kill'd.
>
> > (287–88)

This "demi-devil" will not tell why he "ensnar'd" Othello:

> Demand me nothing; what you know, you know:
> From this time forth I never will speak word.
>
> > (303–4)

He will no longer provide "reasons" or "motives" or "causes," nor will his words infect. In drawing Othello into bestiality Iago loses his humanity and is correctly identified as a "demi-devil" and a "viper."[23]

Now recognized as a "hellish villain" (368) whose "words" have poisoned Othello, Iago will speak no more. Othello is again articulate. He will punish the "uncircumcised dog" that *he* has become. And he will recover the calm, controlled, lyrical and exotic musical purity of a voice that was so tainted. We hear Othello's renewed voice in the play's final moments:[24]

> Soft you; a word or two before you go.
>
> > (338)

He now speaks as he did at the play's opening. He may only be "cheering himself up," but it is more accurate to realize that Othello reasserts his nobility by passing judgment upon his crime. The deep-seated, "curiously compelling"[25] reasons for Iago's appeal need to be recognized and denied in favor of Othello's tragic stature. A terrible and yet triumphant sense of pathos sweeps over the spectators when Othello falls onto the locus of his and Desdemona's marital and death bed.

NOTES

1. Robert Weimann, *Shakespeare and the Popular Tradition in the Theater,* ed. Robert Schwartz (Baltimore: Johns Hopkins University Press, 1978), p. 224.

2. Ibid., pp. 237ff.

3. Ibid., p. 212.

4. Ibid., p. 230.

5. Ibid., p. 230.

6. Michael Goldman, *Acting and Action in Shakespearean Tragedy* (Princeton: Princeton University Press, 1985), p. 47.

7. Robert B. Heilman, *Magic in the Web: Action and Language in "Othello"* (Lexington: University of Kentucky Press, 1956), pp. 45–98.

8. S. L. Bethell, "Shakespeare's Imagery: The Diabolic Images in *Othello*," *Shakespeare Survey* 5 (1952): 62–79. Heilman, *Magic in the Web*, pp. 64–68.

9. Heilman, *Magic in the Web*, p. 45.

10. In Rosalie Colie's *Shakespeare's Living Art* (Princeton: Princeton University Press, 1974), pp. 135–67. In her discussion of sonnet influence Colie cites Harry Levin's "Form and Formality in *Romeo and Juliet*," *Shakespeare Quarterly* 11 (1960): 3–11.

11. Colie, *Shakespeare's Living Art*, pp. 149ff.

12. Colie, p. 150, identifies relevant iconographic sources.

13. Michael Drayton, *Idea*, sonnet 61.

14. Bernard Spivack's *Shakespeare and the Allegory of Evil* (New York: Columbia University Press, 1958) examines the theatrical background. A. C. Bradley's *Shakespearean Tragedy* (London: Macmillan and Co., 1904), pp. 208ff., and Harley Granville-Barker's *Prefaces to Shakespeare* (Princeton: Princeton University Press, 1946–47) 2:98–112, also take the theatrical tradition into account.

15. Arthur Sewell, *Character and Society in Shakespeare* (Oxford: Oxford University Press, 1951), p. 81.

16. A. P. Rossiter, *Angel with Horns and Other Shakespeare Lectures*, ed. Graham Storey (London: Longmans, 1961), p. 19.

17. See Heilman, *Magic in the Web*, pp. 79–80.

18. See Marvin Rosenberg, *The Masks of "Othello"* (Berkeley: University of California Press, 1961), and Goldman, *Acting and Action*, for relevant citations.

19. Heilman, *Magic in the Web*, p. 48.

20. Rosenberg, *The Masks of "Othello,"* p. 15.

21. Goldman, *Acting and Action*, p. 69. As Bradley, *Shakespearean Tragedy*, pp. 177ff., notes, the "accelerating speed of the movement to catastrophe" and the "intolerable spectacle" of 4.1 also contribute to the play's emotional effect.

22. Heilman, *Magic in the Web*, p. 99. In *Shakespearian Players and Performances* (Cambridge: Harvard University Press, 1953), pp. 124–31, Arthur Colby Sprague describes Edwin Booth's portrayal of Iago as a "snake-like" "demi-devil," particularly in the final act but also, in later years, in his earlier soliloquies. Rosenberg, pp. 124ff., offers valuable information on Macready's portrayal of Iago as "a revelation of subtle, poetic, vigorous, manly, many-sided deviltry."

23. See Heilman, *Magic in the Web*, pp. 95ff.

24. On the recovery of Othello's exotic and powerful "voice" see Maynard Mack's "The Jacobean Shakespeare" in *Stratford-upon-Avon Studies: Jacobean Theatre*, ed. John Russell Brown and Bernard Harris (London: Edward Arnold, 1960) 1:11–41; and G. Wilson Knight's "The Othello Music," in *The Wheel of Fire* (Oxford: Oxford University Press, 1930), pp. 97–119.

25. Rosenberg, *The Masks of "Othello,"* p. 171.

7

Othello and Perception

JAMES HIRSH

if thou hast eyes to see

Othello dramatizes the processes by which people perceive one another and their own situations. Perception is the organization of raw sensations into meaningful patterns and encompasses understanding, the stage of this process that occurs at several removes from sensation. To see with the mind's eye is, in fact, the only way to see. At the center of the play is a change in Othello's perception of Desdemona, but Othello is by no means the only character who faces challenges to his powers of perception. Even the shrewd Iago fails to see his own wife's capacity for heroic action. John Bayley went so far as to declare that "No one in *Othello* comes to understand himself or anyone else."[1] Characters are not the only ones who face challenges to their powers of perception at a performance of *Othello*. Playgoers are also confronted with such challenges.[2] Because the topic of perception pervades the play, I will have to limit my focus to two subtopics: Othello's perceptions of Desdemona and playgoers' perceptions of Othello.

Othello formulated his initial perception of Desdemona during the period when he visited Brabantio's house and recounted his adventures, as he recalls when he defends himself before the Senate:

> These things to hear
> Would Desdemona seriously incline; . . .
> [I] often did beguile her of her tears,
> When I did speak of some distressful stroke
> That my youth suffer'd. . . .
> She swore, in faith, 'twas strange, 'twas passing strange;
> 'Twas pitiful, 'twas wondrous pitiful. . . .
> [She] bade me, if I had a friend that lov'd her,

I should but teach him how to tell my story,
And that would woo her. Upon this hint I spake:
She lov'd me for the dangers I had pass'd,
And I lov'd her that she did pity them.

(1.3.145–68)

Othello initially perceived Desdemona as someone who pitied him, and it is this Desdemona with whom he fell in love. But this Desdemona may have been at least partly his own creation. When Desdemona herself speaks later in 1.3, she does not directly corroborate Othello's account of her pitying response to his life story (nor is she on stage to hear that account). Othello himself sees his life as pitiful and is inclined to see Desdemona as someone who shares his perception. As E. H. Gombrich has explained, perception "is always an active process, conditioned by our expectations and adapted to situations. Instead of talking of seeing and knowing, we might do a little better to talk of seeing and noticing. We notice only when we look *for* something."[3]

Even Othello's perception that Desdemona loved him was based, initially, not on Desdemona's explicit declaration, but on the inference he drew from her "hint." And her "hint" may have been an equivocation. She may not have been ready to commit herself to love Othello until he had committed himself to love her, until he had declared his love for her. If so, then Othello's perception of Desdemona's love actually may have preceded her love and may have been a necessary factor that brought Desdemona's love into existence. (Shakespeare has made much ado about a similar creation of something out of nothing in depicting the courtship of Beatrice and Benedick.) In other words, if Othello had not declared his love, then Desdemona's "hint" might have become, retroactively, a red herring. It would have hinted at something that never came into existence. Desdemona's remark may have become a hint of her love because Othello chose to perceive it as one.

Shortly after their marriage, Desdemona gives Othello a new perspective on their courtship: "Michael Cassio, / That came a-wooing with you, and so many a time, / When I have spoke of you dispraisingly, / Hath ta'en your part" (3.3.70–73). A Desdemona who could speak "dispraisingly" of Othello, even in jest, may well seem to Othello inconsistent with a Desdemona "seriously inclined" and moved to tears by Othello's "distressful" account of his life. This new, inconsistent Desdemona might be more lively and interesting than the Desdemona Othello had perceived earlier, but she is not the same Desdemona. Furthermore, if Desdemona seemed to love and pity him, to take him "seriously," but dispraised him, even in jest, behind his back—if (from Othello's point of view) she concealed some aspect of her personality—then Brabantio's parting comment on his daughter—"Look to her, Moor, if thou hast eyes to see; / She has deceiv'd her father, and may thee" (1.3.292–93)—seems to have at least a tiny grain of truth.

To make matters worse, the person to whom Desdemona spoke dispraisingly about him was his military subordinate, a junior officer. And if Desdemona's dispraise were even partly in earnest, then Othello's successful courtship of Desdemona would not have been wholly due to his own account of his life but would have owed something to his subordinate's intervention. Cassio also happens to be a charming man of Desdemona's own nationality, race, and age. And a moment earlier, Othello witnessed this same Cassio leaving Desdemona at Othello's approach. Desdemona is now pleading for Cassio. As someone who regards love and pity as concomitant ("She lov'd me for the dangers I had pass'd, / And I lov'd her that she did pity them"), Othello has "eyes to see" Desdemona's fervently expressed pity for Cassio ("he hath left part of his grief with me / To suffer with him [3.3.53–54]) as evidence that she loves Cassio. Her phrasing seems to include further hints ("Michael Cassio, / That came a-wooing . . . Hath ta'en your part" and so on). Because we cannot see directly into people's minds, we depend on such hints. Othello depended on a hint for his first perception of Desdemona's love for himself. But what do these latest hints hint at? Merely at Desdemona's faint regret that, by irrevocably choosing Othello, she has given up other possibilities for love? Or at an imminent liaison between Desdemona and Cassio? Othello makes a request: "I do beseech thee, grant me this, / To leave me but a little to myself" (84–85). He may well need some time alone to form a new perception of Desdemona that will satisfactorily account for the new pieces of evidence that have disrupted his earlier perception.

Othello is not left to himself when Desdemona departs. Othello's loss of his earlier perception of Desdemona and his current lack of a coherent perception make him vulnerable to Iago's manipulation, and Iago is on stage ready to help him construct a new perception of Desdemona.

One technique Iago uses to manipulate Othello's view of Desdemona is to create red herrings, that is, to plant false clues and then allow Othello himself to draw seemingly obvious and inevitable conclusions. Iago himself engineered the meeting between Desdemona and Cassio in 3.3 and then brought Othello on stage so that

Othello would see them together and infer that they are lovers. In order to encourage Othello to see Desdemona and Cassio as lovers, Iago exclaimed in a feigned aside" "Hah? I like not that" (35). When Othello asked, "What dost thou say?" (35), Iago gave a teasingly unresponsive response: "Nothing, my lord; or if—I know not what" (36). Iago here appeals to Othello's need for closure, which later will become excruciatingly intense ("Would I were satisfied!" [390]). Rather than making an explicit charge against Desdemona, Iago tries to induce Othello to see Desdemona's intimacy with Cassio as the "that" that Iago does not like. A perception of Desdemona's guilt thus is not a perception presented to Othello from the outside but rather an idea Othello himself creates. The process by which Othello sees Desdemona's guilt in response to Iago's hints, however, resembles the process by which he formulated his initial perception of Desdemona's love on the basis of her "hint."

Later in 3.3, Iago urges Othello to keep an open mind: "I speak not yet of proof. / Look to your wife, observe her well with Cassio, / Wear your eyes thus, not jealous, nor secure" (196–98). What Iago asks Othello to do—to perceive without preconceptions—is impossible. Perception "is always an active process, conditioned by our expectations." Iago actually helps Othello to wear suspicious eyes, to accept Desdemona's guilt as a working hypothesis and to seek confirmation of that hypothesis. Earlier in the play Brabantio explicitly advised Othello to wear suspicious eyes ("Look to her, Moor, if thou hast eyes to see"). At that point Othello rejected Brabantio's advice, but that was before his disillusionment. Then he had a confident perception of Desdemona, which has since been undermined by new evidence.

Iago provides Othello with "eyes to see" a guilty Desdemona, with a set of perceptual mechanisms to see anything as evidence of Desdemona's guilt. These mechanisms include social stereotypes and psychological consistency:

> *Iago.* I know our country disposition well:
> In Venice they do let God see the pranks
> They dare not show their husbands; their best conscience
> Is not to leave't undone, but keep't unknown.
> *Oth.* Dost thou say so?
> *Iago.* She did deceive her father, marrying you,
> And when she seemed to shake and fear your looks,
> She lov'd them most.
> *Oth.*   And so she did.
>
> (3.3.201–8)

Iago's argument has the conclusiveness of a double syllogism: (1) Venetian women are deceptive; Desdemona is a Venetian woman; therefore, Desdemona is deceptive; (2) Desdemona deceived her father; people are consistent; therefore, Desdemona is deceptive. While wearing his eyes thus, Othello will not see Desdemona as a complex, unique individual who adopts different behavior in response to different particular circumstances; he will see her as a stereotype (Venetian woman) who acts with mechanical consistency (consistently deceitful). Syllogistic reasoning, furthermore, creates an impression of self-containment and closure that cuts off genuine empirical testing. The conclusion is self-evident, and therefore evidence is unncessary. It is possible to see any new evidence as suspicious if one sees it through suspicious eyes. If one assumes that Desdemona is consistently deceitful, one sees apparently affectionate behavior as hypocrisy, and therefore as evidence of disaffection. It is precisely the danger of the foregone conclusion that prompted Bacon's warnings against the syllogism. Brabantio's similar reasoning—Desdemona could not have willingly eloped with Othello because she was consistently meek and a stereotypical Venetian maiden—was rejected by the Duke: "To vouch this is no proof" (1.3.106).

Because of his insecurity as an outsider among Venetians, Othello accepts the notion that he will not see what Iago sees concerning the Venetian Desdemona until he learns to see with Venetian eyes, to see with Iago's eyes. Othello has faith not only in Iago's honesty and fairness but in Iago's perceptiveness: "This honest creature, doubtless, / Sees and knows more, much more, than he unfolds" (3.3.242–43); "This fellow's of exceeding honesty, / And knows all qualities, with a learned spirit, / Of human dealings" (258–60). Othello feels like a blind man who must trust someone else to be his eyes. In a situation in which the evidence to his own eyes seems so inconsistent, so equivocal, in which plain and uneqivocal evidence is unavailable, Othello needs someone's help in order to see the available evidence in the proper light, even to determine what constitutes evidence. If he is blind, he must choose either to trust Iago blindly or to trust Desdemona blindly, to trust one or the other: "I think my wife be honest, and think she is not; / I think that thou art just, and think thou art not" (3.3.384–85). Othello's choice is not whether to give Desdemona the benefit of the doubt or not, but whether to give Desdemona the benefit of the doubt or to give Iago the benefit of the doubt. Othello's perceptions of Desdemona and Iago become inextricably linked—just as figure and ground are inextricably linked in one's perception of a drawing.

And just as figure and ground can switch in one's perception—for example, in response to the trick drawing in which one sees a vase one moment and two faces the next moment—Othello's perception of an honest Desdemona maligned by a dishonest Iago can switch to a perception of a dishonest Desdemona exposed by an honest and perceptive Iago. Othello never considers the possibility that both Iago and Desdemona may be dishonest; another factor influencing Othello's perception is his presumption of dualism.

Iago did not introduce Othello to the concepts of stereotypes and consistency. Othello's perception of an honest Iago is based on the stereotype of the good soldier. Othello's long service in the army has given him confidence in his judgment of soldiers, and he perceives clearly that Iago is a good soldier. Because by definition a good soldier is honest, it follows that Iago is honest. If reduced to a matter of stereotypes, the familiar category of good soldier versus the very unfamiliar category of Venetian noblewoman, Othello's choice becomes self-evident. Furthermore, Iago has been honest in the past, as far as Othello knows, and Othello has known Iago much longer than he has known Desdemona. Thus, the concept of psychological consistency also favors Iago.

Othello's perception of a guilty Desdemona is a joint creation of Iago and Othello. It is not certain that it would have arisen in Othello's mind without Iago's help, but Iago could not have created it without Othello's predispositions.

In addition to being linked to his perception of an honest Iago, Othello's perception of a guilty Desdemona, like his initial perception of Desdemona, is linked to his perception of his own life as consistently pitiful. This perception may be exacerbated by the sexual anxiety he may now feel as a man considerably older than his wife. In any case, he foresees further pitifulness in his life. On his safe arrival in Cyprus, he declares, "If it were now to die, / 'Twere now to be most happy," for he fears "unknown fate" (2.7.189–90, 193). Hazlitt called Iago an "amateur of tragedy,"[4] but Othello is one as well. A perception of Desdemona's guilt fits in with the consistent pattern he perceives in his life. When he exclaims, "But yet the pity of it, Iago! O Iago, the pity of it, Iago!" (4.1.195–96), he paraphrases the exclamation about his earlier life that he once put in Desdemona's mouth: " 'Twas pitiful, 'twas wondrous pitiful."

It is often argued that the notion of Desdemona's guilt is absurd (because Desdemona has simply not had time to commit adultery). Some critics regard this absurdity as evidence of Othello's inability to think things through. Other critics—double-clock theorists—

excuse the absurdity as something a playgoer would not notice. (They thus explain away Othello's apparent inability to think things through by positing a playgoer's inability to think things through.) But the possibility of Desdemona's guilt is not as absurd as most critics assume. Although Desdemona has not had an opportunity to commit adultery, she did have an opportunity to fall in love with Cassio during the period in which she and Othello were courting. This is precisely the perception that Iago tries to induce in Othello during the following exchange, early in 3.3:

> *Iago.* Did Michael Cassio, when you woo'd my lady,
> Know of your love?
> *Oth.* He did from first to last. Why dost thou ask? . . .
> *Iago.* I did not think he had been acquainted with her.
> *Oth.* O yes, and went between us very oft.
> *Iago.* Indeed!
> *Oth.* Indeed? ay, indeed. Discern'st thou aught in that?
>
> (94–102)

This exchange occurs only moments after Othello's exchange with Desdemona during which he was presented with various sorts of evidence inconsistent with his earlier perception of Desdemona. Othello now is presented with a substitute perception of Desdemona that accounts for all the evidence—for her apparent pity and love during the courtship, for the revelation of her dispraise, and for her intense interest in Cassio's welfare. This Desdemona fell in love with Cassio while pretending to fall in love with Othello and deceived Othello into marrying her in order to advance her lover's career (an advancement already begun by Othello's promotion of Cassio, instead of the more deserving Iago, in return for acting as a go-between in Othello's courtship). It would all fit. It would make sense. Othello can now see the past in a new light. That Desdemona had not yet committed adultery and that she may not even have yet consummated her love for Cassio would be mere technicalities if she never really loved Othello, if she deceived Othello during their courtship about her feelings in order to trick him into marrying her, and if she intends to make a fool of him by pursuing an affair with his subordinate. Such calculating deception from the very beginning of their relationship would be far worse than an act of adultery committed in a moment of weakness. Othello would not see the distinction between intention and deed as significant (to see something as not significant is to remove it from sight); in Othello's eyes, if Desdemona married him to advance the career of her intended lover, she would be an adulteress. Othello is not as thoughtless as

Albert Gerard and others have suggested.[5] But he is in a quandary. It is impossible to prove, with absolute certainty, that Desdemona loves him and him alone and married him in good faith. That Desdemona deceived him cannot be disproven. The perception of a deceitful Desdemona who never loved him and who is using him cannot be simply erased. Indeed, this perception of Desdemona accounts for the evidence available to Othello better than Othello's original perception.

Repeatedly, Othello perceives a guilty Desdemona only to revert, a while later, to his earlier view of her. His mistrust seems complete and final, for example, when he says flatly in a soliloquy, "She's gone. I am abus'd, and my relief / Must be to loathe her" (3.3.267–68). But when Desdemona reenters the stage shortly thereafter, his faith in her revives: "If she be false, O then heaven mocks itself! / I'll not believe't" (278–79). By the time he next encounters Iago, however, his mind has changed once again: "O now for ever / Farewell the tranquil mind! farewell content! / Farewell the plumed troops . . ." (347ff.). Even this extended farewell, it turns out, is not a final farewell to Othello's perception of an innocent Desdemona. Othello is still of two minds: "I think my wife be honest, and think she is not" (384). Othello's suspicion of Desdemona does not gradually increase, nor does his perception at some single decisive moment change irrevocably from an innocent Desdemona to a guilty Desdemona. Instead, until nearly the end of 3.3, he oscillates between perceptions of polar opposite Desdemonas (just as Richard oscillates between polar opposite perceptions of certain victory and of certain defeat in *Richard II,* 3.2). These oscillations resemble the changes one experiences in looking at the trick drawing mentioned earlier. One's perception of the vase does not gradually change to perceptions of facelike vases and then to perceptions of vaselike faces and finally to faces. One's perception changes instantaneously and completely. At a given moment one sees a vase and at another given moment one sees faces. But although the perception of faces is momentarily unequivocal, it is not permanent and can change back, again instantaneously and completely, to the perception of a vase. This occurs because the pieces of evidence presented to one's senses, the marks on the paper, are sufficient for one's mind to construct, with the aid of imagination, a vase, but are also sufficient for one's mind to construct faces. The evidence is insufficient to rule out either possibility. This is Othello's plight. The evidence is sufficient for him to construct either a guilty Desdemona or an innocent Desdemona but is not sufficient to rule out either possibility. Such oscillations in one's perception are painful and can literally be maddening. In response to this torture Othello settles on one of the two perceptions on the basis of his predispositions, which favor a guilty Desdemona, as well as on the basis of evidence. But he must work hard to maintain the perception of a guilty Desdemona and to suppress the perception of an innocent Desdemona.[6]

Shortly after he kills Desdemona, Othello's perception changes again. On what basis? Othello sees an innocent Desdemona when he sees a guilty Iago. Othello's final perception of Desdemona is still inextricable from his perception of Iago. And it relies on a syllogism as dubious as those that earlier contributed to his perception of a guilty Desdemona: Iago has been exposed as a slanderer; Iago made Desdemona appear guilty; therefore, Desdemona must have been innocent. Othello's final perception of Desdemona is not the same as his initial one. But like each of his perceptions of her, it is inextricable from his perception of himself as pitiful. He has been deceived by devilish Iago and will roast in hell. He now sees Desdemona as his victim, whose innocence is inextricable from his own guilt: "This look of thine will hurl my soul from heaven" (5.2.274). Othello's final perception of an innocent and damning Desdemona, like his initial perception of a pitying and loving Desdemona and like his perception of a guilty Desdemona, is based on questionable preconceptions, equivocal evidence, and dubious deductive procedures.

Some critics have argued that the play offers advice about the formation of perceptions. M. R. Ridley suggested that a theme of the play is " 'Reason versus Instinct' " and that "Whenever Othello trusts his instinct he is almost invariably right."[7] But Othello's instinct tells him that Iago is honest and perceptive. An instinct or intuition is merely a guess, and a guess can be mistaken. Other critics, such as Robert Hapgood and Philip C. McGuire, have argued that Othello should have been more rational and empirical.[8] But no amount of evidence could prove that a lover intends to be faithful. The desire for evidence concerning love could be satisfied, could achieve closure, only by evidence of unfaithfulness, and such a desire is inconsistent with trust. And as noted above, even what one sees as evidence and how one sees that evidence will be determined at least in part by how one wears one's eyes. The challenges to Othello's powers of perception are not so easily overcome.

Like Othello, playgoers face challenges to their powers of perception. One such challenge occurs in the opening scene. Ridley noted the following "oddity": "the picture [of Othello] we get, and not unjustifiably think we are intended to get, is surely that of an efficient, perhaps even great, but blustering and erratic, soldier of fortune, of no morals and unsound judgment," but later, when Othello "at last enters, . . . the whole picture at once falls to pieces."[9] What makes this procedure much odder than even Ridley's account suggests is the close similarity between the techniques by which the play encourages us to formulate our initial perception of Othello and the techniques Iago later uses to encourage Othello to perceive a guilty Desdemona. The first speech of the play ends with a cryptic reference to "this"; the speaker (Roderigo) does not like "this." Iago eventually makes his first direct attempt to manipulate Othello's mind by means of a feigned aside, "Hah? I like not that." Just as Othello tries to formulate a picture of "that," a playgoer tries to formulate a picture of "this." Just as Iago is at first teasingly unresponsive to Othello's inquiries in 3.3, so the play is at first teasingly unresponsive to a playgoer's curiosity about "this." Just as Iago provokes Othello's need for closure, *Othello* provokes a playgoer's need for closure.

At the very time it occurs in 1.1, the frustration of playgoers resembles that of one of the characters on stage. The play does to us what Roderigo accuses Iago of having done to him. Roderigo accuses Iago of having withheld information that Roderigo believes should have been divulged as part of their bargain. Playgoers have paid to see a play and expect to be informed as soon as possible who's who and what's what; we cannot begin to wonder what will happen next if we do not know what is happening at first. But the very same information Roderigo accuses Iago of having withheld is withheld from us. We may feel a frustration analogous to the frustration Othello feels in 3.3 when Iago does not promptly and explicitly reveal what is on his mind. Just as Othello's frustration provokes him to grasp at hints and to leap to a conclusion, the frustratingly uninformative opening scene tempts playgoers to leap to conclusions.

In 3.3 Iago supplies hints and creates red herrings to tempt Othello to see a guilty Desdemona in his mind's eye before Iago ever explicitly accuses her. In 1.1 the play provides hints and red herrings that tempt playgoers to perceive a contemptible Moor in their imaginations, even though playgoers have not yet seen him and even though playgoers recognize the bias of the characters who describe him. Most playgoers are able to detect and account for obvious bias ("thick-lips" [66]). But alongside such obviously biased evidence occur less obvious red herrings. For example, the first clear perception we are given of the "this" that Roderigo does not like occurs when Iago tells Brabantio "an old black ram / Is tupping your white ewe" (88–89). Iago assumes that Brabantio has enough imagination to transform this image of a ram and a ewe into a perception of a sordid tryst. But what does a playgoer see? Aware that Iago and his companion are biased against the Moor, a playgoer might see an elopement hidden behind the sordid tryst that Iago wants Brabantio to see. But even those hard-working playgoers who manage to see an elopement still may see a contemptible Moor. It is easy to detect the bias of "thick-lips," but it is not easy to detect the bias of "old" (88). Even if one saw an elopement, one would not see Romeo and Juliet, but May and December. A playgoer can hardly be blamed for seeing Othello in a bad light if that is the only light a playgoer is given.

Some playgoers may ignore these red herrings and see an admirable Moor even in the opening scene by means of the following syllogism: Iago is despicable; Iago is opposed to the Moor; therefore, the Moor must be admirable. This dualistic presupposition is questionable. Some plays, including some other Jacobean plays, portray a bleak world, a world without admirable characters (and in real life two villains could be enemies). Also, this reasoning would tie a playgoer's perception of Othello to the playgoer's perception of Iago, just as Othello's perception of Desdemona is tied to Othello's perception of Iago. Such a linkage in a playgoer's mind between Iago and Othello, like the linkage in Othello's mind between Iago and Desdemona, would obviate the need for evidence: Othello's role as a sympathetic character would be established by Iago's role as an unsympathetic character, and the playgoer sees a despicable Iago as clearly as Othello sees an honest Iago.

A playgoer who resisted the temptation to fall for red herrings and dubious syllogisms, a playgoer who refused to formulate perceptions until presented with full, reliable, and unequivocal evidence, would, on the basis of the opening scene, be unable to form any judgment, any coherent perception, of the Moor at all. Such a playgoer would choose blindness over fallible vision.

As an outsider in Venetian society, Othello later will feel that he must depend on an insider, Iago, to give him his bearings, to help him wear his eyes properly. This makes him vulnerable. As outsiders to the world of a play, we are dependent on the opening dialogue and stage action to provide us with our bearings, to help us wear our eyes properly. Accustomed to plays with conventionally competent expositions, most playgoers are skilled in putting together fragmentary evidence to formulate inferences. We do not expect to be presented with red herrings that may lead us to make false inferences at the very beginning of a play. Even if we were prepared for red herrings, we would not yet have any way to tell the difference between a red herring and reliable evidence. This makes us vulnerable.

An effect of the odd procedure at the opening of *Othello* is to put us in Othello's situation. By the time we witness his struggle to see Desdemona accurately, we have already undergone a similar struggle to see Othello himself accurately. We do not merely witness what Othello experiences, we have an analogous experience ourselves. This empathy should not be confused with sympathy. The play merely puts us in Othello's situation. What we do there is up to us.

After 1.1 we no longer have to rely exclusively on other characters for evidence about the Moor. We get to see him with our own eyes. The Othello we see is poised and eloquent in his confrontation with Brabantio and in his defense before the Senate. He may be middle-aged, but he has youthful vigor and bravado. He is not "old." (A playgoer's perception of Othello as not old is tied to a contrast with Brabantio, whose age Othello himself keeps mentioning.) Even F. R. Leavis, who objected to the sentimentalized Othello of others, saw a "truly impressive" Othello in this part of the play.[10]

Ridley concluded that the most important function served by the misleading opening scene is to set us up for this impressive Othello: Shakespeare "gives us every possible help in making the true picture, which is all the more indelible because it has had to be made after an erasure of presuppositions."[11] If Shakespeare intended this effect, he failed. Far from being "indelible," the picture of a noble Moor is rejected by many critics. The function Ridley saw would also eventually reverse the effect I described above. One's possession of a "true" and "indelible" picture of Othello would distance one from an Othello whose perceptions are fallible. Nevertheless, if Ridley's account accurately reflects his own experience, it does suggest that the play put Ridley in Othello's shoes. Like Othello, Ridley underwent a radical change in his perception. Ridley's second perception of Othello, furthermore, was "all the more indelible" because he arrived at it after undergoing a disillusionment with his first perception. Othello's picture of a guilty Desdemona was similarly made after his disillusionment with his initial perception and thereby seemed all the more convincing. But Othello comes to regret his perception of a guilty Desdemona. The action of the play suggests that one cannot assume that one's perception after a disillusionment is any more reliable than one's original perception. Ridley allowed his perception to be guided by this dubious assumption before Othello does.

Othello eventually mistrusts Desdemona, strikes her and humiliates her in public, treats her as a prostitute, and finally suffocates her—all without conclusive evidence of her guilt. How do Ridley and other critics manage to continue to see a noble Othello despite this evidence? One way is to imitate Othello, to see all this evidence in light of Othello's presumed nobility—just as Othello sees anything Desdemona does in light of her presumed deceit. Thus, A. C. Bradley could see Othello's suffocation of Desdemona as "no murder, but a sacrifice."[12] Just as Othello actively suppresses the perception of an innocent Desdemona in order to hold his perception of a guilty Desdemona, Bradley actively suppressed the perception of a contemptible Othello. Bradley's perception of Othello also was tied to his perception of *Othello* as a tragedy, according to the following reasoning: Tragic heroes are noble; Othello is a tragic hero; therefore, Othello must be noble. Such a perception of a particular character based on an appeal to literary genre resembles Iago's self-validating syllogism: Venetian women are deceitful; Desdemona is a Venetian woman; therefore, Desdemona is deceitful. In each case, one does not draw a conclusion on the basis of evidence, one sees the evidence in light of one's foregone conclusion, in light of a stereotype. Just as Othello's perception of his own life as tragic facilitates his perception of a guilty Desdemona, Bradley's perception of Othello's life as tragic facilitated his perception of a noble Othello. No amateur of tragedy, Bradley was blinded to some features of the play by his expertise. He wore his eyes according to generic presuppositions.

In light of Othello's cruelty to Desdemona, many playgoers come to see him as contemptible. If these playgoers perceive a contemptible Othello on the basis of 1.1 and then perceived an admirable Othello in 1.2 and 1.3, they thus undergo a second disillusionment and revive, with modifications, their initial perception. But just as playgoers inclined to perceive a sympathetic Othello must blind themselves to Othello's cruelty, playgoers inclined to perceive a contemptible Othello not only must suppress their earlier perceptions of his courage, poise, and eloquence in 1.2 and 1.3 but must blind themselves to his ongoing pain. However much he is responsible for his own suffering, he does suffer intensely through the second half of the play and eventually commits suicide.[13] In order to maintain a consistent perception of Othello, each playgoer must ignore or somehow transform some of this evidence. Each playgoer must decide what constitutes evidence and what to make of it. What one sees as evidence will depend on how one wears one's eyes.[14]

Some playgoers wear suspicious eyes after the following exchange:

> *Bra.* Look to her, Moor, if thou hast eyes to see;
> She has deceiv'd her father, and may thee.
> *Oth.* My life upon her faith!
>
> (1.3.292–94)

Those playgoers who have "eyes to see," those that are familiar with dramatic foreshadowing, see the very finality with which Othello treats the issue of Desdemona's faithfulness as an announcement that Desdemona's fidelity will very probably become a major issue, in one of two easily foreseeable ways. Othello's declaration could turn out to be hubris, a blind and unjustified confidence in Desdemona. Or Othello's justified confidence could change to unjustified suspicion. Long before Othello is tempted to allow assumptions about Venetian women to override his perception of Desdemona as an individual, a playgoer is tempted to allow assumptions about what typically happens in plays to override perceptions of highly individualized characters in unique situations in a particular play. Long before Othello is tempted to see hypocrisy in Desdemona's displays of affection, a playgoer is tempted to foresee in Othello's exclaimed confidence in Desdemona's fidelity the eventual loss either of that confidence or of that fidelity. Long before Othello's perception of Desdemona becomes inextricably linked to his perception of Iago—one or the other must be untrustworthy—some playgoers foresee that either Othello or Desdemona will be untrustworthy. A playgoer who assumes, despite this exchange, that Othello and Desdemona will live happily ever after would be in the dark about what the rest of the play will be about (because to live happily ever after is what characters do at the end of a play), and this playgoer would thus resemble the playgoer who chose to be in the dark about the Moor after the opening scene. Some playgoers may go to the opposite extreme and foresee the mutual betrayal of Othello and Desdemona. They would be wearing their eyes with even greater suspicion than Othello later wears his eyes.

A playgoer's perception of Othello is linked to a playgoer's perception of Desdemona for the rest of the play. How one sees Othello's treatment of Desdemona will depend to some extent on how one sees Desdemona. Most playgoers see an innocent Desdemona. How do they arrive at this perception? In my own case, I believe that, when I first experienced *Othello,* I saw an innocent Desdemona by the end of 1.3. My perception was based not on any profound insight into the character of Desdemona, but rather on Iago's declaration in a soliloquy of his intention to slander Desdemona (1.3.383–87). The reasoning behind this perception was the following: Iago is a self-confessed liar; Iago intends to make Desdemona look guilty; therefore, Desdemona must be innocent. This syllogism resembles that by which Othello sees an innocent Desdemona at the end of the play. But these syllogisms are as dubious as those that lead Othello to see a guilty Desdemona. And my syllogism inextricably linked my perception of Desdemona to my perception of Iago, just as Othello's perception of Desdemona became inextricably linked to his perception of Iago. Iago's soliloquy does, however, present some actual evidence of sorts in support of a perception of an innocent Desdemona. Iago believes he will be slandering her; Iago himself perceives an innocent Desdemona. But playgoers who rely on Iago's perception of Desdemona as the basis for their own perception of her do what Othello later does. They accept, before Othello does, that Iago is a good judge of character, that he "doubtless, / Sees and knows more, much more, than he unfolds," that he "knows all qualities, with a learned spirit, / Of human dealings" (3.3.242–43, 259–60). As it turns out, Iago is not even a good judge of his own wife's character. Playgoers who perceive an innocent Desdemona at this point do so on a basis no firmer than the basis on which Othello later perceives a guilty Desdemona.

A playgoer inclined to see things in dualistic terms is also eventually confronted by a set of incompatible syllogisms: (1) Iago is bad; Iago is opposed to Othello; therefore, Othello must be good; (2) Iago is bad; Iago is opposed to Desdemona; therefore, Desdemona must be good; (3) Desdemona is good; Othello kills Desdemona; therefore, Othello must be bad. When one thinks of what Iago does to Othello, one sees Othello as a pitiable victim; when one thinks of what Othello does to Desdemona, one sees Othello as a contemptible victimizer. One can see Othello at one moment as the victim of racism and at another moment as the perpetrator of sexism.[15]

Not all playgoers respond to Iago's soliloquy in the way I did. Those that have noses to smell with would smell dramatic irony. It would be ironic, for example, if Iago's fabricated charge against Desdemona turned out to be true. It would be even more ironic if, in response to Iago' slander, Othello abused Desdemona and drove her, for solace, into the arms of Cassio. (Like Oedipus, Othello would bring about the very thing he feared.) Playgoers who at this point adopt the working hypothesis that Desdemona is guilty would wear their eyes suspiciously, would look for evidence of a guilty Desdemona. The play does contain such evidence—for those with eyes to see. Desdemona encourages Iago's sexual banter, passionately pleads for Cassio, repeatedly uses expressions that seem like blatant Freudian slips, and so on. All these hints could be red herrings, hinting at no more than Desdemona's faint regret that, by irrevocably choosing Othello, she has given up other opportunities for love and sexual gratification. Cassio's effusive praise of Desdemona and his own series of Freudian slips, similarly, may hint merely at frustrated desire for Desdemona rather than at the gratification or the confident anticipation of the gratification of that desire. If Desdemona eventually turned out to be guilty of infidelity, however, these hints, in retrospect, would have been foreshadowings rather than red herrings. But at the time it occurs there is no way to tell a red herring from a foreshadowing. Indeed, a playgoer with sufficiently suspicious eyes may continue to see these hints as foreshadowings of a sort. W. H. Auden saw the potential for guilt in Desdemona: "Given a few more years of Othello and of Emilia's influence and she might well, one feels, have taken a lover."[16]

Just as Iago torments Othello with the possibility of conclusive evidence about Desdemona, the play teases playgoers with the same possibility. For example, the play promises a private meeting between Desdemona and Cassio. Cassio asks Emilia, "Give me advantage of some brief discourse / With Desdemona alone" (3.1.52–53), and Emilia agrees. But when the meeting does occur, Emilia is present. Desdemona has an aside in the middle of her banter with Iago after her arrival in Cyprus: "I am not merry; but I beguile / The thing I am by seeming otherwise" (2.1.122–23). A playgoer wearing suspicious eyes could imagine that she is having second thoughts about the life of deception she has adopted or that the danger to Othello, still at sea, threatens her plan to advance her lover's career. How one sees this piece of evidence depends on how one wears one's eyes. Everything Desdemona says and does could be seen in light of her presumed guilt. Even her speech at 4.2.107–9, in which she declares her innocence, could be regarded, not as a genuine aside, but as a feigned aside, meant to be overheard by the departing Emilia. The suspicious playgoer would recall that, only three scenes earlier, Iago used a feigned aside as his very first tactic to manipulate Othello directly. (The play also suggests that even if we did have reliable access to the thoughts of another person, we still might face challenges to our powers of forming a consistent perception of the person. Othello's soliloquies show as much inconsistency as his outward behavior.) Desdemona's concealment in her dying speech of Othello's responsibility for her death may be seen as evidence of the extraordinary generosity of an innocent Desdemona, but it may also be seen as evidence of the concern of a guilty Desdemona for her posthumous reputation (if Othello were charged with murder, he would attempt to justify his act on the basis of her guilt, and her guilt would then become public knowledge) or simply as evidence of the concern of one or the other Desdemona for Emilia (if Desdemona accused Othello of murder, he might kill Emilia, the only other person present, to keep Emilia from repeating the accusation). A playgoer who perceives a guilty Desdemona is not obliged to abandon that perception; the play never presents unequivocal evidence of her innocence. On the other hand, a playgoer who perceives an innocent Desdemona is not obliged to abandon this perception; the play never presents unequivocal evidence of her guilt. Like Othello, a playgoer who mistrusts Desdemona sees her through suspicious eyes, whereas the playgoer who trusts Desdemona simply because of the lack of unequivocal evidence of her guilt also resembles Othello, who, in the absence of evidence of Iago's untrustworthiness, trusts Iago. *Othello* places us in a situation similar to Othello's: neither we nor Othello have certainty about Desdemona; we either trust Desdemona or do not trust her, and we wear our eyes accordingly.

In trying to perceive Desdemona, Othello is confronted not only with separate pieces of evidence that are inconsistent, but also with individual pieces of evidence that are equivocal. In trying to perceive Othello, playgoers are also confronted with equivocal evidence. A particularly instructive example occurs at almost the precise midpoint of the play, when Othello tells Desdemona, "I have a pain upon my forehead, here" (3.3.284). A majority of editors and critics hear in this line an allusion to cockold's horns and thus perceive at this moment an Othello guilty of mistrust. Horace Howard Furness asserted that it was "scarcely possible in those days to refer to the forehead other than as a groundwork" for cuckold's horns.[17] But if this were so, it is hard to imagine how someone "in those days" would refer to a pain in that part of the anatomy. People in Shakespeare's time presumably sometimes got headaches, especially if they were under emotional stress, as Othello is here. (Indeed, Othello's mental stress brings on a epileptic attack later in the scene; his headache here may be an early symptom, a foreshadowing.) If a man really had a pain upon the forehead, would he lie about it? Furness suggests that "upon" is a giveaway, but the play contains an earlier use of "upon" that shows it was not strictly limited in meaning to "outside": Iago believes Cassio will become quarrelsome if Iago "can fasten but one cup upon him" (2.3.47). Only eight lines before Othello mentions his forehead, he does refer to "this forked plague" (276). But immediately after that evidence of Othello's mistrust, Desdemona enters and he declares, "If she be false, O then heaven mocks itself! / I'll not believe't" (278–79). If only a moment later Othello reverted to a perception of a guilty Desdemona without Iago's presence and despite Desdemona's presence and demonstrations of affection, he would indeed be guilty of profound mistrust—but whether Othello does perceive a guilty Desdemona at this point is the question. Another obstacle to the Othello that Furness perceived in this line is Desdemona, who takes literally Othello's complaint about a headache. Like Othello, Furness created a Desdemona that fit in with his presuppositions: in Desdemona's failure to hear Othello's allusion to cuckoldry, a Jacobean audience "perceived a proof of her unconscious innocence which is otherwise lost on us." But Desdemona does not seem so oblivious to sexual innuendo when she banters with Iago in 2.1 And if Othello's allusion were as obvious as Furness contended, then a Jacobean audience would have been more likely to see Desdemona as simply obtuse. Furness attributed his own perception to a Jacobean audience—just as Othello attributes his own perception of his life as pitiful to Desdemona. In other words, when Othello says that he has a pain upon his forehead, it is possible for a playgoer to imagine that Othello has a pain upon his forehead.

If this is so, then a playgoer who sees cuckold's horns in Othello's mind when Othello says "forehead" wears suspicious eyes. Just as Iago prepares Othello to see anything Desdemona does as evidence of deceit, *Othello* prepares those playgoers with "eyes to see" to see anything Othello does as evidence of mistrust. Othello's reference to "the forked plague" just before his unequivocal declaration of his trust in Desdemona could be a red herring, tempting a playgoer to hear an ulterior meaning and therefore to see a mistrustful Othello when he says "forehead," just as the opening scene of the play contains a series of red herrings that tempt the playgoer to see a contemptible Othello. This episode, in the midst of a scene often called the "temptation scene," tempts playgoers to wear their eyes as Iago eventually gets Othello to wear his eyes, to wear their eyes suspiciously. To assume on the equivocal evidence of Othello's reference to his forehead that Othello has failed to give Desdemona the benefit of a doubt would constitute one's own failure to give Othello the benefit of a doubt. One would be guilty of the very offense one attributes to Othello. The playgoer who assumes Othello mistrusts Desdemona when he refers to his "forehead" does so despite the Duke's dismissal of similarly dubious evidence against Othello earlier in the play: "To vouch this is no proof, / Without more wider and more overt test" (1.3.106–7).

Some of the same critics who have vehemently attacked Othello for assuming on the basis of flimsy evidence that Desdemona is guilty have assumed on the flimsy basis of his reference to his forehead that Othello is guilty of a failure to trust her. Thomas Rymer sarcastically commented: "*Michael Cassio* came not from *Venice* in the Ship with *Desdemona,* nor till this Morning could be suspected of an opportunity with her. And 'tis now but Dinner time; yet the *Moor* complains of his Fore-head. . . . this is very hasty."[18] Rymer found it clumsily improbable that Othello could be suspicious at this moment, yet it is Rymer himself who created a suspicious Othello.

Leavis excoriated both Othello and Bradley for the same offense, for allowing preconceptions to govern their perception of evidence. Othello's "angry egotism" leads him to misperceive Desdemona.[19] Because of "his determined sentimental preconception," his "very obstinate preconception," Bradley was "wearing . . . blinkers."[20] Bradley's account of *Othello* is "grossly and palpably false to the evidence"; "we must not suppose that Bradley sees what is in front of him."[21] Leavis felt it was "easy" to refute Bradley "because there, to point to, is the text, plain and unequivocal."[22] Leavis pointed emphatically to the "forehead" passage: "Even the actual presence of Desdemona . . . can avail nothing against the misgivings of angry egotism. Pointing to his forehead he makes an allusion to the cuckold's horns, and when she in her innocence misunderstands him and offers to soothe the pain he rebuffs her."[23] Leavis saw only the vase and, revealing a trace of angry egotism himself, ridiculed Bradley for seeing only the two faces, for not seeing what Leavis saw, for not seeing what was not in front of either of them. Leavis contended, furthermore, that the behavior of a dramatic character must be "reconcilable with our notions of ordinary psychological consistency"[24] and saw consistent egotism in everything Othello does—just as Iago argued that psychological consistency supported the perception of a deceitful Desdemona. Bradley saw Othello through rose-colored glasses, but Leavis saw Othello through jaundiced eyes.

Jane Adamson resisted the temptation to see a fallen Othello at the moment he mentions his forehead, but she did perceive an ulterior meaning in his words—his pain is the psychological pain of doubt rather than a physical pain—and she saw a fallen Othello a moment later.[25] She agreed with G. R. Elliott about "the intensely symbolic quality of the conversation here"[26] and concluded, "So we cannot miss the significance of the dialogue in which the flickering possibility of restoring their 'bond' is snuffed out, for ever, by Othello's self-mistrust"; "his lingering fears and doubts and self-doubts are such that he rejects the proffered napkin—a token and assurance of her love—as inadequate."[27] Adamson thus saw the handkerchief as evidence of Othello's guilt even before Othello sees it as evidence of Desdemona's guilt. Othello later will see the handkerchief as "a token and assurance" of *his* love and Desdemona's loss of it as a symbol of *her* "snuffing out, for ever" of their bond. If only the behavior of either real people or characters had such a clearly perceptible "symbolic quality," misunderstandings would disappear. But the action of *Othello* suggests that such symbolism is a will-o'-the-wisp. The headache-handkerchief episode could be another red herring. Its superficial triviality could have been constructed precisely to tempt a playgoer to see some ulterior "symbolic" meaning for the headache or for the handkerchief or for both, to turn them into symbols of Othello's guilt. The play thereby tempts some playgoers to do precisely what they are in the process of assuming that Othello is doing. In order to see a suspicious Othello in this episode, one must be suspicious oneself. Like Leavis, Adamson expresses herself in no uncertain terms ("surely," "of course," "we cannot miss," "for ever"). Many critics have suggested that Othello suffered from an intense need for certainty. But we playgoers are not exempt from this need.[28]

Those who have seen an innocent Othello in the forehead-handkerchief episode include Hazlitt and Bradley.[29] George Skillan argued for this perception with as much conviction as Leavis and Adamson argued for their perceptions: "It seems dramatically certain that Othello has conquered his doubts and also that he is in a state of mental exhaustion, unable to conceive of any violent or gross idea."[30] A "supposed allusion to cuckoldry is the project of ingenuity, not art." Othello does not violently rebuff Desdemona's offer of the handkerchief, merely indicates that it is "too little" (3.3.287). The "poignancy of the moment" is "intensified by the contrast" with earlier moments of violence. Skillan's account is no more "certain" than the accounts of Leavis and Adamson; he simply views the same evidence through eyes more sympathetic to Othello. Skillan's assumption that the moment should be "poignant" even resembles Othello's own perception that his life is "pitiful."

The equivocality of this episode puts a playgoer in an awkward position. One can see a suspicious Othello in the episode if one is suspicious oneself—one can blind oneself to Othello's "pain" and see it instead as guilt. Or one can see a trusting Othello if one trusts Othello. One can even oscillate between these perceptions, as Othello oscillates during the course of the play between incompatible perceptions of Desdemona, but at any one moment one will wear one's eyes in one way or the other, and the way one wears one's eyes will correspond to the way one sees Othello to be wearing his eyes. One other choice is to see the episode as insignificant or meaningless, that is, not to perceive it.

Leavis's perception of Othello influenced the 1964 National Theatre production, directed by John Dexter and starring Laurence Olivier. According to Kenneth Tynan's account, "when Othello complains of 'a pain upon my forehead,' he places two fingers above his eyebrows, indicating to us (though not to [Desdemona]) the cuckold's horns."[31] Olivier's gesture eliminated the ambiguity of the passage, but it is not the only plausible theatrical option. Through his facial expression or gesture, an actor could "indicate to us" that Othello here has a genuine headache. Each of these options is legitimate, it seems to me, because each brings to vivid life one of the genuine possibilities allowed for by the text. After seeing each of these equally plausible alternatives well performed, a playgoer (like a viewer of *Rashomon* by Akira Kurosawa, that most Shakespearean of film directors) would be left to make up her or his own mind. It is even conceivable that an actor could perform so as not to eliminate either possibility—so as to convey each *as a possibility.* (Such a performance would not resemble a lifeless performance that failed to convey either possibility and that thereby eliminated both.) It is also conceivable that the King's Men themselves, for their own artistic appreciation and that of their repeat customers, performed the episode in different ways on different occasions.

The editors of most modern editions of *Othello* allow readers to make up their own minds about the state of Othello's mind at this point. Some editors do not supply commentary on the passage and rely on a reader's memory of an earlier note explaining the concept of cuckold's horns to trigger a reader's perception of the possibility that, in referring to his headache, Othello may reveal a belief in Desdemona's guilt. Some editors (including Furness and Skillan) vigorously argue for their own perception and thereby at least tacitly acknowledge that someone else may perceive another possibility. But a few editors flatly declare in footnotes that Othello here alludes to cuckold's horns.[32] These notes eliminate one genuine possibility without vividly bringing to life another possibility (as Olivier's performance presumably did or as extended, imaginative argumentation by Adamson and by Skillan does).[32]

Near the end of the play Othello offers others advice about their formulation of perceptions of himself: "Speak of me as I am; nothing extenuate, / Nor set down aught in malice" (5.2.342–43). He paraphrases Iago's advice to Othello in regard to Desdemona: "Wear your eyes thus, not jealous nor secure." What both Othello and Iago advise, to perceive human behavior without preconceptions, without either sentimentality or cynicism, is impossible. Some evidence cannot be seen at all unless one sees it one way or the other.

By providing individual pieces of evidence that are equivocal and by providing separate pieces of evidence that are inconsistent, *Othello* tempts playgoers to form questionable perceptions and thereby, in one way or another, to do what Othello does. A playgoer cannot make sense of the dramatic action without forming perceptions; these perceptions are the sense the playgoer makes. Precisely because the evidence is equivocal, different playgoers can form different perceptions. Just as Othello's perception of Desdemona at every moment is in part his own creation, playgoers' perceptions of Othello, necessarily, are in part their own creations. (The perception of Othello presented in the early part of this essay is no exception.) Just as Othello oscillates between incompatible perceptions of Desdemona, a playgoer may, because the evidence is so equivocal, oscillate between incompatible perceptions of Othello and continue to do so even after the play is over. But at any one moment one must wear one's eyes in one way or another—it is no more possible for a playgoer to see a contemptible Othello and a pitiable Othello at the same time than it is for Othello to see a guilty and an innocent Desdemona at the same time or for one to see the faces and the vase in the trick drawing at the same time. Because the oscillation between incompatible perceptions is literally maddening, most playgoers end it by trying to suppress one perception or the other. Our experience of *Othello* thus resembles Othello's experience in various ways. Our experience of *Othello* also resembles our experience of the world, in which we form our perceptions of other people on the basis of mere hints; in such a world, if we are to perceive at all, we must wear fallible eyes, we must use our fallible imaginations. *Othello* is a particularly disturbing, thought-provoking, and stimulating play not merely because we witness characters confronted with situations that acutely test their powers of perception, but because we confront such situations ourselves.

NOTES

1. John Bayley, *The Character of Love: A Study in the Literature of Personality* (New York: Collier, 1963), p. 126.

2. Shakespeare seems to have constructed his plays so that situations confronted by playgoers responding to the stage action would in some way resemble situations confronted by characters. This major feature of Shakespearean dramatic technique has been noted by Robert Hapgood in "Shakespeare and the Included Spectator," in *Reinterpretations of Elizabethan Drama: Selected Papers from the English Institute,* ed. Norman Rabkin (New York: Columbia University Press, 1969), pp. 117–36. Analogies between experiences of characters and those of audiences have been explored by Stephen Booth in his landmark essay, "On the Value of *Hamlet,*" in *Reinterpretations,* ed. Norman Rabkin, pp. 137–76; in "*Twelfth Night,* 2.1: The Audience as Malvolio," in *Shakespeare's "Rough Magic": Renaissance Essays in Honor of C. L. Barber,* ed. Peter Erickson and Coppélia Kahn (Newark: University of Delaware Press, 1985), pp.1 49–67; and other works.

3. E. H. Gombrich, *Art and Illusion: A Study in the Psychology of Pictorial Representation,* 4th ed. (London: Phaidon, 1972), p. 148. That perception is an active, dynamic process rather than a passive one has been confirmed by numerous findings of perceptual psychologists. For an overview of these findings, see Julian Hochberg, "The Representation of Things and People," in *Art, Perception, and Reality,* ed. Maurice Mandelbaum (Baltimore: Johns Hopkins University Press, 1972), pp. 47–94.

4. William Hazlitt, *Characters of Shakespear's Plays* (1817), vol. 4 of *The Complete Works of William Hazlitt,* ed. P. P. Howe (1930; repr., New York: AMS, 1967), p. 207.

5. See Albert Gerard, " 'Egregiously an Ass': The Dark Side of the Moor," *Shakespeare Survey* 10 (1957), pp. 98–106.

6. Compare the perceptual quandary Desdemona describes in her very first speech in the play: "I do perceive here a divided duty" (2.3.181). Just as Othello eventually suppresses one of his opposing perceptions of Desdemona, Desdemona has already suppressed one of the conflicting perceptions of her duty—she has suppressed her perception of her duty to her father—in order to act on her other perceived duty, in order to elope with Othello.

7. M. R. Ridley, ed. *Othello* (London: Methuen, 1958), pp. liv, lv.

8. See Robert Hapgood, "The Trials of Othello," in *Pacific Coast Studies in Shakespeare,* ed. Waldo F. McNeir and Thelma Greenfield (Eugene: University of Oregon Press, 1966), pp. 134–47; and Philip C. McGuire, "*Othello* as an 'Assay of Reason,'" *Shakespeare Quarterly* 24 (1973): 198–209.

9. Ridley, *Othello,* pp. xlviii, 1.

10. F. R. Leavis, "Diabolic Intellect and the Noble Hero: or The Sentimentalist's Othello," in *The Common Pursuit* (London: Chatto and Windus, 1952), p. 141.

11. Ridley, *Othello,* p. l.

12. A. C. Bradley, *Shakespearean Tragedy,* 2d ed. (1905; repr., Fawcett, 1965), p. 165.

13. In order to make the following comments on Othello's final speech, T. S. Eliot—in "Shakespeare and the Stoicism of Seneca," *Selected Essays,* new ed. (New York: Harcourt, Brace and Co., 1950), pp. 107–20—must, I think, have blinded himself to certain features of the dramatic context: "What Othello seems to be doing in making this speech is *cheering himself up.* He is endeavouring to escape reality. . . . nothing dies harder than the desire to think well of oneself" (p. 111). If one recalls what Eliot does not mention—that at the end of the speech Othello stabs himself—some of these comments seem like Freudian slips. (Someone who commits suicide could indeed be said to be "endeavouring to escape reality," for example.) In stabbing himself, Othello retroactively equates himself with the "malignant" enemy, the "dog" whom he stabbed "in Aleppo once" (5.2.353, 355)—his desire to think well of himself seems to have died. Even Othello's self-characterization early in the speech may constitute deception rather than self-deception. Othello would have an obvious motive to pretend to cheer himself up. On two separate occasions earlier in the scene, Othello has been disarmed before he could use a weapon against Iago. He has also revealed a suicidal intention: "Here is my journey's end" (267). His self-consolation thus may be a ploy: if he can convince his on-stage auditors, his captors, that he is no longer suicidal, they may relax their guard just enough so that this time he will be able to use his weapon, now against himself, before they can stop him. Throughout the play, Othello does show, in Eliot's words, "the human will to see things as they are not" (p. 111), but this "weakness" is "universal" (p. 110), as Eliot acknowledges, and Eliot shows signs of it himself.

14. The mental processes by which we perceive the hypothetical personalities of dramatic characters on the basis of evidence provided by a play are not essentially different from the processes by which we perceive the personalities of actual people on the basis of their words and actions and what others say about them. Compare Tzvetan Todorov's observation—in "Reading as Construction," trans. Marilyn A. August, *The Reader in the Text: Essays on Audience and Interpretation,* ed. Susan R. Suleiman and Inge Crosman (Princeton: Princeton University Press, 1980), pp. 67–82—that " 'Fiction' is not constructed [in one's mind] any differently from reality' " (p. 81). And like the perception of "reality," an audience's perception of the hypothetical world of a play and the characters that occupy that world is an active, dynamic process, not a passive one. For a theoretical discussion of this last point, see Wolfgang Iser, *The Act of Reading: A Theory of Aesthetic Responses* (Baltimore: Johns Hopkins University Press, 1978), pp. 3–52.

15. Compare Paul Robeson's eloquent commentary, "Some Reflections on *Othello* and the Nature of Our Time," *American Scholar* 14 (1945): 391–92, with Carol Thomas Neely's equally eloquent essay, "Women and Men in *Othello:* 'what should such a fool / Do with so good a woman?' " *Shakespeare Studies* 10 (1977), pp. 133–59.

16. W. H. Auden, "The Joker in the Pack," in *The Dyer's Hand* (New York: Random House, 1948), p. 269.

17. Horace Howard Furness, ed., *A New Variorum Edition of Shakespeare: Vol. VI: Othello,* (1886; repr., New York: Dover Publications, 1963), p. 193. All passages subsequently quoted from this text also occur on p. 193.

18. Thomas Rymer, *A Short View of Tragedy* (1693), in *The Critical Works of*

Thomas Rymer, ed. Curt Zimansky (New Haven: Yale University Press, 1956), p. 150.

19. Leavis, "Diabolical Intellect," p. 146.
20. Ibid., pp. 139, 140.
21. Ibid., pp. 136, 137.
22. Ibid., p. 138.
23. Ibid., p. 146.
24. Ibid., p. 157.
25. Jane Adamson, *"Othello" as Tragedy: Some Problems of Judgment and Feeling* (Cambridge: Cambridge University Press, 1980), p. 167.
26. G. R. Eliot, *Flaming Minister: A Study of "Othello" at a Tragedy of Love and Hate* (Durham: Duke University Press, 1953), p. 126, quoted in Adamson, p.1 67.
27. Adamson, *"Othello" as Tragedy,* pp. 167, 168.
28. Other recent critics who have seen a guilty Othello in this episode include Carol McGinnis Kay, "Othello's Need for Mirrors," *Shakespeare Quarterly* 34 (1983): 265; and Eamon Grennan, "The Women's Voices in *Othello:* Speech, Song, Silence," *Shakespeare Quarterly* 38 (1987): 287.
29. See Hazlitt, *Characters,* pp. 202–3, and Bradley, *Shakespearean Tragedy,* pp. 162–63.
30. George Skillan, ed. *Othello* (London: French, [1936]), p. 48. All passages subsequently quoted from this text occur on p. 48.
31. Kenneth Tynan, *"Othello": The National Theatre Production* (London: R. Hart-Davis, 1966), p. 8.
32. See, for example, George Lyman Kittredge, ed. *The Tragedy of Othello. The Moor of Venice* (Boston: Ginn, 1941), p. 191; Ridley, *Othello,* p. 110; Alice Walker and John Dover Wilson, eds. *Othello* (Cambridge: Cambridge University Press, 1960), p. 187; Alvin Kernan, ed. *Othello* (New York: New American Library, 1963), p. 103; and Norman Sanders, ed. *Othello* (Cambridge: Cambridge University Press, 1984), p. 126.

8

Audience Response and the Denouement of *Othello*

KENT CARTWRIGHT

Performance-oriented criticism of Shakespeare appears limited because tied to dramatic choice—the actor's need to choose one meaning for a word, one gesture for an action, from a range of compelling possibilities. Other critical avenues, however, such as rhetoric, can unearth the mutiplicity of meanings, the ideas of amplification, accusation, and delay, for example, implied by the word "dilation" in *Othello* as these various meanings arise, qualify, and undermine each other in shaping the play.[1] Yet from the perspective of performance, closely juxtaposed differences in stage geography, locomotion of actors, levels of characterization, and acting styles (all as cued by the text) can create for the spectator a multivalent collage of emotional, moral, and intellectual experience. The stage offers its own copious rhetoric. The bi-polar rhythms of *Othello*'s ending, as a case in point, invite a progressive, fluctuating, double response in the theatrical audience, engagement seesawing with detachment. "Engagement and detachment," first applied to Shakespearean tragedy by Maynard Mack, offer terms for analyzing what Edward Bullough distinguished as "psychical distance," the manner in which a work of art impinges upon its viewer.[2] "Engagement" in drama refers to the spectator's surrender of self-awareness. It connotes that immediate, sympathetic response, physical and emotional, which we make to character, acting, language, or action, the sense of being absorbed, lost in the event, "rapt out of" ourselves.[3] Detachment in drama refers to the spectator's heightened self-consciousness. It includes our interpretive responses aroused from moment to moment, our sense of remove from the point of view of any single character, our contrasting of events and attitudes, our awareness of illusion, and our moral and intellectual judgments as invited by the dramatic context. Detachment is not a lack of emotional response so much as recognized or deliberated emotion. "To empathize is the natural human impulse," John Styan observes, "but in alienation lies the drama."[4] At the heart of engagement resides awe; at the heart of detachment, doubt.

Spectators of *Othello* have responded with an awe and doubt that diverge in the farthest extreme, such as the audience moved to tearful pity for Desdemona during a performance at Oxford in 1610, or the "very pretty lady" sitting beside Pepys at the Cockpit in 1660 who called out "to see Desdemona smothered," both reactions contrasting sharply to Rymer's savaging of the plays' inanities later in that century.[5] Of course, all spectators need not fall into such opposing camps. Rather, I would argue, the play invites throughout a shifting and reshifting of spectatorial empathy and intellectual disturbance. Othello himself experiences something of the same. Twice he pauses in a wonderment fashioned of joy and disbelief, awe and doubt: first in his unexpected discovery of Desdemona waiting at Cyprus: "It gives me wonder great as my content / To see you here before me" (2.1.183–84); second as he watches Desdemona leave the "temptation" scene: "Perdition catch my soul / But I do love thee!" (3.3.90–91). In the denouement's scenic rhythms, spectators perhaps finally achieve, as they shed Iago's early domination of the play, a consciousness in themselves analogous to Othello's opaque and irreducible experience of his own world. Distinct from any "development" of its tragic hero, *Othello* may aim also at the development of the audience.

Othello opens the door of the murder chamber, and the world, in the form of Emilia, rushes in (5.2.105). I mark *Othello*'s denouement from that point, for Emilia's harsh and disruptive voice commences the unraveling, the Aristotelian reversal and recognition, of the play. And such reversals and recognitions! Their sensationalism will engage any audience: entrances and exits; hidden weapons; murder attempts and a killer's escape; letters of revelation and a demonic unmasking; poetry of exalted suffering; and a suicide approaching prestidigitation. But sensationalism can also leave the audience just *watching,* agape with wonder yet externalized, involved yet adrift for meaning. Spectacle can overwhelm understanding. The sensationalism of *Othello*'s denouement comes in its rapid-fire and sometimes simultaneous stage events and in the passions of its characters, such as Emilia and Othello himself. But the ending limits spectatorial empathy: Emilia speaks too coarsely, Othello speaks too obliquely, and Iago speaks finally not at all. In terms of detachment, on the other hand, the denouement denies the audience the illumination and perspicuity that mark some of tragedy's richest experiences. Yes, the final episode boils over with "judgments." But the principal thrust of judgment, that Othello has played the fool, hardly satisfies our sense of the temptation scene's tragic unfolding. The structure of the denouement thus evokes a double response from the audience. That double response—figured in the rhythm of delays, quick shifts, and incomplete points of view—consists of an engagement that falls short of empathy and a detachment that falls short of clarity, an excitement of passion and a doubt of understanding—something like Othello's own wonder.

The denouement maintains a tension between sympathetic engagement and detached understanding which can lead the audience to recognize the experience of audiencing itself. The ending of *Othello* divides the audience's response through techniques of speech, stage configuration, and acting,[6] such as: (1) the vehement accusations against Othello-as-fool; (2) the relief yet irritation of Emilia as an audience-figure; (3) the unfinished kinesthetics of violence; (4) the centering or moral indignation on Iago and the visual severing of Othello from him; (6) the obtrusive otherness represented physically by the bed; and (7) Othello's presentational and representational acting.[7] Assessments of Othello's character have often separated into intense camps of sympathy and detachment: the Bradleyan noble Moor against the traitor-within-the-gates of Leavis and Eliot.[8] No wonder the problem of "judging" Othello has consumed critics, for that problem consumes much of the dialogue and hysteria of the last scene. Judging Othello amounts to the overt subject of the close (as "thought" has of the temptation scene). Here character upon character echoes the same revisionist interpretation, Othello-as-fool. What *Othello* presents as the hero's irresistible attraction to jealousy in the temptation scene it detoxifies to blindness and folly in the denouement—inviting the spectator to forget. Much of the scene's audience-engaging sensationalism arises from the characters' indignation at Othello's folly. Yet characters express this revisionist judgment with a passion so great as actually to undercut it. The divided denouement confronts spectators with their own desire for simple clarity and judgment toward the hero, yet for all its sensationalism, the tragedy leaves Othello nearly as opaque to them as the body of Desdemona, pale and cold, looms for him.

The downsizing of the general into a fool culminates with Othello's final extenuation of himself: "Then must you speak / Of one that lov'd not wisely but too well; / Of one not easily jealous, but being wrought, / Perplexed in the extreme . . ." (343–46). Othello's verbs, "wrought" and "perplexed," hint at what T. S. Eliot considered an "aesthetic rather than a moral attitude."[9] "Wrought" connotes emotional agitation, of course. According to the *Oxford English Dictionary,* Jacobeans also applied the word to commodities—textiles, leathers, metals, and scores of hand-manufactured wares—to emphasize the fashioning, shaping, and finishing that distinguished them. Othello suggests, that is, that he has been as finely "worked upon" by Iago as he is "worked up." "Perplexed" conveys a similar susceptibility. For early seventeenth-century meanings of "perplexed," the *Oxford English Dictionary* cites "Involved in doubt," "bewildered," "puzzled." As with "wrought," "perplexed" also applied to material objects and specified intricate intertwining and entanglement. "Perplexed" used in its agonistic sense, as in "tormented" or "vexed," emerged later in the seventeenth century. Othello's present bewilderment falls short of his earlier wonder, such as his "content" upon seeing Desdemona at Cyrpus, a wonder whose conjoined awe and doubt express his greatness of heart. Now Othello sees himself in his valedictory as a figure of extreme confusion, crafted so by Iago. Such language depicts Othello as baffled (like a comic antagonist) and victimized.[10]

Verbal anticipations of Othello's "wrought" and "perplexed" go off early in every corner of the play's ending, like navigational lights defining the terrain. Secondary characters, especially Emilia, who stand as "response-regulators"[11] to the audience, repeat this vision of the victimized Othello. Emilia transforms into one of the play's voices of truth, lifted almost to tragic stature as she uncovers her husband's evil. She assumes Desdemona's mantle of heroic womanhood, her self-discovery and martydom—"I'll kill myself for grief" (192)—privileging he own point of view. Instantly shocked over Desdemona's murder, Emilia brands Othello "devil" (131, 133). That tone shifts, however, with her first glimmerings of Iago's treachery, to accusations of "O gull, O dolt, / As ignorant as dirt!" (163–64). "Gull" and "dolt" are epithets that dismiss Othello's independent power of decision, like the bafflement implied in perplexity. "O thou dull Moor" (225), Emilia charges as preamble to revealing the truth about the handkerchief. Even as she affirms her own veracity against Iago's "thou liest," she repeats her verdict upon Othello: "O murd'rous coxcomb, what should such a fool / Do with so good a wife?" (233–34). Emilia is not alone. As she falls, the theme of Othello-as-fool continues symphonically in Lodovico, who steps forward as the voice of Venice and authority. "Where is this rash and most unfortunate man?" (283), he demands on reentering, and, again, after Othello is once more disarmed: "O thou Othello, that was once so good, / Fall'n in the practice of a damned slave, / What shall be said to thee?" (291–93). Othello completes this picture of himself: "O fool, fool, fool!" (323).

Wrought, perplexed, gull, dolt, ignorant, dull, fool, unfortunate, practice—such language inveigles the spectator to see Othello as more dupe than engineer, more victim than self-victimizer. The portrait is appealing yet reductive. It appeals because it erects a sharply etched, public interpretation of Othello's jealousy, allowing him the tragic stature of flawed nobility. It diminishes because Othello-as-fool comprises too small a vessel for the characters', and our, abhorrence of the recently experienced murder of Desdemona. The tragedies have their fools—Roderigo, Polonius, Rosencrantz and Guildenstern, even Gloucester—who die for their folly. But the shallowness of their souls disarms our anger at them or our interest in calling them to a harsh accounting. Emilia sputters her outrage repetitiously and to inarticulateness: "O gull, O dolt, / As ignorant as dirt! Thou hast done a deed—" (163–64). "[M]urd'rous coxcomb" is almost oxymoronic. Words can barely express her anger, so that we sense subtextually a frustration with speech itself. The audience thus can experience both the most intense emotion and the insufficiency of its terms, sensationalism denying understanding. The language of Emilia, Othello, and Lodovico offers one latticework of "judgment" about the victimized Othello; it also wobbles like thin planking in a high wind.

Emilia's freighted words launch a series of emotional justapositions in the rhythm of *Othello*'s ending that establish the bipolar or divided awareness in which the audience concludes the play. Alone after the murder, Othello staggers (probably physically) to see what he has done: "O insupportable! O heavy hour!" (98), thinking that the universe should respond to his deed with earthquake and the "huge eclipse / of sun and moon" (99–100). His solipsism may startle spectators (yet not, I think, provoke them in the Leavisian sense). But to Othello's call the universe returns Emilia, boisterous, prosaic, heated, coarse, hurrying her way from act 4. Emilia's reactions to Desdemona's death and Othello's confession are courageous, immediate, and intuitive: "Help, help, ho, help! O, lady, speak again!" (120); "Thou dost belie her, and thou art a devil" (133); "I'll make thee known, / Though I lost twenty lives. Help, help, ho, help! / The Moor hath kill'd my mistress! Murther, murther!" (165–67). Emilia stands here as an audience-figure—perhaps not so much a response-regulator as a response-ventilator.

Reacting to the murder of Desdemona, so bloodless, so cold, and so recent, spectators need the loud, commonsensical, aggressive, and heedless burst of outrage that Emilia provides. She perfectly captures the audience's reflexes, its utter intolerance of any of Othello's defenses and its need to have the murder shouted from the rooftops.

Audiences may be particularly desperate for explosive relief, since Othello's murder of Desdemona, as an act of violence, lingers as maddeningly incomplete. Though he has promised to spill her blood moments earlier (5.1.36), he declines the full expression of the sacrificial act: "Yet I'll not shed her blood, / Nor scar that whiter skin of hers than snow" (3–4). Indeed, Othello fails to complete the smothering, and his language (as well as the Desdemona-performer's movements) can leave the audience in an agony of unknowing as to whether Desdemona really is dead: "She's dead. / . . . Hah, no more moving? / Still as the grave . . . / I think she stirs again. No" (91–95). The murder scene swings the spectator's attention back and forth between the knocking Emilia and the questionably dead Desdemona four distinct times—as the audience wonders, perhaps, if Desdemona's signs of breathing refer to the character or merely to the acting. Such unresolved tension typifies the last scene. Here, also typically, the release comes not in the action of murder itself but in a dislocation, a projection, as it were, of the need for release sideways into Emilia's bellicosity.

Audience tension demands an Emilia. Yet Emilia also divides our response, for she constitutes the character perhaps least capable in the play of understanding Othello. The complexity of his fall not only exceeds her knowledge, it also exceeds her psychology. That Emilia exposes Othello in itself condemns him. Of visions of the noble Moor she will remain forever innocent; she is no Bradleyan. Emilia's unshakable faith in Desdemona, her cutting accuracy regarding Othello, and her unmasking of her own husband puncture Othello's "self-idealization." But the point is not simply that Emilia demonstrates to Othello the virtues in which he has failed; equally to the point, it is Emilia who does so. Her very philistinism tarnishes Othello, for a sensibility cruder and yet less erring than his own dismisses him on behalf of the play. But some audience members will already dislike Emilia for her service to Iago and her tawdry opinionating with Desdemona; even her first appearance tags her as sharp-tongued (2.1.103–7).[12] The right truth, the wrong messenger: just the way we so often experience Iago, as when, for example, he exposes Cassio's fatuousness in the Cyprian arrival. Indeed, Emilia's character rightly belongs to comedy (where servants know the truth), and, in a context less pathetic, her repetitions of "My husband?" ("What needs this iterance, woman?" [150]) would have the effect of a comic double-take. Emilia lacks exotic romanticism and Signiorial reason; Shakespeare chooses her both to expose Othello's arrogant self-righteousness and simultaneously to disrupt spectatorial perspective. The play refuses to unravel and judge Othello's crime on the level of Othello's sensibility—a dislocation typical of the fascinations and frustrations of this tragedy. Emilia's juxtaposed point of view will temporarily displace Othello's for the audience, particularly as the drama focuses more and more upon her discovery of Iago, her self-recognition, and her heroism. Yet *Othello* creates, contrasts, and destroys its own perspectives: when Emilia dies, the audience largely loses the independent voice of outrage, the passionate commentator who stands slightly to the side of the principals and sees the "truth."

Othello's exchange with Emilia completes Desdemona's murder emotionally, yet it also continues the pattern of tension aroused and unrelieved. The physical action of the last scene presents a series of failed attempts at kinesthetic release. In tragedy, spectators generally expect violence in the final act not only to resolve the play's conflicts but also to purge those aggressive tensions soaking into their very musculature. But *Othello* gives us half-gestures: Othello threatens Emilia with physical harm but halts (158–59); Iago reaches for his sword against Emilia but Gratiano forestalls him (223–24); then, only in Othello's aborted rush at him (235), does Iago succeed in fatally wounding her (236); Othello threatens Gratiano with his Spanish blade but collapses in mid-declamation (264); he wounds but does not kill Iago (287), and is disarmed for a second time (288). These assaults excite the audience repeatedly, but their frequent failures deny it the visceral satisfaction of completed physical confrontation. Before Othello's suicide, the only successful acts of violence are against women. Desdemona's murder repulses the audience morally yet also feels too bloodless and too uncertain to release us kinesthetically. Emilia's death hardly satisfies more, for she is no sooner wounded than forgotten. "The woman falls," says Gratiano, and then, in a remarkable leap to conclusion, "sure he hath kill'd his wife" (236). Emilia, of course, possesses enough life to agree: "Ay, ay! O, lay me by my mistress' side" (237), upon which Gratiano delivers into the perfect tense the manifestly undead Emilia: "He's gone, but his wife's kill'd" (238). Immediately the Venetians rush off stage, leaving Emilia unattended in the last throes of agony: even Othello barely seems to notice her. These passages may be more weird in the reading than in the rapid-fire of the theater, but they are, at best, awkward. And callous, I think, from the audience's perspective, since we are left suddenly to watch Emilia die alone, unremarked. Emilia's Willow song heightens the pathos of her desertion; likewise she must lengthen out the announcement of her real death because no one else in the play marks it: "So come my soul to bliss, as I speak true; / So speaking as I think, alas, I die" (250–51). Were Emilia expiring in a crowd, such speech might strike the audience as presentational acting, but her isolation actually privileges the self-dramatization. The spectacle barely pauses. Indeed, the moving camera lingers upon Emilia long enough to register only that her death will be our forgetting.

In Shakespeare's tragedies, a crucial form of audience fulfillment accompanies last-act acknowledgments, those moments when characters pay tribute publicly to the worth of others, even adversaries. Acknowledgment has both moral and psychological value. It confirms, within the society of the play, the generous stirrings that the audience may have felt toward characters, often through glimpses accessible only to them. Thus the justice of the tragic world comes not only in heroes exalted or villains punished, but in a recognition of characters by each other that reaches deeper than the paradigms by which they have lived. Before the duel, Claudius observes Hamlet's free and generous nature; at the duel Hamlet acknowledges Laertes' honor with his apology; later Horatio lingers over Hamlet's body with words of recognition that leap beyond the surrounding carnage: "Good night, sweet prince, / And flights of angels sing thee to thy rest!" Lear dies in a long tribute to Cordelia; indeed, his capacity to appreciate her measures his own greatness. True, tragedies do not always achieve the recognition of characters that the spectator might desire. But the absence becomes part of the effect of the play. *Macbeth* makes that point unmistakably. When Macbeth receives news of his wife's death, he pauses long enough to underscore his inability to acknowledge: "She should have died hereafter; / There would have been a time for such a word. / To-morrow, and to-morrow, and to-morrow. . . ." In *Othello,* the women, Desdemona and Emilia, never receive in life or in death sufficient acknowledgment. Such silence, I would argue, speaks profoundly to the audience.

The forsaking of Emilia demonstrates the denouement's masterful switching of points of view—from character to contrasting character, from group to individual—and its residue of mixed spectatorial feelings. Corollary to its revision of Othello from traitor-within-the-gates to victim and fool, the play isolates its moral indignation on Iago. Though in act 3 Othello joined his ancient in a brotherhood of murder, here the action severs Othello from Iago in our judgment and our eyesight. Emilia, the audience-surrogate, directs our attention to her husband: "You have done well, / That men must lay their murthers on your neck" (169–70). Emilia asks the quintessential question—"But did you ever tell him she was false?" (178)—though the question's very literalness (from the literal-minded Emilia) inevitably misses the quintessential truth, the synergy of the temptation scene. Even as Emilia announces the murder of Desdemona, she also rechannels audience attention to the unmasking of Iago: "My mistress here lies murthered in her bed— / . . . . And your reports have set the murder on" (185–87). Emilia likely will have crossed the stage toward Iago ("Disprove this villain . . ." [172]), who has just entered with Montano and Gratiano; Othello's lines position him near the bed. While Emilia on one part of the stage (perhaps centrally) contests her husband with impassioned heroism (190–97), Othello, on another part, commences to fall upon the bed in roaring desolation ("O, O, O!" [198]) and then to rise again in self-righteousness ("O, she was foul!" [200]). This is heady stuff, and the audience has the excited sense of leaping between two electrically charged currents. Not the least of these effects, the play successfully splinters Othello's fate from Iago's; their physical locations diverge on stage, and Iago no longer stands, quite, as the "explanation" of Othello.

In the denouement of *Othello,* characters—Emilia, Othello, and Iago—become less and less accessible by reference to each other; their juxtaposition renders them opaque. Much of the action of unraveling remains, perhaps for that very reason, emotionally external to the audience, something we observe as much as participate in. Part of this externalizing, distancing effect comes in the exposure of the mechanics of Othello's fall, for those characters who step forward with pieces of the truth focus the spectator's attention upon the action reduced to objects: the handkerchief, the letters in Roderigo's pockets. Indeed the handkerchief now cues Emilia's denunciation of Iago (214–22) and Othello's attempt on him (234–35). Othello will return to the handkerchief later with Cassio (319–23). Likewise, Lodovico pulls out one and then another of Roderigo's letters (with the casual information that Roderigo also has died twice), explaining to Othello, "Sir, you shall understand what hath befall'n, / Which, as I think, you know not" (307–8). Othello understand?—Right.

While Othello's responses may be passionate and spectacular, we scrutinize him for signs of self-realization, for acknowledgments of Desdemona. Othello's dialogue consists largely of self-extenuations and accusations ("She turn'd to folly, and she was a whore" [132]), outbursts of grief ("O, O, O!" [198]), or expressions of emasculation ("Man but a rush against Othello's breast, / And he retires" [270–71]). To grasp what Othello comes to understand, we might well turn to what Othello actually does. From his line "Peace, you were best!" (161) through the entrance of Gratiano, Montano, and Iago, through the announcement of Desdmona's murder, to his exchange with Gratiano ("O, she was foul!" [200ff.]) almost forty lines later, Othello has two lines: "Nay, stare not, masters, it is true indeed" (188) and "O, O, O!" (198). Emilia and Iago run with the dialogue; what behavior does the text invite from the Othello-actor? Othello becomes angered enough by Emilia to reach for his sword ("I care not for thy sword" [165]), but to Montano's greeting, "How now, general?" (168), he offers no verbal response. Later, as we have noted, he roars out and falls upon Desdemona's bed (198), then rises again to accuse her. Yet Othello's falling and rising happen in a private world of grief independent of the evolving conflict between ensign and wife. When Emilia exclaims, "O thou dull Moor" (225), she may be addressing not only his folly but a physical dullness at that moment, a remoteness, his mind "lost in thought." Othello's "O"s are the culmination, one might infer, of his intense concentration on the dead Desdemona. His comment to Gratiano and Montano, "Nay, stare not, masters," suggests that he remains physically close to the bed. Emilia's "I will ne'er go home" (197) may trigger a parallel recognition in Othello, and open the floodgates of his loss. Such distraction suggests Othello's earlier "wonder" at Desdemona, neutered into "perplexity." While the audience can watch Othello's face, however, it cannot precisely know his mind.

The bed exercises a magnetic, trancelike power over Othello, it attracts and holds him, vitiates him. As a prop, the bed stands out as unusual, perhaps unique, in the tragedies. It possesses an anthropomorphic presence quite beyond that of the other properties and settings of tragic endings—Claudius's throne or Juliet's tomb or Cleopatra's monument. Against the rushing of characters to and fro, the bed steadfastly keeps the stage.[13] It holds the pathetically dead Desdemona and draws more bodies to it. Ultimately the object acquires the potency to poison sight; it becomes the physical embodiment of *Othello*'s horror. As an object on stage, the bed appears in the last scene with a prior functional identity—a marriage bed—whose meaning then falls prey to corrosive amending by language and action. Because it will never lose its initial visual significance even as it becomes loaded with tragedy, the bed accumulates poignance, best realized on stage, from the tension between its pictorial form and the action debasing it.[14]

Othello's own fixation upon Desdemona's bed, furthermore, expresses a key facet of his character in the last scene. If the denouement of *Othello* as a whole tends, for the audience, to both sensationalize and externalize, one might say, too, that Othello's own mind moves to the rhythm of external objects present to sight or imagination. Othello's mind is much in the physical world. The abstract address and speculation of "To be or not to be" are not his idiom. In "It is the cause" (1–22), Othello, to have a voice, must locate something to address—first "my soul," then "you chaste stars," then the candle in his hand, then the sleeping Desdemona herself. Indeed, the very rhythm of his thought, its object-centeredness, as much as its particulars, brings him to the smell and touch of Desdemona. Othello must imagine an audience in order to speak. He relates directly with the world in its concreteness, discovering an immediate, external focus of attention, as the springboard to speech, self. Here Othello marks the sensibility toward which the audience itself evolves.

The power of the bed as the object of Othello's object-centered attention explains his collapse of valor in "Behold, I have a weapon" (259–82). "Be not afraid," he says to Gratiano, "Here is my journey's end, here is my butt / And very sea-mark of my utmost sail" (266–68). Destination, target, and peninsula: they are the bed, whose sight (recollections of his arrival at Cyprus) melts Othello's martial resolve. The bed across the stage, indeed, is where Othello goes in asking "Where should Othello go?" (271). He addresses Desdemona externally: "Now—how dost thou look now? . . . / Pale as thy smock!" (272–73); he seems to touch her, "Cold, cold, my girl? / Even like thy chastity" (275–76). Her deathly beauty haunts him: "Whip me, ye devils, / From the possession of this heavenly sight" (277–78). The audience desires in Othello an appreciation of Desdemona's virtue commensurate with his earlier dread imaginings, something beyond the material reductiveness of "cold as thy chastity." The play denies us this public recognition, in the way that it consistently keeps obscure Othello's self-realizations. Yet in its stead the denouement provides a passionate, harrowing expression of utter loss from a soul that knows itself largely by knowing the material world around it: "O Desdemon! dead, Desdemon, dead / O! O!" (281–82). Perhaps the most telling moment in the scene comes when Othello feels Desdemona's still flesh—"cold"—a gesture that can unnerve members of the audience and illuminate the physical separateness of Othello inside his grief.

Othello is rich in such great theater (and it is no surprise that historically the more successful Othello-actors have been, like

Kean and Salvini, the more passionate). The ending of *Othello,* like other of its moments, those dealing with witchcraft or the hand-kerchief, for example, invests the physical universe with a preter-natural power (here realized in the bed and Iago's demonism). That primitivism enhances the ending's sensational immediacy and its mystery. The dialogue's hints for the stage movement of the Othello-actor suggest, as well, a kind of physical possession. While he will stand almost entranced for one or two intervals, Othello's language at other times invites convulsive movement by the actor, as if "driven": "Whip me, ye devils . . . Blow me about in winds! roast me in sulphur! / Wash me in steep-down gulfs of liquid fire!" (277–80). Beyond Othello's frozen concentration on the bed, the scene's imagery and kinetics project him as whipped, blown, washed, and hurtled about from revelation to revelation, passion to passion, falling on Desdemona's bed, rising to accuse her, rushing at Iago, attempting an escape, collapsing again at the sight of Desde-mona, recovering himself before Lodovico, wounding Iago, crying out at each new unraveling of the details of villainy, berating him-self, gathering together every ounce of heroic composure for the valediction. If not a noble Moor, he is certainly a busy Moor, and one is not surprised that even Eliot and Leavis acknowledge the audience-winning high theater of the last speech. Such action in-vites broad acting, and the ending of *Othello* strikes me as highly gestural, successfully "presentational." Desdemona's killing may anticipate what comes later. There Othello rolls his eyes mur-derously (37–38) and gnaws his nether lip (43); his whole frame shakes with bloody passion (44); he loses his temper (79). Othello's violent jealousy likely called for highly conventionalized, histrionic Elizabethan acting, corresponding in many details to Burton's cata-loguing of the jealous humor, much grimacing and agitation.[15] Act-ing, indeed, marks Othello's career in the play. The general, so self-possessed in the play's opening acts—"Keep up your bright swords, for the dew will rust them" (1.2.59)—now behaves as if possessed himself. The externalizing of Othello's passion launches consider-able kinesthetic excitement at the audience, a volley of sympathetic muscular sensations crying for relief. These emotional gestures succeed in engaging the spectator, just as the denouement as a whole can absorb us and yet block the door to Othello's or Iago's psyche.

Acting obscures psychological action to greatest effect in Othello's valediction. The speech comes as an afterthought, for Othello has already been invited to one self-summation: "O thou Othello, that was once so good, / . . . . What shall be said to thee?"

(291–93). The parade of shocks and revelations now seems halted. Cassio ties up the loose ends of Iago's machinations. Lodovico (like the Albanys and Malcolms) lays our expectations to rest by telling us what will come next and directing the characters off stage. But Othello forestalls that exit, that version of the end: "Soft you; a word or two before you go" (338). He must call us back into his own play. He faces now the dramatic predicament of his identity ("That's he that was Othello; here I am" [284]). The psychological action of his suicide speech will be his reconstruction and commemoration of himself, the regaining of his "occupation." The speech is both grand and incoherent. While Othello calls for reportage in the plain style—"Speak of me as I am; nothing extenuate" (342)—he will instead present himself indirectly through simile and analogy. He aspires to a prelapsarian idealized self. Though Othello has, moments before, imagined himself as victim of a fate beyond his control and still considers himself "unlucky" (341)—ill fortune is an interpretation that Othello repeats early and late in the scene[16]— he now lays claim to his atrocities. In doing so, his valediction runs counter to the patronizing of his folly sounded by Emilia and Lodovico. For here, finally, Othello assumes his double role as both Bradleyan victim and Leavisian victimizer:

> And say besides, that in Aleppo once,
> Where a malignant and a turban'd Turk
> Beat a Venetian and traduc'd the state,
> I took by th' throat the circumcised dog,
> And smote him—thus.
>
> (352–56)

Those lines are the play's most striking effort to resolve the conflict of "judgments" between acts 3 and 5, for the self-distancing language and the action make Othello both wrongdoer and the party wronged.

But Othello presents himself as a sinner twice, in metaphors that divide rather than unify our understanding. Though one vision is of the malignant, violent, and blasphemous Turk, the other is

> of one whose hand,
> Like the base Indian, threw a pearl away
> Richer than all his tribe; of one whose subdu'd eyes,
> Albeit unused to the melting mood,
> Drops tears as fast as the Arabian trees
> Their medicinable gum.
>
> (346–51)

The base Indian recalls for us the unworldly savage, the natural man too naive and unsophisticated to recognize the pearl of civilized value.[17] This image evokes, as does the Arabian-tree-like mourner, a passionate and unaffected simplicity.[18] Indian and mourner suggest the innocence of ignorance. But that innocence contradicts rather than supports the image of the malignant Turk, who is evil by nature.[19] These two opposite representations of Othello stand side by side, joined by proximity, if not by logic. Indeed, the rhetoric of Othello's last speech tries simply to have it both ways, making him too innocent to be evil and too evil to be innocent.

Othello's valediction sounds narrated, "written." Leavis found in it the "self-dramatizing trick" marking Othello's egotism, failure of self-comprehension, and sentimentality ("an attitude *towards* the emotion expressed").[20] Leavis's objections are essentially moral. Differently, how does the valediction play as acting, the self-dramatization as drama? Othello himself performs a species of acting. He must die publicly: the nature of Othello's self is that it requires an external point of reference—an object, an audience—to reveal itself. Othello will say, then, what the presence of an audience most invites; his personality will tilt emotion toward oratory, self-revelation toward rhetoric. Othello speaks as a reporter to other reporters (or a priest at a funeral), objectifying himself as an absent third party: "Then must you speak / Of one . . . Of one . . . Of one . . . Set you down this" (343–51). The manner is descriptive (the evening news) rather than expressive, the acting presentational rather than representational. "Of one that loved not wisely, but too well" may tip off the audience in the theater that Othello will construct his persona as he memorializes it. The final gesture of suicide, the closing of acting into action, the sudden leap across the paradox of re/presentation, thrills the audience with its heroism. At the same time, however, the gesture argues that all that preceded it was contrived for this *coup de théâtre;* the moment of realism reconfirms our sense of artifice and trickery. The suicide, then, is inescapably double-edged, both authentic and manipulated.

Thus the spectator may make a double response to Othello's valediction, feeling first with Gratiano that "All that is spoke is marr'd" (357), alternately with Cassio that "he was great of heart" (361), and back again with Lodovico that "The object poisons sight" (364). The audience watches Othello imaginatively create himself in the valediction; heretofore he has simply inhabited the heroic self already created.[21] The speech may be the play's ultimate instance of the divided response, for it detaches the spectators, in reaction to the sentimental, self-serving, and presentational in

Othello, at the same time that it engages them in the heroism of his self-fashioning. What ought to conceal, also reveals. Our experience may be not unlike the awe and doubt of Othello's own lost wonder. The valediction charms the audience on a second level, too, for it occasions an actorly tour de force and a spectatorial pleasure in the virtuosic delivery of vivid language, passionate tears, and the niftiest suicide in Shakespeare. Even Leavis could not resist the vicarious thrill of such a great actorly event: "Who does not (in some moments) readily see himself as the hero of such a *coup de théâtre?*"[22] While Othello's suicide speech is teasingly problematic as a dramatic action, it is irresistible as acting, the "presentation" serving up the delight of the deeper "representation."

The denouement of *Othello*—its various "judgments," switched focuses, kinesthetics of delay, and visual isolations, all culminating in the hero's valediction—challenges the watcher with the difficulty of sense-making. The very spectacle keeps its characters at a distance from the audience, the chug of passion, action, and change seldom deviating into explanation. Perhaps the most sweeping effect of the ending is to structure the spectator's consciousness ultimately like Othello's: the play comes in its details, its objectness, its concrete otherness, always opaque. Inside this consciousness, we experience not so much understanding as the presences and absences by which we know its "world," where the fullest acknowledgment must be only the most sensate: "dead, Desdemon! dead! / O, O!" Spectatorship of *Othello* finally turns Othello-like, and the progressive unfolding of *how* onlookers know the play brings them deeper into a perspective analogous to that of the protagonist. Renaissance audiences—who, it is sometimes argued, favored spectacle and pathos as against realism, psychology, and "interpretation"—may have been more pleased with *Othello* than are some of their modern heirs. In the twentieth century, we find frustrating the play's and the hero's final inscrutability. Perhaps that unease tells us how we moderns experience drama. Michael Goldman observes that "Action is a notion that allows us to think of a person as having what he does."[23] The tragic protagonist possesses his or her world through action. For the theatrical audience, empathy provides a groundwork of interest, a calling, while the creative insight of detachment completes the possessing a play. Spectators make the tragedy most fully their own in the action of interpretation—as Othello comes in his valediction to possess himself. *Othello*'s sensationalism arouses, through a form of deferral, the audience's longing to understand. That spectatorial experience can confer a certain liberty, a discovery of choice. *Othello* works to enlarge its spectators by re-creating Othello's most noble perspective inside their own, yet provoking, too, the comprehension, exceeding any inside the play, of what it means to be Othello.

NOTES

1. See Patricia Parker, "Shakespeare and Rhetoric: 'dilation' and 'delation' in *Othello*," in *Shakespeare and the Question of Theory,* ed. Patricia Parker and Geoffrey Hartman (New York: Methuen, 1985), pp. 54–74.

2. Maynard Mack, "Engagement and Detachment in Shakespeare's Plays," in *Essays on Shakespeare and Elizabethan Drama in Honor of Hardin Craig,* ed. Richard Hosley (Columbia: University of Missouri Press, 1962), pp. 275–96. For Bullough's groundbreaking discussion of "distance" as an aesthetic principle, see " 'Psychical Distance' as a Factor in Art and an Aesthetic Principle," *British Journal of Psychology* 5 (1912): 87–118; repr. in Edward Bullough, *Aesthetics: Lectures and Essays,* ed. Elizabeth M. Wilkinson (Westport, Conn.: Greenwood Press, 1977), pp. 91–130.

3. Mack, "Engagement and Detachment in Shakespeare's Plays," p. 276.

4. J. L. Styan, *Drama, Stage and Audience* (Cambridge: Cambridge University Press, 1975), p. 228.

5. Gamini Salgado, *Eyewitnesses to Shakespeare: First Hand Accounts of Performances 1590–1890* (London: Sussex University Press, 1975), pp. 30, 49; Thomas Rymer, *A Short View of Tragedy* (London, 1693); repr. in Curt Zimansky, ed., *The Critical Works of Thomas Rymer* (New Haven: Yale University Press, 1956), pp. 132–64.

6. For an unusually stimulating essay which, by comparing historical performances, illuminates many of the clues to staging and audience response embedded in Shakespeare's text, see James R. Siemon, " 'Nay, that's not next': *Othello,* V.ii in Performance, 1760–1900," *Shakespeare Quarterly* 37 (Spring 1986): 38–51.

7. By "presentational" I mean "formal" acting, the "large" style, with an emphasis on gestures or actions that point at the fact of acting itself, announcing emotions rather than simply expressing them. By "representational" I mean "naturalistic" acting, "doing" rather than stating or describing the emotion. Presentational acting tends to detach the audience, representational acting to engage it.

8. A. C. Bradley, *Shakespearean Tragedy* (London: Macmillan and Co., 1904), pp. 169–98; F. R. Leavis, "Diabolical Intellect and the Noble Hero," *The Common Pursuit* ([1952] repr., New York: New York University Press, 1964), pp. 136–59; and T. S. Eliot, "Shakespeare and the Stoicism of Seneca," in *Selected Essays 1917–1932* (London: Faber and Faber, 1932), pp. 129–31.

9. T. S. Eliot, "Shakespeare and the Stoicism of Seneca," pp. 130–31.

10. For a very recent "lexical" study of *Othello,* see Martin Elliott, *Shakespeare's Invention of Othello: A Study in Early Modern English* (London: Macmillan Press, 1988). Elliott examines "wrought" and "perplexed" similarly to the treatment here, with Othello imaging himself as the handiwork and at least partial victim of the artificer Iago, his words suggesting a passive view of himself and his actions. See pp. 82–83.

11. I take this term from E. A. J. Honigmann, *Shakespeare: Seven Tragedies: The Dramatist's Manipulation of Response* (London: Macmillan, 1976), pp. 27–28.

12. Emilia's exposure of Othello also raises response issues of social class. The plebian members of a Jacobean audience, for example, might have reacted quite differently to her exposure of this upper-class general than would one of Shakespeare's "privileged playgoers."

13. For the argument that the bed was not contained within the "discovery space" of the Elizabethan stage, but was "thrust out," or carried forward, onto the stage, see Richard Hosley, "The Staging of Desdemona's Bed," *Shakespeare Quarterly* 14 (Winter 1963): 57–65.

14. For a discussion of dramatic tension between picture and language, see Bert O. States, *Great Reckonings in Little Rooms: On the Phenomenology of Theater* (Berkeley: University of California Press, 1985), pp. 53–54.

15. Daniel Seltzer, "Elizabethan Acting in *Othello*," *Shakespeare Quarterly* 10 (Spring 1959): 201–10.

16. I.e., "It is the very error of the moon, / She comes more nearer earth than she was wont, / And makes men mad" (109–11); "Who can control his fate?" (265); "O ill-starr'd wench" (272).

17. I accept, as do most editors of *Othello*, "Indian" as opposed to "Iudean." For a summary of the problem, see Norman Sanders, ed., *Othello* (Cambridge: Cambridge University Press, 1984), pp. 191–92.

18. Sanders, in the New Cambridge *Othello*, pp. 191–92, prefers a reading of 'base' as low in rank or in the order of creation, rather than as 'vile.' M. R. Ridley, editor of the New Arden *Othello* (London: Methuen, 1958), notes 348–49, pp. 195–96, follows a similar line, suggesting that Othello's image parallels "a current traveller's tale of an Indian who, in ignorance of its value, threw away a priceless pearl."

19. For the view that sees the Turk and the base Indian/Judean as connotatively similar, see, for example, Alvin Kernan, ed., *Othello* ([1963] repr., New York: Signet, 1987), p. xxxiii.

20. Leavis, "Diabolical Intellect and the Noble Hero," p. 143.

21. For an illuminating discussion of Othello in this regard, see Michael Goldman, *Acting and Action in Shakespearean Tragedy* (Princeton: Princeton University Press, 1985), pp. 62–70.

22. Leavis, "Diabolical Intellect and the Noble Hero," p. 153.

23. Goldman, *Acting and Action in Shakespearean Tragedy,* p. 7.

9
Objects in *Othello*

FRANCES TEAGUE

BACKGROUND

When Shakespeareans examine the plays in terms of the theater, rather than the library, they have traditionally turned to records of specific productions. In the past, performance history has often enriched critical understanding of a play like *Othello*.[1] A recent approach that is also rooted in the theater might be called performance criticism, rather than history. Performance criticism tries to provide insight into the plays as art processes (rather than art objects). During the past twenty years, such stage theorists as Beckerman, Styan, Dessen, Slater, and Bevington have taught scholars how to understand the dynamics of Shakespearean performance and to read the signals placed inside the text by Shakespeare and his company. By analyzing such nonverbal art, Shakespeareans learn *how* things mean—how the actions or gestures of a play may be vehicles of meaning just as surely as the verbal text is.

I have been working on the properties that Shakespearean text specifies—trying to answer the question of why the property lists for quarto and folio texts vary, for example, or how one might translate what Bevington has called "the language of . . . hand properties."[2] In my work I have noticed that the canon uses properties in certain characteristic ways; taking *Othello* as my example, I will describe some of those techniques: time-place marking, symbolic infusion, presentational imagery, and deliberately ambiguous meaning. (A property list for the play is given at the end of this chapter.)

TIME-PLACE MARKERS

One way that a Shakespearean play often uses properties is to signal where a scene is set in time or place. In *Othello,* the action occurs in two settings: first Venice, then Cyprus; furthermore, the play compresses time to suggest that events are moving too quickly to be controlled. The problems of double time are easily stated: Othello should be far more skeptical about Iago's charges if the action only occupies a few days, for how could Desdemona have found the leisure to go to Cyprus for an adulterous affair?[3] *Othello* uses properties, particularly the light and document properties, to establish both the divided place setting and the dual time scheme. Such time-place markers often work on several levels.

The place markers take a number of forms, the most obvious being the play's document properties. Letters arrive in 1.3, 3.2, 4.1, and 5.2. While the last set of letters simply ties up loose ends in the plot, the others keep up communication between Venice and Cyprus, allowing characters in one setting (and the audience) to know what is happening elsewhere. (Another document property, the proclamation in 2.2, seems to exist solely for expository purposes.) The letters have structural importance as well: on three occasions, the letters signal a critical point in Othello's marriage and a turning point in the action. Like messengers in Greek plays, the letters in *Othello* suggest to the audience a change in direction—even before their message is heard. In dramatic convention, a letter is a visual signal not only of a report, but also for a shift that is usually of crucial consequence. Thus the senators' consideration of the letters from Cyprus helps ensure that they will approve Othello's match with Desdemona because they need his help. When Lodovico brings letters from Venice in 4.1, Othello strikes Desdemona, the first open break between them. Finally, the letters found on Roderigo's corpse help Othello "understand what hath befall'n" to make him betray himself (5.2.307).

In addition to the documents, the place markers include the stage properties of the Senate table and Desdemona's bed, which establish that certain scenes are set indoors.[4] That latter property marks both time and place, as do the nightgowns,[5] which indicate both that a scene occurs at night and that characters are indoors rather than out-of-doors. None of these properties does as much to indicate time, however, as the light properties do.

The play specifies torches in act 1 to establish the night setting, no torches or lights in acts 2 through 4 since most of that action is set in the day, and lights for the act 5 night setting. (Although no lights are specified in the drinking scene, 2.3, the text repeatedly refers to night.) In other words, the light properties combine with the verbal text to suggest that the action lasts only three nights and two days, though no indication is given that this time is consecutive.

Like the letters, the light properties not only help establish time-place settings but also have other functions. The torches, lanterns, and candles signal a nighttime setting as well as providing visual reinforcement for the play's pattern of verbal light-dark imagery. As Rosenberg writes:

> The light and dark playing against each other in *Othello* give a special molding to the tensions of action and character: the black or tawny Moor in the white robe; the dark lover, the white bride; shadowy evening, full of passion, conflict, or violence closing in on the day. . . . At the Globe, of an afternoon, it took a word and the flicker of a torch or candle to make darkness of daylight in the minds of an audience; but in indoor theaters, and in the Globe at night, there was perhaps some use of ambient darkness to shadow the play's emotional conflicts.[6]

And a number of critics have discussed the stage darkness as a literal representation of the metaphoric confusion in act 5.[7]

SYMBOLIC INFUSION

One light property is particularly important, for it not only signals a time setting but also becomes infused with symbolic meaning by the language that Othello uses. This property is the light that Othello carries when he comes to Desdemona, saying "put out the light, and then put out the light" (5.2.7). However one punctuates this line,[8] the equation between Othello's light and Desdemona's life is clear. As in Macbeth's famous speech, life is like a brief candle, easily extinguished. John Styan describes one path by which this time-place marker acquires symbolic force:

> . . . the actor takes up the taper which is at once to mark the dead of night and the Moor's impulse to offer prayer, and its visual suggestion of light and darkness becomes associated with the issue of the life and death of a Christian soul and the murder of a young woman in her vital beauty:
>
> But once put out thy light,
> Thou cunning'st pattern of excelling nature,

I know not where is that Promethean heat
That can thy light relume.

(5.2.10–13)

This taper makes of her death-bed a sacrificial altar, one upon which man's love of life and hope of heaven are annihilated.[9]

Othello associates Desdemona's brief life, her ardent love, and her fragile beauty with the light that he carries. The audience accepts his equation in part because his language justifies it, in part because torches have, throughout the play's first act, appeared in association with discussions of Desdemona and her marriage to Othello. (Torches and lights are specified at 1.1.160, 1.2.1, 29, 55, and 1.3.1; this association of torches and Desdemona's marriage may be an ironic version of the conventions of epithalamia.) In a manner of speaking, the audience has been trained to link the appearance of a light property with discussions of Desdemona's character (discussions that have usually misassessed her worth). The violence in 2.2 and 5.1 establishes a second, more ominous association: in this play, lights appear when violence occurs. Violent acts take place in a dark setting, although staged in the afternoon on an open-air stage. During the closing nighttime scene, the appearance of the light offers a presentational image cluster. The light property is associated both with Desdemona and with violence by means of Othello's speech, so that the central symbolic representation of Desdemona's murder becomes the light.

ANOTHER GROUP

The weapons, like documents or lights, stand out because there are many of them. In part, of course, weapons are common because this play is a violent one. Furthermore, the swords are tokens of identity—men who wear these weapons are soldiers, and *Othello* is a play about wartime. One function that the weapons serve, then, is to tell the audience what kind of play this is. They also function to help create Othello's character.

Paradoxically, although Othello is a soldier, his stature is conveyed by his refusal to display a weapon in the opening scenes. Every other character—even the civilian Brabantio—waves a sword around, but Othello never displays his. Indeed when Othello tells Brabantio and his party, "Keep up your bright swords, for the dew will rust them. . . . / Were it my cue to fight, I should have known it / Without a prompter" (1.2.59, 83–84), he shows the attitude of the professional soldier. As Norman Sanders says, this speech shows Othello's "crushing scorn of civilian streetbrawlers."[10] Swords are phallic; when every male carries and displays a sword, Othello's refusal is either a sign of emasculation or of strength (one recalls Gary Cooper in *High Noon*). As Othello's speech before the Senate reveals, he is an exemplary soldier and a model wooer, both roles that suggest his masculine potency. The duke tells Brabantio to make the best of his daughter's match because Othello has conquered him (Brabantio) and broken his weapon.

> Good Brabantio,
> Take up this mangled matter at the best;
> Men do their broken weapons rather use,
> Than their bare hands.
>
> (1.3.172–75)

But the comment is double-edged: Othello is not as good as a whole weapon; Brabantio must make do with his daughter's choice. It is also ironic: unlike most men, Othello prefers to use his bare hands instead of a weapon, broken or not, when he kills his wife.

Throughout the play, Othello commands easily without displaying a weapon, although every other major male character draws a sword or rapier. When he does finally use weapons, he is weakest, furthest from his identity as a soldier. As Dessen has pointed out, in act 5 he cannot use weapons successfully because "Othello's occupation's gone" (3.3.357):

> . . . Othello, who once might have triumphed over "more impediments / Than twenty times your stop," now twice loses his weapon to lesser men (including Montano, one of the figures controlled by the Moor in 2.3). In terms of the imagistic or symbolic progression, Othello at this point has lost his occupation, destroyed the best part of himself, and extinguished the light within, so that his sword, formerly the expression of his stature and strength, has become subject to "every puny whipster."[11]

Yet he remains in the end a soldier who manages to reach three weapons despite the attempts to disarm him. They are his tools; though he has said farewell to his occupation, he still retains enough power as a soldier and as a man to produce more weapons than any other character does.[12]

MULTIPLE MEANINGS

While the weapons are probably the most important category of property because of what they tell the audience about Othello's character, Desdemona's handkerchief, inherently a trivial object, is the play's single most important property. It is also the hardest to understand: "the handkerchief, so emotionally loaded by Othello, is simultaneously the precious gift to Desdemona and yet a trifle light as air . . . which Cassio's possession transforms into what it is not."[13] Characters talk repeatedly about the handkerchief, investing it with emblematic and symbolic meaning throughout the play. The first way to understand it is as an index to character. Thus Othello speaks of its magic:

> That handkerchief
> Did an Egyptian to my mother give;
> She was a charmer, and could almost read
> The thoughts of people. She told her, while she kept it,
> 'Twould make her amiable, and subdue my father
> Entirely to her love; but if she lost it,
> Or made a gift of it, my father's eye
> Should hold her loathed, and his spirits should hunt
> After new fancies. She, dying, gave it me,
> And bid me, when my fate would have me wiv'd,
> To give it her. . . .
> . . . there's magic in the web of it.
> A sibyl, that had numbr'ed in the world
> The sun to course two hundred compasses,
> In her prophetic fury sew'd the work;
> The worms were hallowed that did breed the silk,
> And it was dy'd in mummy which the skillful
> Conserv'd of maidens' hearts.
>
> (3.4.55–65, 69–74)

To Othello the piece of cloth represents his life. He regards the handkerchief as a symbol of himself, a self that he has given into Desdemona's keeping. Standing in place of his parents' marriage and its product, himself, the handkerchief has the magic to maintain his own marriage.

Desdemona, of course, understands the handkerchief differently. To her it signals her husband's sudden shift in behavior:

> *Emil.* Is not this man jealous?
> *Des.* I nev'r saw this before.

> Sure, there's some wonder in this handkerchief;
> I am most unhappy in the loss of it.

(3.4.99–102)

Having heard Othello's account of the handkerchief's power, Desdemona initially reacts by rejecting what she hears, for she fears its importance and his jealousy:

> *Des.* I' faith! is't true?
> *Oth.* Most veritable, therefore look to't well.
> *Des.* Then would to God that I had never seen't!

(3.4.75–77)

When she says this, Desdemona rejects the terrible power that Othello claims for the handkerchief, but Othello thinks she rejects the handkerchief itself and thus symbolically rejects him. Later he inverts this rejection by equating the handkerchief not with himself but with his wife's honor:

> *Iago.* . . . But if I give my wife a handkerchief—
> *Oth.* What then?
> *Iago.* Why then 'tis hers, my lord, and being hers,
> She may, I think, bestow't on any man.
> *Oth.* She is protectress of her honour too;
> May she give that?

(4.1.10–15)

If, as Othello implies, Desdemona's honor and her handkerchief are the same, then either loss or rejection has the same alienating effect. He and Desdemona both understand something different by the piece of cloth, a difference in understanding that helps precipitate their tragedy.

Another way of understanding the handkerchief is emblematically, as a Renaissance viewer might have recognized. The handkerchief is "spotted with strawberries" (3.3.435), the fruit sometimes used in emblem books to signal treachery because serpents hide beneath the attractive leaves to poison any unwary person who picks the sweet berries. Shakespeare knew the emblem: he uses strawberries not only in this play, but also in *Richard III*, when the Bishop of Ely is sent away to fetch strawberries before Richard betrays Hastings. Like Richard, Iago is treacherous. He uses the attractive appearance of an honest soldier to conceal the poison of his nature; specifically, he uses the pretty handkerchief to deceive Othello and destroy his happiness.

Yet one other way of understanding the handkerchief is neither as a symbol of Othello or his jealousy nor as an emblem of treachery, but as a genuinely magic web. Once Desdemona loses Othello's handkerchief, the charm is broken and their marriage has been lost. Thus it is futile for Desdemona to try to deny Othello's accusations, just as it is pathetic when she asks Emilia to make the bed with her wedding sheets. The sibyl's curse already lies over her marriage: no matter what Desdemona says or does, Othello's eye "should hold her loathed" (3.4.62). In this case, the property of the handkerchief has neither symbolic nor emblematic value, but instead signals literally tragic enchantment. The symbolic property in this reading is the wedding sheet. A wedding sheet is inherently symbolic of the bride's virginity, of course, but in the context of this play, the wedding sheet becomes another version of the handkerchief. Each is a white cloth stained or spotted with red and associated with Desdemona's honor as a wife. In the last scene the bed with its wedding sheets is a sign of marriage destroyed by false suspicion. Othello vows, "Thy bed, lust-stain'd, shall with lust's blood be spotted" (5.1.36); and indeed, the nuptial bed, which Othello imagines the virtuous Desdemona has betrayed, becomes a deathbed for them both.

Desdemona's handkerchief, like Richard II's mirror or Yorick's skull, is one of a small group of properties in Shakespeare's canon that become so heavily loaded with meanings that no one can specify which meaning is "correct" at any given moment. But each play handles the various levels of meaning differently. In *Hamlet,* the property of the skull accretes meaning during the graveyard scene. No symbolic value is lost as the scene progresses; instead the meaning deepens so that the skull transcends the conventional symbolism of the *memento mori.* In *Othello,* however, the handkerchief has a range of potential meanings that are mutually exclusive: symbol of self or of jealousy, emblem of treachery, and literal magic token. The play denies none of these meanings, but it does not specify one either. The meaning of the handkerchief is kept deliberately ambiguous.

IMPLICATIONS

I have tried to show that it can be useful to examine an isolated element of production, like property use, even though little is known about the actual conditions of performance on Shakespeare's stage. The instances of Desdemona's handkerchief or Othello's candle suggest one reason for undertaking this kind of study. The plays have a few properties that are so powerful that they actually transcend meaning. James Siemon has argued that such transcendence is more common in Shakespeare's plays than critics have realized; his view is supported by examining the objects that are invested so richly with meaning.[14] But it is hardly original to notice properties of such obvious importance; what could be useful, however, is to look at each as part of a group. Such an analysis demonstrates how a property's meaning depends both on its immediate context and on the way in which similar properties appear. In the case of the light that Othello carries in act 5, for example, the property gains one meaning from his speech, but a rather different meaning from the way it operates as one of a series of light properties. It may also draw on associations established in other plays: the candle in *Macbeth,* for example, or the little candle Portia sees at the end of *The Merchant of Venice*. Although the handkerchief does not fit into a category of properties in quite the same way, there is some congruence between the handkerchief and the wedding sheets; other important handkerchiefs are the bloody napkins that serve as frightening tokens of identity in *3 Henry VI* and *As You Like It*. To study property use in Shakespeare's plays is to recognize how much of a theatrical craftsman he was. The examples of the weapons and the torches demonstrate that he had an intense awareness of how stage business works and of how to use it to best effect. (Another piece of business that depends on properties occurs in 3.1, but I lack the space to discuss the way that the bagpipes parody associations between lovemaking and music or draw on charivari conventions.) Critics have complained of *Othello* as a play that suffers from too many loose ends in its plotting, but it has no such loose ends in its theatrical structure. Instead the play shows deliberate placement and patterning of such properties and costumes as lights, letters, nightgowns, and weapons in acts 1 and 5.

Indeed, if one looks at the play's property list and at which properties are most frequent, it becomes clear that acts 1 and 5 have been made parallel, at least in terms of properties. At the beginning and end of the play, actors often use properties, and those properties are apt to be weapons, lights, or documents. In acts 2, 3, and 4, actors use relatively few properties, which fall into no particular category. That finding in turn raises a question. Some scholars have argued that the composition of the play was interrupted. While motivations and plot elements may be inconsistent between acts 1 and 5, however, the property use is both consistent and consciously patterned in these acts. How should one reconcile the inconsistency of Cassio's marital status and Iago's motives with the consistency shown in displays of nightgowns or weapons?

Traditionally, Shakespeareans have welcomed theater history because an account of a significant performance can reveal fresh meaning in a play like *Othello*. The way an actor like Olivier or Robeson says a line or walks across a stage can enlighten an audience, helping it to understand who Othello is and why he behaves as he does. If performance history is worthy of one's consideration, so too is performance criticism. An analysis of the performance elements in a play can reveal that the playwright planned more deliberately than scholars had realized, creating powerful structures that went unnoticed before.

NOTES

1. The New Cambridge edition of *Othello* gives a good brief stage history: ed. Norman Sanders (Cambridge: Cambridge University Press, 1984), pp. 37–51. Several books illuminate the production work of particular artists: Kenneth Tynan, *"Othello": The National Theatre Production* (New York: Stein and Day, 1966), discusses Olivier; Arthur Colby Sprague, *Shakespearian Players and Performances* (Cambridge: Harvard University Press, 1953). Edmund Kean and Edwin Booth; and Constantin Stanislavsky, *Stanislavsky Produces "Othello,"* trans. Helen Nowak (London: Geoffrey Bles, 1948), his own production. Two books describe how performance both shapes and is shaped by criticism: Carol Jones Carlisle, *Shakespeare from the Greenroom* (Chapel Hill: University of North Carolina Press, 1969); Marvin Rosenberg, *The Masks of "Othello"* (Berkeley: University of California Press, 1961). James L. Calderwood's *The Properties of "Othello"* (Amherst: University of Massachusetts Press, 1989) is concerned with property as ownership, not as an object in performance.

2. David Bevington, *Action is Eloquence: Shakespeare's Language of Gesture* (Cambridge: Harvard University Press, 1984), p. 35.

3. Good summaries of the problem may be found in the New Cambridge edition, pp. 14–16, and in the Arden edition of *Othello*, ed. M. R. Ridley (1958; rev. London: Methuen, 1964), pp. lxvii–lxx (hereafter cited as Arden).

4. Lawrence Ross, "The Use of a 'Fit-Up' Booth in *Othello*," *Shakespeare Quarterly* 12 (1961): 359–70, argues that the bed "brings the locale of a bedroom with it, by implication," p. 362; Richard Hosley, "The Staging of Desdemona's Bed," *Shakespeare Quarterly* 14 (1963): 57–65, also implicitly discusses the bed's function as a place marker.

5. Alan C. Dessen, *Elizabethan Stage Conventions and Modern Interpreters* (London: Cambridge University Press, 1984), has some useful comments on what the nightgowns mean—"unreadiness, vulnerability" (48)—and how they link 1.1, 2.3, and 5.2. Obviously the costumes and properties function in similar ways, but because my space is limited, I shall omit discussion of costuming.

6. Rosenberg, *The Masks of "Othello,"* p. 230.

7. Dessen, for example, *Elizabethan Stage Conventions,* pp. 80–83.

8. One may punctuate the repeated phrase as declarative or interrogative (i.e., "Put out the light, and then—Put out the light?"); see Ridley's discussion in the Arden edition, p. 177.

9. J. L. Styan, *Shakespeare's Stagecraft* (Cambridge: Cambridge University Press, 1967), p. 33; Alan Dessen has a similar reading, as does Ann Pasternak Slater, *Shakespeare the Director* (Sussex: Harvester Press, 1982).

10. Sanders, *Othello,* p. 22.

11. Dessen, *Elizabethan Stage Conventions,* p. 119.

12. In Olivier's production, he turned the final embrace with Desdemona into the opportunity to cut his throat; that soldier, when his weapons were taken away, could create weapons from decoration. Kenneth Tynan, *"Othello": The National Theatre Production,* shows performance photographs of the moment, pp. 94–95.

13. Sanders, *Othello,* p. 33. Robert H. Heilman, *Magic in the Web: Action and Language in "Othello"* (Lexington: University Press of Kentucky, 1956) offers a good discussion of the range of meaning that the handkerchief has, although his critical approach is to try to fix rather than to diffuse meaning.

14. James Siemon, *Shakespearean Iconoclasm* (Berkeley: University of California Press, 1984).

PROPERTIES IN *OTHELLO*

List omits sound effects (such as the bell) and references to peripheral stage areas (such as the bulk). The following abbreviations apply: l = light; w = weapon; d = document; r = riches; o = other; * = prop omitted in this text.

Kind	Folio	Quarto	Riverside	Property
o	*	B3r	1.1.160	Brabantio's gown
l	0175	B3r	1.1.160	torches
l	0203	B3v	1.2.1	more torches
l	0233	B4r	1.2.29	more torches
l	*	B4r	*	other lights
l	0269	B4v	1.2.55	lights
w	*	B4v	1.2.55	weapons
w	0276	B4v	1.2.59	swords
o	*	C1r	1.3.1	table
l	*	C1r	1.3.1	lights
d	0327	C1r	1.3.3	letters
d	0328	C1r	1.3.4	more letters
d	0329	C1r	1.3.4	more letters
d	1097	E3r	2.2.1	proclamation
o	1141	E3v	2.3.30	stoup of wine
o	1182	E4r	2.3.69	canikins
w	*	F1r	2.3.164	weapons
w	1348	F2r	2.3.227	Cassio's sword
o	1518	F4r	3.1.1	bagpipes
r	1529	F4v	3.1.11	money
r	1543	F4v	3.1.24	gold piece
d	1581	G1r	3.2.1	Othello's letters to Senate
o	1920	H1v	3.3.28	Des.'s handkerchief
o	2198	H4v	3.4.52	another handkerchief
d	2607	K2r	4.1.218	senator's letters to Oth.
r	2793	K4r	4.2.93	money
o	2990	L2v	4.3.21	pins (for hair?) jewelry
w	3084	L3r	5.1.2	Roderigo's rapier
w	3109	L3v	5.1.26	Cassio's sword
l	3138	L3v	5.1.47	Iago's light
w	3139	L3v	5.1.47	Iago's weapon
o	3184	*	5.1.82	garter
l	3190	L4v	5.1.88	another light
o	3203	L4v	5.1.98	chair
l	*	M1r	5.2.1	light
o	3239	M1r	5.2.1	bed with curtains
w	3442	M3v	5.2.165	Othello's sword
w	3515	M4r	5.2.224	Iago's sword
w	3553	M4v	5.2.254	Othello's second sword
d	3614	N1v	5.2.308	Roderigo's letter
d	3616	N1v	5.2.310	Roderigo's second letter
d	3621	N1v	5.2.314	Roderigo's third letter
w	3667	N2r	5.2.356	Othello's dagger

Total: 36 in F, 42 in Q. Light: 6F, 9Q. Weapon: 9F, 11Q.
Document: 9F, 9Q. Riches: 3F, 3Q. Other: 9F, 10Q.

10

Othello on the Edwardian Stage
Beerbohm Tree's Revival, 1912

B. A. KACHUR

Writing of Tree's career at His Majesty's Theatre, Macqueen Pope described it as "the very essence of the Edwardian theatre . . . the last word in everything theatrical at that time."[1] And so it was. Ease, luxury, and refinement characterized Edwardian London, and both Tree's theatre, built and decorated for him in the tasteful Regency style and regarded as the "handsomest playhouse in London,"[2] as well as the revivals staged there, the most spectacular Shakespearean productions in British theatre history, culturally epitomized the social milieu. From the opening of His Majesty's on 29 April 1897 until his death in 1917, Tree worked indefatigably to popularize Shakespeare with the general theatregoing public, and his success in doing so is evinced by an impressive production record which no West End compeer could match: 16 revivals which earned unprecedented audience attendance and averaged initial three-month runs, many successful enough for periodic revivals during subsequent seasons, and an annual Shakespeare festival which featured over two hundred performances by His Majesty's Theatre company and other acting corps during its nine-year existence (1905–1913).[3] Tree garnered this career tally by guiding his actor-directorial decisions along one significant tenet espoused early in his career; writing in 1900 on Shakespearean staging, Tree insisted that if his plays were to be made accessible to spectators, then "we must look at him with the eyes and we must listen to him with the ears of our own generation."[4] Though Tree was in part justifying his popular method of scenic verism, he was also stating that for Shakespeare to be appreciated by and applicable to theatregoers, his plays must be translated theatrically and thematically in ways that made them accessible to contemporary theatregoers.

In the case of his 1912 *Othello,* affording such accessibility to
playgoers would be, more so than for any of his previous productions, a herculean task. Indeed, Tree's *Othello* invites particular
attention, for it provides an interesting glimpse into both Edwardian
attitudes and ideologies as well as the manner in which Tree responded to these attitudes in his effort to make appealing a play
which had not, since the midnineteenth century, met with much
success at the hands of British actor-managers.[5]

The major question for Tree, one which the *Morning Post* (10
April 1912) expressed when echoing his colleagues' reservations
about *Othello,* was, "Can the play ever again be to us what Shakespeare meant it to be?" A pertinent question, for it implies not only
that Tree failed to convey the playwright's intent to his Edwardian
audience, but also, and more to the point here, that he was not
expected to do so. Why? Critical response hints at a few reasons, all
indicating irrefragably that English seventeenth-century *Zeitgeist*
had long passed and in its place was an Edwardian mind-set—a
different aggregate of social attitudes and theatrical expectations
which made *Othello* thematically and dramatically remote to many.
Certainly Shakespeare intended *Othello* as a tragedy of Aristotelian
proportions with a noble tragic hero who, through ignorance (both
of self and the world in which he operates), succumbs unwittingly
to the inexplicable workings of some elemental force—Fate. The
Sophoclean implications intended by Shakespeare, however, had
now become obscured by decades of prejudice. By the Edwardian
era, audiences had come to view the play reductively as "a tragedy
of race" in which Shakespeare "divined that there were unions
forbidden by Nature and doomed to disaster."[6] Othello's color no
longer symbolized the character's basic, elemental nature, foreign,
naive, and vulnerable to the guile of the real world embodied by
cosmopolitan Venice, but rather signified the direct cause of his
reversal, viz., his color *was* his flaw. His downfall occurred then not
because of some particular *hamartia* identifiable to audiences, but
rather because, as the *Daily Mail* (10 April 1912) stated with conviction, he "outraged all the laws of caste." Thus, racism, and its
attendant misinterpretation of Othello's color, had robbed the protagonist of heroic stature and tragic flaw, in turn minimizing the
likelihood of evoking the requisite pity and terror; moreover, it
engendered the myopic view of the tragedy as a dramatic caveat
against miscegenation—a view that could hold little relevance for
Tree's exclusively middle- and upper-class patrons. The *Daily
Chronicle* (6 April 1912) conflated the problems of character and

thematic accessibility a bit more crassly: "the play can have little meaning to the person who still regards him as a lynchable negro."

While bigotry undermined accessibility to theme and alienated empathy for Othello, so, too, did Othello's decorum fissure sympathy; his yielding to extreme passion and torment rang excessive and foreign to the Edwardian, who, as the *Era* (10 April 1912) intimates, held tenaciously to a curious, pretentious emotional reserve:

> The real difficulty of treating the piece at the present day is that we have to present a demonstrative hero to a reticent nation and generation. To the self-controlled, self-respecting Englishman, the unadulterated Othello appears unworthily emotional. In the Elizabethan period the real heroes were . . . grandly ebullient and demonstrative. . . . This change in national bearing, if not national temperament, makes some of the scenes in *Othello* almost 'too much' for London twentieth-century audiences.

Echoing these sentiments, the *Daily Chronicle* (10 April 1912), which thought also that Salvini "overdid it in the last act," averred that Othello's "frank revelations of graduated agony . . . are dead against our modern English temperament," while another captious critic declared his "fierce passions . . . somewhat foolish" and concluded that this play "more than most [of Shakespeare's] calls upon us to enter the Elizabethan frame of mind."[7] Clearly, the Edwardian envisaged himself as socially refined, emotionally civilized, more modern and complex than his Globe counterpart, and "the complex modern [man] does not work himself into jealous frenzy on flimsy evidence"—indeed, especially since "two minutes' straight talk with Desdemona . . . would have dissipated [Othello's] suspicions"[8] and obviated her sacrifice. The matter-of-fact Edwardians, who eschewed publicly either admission or demonstration of emotion and contained their passion beneath a "thinly veiled skin of modernity," as the *Daily Graphic* (10 April 1912) called it, had different attitudes—or rather affectations—about plausible and civil behavior that anesthetized many to Othello's torrential anguish.

Of course these verdicts on *Othello* had been passed decades earlier. Lamb expressed repulsion toward a black Moor and found "something extremely revolting in the courtship and wedded caresses of Othello and Desdemona,"[9] and, similarly, nineteenth-century social conventions influenced Irving, Macready, and Fechter to redefine Othello, as Rosenberg demonstrates, to suit the "repressed Victorian: a quieter Othello, a 'troubled person,' more controlled—and contrived—in dignity and passion."[10] The polemic over Othello's color and nature continued into the Edwardian era, but now, with the current influence of both sociology and thesis dramas, audiences ineluctably dissected plays for sociological pathology—hence, the misplacement of theme as the violation of social laws (a mixed marriage). Concomitantly, the seeds of Victorian repression had now burgeoned into an acute pretense of sophistication and civility which cut across all social classes—"the top hat and jingling hansom," says A. E. Wilson, formed the symbols of the Edwardian era, and even "the city clerk, the ill-paid shop assistant, clung to their top hats and starched cuffs"[11] as an outward show of respectability and reserve—a self-image perpetuated by gentlemanly heroes in contemporary drawing room dramas. Thus, while the problems plaguing Tree had surfaced already, they developed into differently critical social and theatrical perspectives that altered perceptions of the play's tragic import and the protagonist's dramatic impact.

How then was Tree to respond to these prejudices, predispositions, and expectations in order to make Othello appeal to the "eyes and ears" of his discriminatory West End playgoer? Clearly the success of Othello pivots on audience compassion for the protagonist, and although Tree could not replicate the Elizabethans' racial and emotional mind-set to ensure such receptivity to both character and text, he could rework his stage version and his characterization to gain accessibility by shaping them to suit his audiences' tastes and sensibilities, doing so by mitigating or removing details that would have short-circuited empathy and orchestrating all production elements to manipulate sympathy for the ill-fated lovers. This is precisely what he attempted, but a close study of extant documents[12] reveals that by so governing his directional approach, Tree, in procrustean fashion, created a revival that mirrored the Edwardian image of self: he reshaped Othello into a readily recognizable genre still much in vogue for the mass theatregoer—the romantic tragedy. To this end, he aimed every element of sight and sound—script, sets, costumes, music, and characterization—to accommodate the Edwardian preference for decorous, sentimental lovers and to envelop the action in an apposite atmosphere of romantic picturesqueness and exotic luxury. Indeed, had it not been for the fifteenth-century mise-en-scène, the action could have been transposed easily to an elegant drawing room of an upper-class Edwardian couple.

Before detailing the specifics of Tree's Othello, a look first at his handling of some production details will afford an overall view of how his romantic, sentimentalized version of *Othello* took shape, as well as provide the necessary context for later points of character discussion. In general, Tree staged *Othello* to suit the conventions of his theatre and the expectations of his audience: an abbreviated script and realistic scenery. Abridged Shakespearean stage editions were now commonplace to allow time for scene changes, and Tree, after jettisoning a hefty 44 percent—1450 of the original's 3310 lines—amalgamated the Folio's fifteen scenes into a four-act, ten-scene version which compared to Shakespeare's as follows:[13]

     Act 1
Scene 1: A Street in Venice (1.1)
Scene 2: A Square Outside Othello's House (1.2)
Scene 3: The Court House (1.3)

     Act 2
Scene 1: Cyprus. The Sea Port (2.1.1–212)
Scene 2: The Open Street (2.1.213–313)
Scene 3: Cyprus. The Sea Port (2.2, 2.3)

     Act 3
Scene 1: The Loggia of the Castle (3.3, 3.4.1–165a)

     Act 4
Scene 1: The Bedroom (4.3.11–21, 4.2.106–71, 4.3.22–56)
Scene 2: A Narrow Street (4.2.172–239, 3.4.169–200, 4.1.60b–201, 4.2.47b–64, 4.1.204–12, 5.1.1–129)
Scene 3: The Bedroom (3.2.1–359)

The first two acts corresponded to Shakespeare's and compassed the action up to Cassio's discharge, while act 3 neatly contained the scenes showing the inception, development, and culmination of Othello's jealousy, beginning with Iago's first insinuations and concluding with Desdemona's failure to produce the handkerchief. The fourth act, a patchwork of Shakespeare's last two, opened with a bedroom scene, the dialogue beginning with Desdemona's request that Emilia "unpin" her (4.3.10), then came Iago's entrance and Desdemona's request that he intervene on her behalf, Emilia's final dialogue with Desdemona ("I have laid those sheets you bade me on the bed" [4.3.11]), the scene finally concluding with the Willow song. The Narrow Street, containing just enough action to tie up loose ends and give Othello his "ocular proof," started with Iago and Roderigo plotting Cassio's murder and followed with the first Cassio-Bianca scene, Othello's entrance to observe Iago with Cas-

sio, Bianca's entrance to return the handkerchief, Othello's determination to kill Desdemona, and ended with the brawl. The last
scene was Shakespeare's fifth act resolution, the curtain falling on
Othello's suicide.

Although Tree's cutting, merging, and transposing scenes would
be deemed vandalous by our standards, it must be kept in mind that
he staged Shakespeare for the *average* theatregoer who, like his
counterpart today, was not an inveterate reader of Shakespeare
familiar with line and verse of each play.[14] Thus, even though the
stage version did create confusing time leaps (Desdemona loses
and looks for her handkerchief in the same 45-minute scene) and
rob Othello of emotional momentum (particularly by the fourth act
omissions), only a few critics caviled,[15] while most thought "from
[the] modern playgoers' point of view the version is even an im-
provement on the original" with "nothing of dramatic moment . . .
omitted,"[16] and *People* (14 April 1912) even went so far as to
recommend it "become a standard for the stage."

Tree's cuts included the standard bowdlerizations—gone altogether was the Clown as were Iago's prurient banter and sexual
metaphors, though to Tree's credit he did reinstate the Bianca
scenes, often deleted for propriety's sake. The majority of deletions,
however, served to focus the action solely around Othello and
Desdemona and relegated everyone, save Iago, to the background;
most harmed were Cassio, Emilia, and Roderigo, each whittled
down to mere shadows. Though no entire scenes vanished, large
segments extraneous to the plot were expunged, such as most of the
details of the Turkish invasion. Tree's most drastic omissions came
after the third act, which created a speedy resolution after the
temptation scene: of the remaining 1348 lines in acts 4 and 5, Tree
removed 769 (more than half of the total lines deleted), the biggest
chunks coming from the deletion of the Venetian embassy's arrival
and Othello's recall (4.1), and the brothel scene (5.2); these latter
omissions not only had a deliberate effect on Othello's character, as
discussed below, but also deleted any meeting of Othello and Desdemona between the temptation and murder scenes, thereby pre-
cluding any quibbling over Othello's failure to question his wife
about Cassio—he had no opportunity. Tree's handling of the last
scene best denotes the sympathetic and sentimental tenor of his
revival; in the closing scene, Tree retained but 90 of the 230 lines
between Desdemona's murder and Othello's suicide, in order to
effect, as he had done with *Antony and Cleopatra* (1906), a more
poignant ending—the near-simultaneous death of the lovers. By the
diminution of all other characters and the elimination of much of

the martial background, in particular the arrival of the Venetian embassy, Tree removed reminders of the world outside the castle walls, as well as the implication of greater consequences to that world by the death of Othello and Desdemona—lending to the action the air of insularity and domesticity.

Just as Tree arranged the text to throw into boldest relief the tragic romance of Desdemona and Othello, so, too, did his designers provide romantic pictorial canvases. Tree, in an interview with *Pall Mall Gazette* (25 March 1912), stated his design concept as "picturesque but simple," though he did nothing so radical as to adopt Elizabethanism, for, despite the advent of the new scenographic methodologies of Craig and Poel, pictorial illustration and antiquarianism remained the desiderata to West End theatregoers.[17] To achieve a more picturesque mise-en-scène, Tree antedated the play by one century, placing the action in 1488, a time when Venetian influence still had considerable sway in Cyprus before the Turkish invasion in 1573. The change in era enabled a blend of semi-Oriental and semi-Venetian appointments which, as Percy Anderson, the costume designer, noted, best suited "the sentiments of this tragedy."[18] For the Venetian costumes, Anderson culled from fifteenth-century painters like Carpaccio and Botticelli, while his exhaustive research led him to dress the Cypriotes as a melting pot of French, Armenians, Syrians, and Italians, which injected an exoticism into the later scenes. The scene designers, Harker and Craven, aimed less at replicating antiquarian details and more at vivifying a romantic environment. Conspicuously absent in reviews are details of scenic exactitude; rather, critics rhapsodized on the ambience created by the Venetian moonlit scenes with canals, starlight skies, and "their ever-present sense of mystery and romance,"[19] or the Cyprus locales which captured the "atmosphere of brightness" of this "fairyland of the East"[20] with their picturesque vistas of "mountains and seas and dark trees as they would appear under the shimmering sun."[21] Grein summed up the scenery's aesthetic function: "the views of nocturnal Venice and of luxurious Cyprus formed a perfect frame to the romance of the play" (the *Sunday Times*, 14 April 1912), while the *Standard* (10 April 1912) extolled the sets as "ablaze with colour, splendid and beautiful," and the *Athenaeum* (13 April 1912) was impressed with their "beauty and fitness." The significance of this romantic background is underscored by Tree's *Macbeth* the year prior in which he used quasi-expressionistic lighting effects to project the phantasmagoric nightmare within Macbeth's tortured psyche. For *Othello,* on the other hand, he employed scenery to project "a world of boundless vigour, a world glowing with passion and energy,"[22] a world of beauty, resplendence, and luxury—an environment befitting his treatment of the tragedy.

In directing his revival toward a more sentimental presentment of text, Tree made full use of the most emotionally manipulative production element: music. Throughout Tree aimed at the murder of Desdemona—using the tragedy's victim, if you will—as the source of most of the pathos and as a ready means to secure indirectly sympathy for Othello. Othello's calm behavior served by contrast to intensify the murder, the abridgment of text pushed the audience relentlessly toward it, and the handling of the finale, both in terms of the simultaneous deaths and the special staging effects, functioned to make the resolution the revival's most pitiful scene. That Tree, taking full advantage of audience general familiarity with the climax, focused on the fate of Desdemona for such empathic gains is nowhere more evident than in his choice of musical accompaniment. Typically, Tree used music of near-Wagnerian proportions—from establishing atmosphere to reflecting major themes or the protagonist's central conflict. For *Othello,* however, Tree commissioned a score from Coleridge Taylor which, curiously, lacked any noticeable suggestion of what would be deemed Othello's major conflicts. There was no motif suggesting his fierce jealousy or Iago's fiendish malignity, as one might expect; instead, the music was characterized by an almost continual melodiousness suggesting the "tenderness and grace of Desdemona."[23] The overture, with its strains suggesting the soldier-warrior Othello and "the pathos surrounding the unfortunate Desdemona," struck "a note of pageantry rather than of tragedy," accentuating "the martial and pathetic elements rather than the sinister and tragic factors."[24] The prelude for the third act temptation scene began with the 'war' motif which was then "calmed by the melody of the Willow Song," while the last entr'acte, again "avoiding any suggestion of the culminating tragedy," opened with the Desdemona motif, "a mournfully strenuous vein" of "winsome pathos" which segued into the "light and graceful" Willow song melody and finished with a return to Desdemona's theme, the latter providing the chief accompaniment for the finale.[25]

Within this romantic environment so carefully contrived by Tree's designers and composer, Tree placed what would be the most sentimental and temperate Othello in stage history. Given his audiences' predispositions, Tree, in an effort to engender sympathy and ameliorate receptivity, sought to present Othello along lines consonant with theatregoers' expectations of heroic behavior. Contemporary literary criticism, specifically the writings of A. C. Bradley, could buttress Tree's characterization, and, in fact, though Tree nowhere credits Bradley's influence, as he had done with *Macbeth* (1911),[26] he enacted and defined Othello in terms strikingly reminiscent of this Edwardian critic. Bradley limned Othello's basic traits as a "greater dignity than any other of Shakespeare's men," and an inordinate amount of "self-control."[27] Tree, similarly enumerating Othello's character, summed the keynotes of his performance: "a gentle creature, the "finest gentleman Shakespeare ever drew," and the "noblest of all Shakespeare's heroes . . . with a matchless command of his emotions even in the midst of tragedy"[28]—characteristics coincidentally analogous to the self-envisaged Edwardian decorum and reserve. Throughout Tree's performance, Othello's noble and dignified behavior was translated into gentility, "tenderness and restraint" (*Era,* 10 April 1912): even in the temptation and murder scenes, when passion gets the best of him, he struggles to contain it rather than succumb, and after his few demonstrations of fury, he showed shock at his potential for unchecked and destructive violence. In so underscoring Othello's gentle and noble nature to enlist audience sympathies, Tree had either to remove or mitigate behavior that would have aborted audience empathy and diminished the protagonist's noble stature. To this end, he removed any business promoting the "black savage" theory, deleting actions that his audience would have regarded as distasteful or indecorous. Thus, gone was Othello's epileptic seizure, his reviling of Desdemona and flinging money at Emilia, and his striking of Desdemona in front of the Venetian embassy. In fact, his only act of brutality, save the obligatory murder, was seizing Iago while demanding "ocular proof." By removing Othello's demonstrations of ferocity, Tree could, as he intended, throw into greater relief his one ultimate act of violence—Desdemona's murder. For some, such as William Archer (the *World,* 16 April 1912), suppressing these segments, in particular the striking of Desdemona, made Othello nothing more than "extremely vexed" and "weaken[ed] the impression of him being to all intents and purposes mad with jealousy and utterly irresponsible." Others, contrarily, thought the business "ugly and better banished" (*Daily Telegraph,* 10 April 1912), and the aforementioned *Era,* which spoke of Edwardian reserve, was "thankful to Sir Herbert for moderating and curtailing some of the 'agony.'" Of course Archer was correct, but Tree was after other game—to present a contemporary gentlemanly lover whose devotion to his wife, as Tree stated, "was the mainspring of his whole existence" (*Evening Standard,* 8

February 1912), and surely such a modern gentleman would be incapable of striking his wife—at least in public.

Tree attacked the most crucial problem in securing a sympathetic and noble Moor—the racial issue—by deemphasizing it. Cognizant of "a certain sexual revolt from a purely black Othello,"[29] as he admitted in an interview, Tree lightened Othello's complexion to tawny (as did Edmund Kean first in 1814), rationalizing that "Shakespeare meant Othello to be an Oriental and not a negro . . . a stately Arab of the best caste," and, moreover, that he was "only 'black' by contrast with the white Venetians."[30] An extant photograph shows Tree only slightly tanned compared to Phyllis Neilson-Terry's Desdemona. In lieu of color as motive for Othello's jealousy and insecurity, Tree stressed the character's age. He explains: "It accounts for so much—that he is no longer young. His jealousy of Cassio is subconsciously the jealousy of the middle-aged of the younger man—of the youth calling to the youth of his wife."[31] Tree's portrayal of Othello as "declined in the vale of his years," was a "violent change," remarked the *Church Times* (19 April 1912), "from what we have expected from the traditions. . . . It is a new revelation of jealousy. The Eurasian problem," continued this reviewer, "is brought out in a way which is not possible with a beautifully young Othello." Tree's Othello, an elderly man (fifties, said Tree—*Evening Standard,* 2 February 1912) in whom youthful passion was no longer at its zenith, showed a gentle, uxorious devotion toward Desdemona, and by establishing a quasi-paternal rather than passionately sensual relationship between them, Tree circumvented audience reflection on their sexuality, thus palliating the repulsion, "the underlying feeling," stated the tendentious *Reynolds's Newspaper* (14 April 1912), "that there is something unnatural and inexcusable in the union."

Having minimized the racial, brutal, and sexual aspects of Othello's relationship with Desdemona, Tree had perforce to emphasize the foreign elemental—rather than singularly racial—nature which worked as the mainspring for his actions. To explicate Othello's behavior as motivated by an innately different ideology, Tree stressed Othello's Arabic descent by loading his revival with Moorish details: all his costumes—even the armor worn at Cyprus—had Arabic motifs, and he located his character via Moorish gestures—the promptbook marginalia, particularly in the temptation and murder scenes, is peppered with notations for Oriental gestures, like the brandishing of clenched hands against each other as well as upon the forehead and against the breast.

By redefining Othello to suit the sensibilities of his patrons, Tree

created in essence, a twentieth-century *amoureux,* a lightly complected, gentlemanly lover, uxorious and deferential, who is "always straining his wife to his breast"[32] when unsuspicious, and
pines for the object of his affection when she is absent. This Othello
is never brutal, always controlled, and, even when the fire of suspicion and jealousy ignites, it metamorphoses not into ferocious,
blind rage directed at others but rather into an agonizing, self-
centered passion. It is Othello with a light touch, with none of the
wild frenzy that could alienate audience receptivity but with all the
"dignity and pathos, infinite pathos" (*People,* 14 April 1912) to
evoke empathy.

All these details provide a general overview of Tree's actor-
directorial choices for *Othello,* but to afford a more imaginative
experience of how these various elements took shape as a performance, a look at salient scenes is called for. To best serve this
purpose, the following reconstruction of Othello's key scenes is
provided.

For the first act's second scene, "The Square outside Othello's
House" where Othello makes his first appearance, Harker designed
"a mystic and wonderful" moonlit square with "deep blue skies
glimmering with stars" and at back a lagoon with "soft lapping
waves" shimmering under the moonlight.[33] Tree's Othello, a "tall
and commanding figure" dressed in a hooded white robe embroidered in gold and a camel's hair caftan, with long dark hair,
moustache, beard, large gold earrings, necklace and bracelets, cast
"a striking portrait" of "a true Oriental."[34] Tree insisted on
Othello's "calm dignity" at the outset, noting, as did Bradley,[35] that
Othello aborted the brawl by just his command (*Era,* 16 March
1912). Thus, as the inflamed Brabantio rushes in with his twelve
guards who draw swords against Cassio's ranks, Othello, without
the slightest gesture, stops the melee with "Keep up your bright
swords, for the dew will rust them." Moments later, when Brabantio's guards step forward to seize Othello, he need only speak,
"Hold your hands," and the soldiers, as the promptbook notes,
"fall away a bit." Here Tree, as the *Daily Mail* (10 April 1912)
lauded, "suggested admirably the stateliness, dignity, and calm of
Othello and the authoritative manner of one accustomed to command"—all without gesticulation or facial expression.

In his meeting with the Duke, played at Harker's Court House, a
grand, scarlet-draped hall with a half-circular council table at center and an upstage window cut cloth giving view to the moonlit sky,
Othello's bearing, as Tree affirmed, was once again "calm and
dignified."[36] From stage left of the table, Brabantio makes his

accusations as Othello, down stage right, back to audience, stood in place. To vocally animate the charges and countercharges between Othello and Brabantio, Tree used the Senators as a chorus, and with their murmurs of "surprise" and "general murmurs," as the promptbook indicates, created a commotion that accented by contrast Othello's control as he stands still and puts his case in modulated tones, "with impressive dignity."[37] His speeches to the Duke are "so mild and dignified," said one observer, that he "made the blustering of Desdemona's father seem futile and weak."[38] His "round unvarnished tale" was delivered with characteristic reserve, but "at the end of it there comes almost a crooning sweetness"[39] as he speaks of Desdemona. Brabantio's warning evoked no signs of incipient jealousy; rather Othello joyfully attests, "My life upon her faith," as he embraces Desdemona.

Act 2 opens at the Cyprus seaport, a deep set replicating a vine-trellised harbor with steps leading to the shore below, and at right the castle with its Cypriote architecture—all this backed by a "picturesque cerulean bay."[40] To open this Cyprus action, where Othello wrestles with his emotional furor, Tree inserted a special effect as much realistic as it was symbolic. In a pre-opening interview with the *Pall Mall Gazette* (25 March 1912), Tree described Othello as "an elemental man. He is not easily jealous, but there comes this terrific storm in his life through which he is shipwrecked." Taking this analogy as his cue, Tree began this act with a raging storm, a "touch of symbolism"[41] as he called it—prefiguring the emotional tempest, the "Pontic sea" surge of elemental emotion that relentlessly rages in Othello. The curtain rises on the entr'acte music simulating howling winds and crashing thunder as prelude to the sight of "great waves beating upon the shore."[42] The *Daily Telegraph* (10 April 1912) detailed with some awe the effect's extraordinary realism:

> First, the moaning of the wind and gathering clouds, then a distant rumbling of thunder, then, all in a moment, blinding light across the black sky and crashing roar upon roar echoed and re-echoed from the dim, dark peaks afar, while the air is all blinding, stinging hail, and you watch and wonder and listen, every nerve tingling, while each instant the flashes stab more keenly and the peals boom louder.

During the turmoil, the brightly dressed and turbaned Cypriotes rush about for shelter as Montano and the First Gentlemen shout reports of the vessels at sea. Slowly the clamor subsides; "the *elements* are at peace again," declared Tree, "as the sun breaks

Othello and Desdemona at the gates to the Citadel in the Herbert Beerbohm Tree production. Reproduced courtesy of the University of Bristol Theatre Collection.

through the clouds and beneath its fierce glow the white houses stand out in bold relief"[43] against the deep-blue sky. This portentous storm—with all its implications of pathetic fallacy—will return again to punctuate Desdemona's murder.

Surrounded by an excited and cheering mob, enter Othello the soldier, dressed in gold damascened armour (after Raphael and Perugino), with the note of elementalism sustained in the Oriental nose-guard and mail hood, rather than the European armet.[44] The reunion of Desdemona and Othello was "an absorbing adoration," recalled the *Licensed Victualler's Gazette* (12 April 1912). Desdemona was "all joy again in Othello's arms" while he, with a "note of utter surrender to his love," held her with "the little touch of the half-paternal solicitude that comes quite naturally from a man in love with a young girl."[45] Othello silenced the riot and cashiered Cassio without rage or noticeable gestures, and after comes a bit of "paternal" business borrowed from Salvini: he and Desdemona "retired cuddling close together, Othello sheltering his wife with his cloak from the gaze of the Cypriote throng."[46] By the end of act 2, Tree had "painted with fine, deep colours the simplicity and grandeur of Othello"[47] and had shown his singular devotion to Desdemona.

The lengthy temptation scene occurs at the castle loggia with an upstage balustrade and walkway giving view of dark cypresses "against the blue sea."[48] The set's blend of Arabic details, such as the archivolts and Moorish stool, and Venetian appointments, like the richly embroidered tapestries and ornamented divan, vivified the cultural clash between Othello's foreign naiveté and Iago's sophisticated duplicity: the *Daily Telegraph* (10 April 1912) noted "the fashion of the furniture, the emblems upon it, all have their tale to tell."

In this scene Tree would follow Bradley's lead, depicting Othello as "not easily or naturally jealous" (*Evening News,* 10 April 1912), slow to anger and rage, and, in the latter moments, once his suspicion is aroused, fighting to control a demonstrative rage which boiled under his outward civility. Tree's lack of gesticulation in the preceding acts now enabled him "to be powerful without ever forcing a line" (*Sporting Life,* 10 April 1912), and served him well to underscore by contrast his writhing and sobbing, which bespoke Othello's ferocity and anguish. Here Tree's sentimental portrayal was most evident. His "sobs and groans and gasps conveyed a self-pitying weakness" and when he finally breaks under the emotional strain "it was the anguish of his rage and not his maddened passion that you felt most."[49] Behind it all "was the sob of a broken heart"

**A sketch of the set for Act III, scene iii, in the Herbert Beerbohm Tree *Othello*.
Reproduced courtesy of the University of Bristol Theatre Collection.**

(*Sporting Life,* 10 April 1912), and though there was no "sheer terror and blistering horror," recalled the *Evening Standard* (10 April 1912), "we do, notwithstanding, feel the tremendous pity of it, the dreadful sorrow." The emotional distress Othello suffered erupted from his loss of faith in Desdemona, a self-pitying anguish that never culminated in brutal ferocity and anger but rather smoldered in a comparatively reticent and heartbroken agony. There was little volcanic fury, no sweeping up by the full tide of passionate intensity, only a sinking into a paroxysm of self-centered, lachrymose sentimentality.

Othello, now dressed in a black robe with silver striping and "cabalistic figures on it,"[50] sits with Iago at the table down right, preoccupied with papers of state as Desdemona importunes on Cassio's behalf. Their exchange is lovingly playful, "subtly and beautifully played," with Othello again exhibiting "something of the elderly man with a young wife":[51] he pats her cheek, kisses her tenderly, but tries to resume working as she takes his pen away and finally snatches the papers until she coaxes from him "I will deny thee nothing." She gives Othello a symbolic red rose and exits up left as the Desdemona motif plays. Othello attempts to work but cannot; he pauses, sighs, tosses the pen down and moves up to the center opening to look off in Desdemona's direction: "Perdition catch my soul, / But I do love thee! and when I love thee not, / Chaos is come again." Othello sighs Desdemona's name; his preoccupation with her is all-consuming. Happy and content, Othello "cheerfully returns to table" (*O* 97) where Iago begins his insidious poisoning. At first the Ensign does not have an easy time of it, for Othello defends Cassio's honesty "almost joyously" (*O* 97) and eagerly settles back to work "as tho' dismissing the whole thing." He is amused at Iago's admonition; he laughs, "Think'st thou I'ld make a life of jealousy," and crosses downstage speaking "proudly" of Desdemona and the compliments others pay her. He laughs again, "Away at once with love or jealousy" and returns to the table, picks up the rose, kisses it and then resumes writing. Iago must now begin with his more direct approach and "franker spirit." His barbed reminder that Desdemona did deceive her father cuts Othello deeply—a pause while the Moor no doubt recalls Brabantio's earlier warning—and then "as in a dream" admits bewilderedly, "And so she did." The fire of suspicion now ignites, but Othello, the self-controlled commander and soldier, abhors showing emotions in front of a subaltern; Tree notes in his rehearsal book that until Iago's exit, "Othello's attitude has been that of a man of superior rank not wishing to show his heart too much." Othello "laughs through a sob," holding back tears at his denial, "Not a jot." Left alone, Othello, so far "sitting on the safety value of his passions," wrote Tree (*O* 97), can finally given vent to passion: "beating his hands together" in Oriental fashion, he throws himself on the divan down left and tosses "to in fro in agitation" (*Era,* 10 April 1912)—not in a rage of jealousy but in confusion, disquietude, and suspicion. The soliloquy (3.3.257–73a) is delivered with alternations of quiet and bursts of despair at which he attempts "calming himself" (*O* 97). At the end, he bitterly curses his marriage, and then "covers his face with his hands and groans" (*O* 97). At his exit with Desdemona he remains tender, doting, and hopeful: "he takes her hand & draws her to him, looking into her eyes" (*O* 97) as if searching for some hint of her fidelity, some truth to disprove Iago's insinuations and to dispel his doubts.

A more agitated Othello reenters, for he has had time, as Bradley opines, to mull things over. "The hitherto placid man," remarked Grein (the *Sunday Times,* 14 April 1912), "became gradually a powerful incarnation of human wrath, descending to blind ferocity of the savage beast." With "clenched hands on lips as tho to choke back the words," he utters, "False to me?" So self-engrossed, Othello does not notice Iago up left, and his words startle the Moor, who still struggles to control his rage—he puts "his hands behind him as tho' he fears to strike Iago in his agitation." Othello's voice quavers, "What sense had I of her stol'n hours of lust?," and in perturbation paces the hall, spitting at the mention of Cassio's kisses. He now works himself into a lachrymose collapse: self-absorbed, he moves slowly down right, "I had been happy . . . / So I had nothing known," and when he reaches the table he "throws himself on knees at side of it, his head on his arms." A sob-filled pause ensues; then, after collecting himself, he stares out into vacancy as if transfixed by memories of a quieter time and, with a more sorrowful, self-reflective calm, he bids farewell to his tranquil mind. The *Daily Telegraph* (10 April 1912) reported that "his very soul was torn asunder when he sank down to groan out 'Farewell the tranquil mind! farewell content!' " He rises and so, too, does his anguish: "O you mortal engines," he presses "the back of his hands to his brow," trying to crush the mental pain, cries out his farewell to his occupation, and then lets his arms "fall listlessly to his sides." He is vanquished. In his stupor, he "has forgotten Iago's presence," but when the Ancient speaks, Othello, no longer able to contain his wrath, lunges at him, grabs him by the throat, forces him to one knee, and demands "ocular proof." He has no sooner grasped Iago than he pushes him away, staggers back to the table, "horrified at what he has done." His safety value has broken—the calm is now lost. With Iago's recounting of Cassio's dream, the incalescent "wild animal" erupts: he stops his ears, tears the papers on the desk, and comminutes the rose—"I'll tear her to pieces"—and again paces the hall, "wringing his hands, tearing his hair, beating his breast,"[52] then returns up stage and stands in the arch, and, "as a brute escaped from the forest," thought Grein (*Sunday Times*, 14 April 1912), cries out for "blood, blood, blood!" He seals his sacred vow with Iago bowing "head to dust in Moorish fashion," then, in a "½ whisper," speaks of Desdemona's "swift means of death," and exits quickly with Iago up left.

Desdemona enters immediately searching for her handkerchief and when Othello recounts its magic, he menacingly "drives her to the end of the seat" at left, resisting, as the *Liverpool Courier* (10 April 1912) observed, "the temptation to strike Desdeomona." She moves away, denying it is lost, and Othello "makes exclamation of joy, he follows & catches her right hand," and then "with gestures of infinite tenderness, he almost takes his wife to his bosom, overpowered by the craving of love."[53] But this note of hope shatters when Desdemona speaks of Cassio; Othello flings her hand away and "looks like killing her," yells "Away!" and, for her protection, slowly backs out the left lower entrance, suggesting that if he were to remain he would do her harm. The act ends with a frightened, confused and tearful Desdemona exiting with Emilia to find Othello, as harp music fades in. In Tree's version, this would be the last meeting between the lovers until the murder scene.

During the course of the revival, the melodious music and the repetition of Desdomona's theme kept this character in the action's foreground, pointing continually, especially through the repeated use of the Willow song, to the tragic conclusion. Tree's intent to accentuate the murder over any other segment, to eke from it the utmost pathos, is evinced by his staging of this scene, which included its sound effects and set design. In addition to reintroducing the storm—which literally began at the first Cyprus scene and figuratively on the Loggia—to find its symbolic resolution as it intensified the murder, Tree additionally accented the deed by his placement of the bed. Early rehearsal promptbooks indicate that Tree initially located the bed in a recessed alcove up center, but in his effort to accentuate the climax, he altered its position to down left center closer to the footlights, making the murder "more painful than ever for the simple reason that it was more prominent."[54] The rest of Harker's set, a spacious apartment decorated in symbolic reds and purples "emphasizing," noted the *Daily Telegraph* (10 April 1912) among others, "the deep note of tragedy at its climax," showed two doors (up center and right), and at left a broad terrace window opening onto a "garden where the cypresses stand beneath a sky of southern blue and sparkling stars."[55]

Othello's killing of Desdemona had often been played so brutally (as with Salvini who violently and physically terrorized Desdemona before he murdered her) that it characterized the Moor as little else than a hateful, vengeful monster bent on cold-blooded murder, but Tree inveighed against such butchery and brutality, insisting, as did Bradley, that Othello "goes to her bedroom as God's executioner," performing an act of immolation rather than hateful revenge. "There is no wild rage, no insatiable revenge," commented Tree. "Believing Desdemona to be guilty," he continues, Othello "kills her because honour requires that he should sacrifice her. . . . His love still 'aches at her sweetness.' "[56] Tree played with restraint and tenderness, losing his calm only when Desdemona asks for Cassio, and his performance in the finale most impressed critics. The *Licensed Victuallers' Gazette* (12 April 1912) found "his overmastering love of his wife mixed with overwhelming loathing for her apparent faithlessness . . . profoundly moving," the *Era* (13 April 1912) thought "the pathos, the power, and the passionate intensity of this part of his performance . . . triumphed in a climax of intense and tremendous tragedy," and the *Referee* (14 April 1912), stated "in the closing scene of the cold blooded murder of Desdemona the Moor claims our sympathy in his anguish, even as we pity the pure, sweet innocent creature so cruelly used."

Before the curtain rose on the final scene, the audience was reminded once again of the innocent Desdemona's pitiful fate by the orchestral repetition of the Willow song, sung at the end of the first bedroom scene by Neilson-Terry "as though she has become spiritualized with grief," said Archer (the *World,* 16 April), with "catches in her voice," recalled the *Evening Times* (15 April 1912) "because she knew that death was knocking at the door." Left with this last impression, this pitiful and "quite haunting"[57] picture of her sitting heartbroken on the window seat looking out over the still Cyprus night and waiting for Othello, the audience was now emotionally primed to witness with sympathy the horror of her murder.

The curtain went up slowly as Desdemona lies sleeping, moonlight from the terrace window flooding her bed. Othello, now garbed in his Oriental-motifed black gown, enters quietly up left to the sound of distant thunder. "It is the cause"—he gives an "Oriental gesture," notes the promptbook, and raises his scimitar; it shines in the moonlight. "I'll not shed her blood," he lays the weapon aside. Othello puts out the candle, kisses her gently, and locks the door; she stirs. From the foot of the bed he solemnly intones her death sentence: "I would not kill thy unprepared spirit." Thunder rolls again. Desdemona's voice falters, "Talk you of killing?" Wide-eyed and fearful, she kneels at his feet, "Clasping at Othello with restless longing hands,"[58] imploring his mercy and insisting Cassio found the handkerchief. She asks for Cassio and retreats for the door only to find it locked. Moving cautiously to Othello, she insists, with a mixture of "fear and outraged love in her very movement,"[59] that Cassio found the handkerchief and that "He is betrayed and I undone." Suddenly the sky darkens, clouds obscure the stars, and thunder peals louder as Othello, angry at her tears for Cassio, throws her on the bed and pulls the curtain closed. Then comes the struggle and a faint voice crying for mercy, for half an hour, for one prayer. In a second, all is unnervingly quiet—the storm is over. Emilia's knocking comes as a welcomed relief from the strained evening silence and the scene of horror.

With only ninety lines remaining, Othello's death follows apace. As Emilia continues banging, he backs to the door "as in a dream" and unlocks it, then "staggers to the table RC & supports himself"—stupefied and shaken by his heinous deed. When Desdemona's innocence is finally confirmed, Othello's maudlin torment returns. "With a tear in his voice and agony on his face,"[60] he falls on the bed and anguishedly cries, "Whip me, ye devils / From the possession of this heavenly sight," as he lifts Desdemona's lifeless body, now lost to him forever, gently rocking her in his arms, straining her to him one final time, and caressingly stroking her hair—a poignant bit of business that sent a shudder through the house. In a quick moment, Othello grabs Montano's dagger and all rush toward him, but it is too late—in front of the bed he drops to his knees. A beat, then Cassio softly touches his shoulder and Othello falls supine. The final curtain comes down quite appropriately to the sound of Desdemona's plaintive motif and the picture of Othello lying beside Desdemona's deathbed.

Tree, the West End's regnant Shakespearean actor-manager most responsive to the expectations and attitudes of his day, sought to make *Othello,* one of Shakespeare's most controversial plays, accessible to a general theatregoing public (and not a coterie audience of bardolaters) with clearly demarcated racial and social biases by satisfying their aesthetic sensibilities. The Edwardian taste for luxury and preference for beauty and refinement could only result in magnificent idyllic scenes with realistic staging effects and, more significantly, in a title character whose nature paralleled contemporary concepts of emotional decorum and social civility. All of Tree's directorial and histrionic choices—the music, costumes, sets, and characterization—coalesced into a picturesque and romantic revival as the encomiastic *Daily Graphic* (10 April 1912) aptly described:

> The whole thing is realised with such perfection as to live and palpitate in the memory—the sway and rustle of the women's trailing gowns, the beauteous faces, the murmur of the crowds, the melody of distant music melting into the twilight, the pain and passion and sweetness of it all throbs with the life's blood of romance.

Tree's strategy for combating the aesthetic dispassion and for allying imaginative sympathies with the Moor was to redefine him—to diminish his brutality and imbue him instead with the noble, calm, gentle behavior congenial to Edwardian concepts. Did his strategy work? Critics were divided. Some reviewers, those who wanted an inflamed Othello who could "tear passion to a tatters with zest" and would be "overwhelmed by the torrent of emotion that he could not control,"[61] found his understated and reserved Othello in the temptation scene "lacking the all compelling fury which like a volcano burns up his pity, and in sheer elemental revenge compasses the death of Desdemona" (the *Globe,* 10 April 1912). Tree's "anger did not blast" in the view of the *Pall Mall Gazette* (10 April 1912), while the *Standard* (10 April 1912), though consenting that "the humanity and utter sorrow of it have never been more convincingly presented," lamented that "the onrush, the avalanche of tragedy, its epic quality were missing," and the *Illustrated London News* (13 April 1912) argued that Tree's Othello "never takes you by storm, never carries you away . . . by dint of passion and animal ferocity." Others, however, preferring Tree's sentimental and reserved portrait of Othello, lauded his nonviolent performance as "a triumph in sympathy and restraint," and "epic sorrow, not the frothings and ravings of a savage run amok."[62] From the standpoint of these reviewers, like the *Evening Standard* (10 April 1912), who was "carried away by its emotion and its grief," Tree created "a striking, powerful, and very human Othello," and raised a "whirlwind of passion" (*Referee,* 14 April 1912), which crescendoed into a "ferocious thing, approximating the wild-animal theory" (*Westminster Gazette,* 10 April 1912). Equal to the division among critics over Tree's presentment of Othello's emotional nature was the reaction to the racial issue. The lighter-complected Othello, a maneuver to evade racism, increased receptivity and empathy for some spectators. The *Evening Times* (15 April 1912) explains the effect with characteristically unabashed prejudice:

> [H]is Othello is the finest conception I have ever seen. . . . I am a man with the colour sense abnormally developed. I believe in lynchings, and I do not sit in a restaurant with negro men, yet Tree made me understand Othello, made me cross the colour line. Made me understand how such a man might inspire love.

Tree's gentle, avuncular, lightly complected Othello, though less jarring on the sensibilities of some, which made "crossing the color line" much easier, did not mitigate everyone's racism. Surely there were those spectators concurring with *Truth* (17 April 1912), who, in terms reminiscent of Lamb, sympathized with Brabantio: "It was as horrible to me as it was to him to see this lily-fair beauty in the arms of this swarthy warrior, no matter how dignified his demeanour or how lofty his love."

Thus, we come full circle, back to the *Morning Post*'s question about the play's viability. Certainly any classical drama, if it is to succeed, can only do so when staged according to the expectations and aesthetics for whom it is produced. For all Tree's efforts to reconcile the play with his audience's attitudes—the orchestration of the music, the starlit evening scenes, the less ferocious and gentle Othello, the underscoring of the Moor's elemental nature via storm effects, costumes, and gestures, as well as the toning down of his color—he could not expunge entirely the underlying prejudice which, according to some reviewers, implies a reciprocal racism on the part of readers. The inherent problems in *Othello* plagued performers as early as the late eighteenth century, and the propelling force behind the failure of actors was the bigotry against a black Othello. Had Tree blackened his face and retained Othello's demonstrative rage, he would have been as the *Daily Chronicle* (10 April 1912) implied, "a lynchable negro who has committed murder in the frenzy of jealousy." By lightening Othello's complexion and jettisoning all his brutality, Tree reduced the play to a sentimental melodrama—certainly not, as the *Morning Post* suggested, the play that Shakespeare intended. As intimated by this critic, and adamantly averred by the *Daily Chronicle* (10 April 1912), "It is Shakespeare's and not Sir Herbert Tree's fault that Othello can never claim quite the same passionate sympathy." Tree, like Irving and others before him, could not succeed in accurately translating *Othello* to the stage regardless of his subdued character or his picturesque mise-en-scène, because the very ideologies that informed every aspect of this play for Elizabethan theatregoers were no longer operative points of reference in Edwardian London. Indeed, even more recently, racism drove a wedge between Othello and his audience: at the 1979 Alliance Theatre Production spectators grasped audibly when Paul Winfield kissed Dorothy Fielding in the Cyprus scene,[63] proving that impenetrable racial barriers to understanding Shakespeare's Moor could still create a fissue between text and audience.

Othello was Tree's briefest revival, running from 9 April to 18 May 1912, at which time he withdrew it to stage his eighth annual Shakespeare festival where it appeared for two performances (25 May 1 June). It never surfaced again. Clearly the short run and absence in later seasons connote the lack of audience support, but in all Tree did make *Othello* more accessible than many prior actor-managers. Though his performance as Othello can never rank with his superb Richard II or Shylock, his revival did have a positive and dramatic impact on a good percentage of spectators:

It took a modern audience by storm. It held them breathless and alert from start to finish; it caught them up and swayed them in its deep tides of human rapture and agony. It clutched our interests and drew upon our sympathies with a force and power that would not be denied.[64]

For some of his Edwardian patrons, Tree had so arranged and staged the play that "though you may know it by heart," as the *Daily Telegraph* (10 April 1912) declared, "it thrills you as though you had the good luck to see it for the first time"—surely a significant accomplishment for a play familiar to most, and unquestionably the aim of any director—who would undoubtedly face similar racial barriers—staging this tragedy today.

NOTES

Research for this essay was funded by a Summer Research Grant from the University of Missouri-St. Louis.

1. Macqueen Pope, *Carriages at Eleven* (London: Hutchinson, 1947), p. 31.
2. Hesketh Pearson, *Beerbohm Tree* (London: Methuen, 1956), p. 101.
3. For example, Tree's first Shakespearean production at Her Majesty's (*Julius Caesar*, 1898), attracted 242,000 spectators during its 165 consecutive runs; *King John* ran from 20 September 1899 to 6 January 1900 and brought in 170,000; *Henry VIII,* Tree's longest running revival, had 254 consecutive runs from 1 September 1910 to 8 April 1911 (Tree, *Thoughts and Afterthoughts* [New York: Wagnalls, 1913], p. 46.)
4. Tree, *Thoughts and Afterthoughts,* p. 41.
5. Ruth Cowig, "Actors, Black and Tawny, in the role of Othello—and Their Critics," *Theatre Research International* 4 (1979): 143; Marvin Rosenberg, *The Masks of Othello* (Berkeley: University of California Press, 1961), p. 70.
6. *Reynolds's Newspaper,* 14 April 1912; the *Morning Post,* 10 April 1912.
7. *Morning Post,* 10 April 1912.
8. *Daily Express,* 10 April 1912.
9. Joan Caldwell, ed., *Charles Lamb on Shakespeare* (England: Colin Smyth, 1978), p. 38.
10. Rosenberg, *Masks of Othello,* p. 70.
11. A. E. Wilson, *Edwardian Theatre* (London: Barker, 1951), pp. 11, 15.
12. Details of Tree's revival are taken from an opening night program (9 April 1912) from the Raymond Mander and Joe Mitchenson Collection, a rehearsal promptbook at the Folger Shakespeare Library (Shattuck 98), and the following documents at the Beerbohm Tree Archive, University of Bristol Theatre Collection: two identical promptbooks copiously annotated with groundplans (95a and 95b, the latter an inked transcription of the first, completed through only three acts), Tree's preparation books (96, 97), rehearsal copies (99), various production papers, and a program dated 11 May 1912. Unless otherwise noted parenthetically, promptbook quotes are from 95a and 95b.
13. As the opening night program and early promptbooks show, the last act contained all the action described, but only in two scenes: The Narrow Street and The Bedroom; by 11 May (the date of a later program), Tree changed the last act to three scenes.

14. Desmond MacCarthy, "From the Stalls," in Max Beerbohm, *Herbert Beerbohm Tree: Some Memories of Him and His Art* (London: Hutchinson, 1917), p. 218.

15. E. A. Baughan, *Daily News,* 10 April 1912; *Glasgow Herald,* 10 April 1912.

16. *Vanity Fair,* 10 April 1912; *Licensed Victualler's Gazette,* 12 April 1912.

17. Victorian and Edwardian appetence for pictorial illustration has been well documented by Michael Booth, *Victorian Spectacular Theatre, 1850–1910* (London: Routledge & Kegan Paul, 1981).

18. *Evening Standard,* 9 April 1912.

19. *Daily Graphic,* 10 April 1912.

20. *Evening Standard,* 9 April 1912.

21. *Church Times,* 19 April 1912.

22. *Daily Telegraph,* 10 April 1912.

23. Ibid.

24. *Musical Times,* May 1912; *Referee,* 14 April 1912.

25. *Referee,* 14 April 1912; *Stage,* 11 April 1912; *Daily Telegraph,* 10 April 1912.

26. In his program note (5 September 1911, Beerbohm Tree Archive) Tree wrote: "Among the many instructive works written upon the subject of Macbeth, none is more inspiring than that of Dr. Bradley."

27. Leonard F. Dean, *A Casebook on Othello* (New York: Crowell, 1961), pp. 139–46.

28. *Pall Mall Gazette,* 25 March 1912; *Daily Express,* 25 March 1912; *Evening Standard,* 8 February 1912.

29. *Pall Mall Gazette,* 10 April 1912.

30. *Daily Express,* 11 April 1912; *Star,* 25 March 1912.

31. *Star,* 25 March 1912.

32. *Illustrated London News,* 13 April 1912.

33. *Evening News,* 10 April 1912.

34. *Glasgow Herald,* 10 April 1912; *Globe,* 10 April 1912.

35. A. C. Bradley, *Shakespearean Tragedy: Lectures on Hamlet, Othello, King Lear, Macbeth* (London: Macmillan and Co., 1904), p. 190.

36. *Era,* 16 March 1912.

37. *Scotsman,* 10 April 1912.

38. *Glasgow Herald,* 10 April 1912.

39. *Evening Standard,* 10 April 1912.

40. *Morning Advertiser,* 10 April 1912.

41. *Star,* 25 March 1912.

42. *Morning Advertiser,* 10 April 1912.

43. *Star,* 25 March 1912. Emphasis added.

44. *Evening Standard,* 9 April 1912; Percy Anderson interview.

45. *Daily Telegraph,* 10 April 1912; *Evening Standard,* 10 April 1912; *Daily Express,* 10 April 1912.

46. *Pall Mall Gazette,* 10 April 1912; see Rosenberg, p. 106.

47. *Evening Standard,* 10 April 1912.

48. *Westminster Gazette,* 9 April 1912.

49. *Reynolds's Newspaper,* 14 April 1912; *Daily Telegraph,* 10 April 1912.

50. *Daily mirror,* 10 April 1912.

51. *Daily Mirror,* 10 April 1912.

52. *Sunday Times,* 14 April 1912.

53. *Era,* 10 April 1912.

54. *Times,* 10 April 1912.

55. *Daily Telegraph*, 10 April 1912.

56. *Daily Chronicle*, 6 April 1912.

57. *Truth*, 17 April 1912.

58. *Daily Telegraph*, 10 April 1912.

59. *Bristol Times and Mirror*, 14 April 1912.

60. *Sunday Times*, 14 April 1912.

61. *Daily Express* 10 April 1912; *Reynolds's Newspaper*, 14 April 1912.

62. *Referee*, 14 April 1912; *Daily Graphic*, 10 April 1912.

63. Charles B. Lower, "Othello as Black on Southern Stages," in *Shakespeare in the South: Essays on Performance*, ed. Philip C. Kolin (Jackson: University Press of Mississippi, 1983), p. 231.

64. *Daily Graphic*, 10 April 1912.

11

Kiss Me Deadly; or,
The Des/Demonized Spectacle

BARBARA HODGDON

When was Desdemona like a ship?
When she was Moored.
—Minstrel Show joke

As the opening night of Giuseppe Verdi's *Otello* in 1887 neared, all Milan prepared for the return to La Scala, sixteen years following *Aida,* of the long-awaited work by the septuagenarian composer whose name had become synonymous with an Italian operatic tradition of melodic lyricism and who acknowledged Shakespeare as "Papa . . . the master of the human heart."[1] In a collection of letters to Wilkie Collins, Blanche Roosevelt reports that Milanese society women took hairdresser's appointments whenever they could get them, even if this required rising at dawn and spending the remainder of the day protecting their elaborate coiffures for the evening's gala appearance; one hotel maid, refused permission by her employer to attend, lost her job rather than miss the occasion.[2] Such anticipatory rituals and sacrifices, whether involving simply a disruption of convenient routine or, more threateningly, of economic security, share a remarkable similarity to those of Desdemona herself, who (nearly a century later, in Franco Zeffirelli's 1978 staging of Verdi's opera) sits at her dressing table while Emilia removes the pearls from her hair and arranges her flowing blonde tresses over her shoulders, preparing her for, and also *as,* a final spectacle in which her own occupation, as Othello's wife, is at risk. Insofar as this scene positions its women characters in a space that might be considered a room of their own, represents women's daily, lived experience, and details a conversation that reveals sharply polarized attitudes toward the double standard and marital fidelity, it not only affords its characters a potential sense of agency but commands particular recognition from female spectators.[3] To describe the scene in this way begins to imagine an un-author-ized *Othello*—an *Othello* as the story of a fatal attraction, haunted by murder and *seen,* if not *constructed,* from a woman's point of view. Such a project would connect Shakespeare's playtext as well as Verdi's opera with women's melodrama and soap opera, genres which, in representing social realities from a gendered point of view, attempt to negotiate a space within patriarchal domination that exposes and contests its power over the female body and voice.[4] I want to linger briefly on such a rewritten vision of *Othello,* to see it as a transient possibility which this scene inscribes by weighting both the female voice and body with special privilege and thus according women viewers particular aural as well as visual competency. On the one hand, we hear Emilia contest patriarchal law by calling adultery "a small vice," one not only patterned on male behavior and attitudes but possible because women are *like* men, sharing their "sense" and "desires for sport"; on the other, Desdemona not only confirms her inability to imagine, or commit, such a vice but suggests, especially through her song, her immobilization in a masochistic scenario.[5] And what we see—a maid helping her mistress prepare for bed—represents an instance where a woman spectator can, if she so chooses, separate her gaze from the sexualized male surveillance of the play's inscribed spectators, which endorses that of its viewing audience, and so escape being constructed as "to-be-looked-at-ness" by owning a (potentially) desexualized look at a woman's body.[6]

Theorizing a female spectator and a specifically gendered gaze[7] for this spectacle of women's community assumes not only that the sexual difference so heavily inscribed within society (whether Renaissance or contemporary) also applies to spectators but that *Othello* turns both spectacle and gaze into theatrical conventions that interrogate propositions of value and integrity concerning bodies—especially female bodies. In an essay that positions *Othello*'s obsessive concern with the possessive (and I would add pathological) enclosure of the female body within patriarchal territory, Peter Stallybrass analyzes that phenomenon primarily as "a function of the antithetical thinking of the developing Renaissance state and as a target of the displaced resentment of the subordinated classes."[8] Although he acknowledges that the play's structure overdetermines Desdemona's subservience (which, contradictorily, Emilia serves to elevate as the more honorable of two choices), Stallybrass points to Emilia's functions, not only in this scene, as she voices the invisible assumptions that drive the play, but later, as the "agent of truth, who open[s] the closed mouth, the locked house," and conjectures a position that extends her subversive resistance beyond the play, gives it interventionary agency, sees it responsible for the literal destruction of historical enclosures.[9] Certainly the position Stallybrass imagines not only constructs a space within which women can, however surreptitiously, refuse their containment but offers a woman spectator potential mastery over the foreclosed vision *Othello*'s ending seems to enforce. But, at least in terms of particular performance texts, its considerable appeal is also considerably limited. For, although reading (beyond the playtext) can reveal the contours of a potentially pleasurable subversive space, in the case of particular performance texts of *Othello*, "visual pleasure" exists primarily in terms of *intellectual* mastery. And it is this lack of visual pleasure, and of the subversion often associated with performance, that I wish to investigate further.

Here, I see a useful connection between the models generated by recent feminist film theory which assign gender to as well as psychoanalyze the relations between spectacle and gaze and Katharine Maus's provocative conjectures about the relations between an eroticized Renaissance spectacle construed, by antitheatrical commentators, as a "whorish female" and the jealous male's scopic project as one figure for the Renaissance spectator "at his most agonizingly involved and his most scandalously marginalized."[10] Not only is a double standard of spectatorship that positions the male as perceiving subject and the female as perceived object common to both, but the deeply gendered split in subjectivity that both take as a given constitutes a terrain endemic to *Othello*'s plot, in which the look and looking map a progression from Brabantio's "Look to her, Moor, if thou hast eyes to see" to Othello's "Give me the ocular proof" to Lodovico's "the object poisons sight." Indeed, *Othello* carries the tyranny of the male look to extremes. Even the earliest records of *Othello*'s eyewitnesses confirm the gender difference theory proposes: at a performance in 1610 at Oxford, a (male) spectator reports that "Desdemona, killed by her husband, in her death moved us especially, when, as she lay in her bed, her face only implored the pity of the audience."[11] Fifty years later, Samuel Pepys mentions seeing "The Moor of Venice" at the Cockpit, where the diarist's ever-prurient eye, simultaneously alert to offstage as well as on-stage sights, noted that "a very pretty lady that sat by me, called out, to see Desdemona smothered."[12] Together, these comments sketch out a potential fracture in gendered spectatorship—the man who is moved to appropriately classical tragic emotion by the female spectacle, the woman who cries out at precisely the moment when Desdemona loses her voice.

My own voice serves here to chronicle the sights and sounds of *Othello*'s ending, trace its commodification as the story of a desiring male subject and, finally, reveal some partial fissures along the lines of sight. In exploring the contours of *Othello*'s ending in a number of performances *of* and performances *on* Shakespeare's playtext (itself a rewriting of Cinthio's tale),[13] I do not mean to insist, or even suggest, that all be compared on the same level or that all have equal value. None, certainly, has the status of a defended text; indeed the very existence of so many different *Othello*s proves the plurality of that (infinitely desirable) text by demonstrating its ability to be reproduced in another form. Rather, what interests me is the confrontation between *Othello*s that aspire to privileged authority as cultural commodities and ones that occupy a more marginal territory.[14] For it is the connections—the "knee play" or joints between these—which call into question the crucial issues of representation, spectatorship, and the gendered relations of body and voice I want to raise. Thus, although I do not offer a precisely chronological history of what one might call the colonizing of Shakespeare's playtext, my analyses attempt to demonstrate how that playtext, like Desdemona herself, becomes a textual body which is signified upon in order to legitimate or resist strategic, shared cultural assumptions, fantasies, and obsessions concerning male subjectivity and female objectification.[15] To give *Othello*'s ending a reading that assigns to it a particular local habitation and a name constitutes, then, a kind of new historicism of the recent past and, even, the present. And it is precisely the *use* of Desdemona's voice and body, binding her either with a masochistic scenario or positioning her as the central term in a system of male exchange, which activates that reading.

Consider, first, two apparently diverse *Othello*s—Verdi's opera and Orson Welles's 1952 film. Although each occupies a discrete cultural space, and although neither can be strictly considered "Shakespeare's *Othello*," each participates equally in according both "Shakespeare" and *"Othello"* singular cultural authority.[16] And both constitute equally radical appropriations of Desdemona which construct her—within the aural economy of Verdi's opera; within the visual economy of Welles's film—not only to serve male subjectivity but, more especially, to perpetuate the hegemony of male artistic practice.

By condensing *Othello*'s two Desdemonas—the one an outspoken woman, aware of her own agency; the other a "maiden never bold"[17]—into a rarefied heroine, Verdi-Boito's *Otello* gives particular cachet to a socially imbedded male fantasy—the extravagant trust and reverence accorded to women which, in constructing them as enclosures of perfection, opens them to victimization as well as to the demonic. In a letter to Giulio Ricordi, his publisher, Verdi describes his Desdemona:

> . . . a female who allows herself to be mistreated, slapped, and even strangled, forgives and entreats, she appears to be a stupid little thing! But Desdemona is not a woman, she's . . . the type of goodness, of resignation, of sacrifice! They are creatures born for others, unconscious of their own *ego!* Beings that exist in part, and that Shakespeare has poeticized and deified, . . . types that have never been encountered, except perhaps in Antigone of the ancient theater.[18]

To support Verdi's conception of Desdemona as an ego-less, malleable "being," Arrigo Boito's unusually explicit instructions for the physical performance of an ideal Desdemona call for restraint, "simple and gentle" gestures, all designed to evoke "a feeling of love, purity, nobility, docility, ingenuousness and resignation."[19] Transformed into a passive, guileless, *fin-de-siècle femme fragile* who adores Otello selflessly, Desdemona is *il maestro's* creation: in describing hers as "a part where the thread, the melodic line, never stops from the first to the last note,"[20] Verdi figures her as the epitome of the lyrical Italian operatic ideal, invests her with what had become his own musical signature.

Nowhere in Verdi's score is this perfected melodic strain so foregrounded as in what Joseph Kerman calls *Otello's* "architectural, austere" final act, where the first half—dramatizing Desdemona's preparations for bed—constitutes a monologue for Desdemona, made up of an entrance-*scena* (the Willow Song) and a free-standing *pezzo* (the "Ave Maria")—the first, and only, soprano solos in the entire score.[21] Both had preoccupied librettist and composer equally, especially since it was inevitable that comparisons would be made with Rossini's *Otello* (1816), which also included a Willow Song and a prayer—the most successful and popular arias in the entire opera.[22] And not only did the compositional circumstances arise from male artistic rivalry but Boito's libretto accords primacy, not to Shakespeare's text, but to that of a rival poet. Boito was working from François-Victor Hugo's translation, in which Hugo had transcribed four stanzas of a willow song—those closest to Shakespeare's version—from Thomas Percy's 1765 collection, *Reliques of Ancient English Poetry,* adding them to his commentary together with the implication that they constituted a complete poem and were the original of Desdemona's song. It is these stanzas, not Shakespeare's, which determined both the ordering and the content of Boito's new Willow Song, the most metrically complex text in the opera, and the most difficult to sing: Verdi wrote to Francis Faccio, conductor of the *Otello* premiere, that "the [performing artist], like the Holy Trinity, must produce three voices, one for Desdemona, another for Barbara . . . and a third voice for the '*Salce, salce, salce*" [the "willow" refrain].[23] But Boito's most intriguing changes involve gender: the Percy version inscribes two voices—the narrator and the lover, both male; Boito not only adds a third but regenders the speaker and casts Percy's "She was born to be false, and I to die for love" as Desdemona's *"Egli era nato—per sua gloria, / Io per amarlo e per morir"* ("He was born for glory, / I to love him and to die"), a phrase interrupted by what Desdemona reads as a knock on the door and what Emilia tells her is the wind.[24] Whereas the original wording, complicit with the Iago-Othello demonizing of women, positions them as naturally false, Boito's version positions Desdemona in relation to Otello by mapping out distinctively separate male and female territories—a construction which, in the orchestral score, the wind's "voice" naturalizes, as though complicit with her premonition.

Even more strikingly, however, the scoring for the song—a single cor anglais and woodwinds—is rooted in F sharp minor, a key first introduced (as F major) into the opera by Iago, at Cassio's dismissal in act 1, and next picked up by Desdemona in her climactic act 1 duet with Otello (her first appearance). That Verdi keeps Desdemona in this key throughout the duet initiates a complex musical gesture that develops full significance only at the close: here, not only does her use of F suggest that Iago's venom is already beginning to work, in that she appropriates his vocal register, but her acceptance of F also signifies her transcendent innocence, her inability to imagine the infidelity of which Otello will later accuse her.[25] When the key recurs, in the Willow Song, the shift to a minor register, together with Emilia's two brief questions ("Did he seem calmer?; But why this talk of dying?") and Desdemona's own interruptions, as she speaks her feelings, counter a sustained melodic line, suggesting a diminishment from the tonic expressive of Desdemona's desolation; minimal underlying orchestral accompaniment stresses even further the isolation of her voice and person,[26] and her breaking phrases anticipate the final cutting-off of her voice.

By contrast, the "Ave Maria," scored primarily as an *adagio* for strings and one of the opera's most traditionally conventional compositions, is in A flat major throughout. Set in an old Italian lyric form (aa'ba''), it begins as a vernacular version of the familiar Latin prayer and moves to Desdemona's personal prayer for the weak, afflicted, and innocent; the melody hints at plainsong and, like the Willow Song, finally disintegrates into softly voiced phrases, lacking orchestral support, as Desdemona repeats the first and last words of the prayer, *"Ave Maria. . . . nell'ora della morte. Amen."*[27] Here, even though Desdemona "owns" her own key and prays to a feminine intercessor, the prayer also constitutes a sign of her subservience to an ideological construction: not only is it cued by a line from Shakespeare's *Othello* ("Have you prayed tonight, Desdemona?") but it represents the climax of the devotional iconology with which Verdi, as her surrogate "father," surrounds her. And, during a performance of Verdi's opera, the applause that inevitably follows this aria can seem to wed the soprano's beauty of utterance to Desdemona's apprehensive fear, as though the social conventions of opera spectatorship were complicit with the represented cultural fantasy of entrapped femininity.[28]

The signifying relations between particular key areas with important dramatic associations become even more complex as *Otello* draws to a close. Otello's entrance into the bedchamber is accompanied by a motif built on the notes of the E major triad (a key associated with Otello's greatness, his heroic destiny) which quickly reappears in the key of A, thus incorporating the key of Desdemona's "Ave Maria" and reintroducing the *bacio* theme—the central motif of the closing act 1 duet that expresses Desdemona's and Otello's shared love. There, Desdemona bends down to kiss an Otello who has momentarily collapsed, overcome by his emotions; here, as Otello kisses the sleeping Desdemona three times, that gesture is precisely reversed. Now, the melody turns again to E, followed by a return to C major—the key associated with Iago's control over Otello and which recurs at each stage of his fall—again as in the love duet. But the expected cadence in the key of E fails to appear; instead Desdemona's awakening is accompanied by a sudden modulation to an ominous dominant of F sharp minor, recalling both Iago's voice and the Willow Song, with its premonitions of death. And, in direct contrast to the chromatic harmonies of the act 1 duet, the ensuing exchange between Desdemona and Otello is set in rapid *parlante* with no hint of the melodic line, Desdemona's sign. Boito's libretto radically compresses the relations that follow Desdemona's death, which are handled in recitative and *scena* music punctuated, as she returns briefly to consciousness, with several broken melodic phrases set to string harmonies. Spare recitative again articulates the Otello-Emilia exchange and Iago's escape (Emilia remains alive) before the *bacio* theme recurs for the last time, at the end of Otello's final, intensely charged *arioso*-recitative. Its striking final cadence builds a sequence of descending chords—C major to A minor to F major—over a tonic pedal of E; the last rhyme—*giacio/bacio*—condenses "lie" and "kiss," and as Otello dies, not only does F return to the tonic key of E but Verdi sets the last syllable beneath a rest: no pitched note, just the expiring sound of speech.[29]

That *Otello*—with Otello's final breath—ends in E major implies the return of Otello's glory, which triumphs over the C major triad associated with Iago, and even, perhaps, over the D flat major that signifies Otello's love for Desdemona. The stage picture, however,—only the two bodies, close together within a private space—privileges Otello's restoration as lover, as does the extraordinary link backward, through the recurrent *bacio* theme, to the serene harmony of act 1's closing duet. Although this seems to open up a contradiction, its musical strategy also resolves, as in that duet, the dual elements of Otello's character, linking, in David Lawton's phrase, "the giant and the lover, the soldier and the man."[30] Insofar as the close of Verdi's opera not only privileges Otello's subjectivity and centrality but, through its final plagal cadence, attempts to reconstitute the several aspects of his identity as a whole, it seems to do so at Desdemona's expense. Yet that last return to the *bacio* theme can also be understood as a reprise of Desdemona's and Otello's earlier duet with one voice—Desdemona's—silenced. In *Otello*'s vocal economy, which identifies Desdemona specifically with the lyric tradition of Italian opera and where her voice functions especially to counterbalance Iago's analytic intellect and his desire to annihilate all melody (*"I vostri infrangerò soavi accordi"* [I shall shatter your gentle sounds]), her demonizing and her murder signal the death of that tradition, to which Otello's *"E tu . . . come sei pallida! e stanca, e muta, e bella / Pia creatura nata sotto maligna stella,"*[31] as well as the final harmonic recall, pay homage. At the close, Desdemona's silenced voice may speak even louder than the powerfully romantic *Liebestod*-like stage image or Otello's privileged subjectivity, for her Willow Song and Ave Maria represent, within turn-of-the-century musical politics, a final embrace of, and farewell to, the naiveté and simplicity associated with pure, harmonic melody, and with the past.[32] But so privileging Desdemona's erased voice does not subvert, or even call into question, Verdi's conceptualization of her as the type of goodness, resignation, and sacrifice; rather, whatever potential resistance that erasure generates serves primarily to call *Otello*'s musical innovations into question. Most strikingly, Verdi's musical gestures ally him with Brabantio as well as with Iago, with the most central and most marginal representatives of patriarchal law. Bettering both, his all-encompassing appropriation of Desdemona's "virtue" envelops her in perfect—and *almost* perfectly sustained—melody, which both commemorates his past reputation and ensures the lasting legacy of his own transcendent (male) artistry.

If the aural economy of Verdi's *Otello* situates it as a kind of limit-text, Welles's *Othello* constitutes another, its opposite, which appropriates Desdemona's image within a visual economy. His 1978 documentary, *Filming "Othello,"* almost perfectly exemplifies that appropriation: not only is it organized as a series of male conversations or monologues, with Welles, who played Othello, at its center; but none of the three Desdemonas who worked on the film appears to tell her story.[33] Moreover, the two images of Desdemona inscribed within that film—the opening funeral procession, one of its masterful set pieces, and a haunting single frame of her face in high-angle extreme close up, with gauzy fabric stretched across her features, distorting them into an eerie death mask—show her immobilized in death; both function not to reveal the actress's performance but to advertize the filmmaker's stylistic control. And in *Othello,* one sequence in particular serves as a paradigm for how Desdemona is further dominated by the camera apparatus itself: in the scene where Othello greets the Venetian senators who have come to Cyprus to relieve him of his command, she walks forward into a close-up, looking straight at the camera lens as though it were a character; suddenly, Othello's hand comes into the shot from left frame foreground to slap her face. Here, the camera literally becomes Othello, positioning Desdemona as the object of his gaze and gesture,[34] a shot that is later followed by another characteristic camera move: a track out from the close-up to a long shot which situates her figure at a great distance from Othello as, dwarfed by his presence, her tiny figure exits the shot frame right background, her face turned away from his—and the camera's—look.

Both this obsession with sexual hierarchy and these exaggerated representations of woman as the object of the male gaze are entirely characteristic of classical narrative cinema—constructed by a male auteur to assume an identification with a male vantage point and addressed to a male spectator. To the extent that such cinema is informed, even driven, by a sexual politics that privileges male subjectivity and in which, according to Raymond Bellour, "woman occupies a central place only to the extent that it's a place assigned to her by the logic of masculine desire,"[35] its operations almost perfectly describe, and are uniquely suited to the grammar of *Othello*. For Shakespeare's playtext not only invites audiences to identify with a male point of view, but its scopic project depends on the virgin/whore dichotomy characteristic of woman's representation in classical narrative cinema, an opposition that, ultimately, works to universalize both categories.

Welles's film further exploits this match between two classical forms, tragedy and Hollywood cinema, by reconstructing Shakespeare's narrative to conform to an investigative model not unlike that of his earlier *Citizen Kane* (1941) or the later *Touch of Evil* (1958), using what amounts to an extended (and enclosed) flashback to explain the enigma posed by the opening (and framing) funeral procession. As Welles himself puts it, "My films are all for the most part a physical search."[36] Yet another version of the myth of lost Eden and the fall from innocence that so fascinated and obsessed him, his *Othello* makes Desdemona's body central to that search, a site of spectacle interrogated by the camera's investigative gaze, which, in turn, is allied, especially once Iago convinces him of her infidelity, with Othello's obsessive paranoia. In his documentary, Welles locates Desdemona as part of Othello's knowledge of Venetian society, his dream of woman; and indeed Suzanne Cloutier's Desdemona *is* a dream figure—a luminous "fairy princess" situated within what Jack Jorgens aptly calls a "symbolic geography" that opposes the art and institutions of high Venetian culture to the stark ramparts and labyrinthine spaces of Cyprus's fortress–frontier.[37] Framed initially by images of Venetian art and architecture, she becomes one with its eroticized feminine spectacle, which is controlled by Othello's grandiose presence, expressed in fluid camera movements and coherent editing—what Jorgens refers to as "the Othello style,"[38] once in Cyprus, however, she becomes increasingly subjected to the canted camera angles and rapid, often disorienting montage associated with Iago's style, which eventually transforms and co-opts Othello's own gaze. In terms of the trajectory of Desdemona's body, she moves from being enfolded by one patriarchal enclosure—represented by the formal stability of the Venetian state spectacle—only to be bound up within another—where the natural, but often vertiginously constructed spaces of Cyprus not only problematize patriarchal law but admit, and reveal, its most transgressive, psychotic manifestations.

Just as Verdi's act 1 finale, the Desdemona-Othello duet expressing their shared love, establishes an anticipatory web of sound motifs which consistently recur and are transformed in *Otello*'s close, Welles constructs a series of visual signatures that link marriage to murder and magnifies that connection by repetition as well as by increasing visual and aural exaggeration and distortion to generate a structure of suspense that, during the murder, finally condenses all signs to a nightmare display of excess. Here, two sequences are exemplary: one marks the climax of the Venetian romance; the other a stage in Othello's growing jealousy. The first begins with a stunning long shot of the Piazza San Marco, taken from behind the mechanical clock figures that strike the hour, and cuts to a full shot (accompanied by nondiegetic lute music on the sound track) of Othello parting the gauzy bed curtains and then to a high-angle mid-close-up of Desdemona, dressed in a white nightgown, her blonde hair swirling about her on the bed. In mid-shot, Othello bends over her, and, as the billowing curtains and the barred chamber window cast shadows over the bed, the camera dollies in to a close-up as he kisses her, his hand fondling her hair. Abruptly, the screen goes black, censoring the erotic spectacle, blacking out Desdemona's presence with Othello's and, in the ensuing images, substituting a violent storm, which opens out onto Othello's triumphant arrival at Cyprus, for the consummation of their marriage.

In the second sequence, Othello enters the bedchamber (again in full shot) and (again) parts the curtains; in place of language or lute music, the sound track amplifies the grating noise of the curtain rings moving along the traverse, and the cut reveals a slight high-angle full shot of the bed, its rumpled sheets traced by long shadows from the window grating and the tasseled canopy overhead. Although he himself has recently risen from the bed, Othello now rereads in its disheveled sheets the signs of Desdemona's sexual betrayal, and the concluding shots in the sequence—a low-angle full shot of Othello from the point of view of the site he searches and a tracking long shot of Desdemona floating through the arched spaces of the chapel on her way to pray at the altar—confirm that his paranoia is the product of his own look. Even if it occurred only once (it does not; rather, it *re*curs), the next-to-last shot in this sequence would require comment, since it both conforms to and simultaneously deconstructs the classic shot/reverse shot exchange. For it reinscribes Desdemona's absence as a "gaze" that precisely mirrors Othello's own, reflecting onto the looker his own status as an empty subject. And, especially insofar as the extreme angle associates it with Iago's distorted vision, and thus with his imaginary "ocular proof," it uncannily suggests his use of Desdemona as well as his desired penetration of the site and (contradictorily) his misogynistic mockery of the marriage bed.

The reverse of this shot—elided in this sequence but elsewhere, and especially in the murder, a characteristic element—the high-angle close-up or mid-close-up of Desdemona's body—contributes equally to *Othello*'s uncanny representational strategies. For, whereas a classic shot/reverse shot regime consistently establishes Desdemona and Othello as quite close together, the repeated high-angle shots that so intensify her objectification widen and magnify the distance between them, much as though the camera's eye must evade her, and, in observing her only from an immense height, seek to represent her, not as woman but as an icon of herself. Only once does the film permit Desdemona to reverse the high-angle point-of-view gaze onto Othello: when he accuses her in the so-called whorehouse scene, she stands, looking down at him as he kneels at her feet, caressing the fabric of her skirt ("O thou weed! / Who art so lovely fair, and smell'st so sweet" [4.2.67–68]). But even here, the camera intrudes, breaking her potentially corrective gaze to follow his gesture by panning down her still, column-like figure. Although her fetishized image undermines Othello's verbal attack, Desdemona herself, as the subject of discourse, is absent; rather, it is woman's body which is spoken: her voice, divorced from her own image, belongs to Othello's, and he grants it only limited validity, accuses her of lying, and, eventually, silences her.

Her very fetishization, however, opens up a contradiction. For, in spite of being subjected to expressionistic camera angles and aggressive editing that attempt to inscribe Othello's growing paranoia on the surface of her body, Desdemona's pale blonde beauty resists such (Freudian) perversions: the camera's eye cannot penetrate its opaque surfaces, cannot discover the (invisible) symptoms of infidelity for which it searches. Nevertheless, as the murder scene makes clear, Othello's obsessive attempts to submit Desdemona to a series of sensual tests and to read her moist hand and her failure to produce the handkerchief result in a diagnosis—"It is the cause"—that confirms her identity as a "sick" whore. Such clinical terms seem entirely appropriate here, for the image that opens that scene—a man who carries a light entering to a woman lying on a bed—analogizes the relation between physician and patient in an examining room and invites reading Othello's address to Desdemona's body as his failure to *de*specularize her body, to substitute, for the erotic spectacle that meets his eye, an object lacking identity, confined to her body and knowable only by the name of her illness:

"else-she'll-betray-more-men." In patriarchy, to desexualize a woman's body is, ultimately, to deny its very existence; and, as in the clinical relationship, where the woman patient is both de-eroticized and subjected to an ever-widening (usually) male gaze, her own vision is denied.[39]

Welles's heavily constructed murder scene represents just such a crucial restriction of woman's sight, a denial of her presence. Rapid montage, hysterical camera movements, tilted angles, spatial disjunctures, and disorienting perspectives seem designed to fragment the event, making it resist any coherence except that provided by the camera, which functions much like Foucault's imaginary "speaking eye"—the "pure Gaze that would be pure Language."[40] Pure *cinematic* language, that is, for, although this is a sound film, and although the voice of Welles's Othello dominates the image, Welles's stylistics derive from silent film, more especially from Carl Dreyer's 1928 *La Passion de Jeanne d'Arc,* in which faces float against an empty or stark background space, privileging the human face, and most particularly the look, as the sole register of the internal drama. In *Othello,* although Desdemona's eyes are open as Othello enters the room, she closes them as he approaches the bed; and her body, increasingly fractured and dis-membered by montage that works to destroy the illusion of Renaissance space, is finally reduced to metonymical representation—the bed; the lighted, and then extinguished, candle; the handkerchief. By contrast, Othello is represented, first, only as a massive shadow, a sign of encroaching darkness which then resolves to a seemingly disembodied face and gradually gains three-dimensionality as he moves forward in the shot until, finally, just before the murder, he becomes a grotesque single eye.[41] Reduced to its simplest signs, the sequence opposes that dominant, all-seeing eye—which stares directly at the camera—to Desdemona's sightless face and represents the murder itself as a violation of sight. As Othello draws the lace-edged handkerchief (or wedding sheet) over her face,[42] seen in a high-angle extreme close-up, a nonlinguistic, involuntary humming floods the sound track, increasing in volume as, in a mid-shot, Othello's shadowed bulk obscures Desdemona and, in the ensuing shot, turns again to a shadow against which her face, her mouth and eyes open but now completely covered, is framed by his hands. From this, perhaps the most perfect figure of her complete enclosure as well as her silencing, the film cuts to a low-angle long shot of the castle ramparts, with Iago's prison-cage hanging beside the tower, its window darkened; and the humming noise ends with a chord, which is immediately transformed into the clang of bells, a discordant echo of the Venetian clock-figures that preceded the first image of the bed as erotic spectacle. Finally, the film deprives its viewing audience of the actual moment of Desdemona's death, closing this sequence on a low-angle mid-shot of the trembling bed canopy, which reconstitutes her, not as an icon but, in a last metonymy, and in her absence, as one with the site of the violated wedding bed.

When, later, Othello returns to that site to lift Desdemona's body from the floor and place it on the bed, his gaze becomes locked within a shot/reverse shot exchange of high- and low-angle shots which subordinates his look to that of the Venetians who watch him from a window opening situated high in the ceiling above the bed. Here, too, his all-seeing eye becomes subdued and absorbed within a metonymic equivalent which reattributes all control over seeing to the voyeuristic onlookers who watch his death from a god-like distance. But that control is not complete, for at this point the film articulates two endings before cutting away to reprise the funeral procession with which it began and which functions to mask the murder. In the first, a full shot of Othello holding Desdemona in his arms, the camera holds on the space as he falls out of the frame, and the film mimics that disappearance with a blackout followed by a dissolve, marked by a final chord of the choral anthem that accompanies the sequence. Two shots comprise the second ending: a high-angle shot of the two bodies on the bed, both now immobilized in death, and its by now familiar obverse: a low-angle full shot, from the point of view of the searched space, which gazes at the watchers, far above, who slowly close off the window's omniscient eye.

As one of the final signs of a paranoid text which details masculine subjectivity in crisis, this shot has a double function: not only does it summarize, once again, the emptiness of that subject but it also reasserts Welles's own (absent) presence. Just as it is he who speaks the voice-over narration ("Once in Venice, a Moor called Othello . . .") which, following the initial funeral prologue (itself an homage to another *auteur,* Eisenstein), opens the narrative proper, Welles writes his own visual signature on Shakespeare's *Othello,* rivals him as transcendent author, has the final word.[43] If the last words of his documentary film offer one kind of authorial statement—"I wish I wasn't looking back on *Othello* and I was looking forward—that would be a hell of a picture"—the closing voice-over of his 1942 film, *The Magnificent Ambersons,* more accurately represents his appropriation of both Desdemona's body and the body of Shakespeare's playtext: "I wrote and directed [this film]; my name is Orson Welles." Finally, this statement points the contradiction central to the film: that Welles as the partially deconstructed male subject ultimately comes under the control of Welles the *auteur*.

Authorizing and authority—as both pertain to "Shakespeare's voice" and to the gendered relations of gaze and spectacle—are also at issue in Dmitri Buchovetski's 1922 *Othello,* starring Emil Jannings—one of several postwar films commemorating celebrated Deutsches Theatre productions and making them available to a wider audience.[44] In a curious blend of textual fidelity and erasure, Buchovetski's murder scene focuses so exclusively on preserving the characters' words intact that the "sound" of Shakespeare's language—privileged as imaged speech in frequent intertitles—not only leeches all potential tension from the action but risks becoming an intrusive third presence, an omniscient voyeur who controls and mediates the murder. The film's visual regime, which intercuts omniscient point-of-view shots with mid-shots and mid-close-ups designed to capture Jannings's performance in detail and with high-angle mid–shots and close-ups of Desdemona, rather conventionally sustains Othello's dominant gaze and Desdemona's specular objectification. In addition, editing also functions to protect Othello's subjectivity at Desdemona's expense. Although a full shot shows him about to strangle her, an oddly elliptic cut then eliminates her body to reveal, in the ensuing mid-shot, the foreground figures of Othello and Emilia positioned against a black background. In contrast to the full voicing of the murder's preliminaries, no titles articulate Emilia's revelations: Othello simply throws her from him, as though to make room for Iago's presence and for the accusatory exchange—privileged in close-ups—that follows. Like Desdemona, who appears in only three more shots (two of which privilege Othello's dying kiss), her voice and body become dispensable commodities, subsumed and co-opted by the film's final, radically anomalous renegotiation of the tension between the personal and political that shapes Shakespeare's play-text.

For the concluding sequences eclipse both women altogether through a series of moves which deprivilege "the tragic lodging/ loading" of the bed and replace that spectacle (and Desdemona's body as its center) with the reconciliation of Othello and Cassio. Strikingly, a high-angle long shot of the crowd outside the palace, followed by an intertitle—"Othello is arrested! O woe!"—complies with this denial as well as with the shift to an exclusively male spectacle, one that, by positioning Desdemona as an object of exchange within male subjectivity, heals the breach between general and trusted officer in a transfer of political and erotic power. Their gestures—Cassio kneels to kiss Othello's hand; Othello caresses Cassio's face—culminate as the two stand, foreheads touching, each gazing into the other's eyes. Whether read as homosocial, as homoerotic, or as both,[45] this mirroring look clearly positions Cassio as Othello's substitute, an exchange confirmed when he later appears on a balcony, tells the waiting crowd that Othello is dead, and, in anguish, prays for his soul. Here, the editing pattern alternates between high-angle long shots of the crowd and low-angle full to mid-shots of Cassio, whose gaze and gesture—a Mussolini-like salute—controls, and subjects, the film's inscribed spectators. This *Othello* exploits Desdemona's death as an event that not only regenders spectacle and reauthorizes the male gaze but also reshapes Cypriot-Venetian politics. In the film's final, most interventionary, substitution, Othello's black generalship opens out onto Cassio's dictatorship—and beyond that, onto the black shirts of Italy's National Fascist regime.[46] That such a move toward imposed unity resulted from collaboration between Shakespeare, a Russian émigré director, and a German production company traces an ironically prophetic German-Italian axis over the body of a text central to Britain's cultural heritage.

Although no other *Othello*, to my knowledge, so explicitly alludes to an historical figure's rise to power, Buchovetski's making of Desdemona's murder, and the consequent privileging of Othello's centrality, has a long history in the theatre.[47] Edwin Booth, for example, writes, "I prefer the bed at the side of the stage, with the head towards the audience; it is of more importance that Othello's face should be seen than Desdemona's dead body, and the killing is partly hidden at the same time."[48] And Mrs. Fanny Kemble is even more prescriptive about what she considers "technical difficulties" of representation: "The audience, of course, cannot be expected to sit by and see Desdemona smothered; the curtains of the alcove in which the bed is, are therefore lowered during that operation, but it is very desirable, if not absolutely necessary that she should be both heard and seen when she gasps out her dying exculpation of her husband, and while she is perpetually apostrophized by Emilia, Othello, and Lodovico."[49] This tradition substitutes one spectacle—in Booth's case, the male actor's face—for another in an exchange which not only momentarily erases Desdemona's body but in which sound (or its lack) constitutes the only sign of her murder; even Mrs. Kemble's proposed staging empowers Desdemona in order to enhance Othello's subjectivity (her absolution of him) and to stress her position as a stage-property, the object of others' speech.[50] Certainly hiding the murder insulates spectators from what might be called Shakespeare's authorized view of its deeply gendered subject-object relations, which, with Emilia's death, again punishes women for owning—and activating—the gaze. If one objective here is to protect a social audience from potentially troubling complicity in the murder (men only?) or from its threats (women only?), such a practice also functions to protect Othello's status as a hero, as well as the male project called the play,[51] and thus to circumscribe Desdemona's history (and that of woman spectators) within his "tragedy."

If nineteenth-century theatrical practice tended to refine or repress particular lines of sight, a late twentieth-century *Othello,* Terry Hands's 1985–86 production for the Royal Shakespeare Company, not only exploits the female body but stresses, and further problematizes, gendered looking relations. Hands's performance text makes Desdemona's body the insistent focus of attention from the Willow scene forward, isolating her sleeping body on a downstage left bed, behind which the mirrored black surfaces of the huge raked stage shimmer away into the upstage darkness, where the brawl in which Roderigo is killed and Cassio wounded takes place.[52] But because, in the early Stratford performances, the bed blocked sightlines for spectators in the stalls, it was later lowered to stage level just as the fight began, a change which constitutes a curiously apt emblem of Desdemona's passive compliance—to the needs of spectators, to a male spectacle, to the demands of being "true" to Shakespeare's narrative strategy. Nevertheless, her foreground presence gives a curiously misogynistic spin to her relation to the upstage action, linking her passive body to Iago's betrayals and Roderigo's death—the "cause" (in a sense different from Othello's later usage) of both. Raised once again for the final scene, the white-draped bed, with Desdemona's sleeping, and then lifeless, body, becomes a site that transforms Othello's earlier disjointed utterance, "Lie with her? lie on her!—We say lie on her when they belie her," to reveal "lying" as a code shared by both body and voice, one that Desdemona's last utterance ("Nobody, I myself") turns inside out to confirm Iago's use of her goodness, unmask Othello's final accusation of falsity ("she is a liar"), and, ultimately, precipitate his suicide. Here, as Othello draws his hidden dagger, he feigns a slashing blow at Iago before cutting his own throat and falling on Desdemona to claim a final kiss. Iago throws himself forward on top of Othello's white-robed body but is pulled back, forced by those who restrain him to look at his "work."[53]

Hands's Rembrandtesque final tableau, reminiscent of "The Anatomy Lesson," literalizes closure across the surface of Desdemona's body, opening up fissures along the gendered lines of sight. As Lodovico, covering the bodies with his black cloak, proclaims, "The object poisons sight, / Let it be hid," language and gesture condense, simultaneously calling attention to the male-dominated voyeuristic project of the play and to his refusal—and that of the other males on stage—to acknowledge ownership of the gaze. As though obedient to Othello's own words, he and the others look with "subdued eyes"—a viewing position traditionally accorded to women—a strategy that effectively displaces their desiring gaze, together with all responsibility for the double deaths, onto Iago. And it is Iago's ambiguously homoerotic gaze that constitutes the performance text's final sign of male subjectivity—a last look that appears to fetishize Othello himself (dressed here, as throughout, in a flowing white robe) by positioning him on the side of feminized spectacle. Although the shift that decenters Desdemona as a spectacle in order doubly to privilege males—in directing the lines of sight, constituting the gaze as well as the spectacle—is what Darko Suvin would call an invariant feature of representations of *Othello*,[54] Hands's performance text, like Buchovetski's film, puts that invariant to radical use. However, whereas this *Othello* also positions Desdemona as an exchange within male subjectivity, its final interweave of looks reveals, not a public affirmation of male power, but a hidden ambivalence within male spectatorship. For in demonizing all manifestations of the marginalized Other—women, the "womanish" jealous male (who also represents racial difference)—as well as the homosocial/homoerotic, Hands's performance text seeks to affirm the dominance of the (straight) male gaze but does so at the precise moment when that gaze averts itself, chooses (woman-like) to look away. However potentially homophobic, not only does this ambiguous gesture acknowledge multiple, fluid gender identifications, and thus call into question a theory of spectatorship built on a simple binary oppositions, but it also brings into sharp focus the challenge to male subjectivity central to *Othello*—the loss of self involved in identification, especially identification with the feminine.

If, at the close, Hands's performance text seems to blur, if not altogether deconstruct, the gendered gaze on which *Othello* depends, it does not open up a space, which enables women to resist that gaze. Although it works toward exposing the mechanisms of violence and seduction in looking relations, and thus fosters an understanding, which potentially compromises a male spectator and subverts the hegemony of his gaze, it also suggests that the male gaze exerts power and control even when it looks away. Moreover, because Hands's strongly theatricalized closural composition attempts to contain the drama's energies, it invites a distanced, meditative perspective on the (masculine) tragedy, a highly privileged cultural form. But popular representations of *Othello,* in particular those which either distance themselves (however slightly) from Shakespeare's cultural authority or reappropriate elements of *Othello*'s text, can more easily accommodate the possibility of containment and resistance—what Stuart Hall calls the "double movement" of popular culture.[55] Here, two films—August Blom's 1911 *Desdemona* and George Cukor's 1947 *A Double Life*—offer especially pertinent, and almost diametrically opposed, examples of *Othello*-texts that use Shakespeare's play to interrogate the construction of the male subject. And both narratives articulate this movement by calling attention to the potential dangers of theatrical representation: its ability to confuse the boundaries between appearance and "the real" and, ultimately, to dismantle psychological integrity.[56]

Blom's *Desdemona* transforms Shakespeare's play into a "thrilling modern drama"[57] set in smart haut-bourgeois décors—a partially Ibsenized *Othello* which (at least initially) not only explores Desdemona's desire but also assumes, as well as *represents,* her guilt. Conceived as one of Nordisk Films Kompagni's "shocking"—and immensely popular—scandal films,[58] its story (told in twenty-nine tableaux) of a rather stereotypical affair unfolds within a theatrical milieu: Ejnar and Maria Lowe (Valdemar Psilander and Thyra Reymann) are actors playing Othello and Desdemona in a production of *Othello.* While rehearsing, Preben Winge (Nicolai Brechling), who plays Iago, makes advances to Maria, who rebuffs him; by spying on her in her dressing room and in a restaurant, he discovers that she is having an affair with the monocled Count Brisson (Henry Lauritzen). Throughout, *Desdemona* seems both to anticipate and be constructed for a male spectator: although its early tableaux focus almost exclusively on Maria, her look receives authority and agency in only two close-ups—one of a card from Brisson, the other of a locket, containing his picture—and both represent evidence of her adultery. When Maria returns home from her rendezvous with Brisson, she avoids her husband's questions and his embrace by pretending a headache; retiring to her bedroom, she removes her coat, fixes her hair before a mirror and then poses, center screen, stretching her arms in a deliberately sexualized display of sleepiness directed toward the camera before arranging herself on the chaise longue in left foreground, the locket Brisson has given her clasped in her hands. Meanwhile, in the drawing room, Preben shows Ejnar the card Maria has received from Brisson; stunned, Ejnar enters her bedroom, stares at her sleeping body and, without waking her, discovers the locket, which has dropped to the floor. A second shot of the mirror shows him holding the locket's photo close to his face: in the next tableau, he makes himself up to look like Brisson before returning to the bedroom, where he kneels by his sleeping wife. Awakening, Maria starts to reject him, assuming he is her husband, and then rises, startled to embrace him, betrayed by the double "ocular proof" of her monocled lover's photo and her husband's impersonation—a neat reversal of the then conventional use of disguise in comic shorts or detective films. Ejnar stops himself from striking her, throws her shawl at her and points her toward the door; as she leaves, he puts his hands to his head and kneels in despair by the chaise longue.

That this "modern" melodramatic ending appropriates *Othello*'s so-called whorehouse scene (4.2) to punish a woman's deviance from bourgeois conventions is less revealing, however, than the relations between the fetishistic shot of Maria's body and Ejnar's mirror shot, which inscribes within the film a male gaze that differs from both Winge's and Ejnar's voyeurism—one that not only repositions the identity of the Other and regenders the spectacle but articulates a split within male subjectivity. And it is this split, together with the shift away from Maria as the primary spectacle, that shapes *Desdemona*'s second ending, which takes place in the theatre where Ejnar and Maria are performing in *Othello*. In this final sequence, a conventional long shot of the stage from the theatre audience's point of view shows Desdemona in bed as Othello enters, moves toward her and bends over her; the film then cuts to a full shot of Brisson, leaning forward in his stage-side box, and then rising to stand: the next shot, in which Ejnar-Othello strangles Maria-Desdemona, is a medium-long shot from Brisson's point of view. Whereas the traditional long shot of the stage concerns the drama of Desdemona and Othello, the medium-long shot articulates the offstage drama, which at this point conflates with the staged representation (Maria dies as Desdemona), a process confirmed by ensuing shots: Brisson standing; the stage, where Ejnar's Othello moves forward pointing an accusing finger at Brisson and clenching his fists in anger; Brisson in the box, with the entire audience turned toward him until, subject to their accusing eyes, he

leaves. The last tableau returns to the stage: as two policemen enter
to arrest Ejnar, he wrests away to fall on Maria-Desdemona's body,
hiding his head in disgrace.

Desdemona's finale, with its doubled spectacles, uses Shakespeare's *Othello* to punish marital infidelity and the theatrical occasion itself to recapitulate the earlier mirror scene and to displace
blame, if not for the murder, certainly for the destruction of Ejnar's
marriage, onto Count Brisson.[59] But, although turning the adulterer
into an offstage spectacle results in his public exposure and in a
(potential) shift of audience sympathy toward Ejnar-Othello, it is
Ejnar, not the noble Brisson, who remains trapped in the theatre,
the cuckolded murderer, scapegoat of both real and fictional spectacles. If this confrontation between *Othello* and real-life melodrama refuses, at the close, to address the issues of gender relations
and class privilege it raises or to see itself as anything more than a
kind of early Scandinavian *National Enquirer* tale, its attempt to
psychologize Ejnar's character and to circulate blame through an
exchange of looks certainly calls the scopic project into question,
compromises the male gaze that subjects (and erases) woman by
turning its potentially deadly power on those who seek to authorize
it.

In its central premise—the commonplace but nonetheless threatening assumption that actors become the characters they play—
George Cukor's *A Double Life* seems at first a direct, and entirely
predictable, descendant of Blom's film.[60] Tony John (Ronald Colman), a matinee idol famous for his roles in farce, is persuaded to
attempt Othello, a part he has always desired to play and for which
he has outlined what his agent calls a "brilliant and believable"
strategy for the ending: killing Desdemona with a kiss. As he works
on and performs the role, it gradually takes over his personality, and
the film details his developing paranoia, leading to his eventual
suicide. Less predictably, however, this story of misplaced obsession—for a text rather than a woman, and for one particular moment, Desdemona's death—positions the Tony-Othello figure between two women—Tony's ex-wife Brita (Signe Hasso), who plays
Desdemona, and Pat Kroll (Shelley Winters), an ex-masseuse (from
Boston), now a waitress in the Venezia café—and appropriates
Othello's murder scene (repeating it four times) to threaten one
marginalized stereotype, the divorced, independent woman, and
kill another, the blonde hussy-victim borrowed from film noir.[61]
Indeed, Tony's own doubleness becomes contagious, infecting
every feature of the film.[62] Especially intriguing here is the film-
script's use of Othello's language as an "acoustic mirror" in which

Tony hears elements of himself—his jealousy, his fear of women; so that by anchoring his body and voice to that text he re-en-genders his own subjectivity.[63] Thus the film accords Shakespeare's play-text, as well as its characters, a double life: it is both a stable sign of a discursive authority located at the very center of the filmtext and a register of Tony's unstable, schizoid identity.

Of the four representations of Desdemona's murder, the first, *Othello*'s opening night, relies on entirely conventional relations between sound and image, voice and body. Here, Shakespeare's language grounds the continuity of a staged performance that dem-onstrates Tony's mastery of Othello's voice as well as his control over the image track, which supports the fluid movement of voice across shot boundaries. Only once does Tony's success as Othello seem at risk: as he approaches the bed ("Yet she must die, else she'll betray more men"), the film cuts to a high-angle full shot of Desdemona on the bed, accompanied by Tony's voice-over— "There are two men now, grappling for control, you and Othello" and then to a mid-close-up of Othello-Tony, holding a candle ("Put out the light"). Momentarily startling, the voice-over nevertheless speaks from a point close to events represented in the image track and, since no further splits occur, Tony's Othello achieves com-plete—and satisfactory—embodiment, confirming Tony's psycho-logical integrity. If the single high-angle shot reveals Tony observing himself from an omniscient point of view, elsewhere the sequence attempts to transfer the viewing audience to the stage,[64] generating an illusion of identity with the actor that is further enforced by withholding the traditional long shot establishing audience point of view. Instead, mid-shots and mid-close-ups of theatre spectators are cut in at several crucial moments: as Desdemona pleads, "But while I say one prayer"; after Othello bends to kiss (and kill) her; and after the kiss, as a black veil billows across the bed. Except for one man (who appears in only one of the seven shots), all these watchers are women. Keyed by Desdemona's words, their gaze not only confirms their involvement with her but establishes their com-plicity with Tony's performance—and with a discursive authority derived from Shakespeare—which enthralls and subjects them to his ability to push away and silence the female voice.

But this complex, self-reflexive reference to looking, and to the film as a project directed toward and consumed by women, also alludes to Colman's "real" status as matinee idol—more especially, as a Hollywood star fetishized by the attentive gaze of women viewers. Here, representation most precisely foregrounds one cen-tral problem that theory attempts to address and deconstruct: the extremely ambiguous position of the female spectator as a "mixed sexual body"[65]—desiring to be both Hasso-Desdemona and Colman-Othello. And the conclusion of the sequence makes the act of gendered spectatorship even more problematic by framing both the staged *Othello* and its inscribed spectators with an ironically distanced—and exclusively male—point of view, that of Bill (Tony's publicity man, the Cassio-figure), his agent, and the producer anticipating unfavorable reviews in a bar: "Who murders who?" . . . "He kills her with a kiss" . . . "Tonight he murders his girl; tomorrow they murder him."

Tony's successor, however, is threatened not by bad press but, at *Othello*'s 300th performance (where his acting seems more naturalistic than his initial, rather stagy performance), by Brita. This time, however, although Tony's point of view—an extreme close-up of Desdemona as she speaks, "Alas, he is betrayed, and I undone"—initiates the murder sequence, Brita-Desdemona's point of view (occasionally intercut with that of the backstage crew) dominates; and it is her voice, speaking a text that obliterates Shakespeare's, which betrays and undoes Tony's Othello, undermining the representation at the level of both sound and image. In that what she says—"Oh, Tony . . . Tony, Tony, please . . . Tony, Tony . . . Please stop him"—can express desire as well as fear, Brita's words not only cut through to the (inexpressible) contradiction central to Tony-Othello's identity but, by stopping the performance, assert the power of the female voice to control and disable male subjectivity. On the one hand, Brita's voicing links Tony's inability to perform with his castration fear; on the other, it draws him toward her. Both are made more explicit later when, faced with a wedding cake topped with figures of Desdemona and Othello to celebrate the production's second year, Tony mockingly asks, "Do I get to eat myself?" and then, claiming he is sick of *Othello,* asks Brita to remarry him. When she refuses, he beats on the locked door of her bedroom, his voice-over struggling between self-apostrophe and the Shakespearean phrases that articulate the deepest point of Othello's interior fantasy: "Don't hurt Brita" . . . "But she must die else she'll betray more men" . . . "Go home, you've lost control" . . . "Heaven truly knows that she is false as hell."

The sequence that follows, where Tony goes to Pat Kroll's apartment, represents Tony's actions as the direct consequence of his inability to possess Brita: here, he reasserts his control over both Othello's text and the female voice. And it is Pat's appropriation of Othello's words—"Wanna put out the light?"—which keys his fugue into Othello: her transgressive attempt to own (and regender) male discursive authority results in her death. Here, too, the film becomes momentarily complicit with containing and regulating the female voice by articulating the murder in a single long take and by privileging image rather than sound as the basis for continuity. Except for the (off-screen) sound of an El train passing, the murder occurs in an aural blackout, a strategy that effectively exempts "Shakespeare's voice" from blame. Only when the window curtain blows across the bed, obscuring it as on the stage and in the prompt copy which was the film's initial sign of the *Othello*-text, does that voice return—as Emilia's "My lord, my lord." And that disembodied voice-over becomes absorbed, first, by the (nondiegetic) music behind a high-angle full shot of Brita in bed, fingering her throat, and, then, by the scream of the landlady who discovers Pat's corpse, which is in turn transformed to musical chords. In reaffirming his subjectivity, Tony-Othello's "kiss of death" both silences the woman's mouth and elicits its cry.

The final representation of the murder returns to the theatre and turns Shakespeare's text on Tony-Othello, calling his mastery of it into question. As he becomes aware that the police are watching him from the wings, he attributes double meaning to Iago's "What you know, you know" and Lodovico's "You shall a close prisoner rest" and (twice) cries in his role: at "of one whose hand" and at "of one whose subdued eyes," the Doge must prompt him to continue. Reaching for Tony's hand and seeing her own come away covered with blood, Brita discovers that he has stabbed himself but stifles her scream—a final sign of her submission to Othello-Tony, which protects the integrity of the staged representation as well as his performance; later, at his backstage death, Tony places his reputation in her trust. "Don't let them say I was a bad actor."[66] In the film's initial introduction to Tony's actorly skills—the conclusion of *A Gentleman's Gentleman*, where he plays a valet who, by stealing his master's fiancée, becomes a "lady's gentleman"—the last words of his role, "I hope I've always given complete satisfaction," drew applause. *A Double Life* concludes, however, with a shot that, although it reprises the earlier occasion, defers both satisfaction and applause to offscreen spectators. It is a high-angle long shot, in complete silence, of the empty, spotlit stage, its curtains closing, the safety curtain descending. And, like Tony-Othello, whose absence it describes, this final shot has a double life. Here, the camera's overhead gaze at the empty stage confirms the fusion of actor and role—the one dying as the other; it also describes the deeply gendered fullness of that integrity as a lack, an erasure of the male subject—incapable of being represented, of being responded to, or even named.

If closing on emptiness seems calculated to deprive women spectators, like the ones inscribed earlier within the film, of Tony John's Othello, *A Double Life* does reward them, in the next-to-last shot, with a final glimpse of Ronald Colman. Magically—and across a single cut—Tony's Othello make-up disappears for his backstage death, transforming him from "black" man to white male star—a visual image that not only gives the cinema audience what they desire but, by privileging Colman-as-star-actor, works to overwhelm the disruptive blurring of appearance and "the real" the film attributes to theatrical representation. Moreover, at this point *A Double Life* also reconfirms its distance from and apparent indifference to racial difference, an issue which lies outside the film's scope of address and which has not figured in my analyses either of the gendered relations of body and voice or of spectator positioning. And the absence points to a lack within theory, for the question of race also lies outside a problematic that encodes the ideological in conventions of editing and the operations of the cinema apparatus and proposes a psychoanalytic model of gendered spectatorship in which categories of race (and class) are theoretically disallowed and which, consequently, works to affirm white middle-class norms. Furthermore, such a model also suggests that gender alone determines woman's fate, and thus further mystifies women's reality.[67] Although engaging fully with these questions would require another essay, they are pertinent to the last two *Othello*-texts I wish to consider—Charles Marowitz's *An Othello*, first presented at London's Open Space Theatre in 1972, and Basil Dearden's 1962 film, *All Night Long*. Both make blackness figure prominently in looking relations, and one negotiates a space within *Othello*'s foreclosed patriarchal ending for an historicized female spectator.

Like most of Marowitz's other Shakespearean collages, *An Othello* disjoins language from its flow in Shakespeare's playtext and intercuts one scene with another, reassigning some speeches as well as interposing invented dialogue which unmasks and at times refashions characters' motivations and actions to serve Marowitz's chosen themes—the relations between power, sex, and race that divide and politicize late twentieth-century American culture. The result is less an adaptation or rewriting of *Othello* than a parallel gloss that fractures the surface of Shakespeare's play in order to negotiate space for voices, which speak for black power (Iago as Harlemized activist), patriarchal privilege (Brabantio as Brooklyn

Jew), and white supremacy (the Duke, Lodovico, and Cassio as Southern military gentry).[68] Marowitz's schematic cultural stereotyping positions Othello (an "uppity nigrah" who has achieved power within a white military regime) as the central spectacle, his blackness the object of both black and white male (and female) gazes. Here, the radical anxiety against which he constructs himself is institutionalized as much as sexual jealousy. And Desdemona's whiteness, as well as her sexuality, comes under equal scrutiny, particularly in Iago's labeling of her "Snow White" and "white poon-tang") but most especially in a fantasy gang-bang (on a giant handkerchief) where, as Cassio, Iago, and Lodovico line up, Brabantio counts money while Othello watches, horrified. As commodified objects of appropriation, spectacles defined by the demonizing glaze of others, Othello and Desdemona not only seem mirror images of one another but are put at the service of mythic constructions of black male sexual potency and female infidelity. And the erotic is shown to be, not separate from, but integral to black/white politics: as the Duke, explaining the Great [White] Chain of Being [Command], says to Cassio, "We don't want a bloody coon General trottin' around . . . with a white pussy in tow, and subvertin' the authority of our rule."[69] Moreover, erotic relations become absorbed within power relations to reshape Desdemona's murder as well as its fragmented aftermath, in which the formal disturbances of Shakespeare's text together with stage directions call attention less to the "not said" of Shakespeare's play than to its "not seen"—that is, to spectators' unseeing endorsement of how *Othello*'s close reconstitutes white hegemony.

The murder is delayed, first, by a Faustian dialogue between Iago and Othello over Othello's "black soul" in which Iago attempts to convince Othello that, although killing Desdemona represents revenge for past wrongs against blacks, "when you turn the blade on to yourself, you're doin' whitey's work, . . . just fallin' into his setup," and, then, as Lodovico and Desdemona attempt to eject Iago from the play. Next, Othello sits, silent, his back to the audience, listening as the Duke, Lodovico, and Brabantio praise his "record of achievement," encouraging him to "do what you have to do." As the Duke puts it, "What happens to [Desdemona], if you'll pardon my being blunt, means nothing one way or the other. She's a woman, and she doesn't stand for anything. I'm not being disrespectful, I'm just stating facts. But you are a man, and you *represent* something, and when you fulfill your obligations to yourself you are fulfilling them for everyone else as well."[70] When Othello begins "It is the cause" once again, it is as a staged representation, a play within-the-play during which he repeatedly hesitates, so that Desdemona, who cues his speech, becomes complicit with her own death and with fulfilling Othello's "obligations" as well as those of the play: here, woman's importance lies only in her ability to provoke the hero to action. Just when Othello smothers Desdemona, Iago appears beside him, urging him to accept the "crazy little shiver in the blood [that] a black man feels when he scourges the whiteness in him." And it is Iago's voice that, in sketching out spectators' desire for the play's final, strikingly *known,* action, again invites Othello to resist the demands of *Othello*'s plot:

> Now the best half of your work's done and they're nestlin' in the wings—cozy in the stalls—waitin' for *their* high; the joy of seein' the black man pay his dues, purge his soul, drive three inches of steel into his regret and his remorse, so's he makes his final bloody apology for risin', mixin', makin' it and thinkin' he could carry it off despite all the odds. [*To audience*] Look at 'em all, General—sittin' cool and quietly pantin' for what they know's already theirs—your rich-red, routine-and-predictable blood. Pause brother . . . and reflect before you feed those hyenas what four centuries of black generals have given them *without* reflection . . . without one moment's pause.[71]

From this point forward, *An Othello*'s reconstituted close articulates Marowitz's exposé of *Othello*'s ending and its spectators' assumed complicity with its racism primarily through stage directions that privilege the gaze and enforce a very specific set of looking relations. Othello throws a defiant look at Lodovico, resists arrest, and, in repeated pauses during the Aleppo speech, as Iago looks at him, he "receives the look and its intent." As he stands, knife in hand, a further exchange of looks signals the Duke and Cassio, who ward off Iago and grab Othello: Lodovico cuts his throat, and the Duke completes his speech—"And smote him thus." Briefly, all regard Othello's body before hurrying to end the play as quickly as possible. To cap this Renaissance equivalent of lynching, a final choreography of look and gesture saturates the spectacle with interpretative directions:

> Desdemona rises slowly and takes her place beside the Duke, Lodovico and Cassio. They look for a moment at Othello then towards Iago who is hard and steely-eyed beside the bed. Slowly, Iago approaches Othello's body, bends down and cradles him in his arms. Slowly, heavily and with a curious kind of love, he drags out Othello's body. When he is gone, the others, slight smiles playing on their lips, look from one to the other. Blackout.[72]

An Othello anticipates this spectacle earlier when, at the conclusion of Othello's fantasy of Desdemona's infidelity, she strangles him with the giant white handkerchief and is, in turn, blotted out as the other characters slowly raise it, making her disappear from view. Although here at the end her resurrection restores her gaze, it is co-opted by males to enforce dominant racial relations within a self-satisfied exchange of looks that locates blackness, not woman, as the demonized Other and celebrates the power of white males to punish and expel its threat. Moreover, just as that exchange absorbs the misogynous gaze, it also inscribes on Othello's body a single interpretation: taken over by others—black as well as white—within white power relations, he is shown to be an empty subject. Indeed, Marowitz's ending turns Shakespeare's text into a pliable (feminized) object, remade by white male sight—an excess of showing that works to reverse Lodovico's "let it be hid": here, nothing remains unseen—except for the unconscious sexism of folding Desdemona into a male viewing position. At the close, *An Othello* represents a mirror-image of a white racist audience, reflecting onto its viewers—and folding female spectators, like Desdemona, into a male position—how their own looking relations construct their social reality: racial injustice continues, perpetuated by visual taboos that prohibit the black man's sexual glance. Finally, however, *An Othello* is less about refusing to look at a white female through the gaze of a black man than it is an attempt to make Shakespeare's play acknowledge—if not completely comprehend—the category of the real historical black subject.

If Marowitz's revisionary strategy works to subvert the hold of racial prejudice, the success of Basil Dearden's *All Night Long* (1962)—the only representation of *Othello* I consider in which the Othello figure is played by a black man[73]—ironically depends on pretending that it does not exist. Nevertheless, Dearden's riff on "Shakespeare's voice" generates a radical transformation of what G. Wilson Knight long ago called "the *Othello* music."[74] Indeed, the film is as interested in paying homage to three jazz greats—Dave Brubeck, John Dankworth, and Charlie Mingus—each of whom give solo performances, as in reseeing *Othello*. Rod Hamilton (Richard Attenborough), a playboy jazz afficionado, hosts an all-night party celebrating the first wedding anniversary of black bandleader Aurelius Rex (Paul Harris) and white singer Delia Lane (Marti Stevens), who gave up her career to prove that she put Rex "above everything else in the world." Johnny Cousin (Patrick McGoohan), Rex's drummer, draws Cass (Keith Mitchell), the band's manager, into helping him establish his own band by urging

Delia from retirement and secretly coaching her; with Delia as his lead singer, he can be assured of financial support from Rod as well as other backers. Johnny's desire to make his own music results in, or exposes, a series of betrayals, all of which concern the production of sound: whereas Rod exploits the musicians—and Delia—primarily for his own pleasure, Berger, the producer-backer, sees her return only in terms of profit; and Johnny himself reedits a tape of Delia's voice in order to convince Rex of her liaison with Cass.

Central to all these is the question of ownership and control of Delia's voice, issues the film articulates most clearly in two key sequences. The first occurs when Rex urges her to sing her signature tune, "All Night Long." Although she at first protests ("Will I never get away from that number?"), she then sings, à la Peggy Lee, a smooth, romantic ballad—"Night and day I pray I will hear you say / Take me in your arms, and hold me all night long, where I belong"—directly to Rex, a sign of her willing subservience to him, which the image track supports by positioning her seated below him on a stair, her face lifted up toward him. Here, the spectacle of her body establishes his centrality, while her voice creates a sonorous envelope of nostalgic security—imaging, on the psychoanalytic level, the fusion of child and mother and thus figuring corporeal as well as vocal harmony.[75] Delia's second performance, however (which Rod introduces as "the new, *true* Delia Lane"), calls into question not only who she is but where, precisely, she belongs. It is an Ella Fitzgerald–like number that begins with scat and moves into a verse—"I never knew I could love anybody, honey, like I'm lovin you / I never realized what a pair of eyes and a baby smile could do"—which not only counters the passivity of the earlier lyric but asserts her own knowing subjectivity. This time, too, she stands rather than sits, and the editing pattern links her to Cass, who directs the band and also accompanies her (on the saxophone), and positions Rex as an excluded spectator. Delia's change is doubly transgressive: not only does she credit her performance to Cass but, by appropriating a black jazz style, her voice becomes a mirror in which Rex hears, neither her whiteness nor her need for him, but his own blackness; grabbing her hand, he asks, "What are you?" to which she replies, "I'm your wife." If what he hears perhaps challenges his solitary spot in the professional limelight, it certainly calls his personal ownership of Delia into question—an ownership explicitly associated with silencing her professional voice.

Predictably, and in compliance with Shakespeare's narrative, Rex reacts by attempting to strangle Delia; but at this point *All Night*

Long drifts away from *Othello*'s ending, from the issue of black/ white relations within the jazz world, and from the questions it raises concerning Delia's occupation—whether as singer, "domestic animal," or both. Following an exchange of mid-close-ups detailing Delia's tearful reconciliation with a chastened Rex, the film concludes with a substitute "murder," as Johnny, sitting at his drums, drowns out and then silences his wife Emily's loving voice, punctuating his last words—"I love! You love! She loves! Everybody loves everybody! But I don't, see? I love nobody. . . . Get out of here! Go find somebody else to love?"—with discordant noise. Finally, however, the sound track blends Johnny's solo drums into the nondiegetic improvisations of the jazz combo (presumably the white Brubeck and Dankworth and the black Mingus), and it is their harmony which plays over a dissolve to the film's last image—a high-angle long shot of Delia and Rex, arms around one another, walking down Thames-side—an ending that invites a viewer's eye as well as a listener's ear to integrate *Othello*'s music in a kind of colorblind synchrony absorbing (almost) all difference.

Reading backward, the close of *All Night Long* seems to provide a hopeful sequel to Marowitz's vision of reconstituted racism, if not precisely to signal the end of the struggle to overcome it. Yet Dearden's film represents, at best, a fantasy conversation with late twentieth-century racial politics. For transforming *Othello* to serve the formal demands of a coupling comedy (a black comedy?) involves, first, situating the story in a milieu in which talent, performance skills, and economic success, not blackness, are at stake and, second, decentering Rex, the Othello-figure, to privilege Johnny Cousins–Iago as the film's central subject. And this decision, confirmed by casting—the white Patrick McGoohan, not the black Paul Harris, is the film's known star—rewrites black oppression as white anxiety: it is Johnny's inability to love, his unsuccessful attempts to define his own musical style against a form associated with black history and in which white musicians are Johnny-come-latelys, that drives *All Night Long*'s plot, to which Rex and Delia's story becomes secondary. That the film articulates its "true" ending in the spectacle of Johnny's sadomasochistic self-absorption in an envelope of discordant sound constitutes a displaced sign of that anxiety, which excludes him from any contact with the film's racially problematic figures—either the "new" Delia Lane, whose voice takes on a borrowed blackness, or Rex, in whose piano solos the listener hears the white Dave Brubeck. How, then, does this invite rereading the film's last shot, its imposed "happy ending"? As the distant figures of Delia and Rex walk into the deep space of dockside, they face away from the camera, which not only masks their gaze at one another but makes their color unreadable: costume is its only sign—a white dress for Delia, a tuxedo for Rex. Here, however, even that sign seems emptied of its racial signified; instead, they read as a conventional romantic couple, walking (prophetically?) into the lightening dawn rather than toward the dark. The image, however, is curiously ambivalent, for just as it reveals integration as the resolution of *Othello*'s hidden comedy, it represents the possibility of that social change as an erasure, not an acknowledgment, of blackness.

I said earlier that Dearden's film negotiates a space for an historicized woman spectator, a statement that its ending seems either to invalidate or to reduced to a simple exchange at the level of form, replacing tragic with comic enclosure: remarriage instead of Othello's dying kiss of rebetrothal. But, although *All Night Long*'s final image seems to reposition Delia as the willing "domestic animal" she had earlier claimed to be, elsewhere the film raises questions about her status as a potential subject which destabilize such a pat resolution and sustain the enigma associated with her figure. That such questions are even posed, if not fully addressed, depends, somewhat paradoxically, on the film's anxious strategies of dislocation. Both its white star dynamics and its transparent attempt to defuse the issue of race work against privileging Rex, to make Delia's professional singing career and her reputation, not his, a pivotal plot element. However, if foregrounding Delia's career suggests that women's voices and bodies do not pertain exclusively to sexual difference, that move clearly effects another, equally binding exchange within capitalism, replacing sexual with economic exploitation. But it is also true that in both instances where Delia performs, her image escapes the rule of the look associated with the masculine psychic economy. For even though men do look at her, their gaze is one with, rather than a stand-in for, that of the audience; their look does not *construct* her presence but is subordinated to her own self-construction.[76] And it is precisely those images of woman's self-constructed identity and potential agency which travel forward to be embodied within, if not completely inhabit, *All Night Long*'s otherwise conventional close: that ending, to borrow Laura Mulvey's phrase, "opens up the neat function 'marriage' . . . to ask 'what next?' . . . 'what does *she* want?' "[77]

To position Dearden's film in relation to the other *Othello*-representations considered here is to clarify more precisely what such an admittedly small space (I shall resist calling it a crack) affords a woman spectator. Whereas Verdi, Welles, and Hands transfer

Othello to a transcendent realm that insulates the text from history and suspends issues of gender and race within an aesthetic vacuum, Blom's *Desdemona* relies on a transhistorical misogyny that reads women as naturally false, a notion that *A Double Life* echoes by punishing two versions of feminine independence, both of whom might be considered late 1940s "working girls." And, although Buchovetski's *Othello* and Marowitz's *An Othello* turn Shakespeare's playtext toward particular historical circumstances, the one erases Desdemona altogether to address the rise of an authoritarian political regime, while the other co-opts her to critique white racist supremacy. Among these, *All Night Long* most clearly articulates the interplay between mastery and masochism that expresses the lived contradictions of women in late twentieth-century culture. And, like *A Double Life,* the film acknowledges the apparent impossibility of resolving the two positions by distributing the traits associated with each between its two women characters.

For what is finally most troubling about the invitation to buy into conventionally satisfying romantic closure returns, not to Delia's side of this oppositional tension and to her potential mastery, but to the question of Emilia—in *All Night Long,* Emily, Johnny Cousins's wife, played by Betsy Blair. To evoke the terms of Stallybrass's argument, "elevating" Delia-Desdemona to the status of a comic winner occurs at the "low" Emily-Emilia's expense: among its other strategies of exchange, *All Night Long* implies that one woman's success invites, if not requires, demonizing another, a move that not only echoes Johnny's own perversity but further destabilizes the representation of women's community. Here, Betsy Blair's own history provides an oddly accurate mirror of this exchange: cast as the second Desdemona in Welles's 1952 film and later replaced by Suzanne Cloutier, Welles's final choice, she appears in *A Double Life* as Emilia, where only traces of her body and her disembodied voice register her presence; finally, as *All Night Long*'s Emily, she replaces the film's Desdemona-figure and is once again excluded, her body and voice ignored.

Blair's real-life history, and the question of Emilia-Emily's representation, also recall the *Othello* I imagined earlier—one seen, if not constructed, from a woman's point of view and thus enabling a spectator to experience the difficulties involved *for a woman* in comprehending the enigma of the desiring male subject.[78] And it also acknowledges my own difficulty in reading against the grain, or drift, of these *Othello*-texts in order to maintain the focus on women's bodies and voices with which this essay began. For only two—Welles's film and Hands's Royal Shakespeare Company production—include Emilia's subversive, interventionary voice, her firm refusal to be enclosed within patriarchal territory. The other six not only accentuate that drift but, as though to acknowledge the threat she represents, further restrict her presence: although Verdi's *Otello,* Buchovetski's film, *Desdemona,* and *A Double Life* all include her, Marowitz's *An Othello* erases her altogether, and *All Night Long* shows her to be, much like Desdemona, subjected "to the very quality of [her] lord." Furthermore, except for Hands's performance text, each representation reshapes or repositions *Othello*'s single glimpse of women's community. Verdi's Emilia reenforces Desdemona's willing subservience, and Welles's trance-like Desdemona seems hardly aware of Emilia's words; Buchovetski's *Othello* as well as Blom's *Desdemona* repositions the Desdemona-Emilia scene much earlier in the action, and each recasts both women as (male-constructed) stereotypes—Buchovetski as giggling girls, displaying their bodies for a Peeping-Tom Othello as well as for the camera; *Desdemona* as co-conspirators in keeping Maria-Desdemona's affair with Count Brisson secret. And in *A Double Life,* Emilia is most strikingly represented only by her nondiegetic voice-over following Pat Kroll's murder.

Moreover, Desdemona's Willow Song has an equally curious history of omission and substitution: absent from Welles's and Buchovetski's *Othello*s and from *Desdemona* and *A Double Life,* it appears, rewritten, in Marowitz's *An Othello,* as a soliloquy through which Desdemona affirms both her desire for Othello's blackness and her opposition to Brabantio's conventional notions about daughters and marriage. *All Night Long,* however, not only gives Delia two numbers that may be considered descendants of the Willow Song but also includes a private conversation between Delia and Emily that takes place in a powder room and that reverses the roles of Desdemona and Emilia. That conversation reveals that whereas Delia and Rex seem "perfect for each other," Emily's marriage is not only transgressive—the result of a high-school crush and a drunken weekend—but legislated, not by a father's will but by her *mother's* insistence that she "give it a try" or Johnny will go to jail. Admitting that she wanted the marriage but Johnny didn't, Emily turns herself into a sacrificing mother who feels sorry for him: "he's intelligent and talented [and] has all these plans, . . . but nothing ever works."

Emily's last phrase might easily characterize a project that attempts to discover, and account for, a resistant, if not subversive, space in performance texts deriving from Shakespeare's *Othello* that either omit or radically rewrite those features that articulate the possibility of such subversion. For what these *Othello*-texts seem to reveal, in their emphases on constructing as well as deconstructing male subjectivity, involves not just Emilia's erasure but the disabling of Desdemona's phrase—voiced by Othello—"she wish'd / That heaven had made her such a man." If, however, representations deriving from *Othello* must always demonize her wish to be a speaking subject who can not only tell her own story but command a listener—or spectator—of the opposite gender, perhaps some hint of that wish remains in Desdemona's (nearly) last words—"Nobody, I myself, farewell"—a phrase usually interpreted, especially though not exclusively by male readers, as her final lie.

What strikes me particularly here is that her voice is, both literally and figuratively, heavy with body. And not, I would argue, exclusively with the "nobody" that performances represent as *Othello*'s (deconstructed) male subject but also with her own body as subject. For, just before she commends herself to her kind lord, Desdemona accepts herself as subject, reconfirms her desire to experience narrative[79] and attempts to construct a self distinct from and outside the body Othello and the male gaze would seek to interrogate and immobilize. If indeed, as Katharine Maus argues, the jealous male represents one figure for the spectator of Renaissance drama, Desdemona, I think, represents a figure for the problematic woman spectator of that drama as well as its more contemporary rewritings—the spectator who represents a contradiction in terms, who is and is not herself, who, as in B. Ruby Rich's telling phrase, is "the ultimate dialectician."[80] For it is Desdemona's knowing assertion, together with Emilia's interventionary dissent, that offer a *communal* hinge for the double movement of containment and resistance that would detach woman's voice, heavy with body, from enclosures such as those represented by *Othello*. Such a project must begin, not with presupposing the transhistorical dominance of the male gaze but by attempting to historicize the gender as well as the (various) gender-bendings of looking relations. Indeed, this enterprise might dis-cover—rather than re-cover—whatever visual pleasure may be found by interrogating the construction of the female subject in history. Insofar as that discovery may entail not only considerable perceptual transformation but also the fall of psychoanalytic modes of analysis, it is instructive to remember how Genesis 3:7 articulates the changes involved in another Fall: "And the eyes of both of them were opened."

NOTES

My thanks to Richard Abel and Jonathan Dollimore for extremely helpful comments on an earlier draft of this essay.

1. Accused, after *Aida* (called by his critics *Il Lohengrin Italiano*) of being a Wagner-imitator, Verdi had been hesitant to enter the contemporary musical crisis that pitted the viability of "pure Italian song"—a melodic line of direct emotional expressiveness—against the "Ultramontane complexity and profundity" of the post-Wagnerian tide of naturalism, or *verismo;* fanned by the press, the debate had widened to the extent that national integrity and Italian individuality were at stake (James A. Hepokoski, *Guiseppe Verdi, "Otello,"* Cambridge Opera Handbooks no. 22 [Cambridge: Cambridge University Press, 1987], pp. 48–49). For the comment on Shakespeare, see Julian Budden, *The Operas of Verdi,* vol. 3 (London: Cassell, 1981), p. 305.

2. Blanche Roosevelt [Tucker Macchetta], *Verdi: Milan and "Othello"* (London: Ward and Downey, 1887), pp. 183, 186–89, quoted by Francis Robinson, commenting on *Live from the Met,* the 25 September 1978 telecast of Franco Zeffirelli's staging of *Otello,* James Levine conducting.

3. I draw here from Christine Gledhill, "The Melodramatic Field: An Investigation," in *Home Is Where the Heart Is: Studies in Melodrama and the Women's Film,* ed. Christine Gledhill (London: BFI, 1987), p. 37.

4. These notions derive from Annette Kuhn, "Women's Genres: Melodrama, Soap Opera and Theory," (1984) repr. in Gledhill, *Home is Where the Heart Is,* p. 341. Examples of narratives built around the marriage/murder axis are Alfred Hitchcock's *Rebecca* (1940) and *Suspicion* (1941) as well as George Cukor's *Gaslight* (1944).

5. Laura Mulvey suggests how song, as well as dance, not only breaks narrative flow but can eroticize woman as spectacle. See "Visual Pleasure and Narrative Cinema" (1975); repr. in *Feminism and Film Theory,* ed. Constance Penley (New York: Routledge, Chapman and Hall, 1988), p. 62.

6. "To-be-looked-at-ness" is Laura Mulvey's apt phrase ("Visual Pleasure," p. 62). I call attention to a *potentially* desexualized look in order to negotiate space for a lesbian spectator, for whom the trajectory of the gaze might change significantly. See Lucie Arbuthnot and Gail Seneca, "Pre-Text and Text in *Gentlemen Prefer Blondes," Film Reader* 5 (Winter 1981): 13–23; and Chris Straayer, "*Personal Best:* Lesbian/Feminist Audience," *Jump Cut* 29 (February 1984): 40–44.

7. For the initial theoretical work on the gendered gaze, see Mulvey's "Visual Pleasure" and "Afterthoughts on 'Visual Pleasure and Narrative Cinema' inspired by *Duel in the Sun*" (1981); repr. in Penley, *Feminism and Film Theory,* pp. 69–79. Further studies respond to, extend, and/or qualify her formulations. See, for several examples among many, Mary Ann Doane, "The 'Woman's Film' Possession and Address (1984); repr. in Gledhill, *Home is Where the Heart Is,* pp. 283–98; Linda Williams, " 'Something Else Besides a Mother': *Stella Dallas* and the Maternal Melodrama," *Cinema Journal* 24, no. 1(1984):2–27; Teresa de Lauretis, *Alice Doesn't: Feminism, Semiotics, Cinema* (Bloomington: Indiana University Press, 1984); Tania Modleski, *The Women Who Knew Too Much* (New York: Methuen, 1988); and Naomi Scheman, "Missing Mothers/ Desiring Daughters: Framing the Sight of Women," *Critical Inquiry* 15, no. 1 (1988): 62–89. Pointing to the difficulty of assuming that certain representations are aimed at a female audience, Annette Kuhn draws a useful distinction between spectator and audience by labeling the spectator a "meaning-maker," one who is not only con-

structed by a text but is part of a larger context, the "social audience" ("Women's Genres," pp. 18–28).

8. Peter Stallybrass, "Patriarchal Territories: The Body Enclosed," in *Rewriting the Renaissance: The Discourses of Sexual Difference in Early Modern Europe,* ed. Margaret W. Ferguson, Maureen Quilligan, and Nancy J. Vickers (Chicago: University of Chicago Press, 1986), p. 142.

9. Stallybrass, "Patriarchal Territories," p. 142.

10. Katharine Eisaman Maus, "Horns of Dilemma: Jealousy, Gender, and Spectatorship in English Renaissance Drama," *ELH* 54, no. 3 (1987): 578. For pertinent work in film studies, see the citations in note 7.

11. Quoted by Geoffrey Tillotson in *Times Literary Supplement* (London), 20 July 1933: 494 and reproduced in John Russell Brown's Harbrace Theater Edition of *Othello* (New York: Harcourt Brace Jovanovich, 1973), p. 94n.

12. Pepys diary entry for 11 October 1660, quoted in *A New Variorum Edition of Shakespeare: Vol. VI: Othello,* ed. Horace Howard Furness (1866; repr., New York: Dover Publications, 1963), p. 402n.

13. Shakespeare's playtext considerably transforms Cinthio's ending, in which Iago and Othello arrange Disdemona's death to look like an accident: after beating her to death with a sand-filled stocking, they pull down rotten ceiling timbers on her body. Fearing exposure, Othello cashiers Iago, who, together with Cassio, accuses Othello to the Signory after all have returned to Venice. Tortured, Othello refuses to confess and is banished and later killed by Disdemona's kinsfolk. Iago finds other victims, but is finally arrested and dies under torture. From the summary in *Othello,* ed. M. R. Ridley (1958); repr. (London: Methuen, 1971), p. 245.

14. Recent discussions of "Shakespeare" as cultural authority/commodity may be found in *Political Shakespeare,* ed. Jonathan Dollimore and Alan Sinfield (Manchester: Manchester University Press, 1985); *Alternative Shakespeares,* ed. John Drakakis (London: Methuen, 1985) and *The Shakespeare Myth,* ed. Graham Holderness (Manchester: Manchester University Press, 1988).

15. The terms "subject" and "object" are especially slippery, their meanings often geared to the discourse which evokes them. For an exhaustive examination of the issue, see Paul Smith, *Discerning the Subject* (Minneapolis: University of Minnesota Press, 1988). Smith credits feminist studies with the most careful, precise articulation of the terms.

16. Here, it seems ironic that Welles's film, potentially the more popular—and accessible—of the two media, is not presently available for commercial distribution, whereas a 1987 film of Verdi's *Otello,* directed by Franco Zeffirelli and starring Placido Domingo, makes the opera widely available to a popular audience. As a 1978 telecast on *Live from the Met,* Zeffirelli's production also reached a large audience. But, like the BBC-TV *Othello,* it was shown at the margins of "prime time" and presented as a showcase "special," a media positioning that retains some aura of its status as privileged spectacle, which is enhanced by accompanying explanatory material, interviews, and historical documentation.

17. Among others, Stallybrass notes Desdeomona's doubleness ("Patriarchal Territories," p. 141). See also Carol Thomas Neely, *Broken Nuptials in Shakespeare's Plays* (New Haven: Yale University Press, 1985), pp. 105–35; and Karen Newman, "'And wash the Ethiop white': femininity and the monstrous in *Othello,*" in *Shakespeare Reproduced: The Text in History and Ideology,* ed. Jean E. Howard and Marion F. O'Connor (London: Methuen, 1987), pp. 143–62.

18. Franco Abbiati, *Giuseppe Verdi,* vol. 4 (Milan, 1959), p. 332; trans. and

quoted by Martin Chusid, "Verdi's Own Words: His Thoughts on Performance, with Special Reference to *Don Carlos, Otello,* and *Falstaff*," in *The Verdi Companion,* ed. William Weaver and Martin Chusid (New York: W. W. Norton and Co., 1979), p. 161.

19. From Ricordi's *Disposizione scenica per l'opera* "Otello" (Milan, 1887), which contains prescriptive directorial comments by Verdi, Boito, and Victor Maurel, the original Iago, that outline an idealized version of performance; trans. and quoted by Budden, *Operas of Verdi,* vol. 3, pp. 328–29.

20. In a letter to Ricordi, 11 May 1887, recorded in Abbiati, *Verdi,* pp. 336–37 and quoted by Weaver and Chusid, *Verdi Companion,* p. 161. See also Hepokoski, *Otello,* pp. 179–80.

21. Joseph Kerman, "*Otello:* Traditional Opera and the Image of Shakespeare," in *Opera as Drama* (New York: Alfred A. Knopf, 1956), p. 153; Hepokoski, *Otello,* p. 140.

22. Indeed, the popularity of Desdemona's solos had kept Rossini's rather conventional opera alive: in one of its most affecting moments, an offstage gondolier sings a setting of lines from Dante's *Inferno* concerning Paolo and Francesca, "*Nessun maggior dolor che ricordarsi d'un tempo felice nella miseria*" as Desdemona prepares for bed (Budden, *Operas of Verdi,* p. 303). Rossini's opera casts the story from Desdemona's point of view, omits Cassio and hints at a potentially bloodless ending: Iago botches the murder of Roderigo and is killed, after confessing to his villainy; this news is brought to Otello, just after he has killed Desdemona, by Elmiro (the Brabantio figure), who has come to exonerate Otello and offer his blessing to the marriage (Vincent Godefroy, *The Dramatic Genius of Verdi: Studies of Elected Operas,* vol. 2 [London: Victor Gollancz, 1977], p. 282; Christina Merchant, "Delacroix's Tragedy of Desdemona," *Shakespeare Survey* 21 [1968]: 81).

23. The Willow Song, which makes use of the French operatic *couplet,* is built from three strophes of poetry, the first two parallel and the third disintegrating, expressive of Desdemona's anxiety. Given Boito's penchant for artifice, it is not only possible but probable that the metrics reflect his pseudo-classicizing of an ancient classical meter known as *poesia barbara* (Hepokosi, *Otello,* pp. 43, 142, 184–86). For Verdi's letter to Faccio, see Weaver and Chusid, *Verdi Companion,* p. 159. Cf. Joel Fineman's play with the notion of inscribing authorial persona ("willow/William") in "The Sound of O in *Othello,*" *October* 45 (Summer 1988): 77–96.

24. *Otello,* libretto in English National Opera Guide Series, trans. Andrew Porter (London: John Calder, 1981), pp. 70–71; Peter J. Seng, *The Vocal Songs in the Plays of Shakespeare: A Critical History* (Cambridge: Harvard University Press, 1967), p. 196. In an equally intriguing regendering of voice, Boito transforms Othello's greeting to Desdemona in Cyprus, "O, my fair warrior," into Desdemona's "*O mio superbo guerrier,*" her first telling words to Otello.

25. See David Lawton, "On the 'Bacio' Theme in *Otello,*" *19th-Century Music* 1, no. 3 (1978): 218. See also Frits Noske, *The Signifier and The Signified: Studies in the Operas of Mozart and Verdi* (The Hague: Martinus Nijhoff, 1977), pp. 159–67; and Roger Parker and Matthew Brown, " "Ancora un bacio: Three Scenes from Verdi's *Otello,*" *19th-Century Music* 9 (1985–86): 50–62.

26. See Sandra Corse, *Opera and the Uses of Language: Mozart, Verdi, and Britten* (Rutherford, N.J.: Fairleigh Dickinson University Press, 1987), p. 86.

27. These sentences draw on Hepokoski, *Otello,* p. 140; Budden, *Operas of Verdi,* vol. 3, 3:394; and Noske, *Signifier and Signified,* p. 142.

28. I assume this applause because it has occurred at every performance of the

opera I have seen or heard; its history goes back to the Milan premiere, when the "Ave Maria" was one of two (apparently planned) encores. The other was for Otello's entrance, which follows directly: at the Milan premiere, in fact, Otello went offstage and reentered (Hepokoski, *Otello*, p. 109).

29. This paragraph draws on Lawton, " 'Bacio' Theme," pp. 217–20; Budden, *Operas of Verdi*, vol. 3, pp. 396–98; and Kerman, "Traditional Opera," pp. 145–46.

30. Lawton, " 'Bacio' Theme," p. 220.

31. "And you . . . How pale you are! and weary, and silent, and lovely. / Gentle creature born under an evil star" [my translation].

32. See Hepokoski, *Otello*, pp. 187–89. For a contradictory view, which sees a "decorous, rational, powerfully romantic" ending that "vindicates Thomas Rymer and his friends," see Kerman, "Traditional Opera," pp. 161–63. Cf. Stephen Greenblatt's reading of Desdemona's position in *Renaissance Self-Fashioning* (Chicago: University of Chicago Press, 1980), pp. 251–54. For a feminist critique of opera, see Catherine Clément, *Opera, or the Undoing of Women* (1979): trans. Betsy Wing (Minneapolis: University of Minnesota Press, 1988), esp. pp. 119–25.

33. The following description of Welles's *Othello* is based on a print preserved on videotape at the Library of Congress; the description of Welles's documentary, *Filming "Othello"* (made for West German television), is based on notes taken by Richard Abel at a September 1986 screening of the film in Paris at the Artistic Cinema. I am grateful to Abel for sharing his notes.

34. James Naremore also notes this in *The Magic World of Orson Welles* (New York: Oxford, 1978), p. 216.

35. Janet Bergstrom, "Alternation, Segmentation, Hypnosis: interview with Raymond Bellour," *Camera Obscura*, no. 3–4 (Summer 1979): 71–103; esp. 93.

36. Juan Cobos, Miguel Rubio, and J. A. Pruneda, "A Trip to Don Quixoteland: Conversations with Orson Welles," in *Focus on Citizen Kane*, ed. Ronald Gottesman (Englewood Cliffs, N.J.: Prentice-Hall, 1971), p. 8.

37. Jack J. Jorgens, *Shakespeare on Film* (Bloomington: Indiana University Press, 1977), p. 179. Welles refers to, and praises, Jorgens's analysis of *Othello* in his documentary; that he literally appropriates what Jorgens says as his own words in particularly intriguing—especially from a filmmaker whose use of others' "visual property" rivals Shakespeare's own borrowings. Is this part of the famous Welles-as-master-magician fakery? For other pertinent studies, see Micheál MacLiammóir, *Put Money In Thy Purse* (London: Methuen, 1952); Joseph McBride *Orson Welles* (London: BFI, 1972), pp. 117–22; Peter Cowie, *A Ribbon of Dreams: The Cinema of Orson Welles* (South Brunswick, N.J.: A. S. Barnes and Co., 1973); Lorne M. Buchman, "Orson Welles's *Othello*: A Study of Time in Shakespeare's Tragedy," *Shakespeare Survey* 39 (1987): 53–66; Samuel Crowl, "The Murderous Image: Welles's *Othello* and Post-Structuralism," unpublished paper for the Shakespeare Association of America seminar on "Shakespeare on Film," 1988; Peter S. Donaldson, "Mirrors and M/Others: The Welles *Othello*," unpublished paper for the Shakespeare Association of America seminar on "Shakespeare on Film," 1988; and Anthony Davies, *Filming Shakespeare's Plays* (Cambridge: Cambridge University Press, 1988), pp. 100–118.

38. Jorgens, *Shakespeare on Film*, p. 177.

39. For a discussion of woman's body as located within a medical discourse, see Mary Ann Doane, "The 'Woman's Film,'" pp. 290–93. The operations of this discourse in *Othello* differ considerably, of course, from those in the woman's film.

40. Michel Foucault, *The Birth of the Clinic: An Archaeology of Medical Perception*, trans. A. M. Sheridan-Smith (New York: Vintage Books, 1975), pp. 114–15.

41. Cf. Newman's discussion of Othello and the monstrous, " 'And wash the Ethiop white,' " pp. 143–62.

42. Jorgens also notes this visual ambiguity (*Shakespeare on Film,* p. 182). Certainly the two signs, however variously interpreted and construed, share a signified. For a fine discussion, see Lynda E. Boose, "Othello's Handkerchief: 'The Recognizance and Pledge of Love,' " *ELR* 5 (1975): 360–74.

43. Like Welles's other Shakespeare films, *Othello*'s sound is post-synchronized, and Welles himself not only "voices" Othello but also, at times, Roderigo, Cassio, and (if my ear does not deceive me) Iago. The production was drawn out over a number of years; Welles speaks of *Othello,* in his documentary, as a film "made on the installment plan."

44. See Lotte Eisner, *The Haunted Screen: Expressionism in the German Cinema and the Influence of Max Reinhardt* (1952); repr., trans. Roger Greaves (Berkeley: University of California Press, 1965), pp. 78–79. The following description and analysis is based on a print of the Wörner-Film production with English intertitles in the American Film Institute collection at the Library of Congress. For a complete, though somewhat biased, description, see Robert Hamilton Ball, *Shakespeare on Silent Film* (New York: Theatre Arts Books, 1968), pp. 279–84.

45. The choice, here, points to the probable homophobia of a male spectator and, beyond that, to the strongly homophobic stance of psychoanalysis. For current work that attempts to construct the homoerotic outside psychoanalytic paradigms, see Eve Kosofsky Sedgwick, *Between Men: English Literature and Male Homosocial Desire* (New York: Columbia University Press, 1985); and Jonathan Dollimore's work on "transgressive reinscription," for example, "Subjectivity, Sexuality and Transgression: The Jacobean Connection," *Renaissance Drama,* n.s. 17 (1986): 53–81.

46. Immediately following World War I, Mussolini organized his followers, mostly war veterans, into the *Fasci di combattimento,* which stood for an aggressive nationalism that violently opposed Communism and the socialists; they borrowed the black shirts of D'Annunzio's followers as their uniform. In 1921, Mussolini's election to Parliament prompted the official organization of the National Fascist Party, and in October 1922, backed by nationalists and propertied groups, he sent the Fascists to march on Rome. King Victor Emmanuel permitted their entry and called upon Mussolini, who had remained in Milan, to form a cabinet; as premier, Mussolini transformed the government into a dictatorship. Buchovetski's film was showcased in early 1923 at New York's Criterion Theatre together with a Max Fleischer "Out-of-the-Inkwell" cartoon, a "tempting scenic of the Riviera" and a "diverting animal picture" from the Bray Studios (*New York Times,* 26 February 1923, 15: 1).

47. In "The Earliest Images of *Othello,*" (*Shakespeare Quarterly* 39 [Summer 1988]: 171–86), Paul H. D. Kaplan examines paintings and engravings on *Othello* from the eighteenth and nineteenth centuries, when artists repeatedly selected the murder scene to represent the play; Kaplan concludes that this practice "reveals a taste for the melodramatic, and implies a reading of the tragedy in which Othello's violence assumes the most important position" (185).

48. Furness, *Variorum,* p. 292n.

49. Ibid., pp. 292–93n.

50. I have not ascertained exactly when the practice of hiding the murder began and ended: Marvin Rosenberg, for example, does not trace its history (*The Masks of "Othello"* [Berkeley: University of California Press, 1961]).

51. For the notion of the play as male project—with women as its stagehands, see Scheman, "Missing Mothers/Desiring Daughters," p. 87.

52. My description is of a January 1986 performance at the Barbican Theatre, London. Niamh Cusack played Desdemona; Ben Kingsley, Othello; and David Suchet, Iago.

53. For essays by Ben Kingsley and David Suchet on the roles of Othello and Iago in Hands's production, see *Players of Shakespeare 2: Further Essays in Shakespearean Performance by Players with the Royal Shakespeare Company,* ed. Russell Jackson and Robert Smallwood (Cambridge: Cambridge University Press, 1988), pp. 167–78, 179–99.

54. Suvin defines "invariant" as an element necessary to any performance of a play because dictated by the dynamics of the playtext ("Weiss's *Marat/Sade* and Its Three Main Performance Versions [Contribution to a Theory of Interpretative Pragmatics," Lecture at Duke University, 18 October 1988, forthcoming in *Social Text*]). Suvin disclaims *"intentio auctoris"* as well as *"intentio operis"* by allying his term with Eco's "semiotics of interpretation" (19). Although I find his terms somewhat mechanistic, this final shift within *Othello* to male-centered spectacle seems at least to have the status of a "constant variable."

55. Stuart Hall, "Notes on Deconstructing 'The Popular,' " in *People's History and Socialist Theory,* ed. Raphael Samuel (London: Routledge and Kegan Paul, 1981), p. 228.

56. Although it would, perhaps, push the connection, both Maus and Modleski call attention to the theatre as a site associated with the threat of feminization (Maus, "Horns of Dilemma": 566–70; Modleski, *The Women Who Knew Too Much,* pp. 14, 34–35).

57. *Kinematograph and Lantern Weekly,* 7 March 1912, quoted in Ball, *Shakespeare on Silent Film,* p. 132. The following description and analysis is based on a print of *Desdemona* (Nordisk production) in the American Film Institute collection at the Library of Congress. For further historical information, see Ronald James Mottram, *The Danish Cinema, 1896–1917,* dissertation, New York University, 1980 (Ann Arbor, Mich.: University Microfilms International, 1980), pp. 261–62. See also Ball, *Shakespeare on Silent Film,* pp. 132–34.

58. *Desdemona* is typical of Danish films at this time: a banal story set in a refined milieu, in which money often plays a large part in the plot intrigues; many excelled simply "by virtue of their advanced, bold use of erotic *motifs*" (Ib Monty, "The Danish Film 1896–1960: An unbroken tradition for film-making" in *Danish Films,* ed. Uffe Stormgaard and Søren Dyssegaard, trans. David Hohnen [Copenhagen: Vang Rasmussens Litografiske Trykkeri, 1973], p. 38).

59. Is there a connection here between this character and Adolphe Brisson, the French drama and film critic whose weekly review column in *Le Temps* made him an important early authoritative voice?

60. Cukor's film (Universal-International, 103 minutes; Ruth Gordon–Garson Kanin script) was the second sound adaptation of *Othello.* The first was a 1921 film, *Carnival,* re-released in 1931 with sound (Ball, *Shakespeare on Silent Film,* p. 134). Cukor's film showcased in New York at Radio City Music Hall, together with a review entitled "Yesteryear," starring (among others) Larry Storch and featuring the glee club, the corps de ballet, and the Rockettes (See Bosley Crowther's review, *New York Times,* 20 February 1948, 19: 1). The following description and analysis is based on a complete print in the American Film Institute collection at the Library of Congress.

61. *Mildred Pierce* is the central noir melodrama featuring the divorced woman as sadomasochistic mother. For several studies, see Pam Cook, "Duplicity in *Mildred Pierce,*" in *Women in Film Noir,* ed. E. Ann Kaplan (London: BFI, 1978), pp. 68–82; and Annette Kuhn, *Women's Pictures: Feminism and Cinema* (London:

Routledge & Kegan Paul, 1982), pp. 28–35. Although *A Double Life* certainly draws on the classic film noir story of a man trapped by a woman and destroyed by his own desire, Cukor borrows the stylistics of the genre only for the scenes concerning Pat Kroll. And, unlike the so-called women's films, which dissect female psychosis, *A Double Life* is more like "male weepies" such as *East of Eden, Bigger Than Life* and *Rebel Without a Cause* in which male, rather than female, identity is at issue.

62. In that Tony acts as his own Iago, the film connects with that strain of *Othello* criticism which sees the two characters locked in a tension, both parts of a single, phenomenological whole.

63. I borrow Kaja Silverman's term, "acoustic mirror," and draw on her analysis of the relations between voice and body in cinema, but without reproducing her full psychoanalytic apparatus. She locates the "acoustic mirror" as maternal: "Within the traditional familial paradigm, the maternal voice introduces the child to its mirror reflection . . . ; the child also learns to speak by imitating the sounds made by the mother, fashioning its voice after hers" (p. 80). By equating the acoustic mirror with Shakespeare's playtext, I located the maternal in a paternal text, an inversion which seems compatible with Tony's–and the film's–use of that text as one that fashions Tony's voice and his subjectivity (*The Acoustic Mirror: The Female Voice in Psychoanalysis and Cinema* [Bloomington: Indiana University Press, 1988] especially pp. 72–100). See also Modleski: "For while, as Jean Laplanche and J.-B. Pontalis note, 'it is by means of a series of identifications that the personality is constituted and specified,' there is a danger that the other with whom one identifies may usurp and annihilate the personality—a danger which is especially keen when the other is a woman and hence serves as a reminder of the original (m)other in whom the subject's identity was merged" (*The Women Who Knew Too Much*, p. 55).

64. In an interview with Gavin Lambert, Cukor speaks about asking Milton Krasner, the cinematographer, to halate some lights into the camera in order to produce the effects of blinding stage lights (*On Cukor* [New York: G. P. Putnam's Sons, 1972], p. 197).

65. For one formulation of the hermaphroditic composition of the female spectator as constructed by the text, see, among others, Doane, "The 'Woman's Film,' " p. 295.

66. Cf. Othello's Aleppo speech (5.2.334–52), as well as Iago's "Good name in man and woman, dear my lord, / Is the immediate jewel of their souls" (3.3.155–56).

67. I draw here on Jane Gaines, "White Privilege and Looking Relations: Race and Gender in Feminist Film Theory," *Cultural Critique* 4 (Fall 1986): 59–79.

68. For an analysis of several other Marowitz rewritings of Shakespeare, from which I borrow the notion of disrupting the surface of the text, see Alan Sinfield, "Making space; appropriation and confrontation in recent British plays," in Holderness, *Shakespeare Myth*, pp. 134–37. For the issue of Othello's blackness, see M. R. Ridley's introduction to the Arden *Othello* (London: Methuen, 1958), p. li; and Newman, " 'And wash the Ethiop white.' " esp. pp. 143–49.

69. *An Othello,* in *Open Space Plays,* Selected by Charles Marowitz (Harmondsworth: Penquin Books, 1974), p. 286.

70. Ibid., p. 304.

71. Ibid., pp. 307–8.

72. Ibid., p. 310. The Penguin volume's introduction, by Lionel and Virginia Tiger, glosses the ending this way: "Marowitz brings Desdemona back to life, and

for the finale we leave her about to party it up with the honky officers who've protected the public's peace by shielding her white privates against the Moor's black rod. The harsh elaborate walnut connection between power and copulation, between race and personal efficacy, is flashed before our eyes and the image stays" (p. 255).

73. Although Marowitz's original production had a black Othello as well as a black Iago, it would be possible (though not politically responsible) to cast white actors in both roles.

74. The following description and analysis is based on a complete print (Rank production, 95 minutes) in the American Film Institute collection at the Library of Congress.

75. See Silverman, *Acoustic Mirror*, p. 96. Earlier, the film glances at psychoanalytic theorizing, setting it against the "real" function of music: just before Delia sings, Cass baits Berger, accusing him of having theories about music rather than just listening to it: "You think it's just pure libido, regressive narcissism associated with negros, adolescents and intellectuals."

76. See Mulvey, "Visual Pleasure," p. 65, as well as Lucy Fischer, "The Image of Woman as Image: The Optical Politics of *Dames*," *Film Quarterly* 30, no. 1 (Fall 1976): 2–11; and Maureen Turim, "Gentlemen Consume Blondes," *Wide Angle* 1, no. 1 (1976): 52–59.

77. Mulvey, "Afterthoughts," pp. 74–75.

78. I draw here on Tania Modleski, "Never to Be Thirty-six Years Old . . . *Rebecca* as Female Oedipal Drama," *Wide Angle* 5, no. 1 (1982): 34–41, esp. 38.

79. Cf. Lea Jacobs's reading of female pleasure as connected to narrative in "*Now Voyager:* Some Problems of Enunciation and Sexual Difference," *Camera Obscura* 7 (1981): 89–109, esp. 95.

80. B. Ruby Rich, in Michelle Citron et al., "Women and Film: A Discussion of Feminist Aesthetics," *New German Critique* 13 (Winter 1978): 83–107, esp. 87. Of course, conditions in the Renaissance theatre, where women's roles were played by boys, intensify this problematic; even though the convention was presumably accepted, it suggests fluid, unstable gender difference and thus opens up a choice for women spectators. See Mary Ann Doane, "Film and the Masquerade: Theorising the Female Spectator," *Screen* 23, nos. 3–4 (1982): 74–87; Kathleen McLuskie, "The Act, the Role, and the Actor: Boy Actresses on the Elizabethan Stage," *New Theatre Quarterly* 3 (1987): 120–30; Jean E. Howard, "Crossdressing, The Theatre, and Gender Stuggle in Early Modern England," *Shakespeare Quarterly* 39 (Winter 1988): esp. 435, 439–40; and Stephen Orgel, "Nobody's Perfect: Or Why Did the English Stage Take Boys for Women?" *South Atlantic Quarterly* 88 (Winter 1989): 7–30.

12

Talking Back to Shakespeare
Student-Reader Responses to *Othello*

MARTHA TUCK ROZETT

The prefix *re* seems to be especially favored on the contemporary literary theory scene. Texts are representations, subject to reconstruction and re-readings; they are received, and remembered and reproduced by readers who reinvent them by reacting or responding in terms of their own cultural and personal predispositions. A text, according to this line of thinking, consists of the interaction of written work and reader; far from being fixed or determined, it takes its shape from each new encounter. The effect of all this has been quite exciting for a scholarly community engaged in reading and rereading plays and poems and novels whose potential to generate new meanings seems to be growing with marvelous fecundity. In many cases the process has entered the classroom as well, although, too often, what we do in the scholarly journals and what we do in the classroom seem increasingly remote from one another. I have become fascinated by the only kind of reading I can never again experience—the first reading. As we scholars talk about Shakespeare and colonialism or Shakespeare and patriarchy or Shakespeare and power politics, we are engaged, like Tate and Dryden and Bradley and Tillyard, in bouncing our current values and anxieties off Shakespeare, testing our critical theories and social principles and political hopes and fears against the plays, knowing that they are resilient enough to survive our exertions. Yet when our students, in *their* first readings, do what amounts to the same thing we often seem to be suspicious—perhaps because we feel that they have not earned the right to do so by immersing themselves in the history (which history?) of the period, the literary conventions, the sources, the details of text and performance, and so forth. Once our pedagogy catches up with our theoretical advances, it should become clear to us that, while helping our students bridge the gap of four hundred years that divides them from the play as it appeared to its original audiences, we can get something in return: an unencumbered, unqualified encounter with characters and situations, informed by the very basic and immediate need to understand and render judgments about the characters' treatment of one another.

Historical research, both in its traditional forms and as reincarnated by the new historicists, makes us sensitive to the "texts" and cultural assumptions the Elizabethan audience might have brought to the theater. What "texts," one might ask, do the thousands of American and British students reading Shakespeare today—for, more than any other single author, they are still reading Shakespeare—bring into the classroom along with their Riversides? What personal and political and social assumptions and expectations serve as a lens through which *they* read the plays—and read them for the first time, trying very hard to appropriate, and thus make sense of, what they are reading?

What I have begun to see in first readings, as the following very preliminary and informal study of undergraduates reading *Othello* at a northeastern public university will suggest, are some modified, popularized versions of gender-related criticism, at times feminist, at time informed by popular psychology, but very strongly shaped, I believe, by the dominant forms of discourse in our culture. Childhood reading habits, animated cartoons, and situation comedies have clearly shaped our students' notions of plot, character, and authorial purpose long before high-school English teachers address these subjects. Television, movies, newspaper, and magazines are the "texts" that inform student reading, often in lively and productive ways. Poststructuralist literary theory tells us that our notions of what constitutes a literary text are arbitrary and tradition-bound; for eighteen or twenty-year-old first readers, *Othello* may be no more "privileged" a text than a Judy Blume novel or a movie actress's autobiography or, for that matter, an advice column or a self-help book, which together constitute increasingly prevalent cultural phenomena in American society. Recently, I came across an article in *TV Guide* in which Dr. Ruth Westheimer lectured two characters from a popular show on the absence of commitment and communication in their sexual relationship. The premise of the piece was that fictional characters can be discussed as if they had the motivation and behavioral patterns of real people, and that we, the audience, can learn lessons from their situation that apply to our own lives. This premise was very familiar to me from classroom experience; first readers frequently assume that great literature is a series of cautionary tales, an assumption they unknowingly share with medieval and Renaissance poets, with the difference that students are less likely to consider the ways in which the fictional characters are bound by conventions or "rules" of literature. And so, like Dr. Ruth, they expect them to behave like real people.

In looking at student first readings as a legitimate form of "interpretation" from which we, as scholars, can learn, I am advocating a reader-response approach that considers student first readers as a special class of readers with certain group characteristics that reflect the influence of our social and educational culture. I am not thinking of Norman Holland's "identity themes," an approach which focuses on readers as idiosyncratic personalities, but rather of something like the "positions" identified by William Perry in *Forms of Intellectual and Ethical Development in the College Years.* Perry discovered that the early stages or positions of student development were characterized by "an urge to make order out of incongruities, dissonances, and anomalies of experience." Students confronted with the "dissolution of established beliefs" felt a desire to retain "hometown values," and resorted to a dualistic absolutism that eventually, as they matured, yielded to a more generalized relativism.[1] Although Perry's scheme may not apply precisely to students reading Shakespeare in the early 1990s, more recent research on the reading process suggests a similar desire for this kind of "order." Inexperienced readers tend to "compose" a text "according to the code of [a] conventional narrative"; that is, they view the text as "proof" of the validity of a preexisting story, or formula, derived in part from "classroom structures of reading, but sometimes structures derived from the church or home or from any of the cultures outside our classrooms."[2] First readers try to make the text "mean" something, using what they know best, which frequently consists of received truths and rather prescriptive formulas about human behavior.[3]

Much reader-response theory and pedagogy builds on the work of I. A. Richards, who recognized fifty years ago in *Practical Criticism* that "the personal situation of the reader inevitably (and within limits rightly) affects his reading . . . the dangers are that such recollected feelings may overwhelm and distort the poem. . . ." He adds, however, that the readers' personal experiences "are not to be hastily excluded as mere personal intrusions," but that "they must be genuine and relevant, and must respect the liberty and autonomy of the poem." The question response theorists of the 1980s would ask of Richards is this: who decides what is genuine and relevant? Richards goes on to discuss "stock responses," arguing that in life, as in literature, "an extensive repertory of stock responses is a necessity. . . . Clearly there is an enormous field of conventional activity over which acquired, stereotyped, habitual responses properly rule. . . ." Having said this he notes that stock responses lead readers to object to a poem "for not being quite a different poem, without regard paid to what it is as itself."[4] This, I suspect, is what happens with many first readings of Shakespeare's plays. Faced with the combination of difficult language and seemingly familiar characters and situations, the students resort to stock responses as a way of "obliterating the difference or otherness of literature, domesticating or coercing into 'naturalness' the strangeness which defies and resists understanding."[5] This strangeness, from the first reader's point of view, is especially present in Shakespeare's plays, which are at once poetry, play-texts (words without description of accompanying action or physical detail, and with no accompanying narrative guide), and historically remote fictions. Furthermore, if a student perceives Shakespeare as encrusted with the sanctity of canonization, then the plays are unlikely to receive the same kind of first reading that same student-reader would give to an unknown author writing in a contemporary idiom.

In *The Pursuit of Signs* Jonathan Culler urges a "semiotics of reading [which] should get at differences in interpretive conventions and procedures rather than describing differences of opinion."[6] The interpretive conventions I observed my first readers bringing to the study of Shakespeare seemed to put a good deal of emphasis on characters as responsible members of society, accountable for the consequences of their behavior.[7] These readers have somehow come to assume that reading is a reactive, judgment-making process, one in which the psychology and morality of social relationships tends to crowd out other aspects of the texts. The political and social implications of this approach to Shakespeare— an approach that may be receiving encouragement from teachers and standardized testing—merits more discussion than it has so far received. Alan Sinfield tackles the subject in the British school system. He notes with concern that when historical and theatrical contexts are disregarded in the teaching and testing of Shakespeare, "Individuals [become] the unproblematic source of action and meaning," and the plays are approached either in terms of the universal (e.g., "the problem of evil") or the individual, with "a yawning gulf between the two."[8] Until recently, published work on the teaching of Shakespeare has focused on how to teach the plays rather than on the ways in which they are actually taught, and just

as important, received by the students.[9] Because of work done over
the past decade or so by audience-oriented and writing-pedagogy
theorists, we have become sensitive to the implicit assumptions in
handbooks such as *How to Read Shakespeare,* published in 1971 by
the well-known Shakespeare scholar Maurice Charney. In a section
entitled "Moral conventions in the presentation of character allow
Shakespeare to ignore psychological realities," Charney con-
fidently asserts that "We are willing to accept gaps in the presentation of Shakespeare's characters, quick changes in their
development, and other moral conventions because we are not
committed to seeing them as real people."[10] What scholars and
teachers are now asking, in a variety of ways, is how students as
"interpretive communities" differ from "us" as readers, and how
"we" deal with those differences. Further study of college-level first
readers may tell us more about what students expect of literature,
about the authority and motives they assign to "great" authors like
Shakespeare, and about the way Shakespeare is taught and read in
secondary schools. We may even gain a better understanding of the
extraordinary, enduring popularity of Shakespeare's plays in a society that is increasingly distant from the audience for which those
plays were originally written.

*   *   *

The students in my 100-level Shakespeare class came to *Othello*
by way of comedy; we had spent the preceding three or four weeks
of the semester reading *The Taming of the Shrew, A Midsummer
Night's Dream,* and *The Merchant of Venice.* After only a brief
discussion of the play, I asked them for their reactions (see Appendix A for the list of questions). The *Othello* they wrote about
consisted of two rather different experiences: first they read the
text, and then they watched the well-known British film made in
1965, with Lawrence Olivier as Othello, Maggie Smith as Desdemona, and Frank Finlay as Iago. I was interested in how those two
experiences affected one another, and how, taken together, they
produced an interpretation, or assessment, of the play. I was also
curious about the juxtaposition of *Othello* with *The Merchant of
Venice* and the other comedies; would it prompt a response conditioned, at least partly, by comic expectations? Would they "know
how to react tragically" to a play that, in its first act, is so similar to
comedy, without my preparing them for the shift? In retrospect, I
think I may have "loaded" the assignment somewhat, by focusing
on character and asking the class if they found themselves wondering what they would do in the characters' situations. Every question

serves in some way to organize or direct the response it receives, and so perhaps I appeared to be inviting them to translate the characters into their own world rather than prompting them to undertake the far more difficult "translation" that comes of entering the world of the play. And, by drawing attention to the vestiges of didacticism and implicit moral assumptions in *The Merchant of Venice* and the other comedies, I had given "permission" to see Shakespeare as a moralist, a role in which they were already predisposed to place him.

The assignment elicited very strong responses. Many of my students talked back to Shakespeare assertively and quite critically, approaching the characters as they would their peers. Although the papers contained a variety of readings, I was struck by a recurring "pragmatic" approach, one that resorted insistently to familiar, and by now formulaic principles of social survival concerning such matters as sexual and professional jealousy, misplaced trust, communication breakdowns, and manipulative relationships. The students adopted the posture of advice-givers, proffering bits of received wisdom and personal opinions in a remarkably prescriptive tone of voice; hence they took Othello to task for "acting hastily, without first consulting several people," for not "communicating better with his wife," and for "being so foolish as to let jealousy get the better of him." They frequently assumed the authoritative voice of an advice columnist: "Communication is a vital part of sustaining a relationship," one young woman declared, after asserting that "in Othello's position I can safely say I would have consulted others, but not without consulting Desdemona." Another woman, speaking of "lack of communication" among all the characters, added "misunderstanding between couples is typical." And a young man, who concluded that the whole situation could have been avoided if Othello had listened to Cassio, pronounced the play to be an "example of what can result from lack of communication."[11]

Reading James Calderwood's essay on "Speech and Self in *Othello*" while working on this paper, I became interested in the similar conclusions yet complete differences in language and approach. Calderwood observes that Othello's style is "constitutionally opposed to dialogue," and that "monologue makes its own meaning"; moreover, that Othello is "logocentric" and "lodges all meaning in words."[12] Although my students were unable, or unwilling, to develop their interpretations out of close analysis of language patterns and specific scenes, many of them were, like Calderwood, finding pervasive patterns in the play. Their approaches to the writing process though, were quite different: many, if not most, felt the necessity to see the play as an instructive statement for the audience's benefit, and to imitate or reinforce what they saw as the author's stance by drawing their own moral conclusions. Calderwood, by contrast, never makes a judgmental pronouncement; his role as critic, clearly, is to describe. The closest he comes to the type of reading I have been discussing is his remark that it is "perfectly natural" for Othello, as a stranger among the Venetians, "to situate as much meaning as possible in words, and especially in his own words."[13] In other words, as my students might say, he was not listening to others.

The "pragmatic" responses represent one aspect of the students' reading of *Othello*. But the papers also reveal another, quite different stance. Many of the first-time readers described strong feelings of anger, helplessness, indignation, and disgust as they entered into an emotional relationship with the play.[14] Responding to it became a way of articulating their own anxieties about relationships, their sense that people like Iago do exist and pose a serious threat to social stability, and their frustration at being in a position of knowledge yet unable to intervene. Students found themselves wanting quite literally to talk back to the characters: "I felt like screaming to Othello not to listen to Iago . . ."; "I knew exactly what Iago was going to do, but couldn't yell out and warn anyone. To put it simply, Iago made me feel quite helpless"; "I would have loved to have been there with them in Cyprus, to . . . tell Cassio he was being set up. . . . Shakespeare keeps our attention by frustrating us"; "I really had an urge to enter the play and tell Othello and Cassio of Iago's knavery"; "I wanted to shake [Desdemona] and say: 'Look at your husband and do something to help yourself instead of trying to help Cassio.'" Whether they realized it or not, these five students seemed to be dealing with their reaction to Iago as a "frightening" or "disturbing" character by wanting to oppose him directly. If this response has a certain "naive" quality, suggesting an insufficient distinction between art and life, it also testifies to a strong need to believe in one's own ability to take charge and restore order. Further, it reveals an uneasy relationship with the play's prevailing irony, and a feeling, as one student put it, of being manipulated. *Othello* employs dramatic irony to an unusual degree, and first-time readers sometimes have to go back and look at exits and entrances to remind themselves of how much more they know than the various characters do. Such knowledge can confer a sense of moral superiority, or authority, on students who are accustomed to feeling humbled by the linguistic difficulties of first readings. But knowing more than the characters can also become an emotional burden, one which could, if pushed too far, trigger frustration, impatience, and even contempt. Writing about the play intensifies this effect, for writing can be a form of exerting authority and control over the text, particularly if one can define (or, we might say, redefine) the play's central issues in a familiar vocabulary.

First-time readers are less likely to use quotations from the text to make their point than more experienced readers, resorting instead to a significantly small group of loaded words and phrases. Foremost among those recurring words and phrases were references to order and self-control. One student stated that Shakespeare is telling us that "to avoid tragedies within our own lives we must keep in touch with the events and actions that make up our life." Another, who initially viewed Othello as a clear-headed, even-tempered father figure, said that he felt like a child who discovers that his father is "a bum." "He threw it all away—beliefs, ideas, loyalty, trust, faith, and let himself be manipulated like a piece of clay." He found a similar message in Othello's tragedy: "we must take a step back and reevaluate our conclusions and see how foolish they are." "Even-tempered level-headedness," he felt, "should be our goal." In sum, as one student concluded, "the play expresses a basic fear of the loss of control." At the end of the term, when the students looked back at *Othello* after reading *Hamlet* and *The Tempest,* this emphasis on order and control was, if anything, even greater. Several of the students praised Prospero for his "restraint of emotions" and "evenheadedness" and for his ability to "reason correctly" and arrive at "a rational solution through language rather than violence." Unlike Othello and Hamlet, Prospero, in the words of one student, can evaluate before acting. "Many aspects must be considered and evaluated," the student approvingly generalized, "before extreme steps are taken" (the passives lend a tone of bureaucratic prudence to this utterance). Another student noted that Prospero and Iago shared "an almost perfect control" of their respective plays, while Othello "did not control his situation." Or, as another put it, Othello "was quick to act before he had all the facts" (Hamlet, she said was too slow in acting).

For many of the readers, order and control occur when people talk things out and trust one another. Viewed thus, *Othello* becomes a statement about trust in marriage. One impassioned young man spoke of having "always been taught that when you say 'I do' that means forever. Now if you are going to spend your life with someone you are going to have to trust that person with all your heart and soul. Even if there were a chance of that belief backfiring, I would have to believe my wife over anyone." This trust, he seems to feel, is the only absolute in a perilous world. Even a long, intelligent paper on the way symbolism and imagery shaped our responses to Othello as an "outsider" who elicits our sympathy concludes that "Othello brought his downfall upon himself." In the accents of the marriage counsellor the writer observes that "Any marriage will not survive without trust and honesty on the part of both husband and wife. . . . Everyone who reads *Othello* should examine his mistakes and try to avoid them in his own relationships."

The students in this class tended to ignore historical or cultural differences and regard the characters as if they were our contemporaries. I was surprised to find an almost complete absence of references to racism or racial identity in the papers, especially since we had had a rather lively discussion of Shylock's Jewishness only a week or so earlier. At a time when "cultural diversity" is a catch phrase on college campuses, one possible pragmatic response to Othello might attribute his behavior to his African origins and view the "failure of communication" from a cultural perspective. With only two or three exceptions the students who were so quick to scold Othello for listening to Iago said nothing about his position as a Moor, unfamiliar with the ways of European culture. Nor did anyone mention racism on Brabantio's part, or attribute Iago's behavior to xenophobic or racist motives. One student who did see "a racial issue" in the play wrote that Othello reverts to a "lower, bestial self," but she too resorts to the familiar 1990s psychospeak: Othello's love for Desdemona was not "strong enough," because his "sense of confidence and self-worth were weak," while Desdemona's love was "obsessive and based on novelty." These first readings suggest that the students were not paying much attention to the black/white imagery in the play's opening scene and that the words "Moor" and "Venetian" did not signify much to readers for whom both cultures are equally foreign and without any very clear association. In other words, these responses are quite different from those of a Jacobean audience, which would have presumably come to the play with some acquired notions and prejudices about Venetians and Moors. Similarly, the students seemed to approach *Othello* assuming that troubled marriage relationships were the "fault" of the participants, but that these relationships could be "fixed." As they often do when reading *Hamlet,* the students felt that the principal characters have more control over their lives than they care to exercise.

The film caused many of the students to revise their views, and in retrospect, I wish I had not shown it. Olivier's depiction of Othello is rather dated—one cannot imagine a prominent white actor employing such exaggerated blackface makeup today. Many of the students were uncomfortable with the Othello they saw on the screen, and thus even more inclined to distance themselves emotionally from him. The most articulate remark on the subject of Othello's color noted that "the emphasized bodily movement, eye-rolling, and hand gestures further the notion of an uncultured, primitive black man. This emphasizes the cultural differences between the black and white races, and the inadequacies of a black moor as an effectual leader of a white community." Others simply felt unnerved by what they saw as Olivier's uncontrolled, hysterical, insane Othello, which worked against the respect they initially felt for the noble Moor. One young woman described a radical shift in sympathy as a result of seeing the film: "While reading the play, I felt very sorry for Othello because his good nature and fairness were unjustly played upon." But Olivier's "brash and cocky" and extremely gullible Othello put her off, and she was offended by the rude, self-assured, even mocking attitude of indifference he showed toward Brabantio. She concluded: "I almost felt as though he deserved what he got." Just as exaggerated as his color was the prominent cross Olivier wore in many scenes. "I didn't realize he was so religious," several said, rather than asking, as a more experienced viewer might, why the director chose to make this kind of statement through costume.

Seeing the film also caused many of the students to think more deeply about characters they had not originally paid much attention to. Cassio, Roderigo, Emilia, and Bianca are all less intimidating than the principal characters, and in some ways, more familiar. My class had no difficulty sympathizing with Derek Jacobi's handsome, innocent-looking young Cassio; no one censured him for getting drunk, though they remarked on his apparent flirtatiousness toward Desdemona. A few were bothered by this, but most explained his behavior as youthful devotion to his general and the general's wife. Robert Lang's childish and, I thought, foolish Roderigo inspired more sympathy than I expected; one young woman commented that he would "get so happy and then Iago would screw everything up for him. The hurt I saw in his face was too incredible for me to deal with; my heart really went out to him." This student also said that "I should feel sorry for Othello, but I really don't." The most unexpected response came from a young man who said that the only person he sympathized with was Brabantio: "I tried to put myself in his place; how would I feel if my daughter, who I loved and thought was so honest and trustworthy, just packed up and left one day?" But he added that Brabantio had put his daughter in a difficult position: "she is so high on a pedestal that the slightest thing she does wrong will cause her father's heart to break." It is difficult to know how to "correct" an eccentric reading like this one without seeming to dismiss a serious and heart-felt response to a character who may appear less to blame for his suffering and loss than Othello and Desdemona. This is an instance in which the student-reader resists the "implied reader's" role, by refusing, or being unable to accept the values and adopt the perspective the text requires—in this case, the notion that tyrannical fathers do not have primary claims on our sympathies.[15] This first reader had read *A Midsummer Night's Dream* and *Romeo and Juliet* and heard me discuss the conventional comic, irate father as a character-type who opposes the heroine's desire for autonomy and true love, yet he did not read *Othello* from that perspective. Rather, his reading placed Brabantio in a contemporary "realistic" framework and took him seriously as a developed, sympathetic character. If I were able to talk to this student further, I would try to discover what combination of reading strategies and individual inclinations led him to focus so exclusively on Brabantio.

As I expected, women students paid more attention to Emilia and even Bianca when confronted with them on screen. One spoke of being disturbed by how the men in the play view the three women characters as "simplistic" and physically push and pull them about throughout the film. Another was annoyed that Emilia "just gave Desdemona's handkerchief to Iago. I would have been more loyal to Desdemona, because she treated Emilia better than Iago did." And another spoke of feeling "the pain and guilt Emilia must have felt because she did contribute to Iago's schemes unknowingly." A strong-minded young woman who felt disappointed by Desdemona ("I wish she had been more aggressive, more demanding; everyone lacked bravery and accepted too much") found it easiest to imagine herself in Emilia's role. "I would have questioned Iago and not given him the handkerchief until he gave me a good reason." But she adds, "But I'm not sure I would know whether he was lying to me." Interestingly, one male student spoke passionately of how Emilia risked her life to clear Desdemona, and how it felt "to watch her in agony over the death of her friend, and then discover that her husband is the cause. . . . I didn't expect Othello to murder his wife, but I was really troubled when Iago kills Emilia. This caused me to stop admiring his skill and start hating him."

The words "stop" and "start" in this sentence are revealing; rather than describing simultaneous mixed responses to a character, as a more experienced reader attuned to the complex texture of the play might do, this student records his responses serially, employing black-and-white terms like "admire" and "hate" to do so.[16] It occurred to me, reading the first-time reader responses, that the students and I were operating at cross-purposes. The students wanted to demystify the text, to cut a path through the difficult language and unfamiliar speech patterns to arrive at a clear sense of meaning, whereas I, as teacher, wanted to explore its multiplicities and contradictions. If I saw *Othello* as a floating mass of possibilities, they wanted it to be a solid object against which they, as young adults, could test the moral and social assumptions they were in the process of formulating. Teaching is frequently a dialectical process, whereby students stake out a position and the teacher disrupts or questions it. Thus, once my students had decided that the need for communication was the "message" of *Othello,* my role was to show how communication was in fact being deflected and transformed by Iago's control over situations in which characters tried to read one another's signals. In the process, I tried to dislodge the students from some of their twentieth-century assumptions, by explaining that the formality and distance between Renaissance husbands and wives, along with the language and posturing of courtesy in Desdemona's scenes with Cassio, together conspire to make impossible the frank, open, inquiring "communication" of the type advocated by Dear Abby or Dr. Ruth. They thus began building upon, qualifying, and revising their first readings, but without being required to discredit the deeply held beliefs upon which those first readings were founded.

* * *

Throughout the process of writing and revising this paper, I wondered whether another class would respond to *Othello* as mine had. Perhaps I had elicited these first readings by the way I had taught the course. And so I devised a new list of questions (Appendix B) and asked a colleague to distribute them to her summer-school 100-level Shakespeare class before discussing the play. This class consisted mostly of juniors and seniors whose experience with Shakespeare was limited to a couple of plays in high school; they had read *The Taming of the Shrew, A Midsummer Night's Dream, As You Like It,* and *Hamlet* during the previous three weeks. Although the students had no opportunity to discuss the play either among themselves or in the classroom before answering

the questions, they arrived at remarkably similar patterns of response. I was particularly struck by a recurring phrase used by five
of the twenty-three students to express the play's theme or message.
The phrase, "don't jump to conclusions," encapsulates or "pack-
ages" a stock response in a form easily understood by speakers of
English who recognize the extensive conventional wisdom that lies
behind the cliché. In its epigrammatic brevity, "don't jump to
conclusions" employs a formula familiar to us at least since the Ten
Commandments: by admonishing us *not* to do something, it alludes
indirectly to a pattern of behavior that will make us morally and
socially successful human beings. The five students who used this
phrase, and several others, spoke urgently of the importance of
checking the facts, rejecting rumors or hearsay, and being careful
about whom you trust. As in the student responses I had looked at
earlier, the tone was frequently prescriptive and sounded rather like
an official document; for example, "Do not always take what
'seems' to be true for being so and do not react without thoroughly
contemplating end results," said a student who viewed the play as a
statement about trust, both in others and in one's own judgment.
Another remarked that "this play reaffirmed my belief that you
should never listen to rumors and always get the story from the
source." She added, "we should not let the passion of jealousy and
revenge take us over"—like so many of her generation of first
readers, she seems to believe that we can control our emotions.
Several students defined tragedy as a situation that could have been
avoided. In *Othello,* as one young woman put it, people died "who
didn't really need to"; there could have been a way of "working out
the misunderstandings." Another proclaimed that "Jealousy is inherent in human nature, so all must learn to control it." These
readers shared my earlier class's concern with order and control,
though as a group, they put less emphasis on the issue of communication and trust in marriage and more on Othello's susceptibility to
Iago's machinations. One of my questions invited them to explore
the relevance of *Othello*'s themes to their own lives, and some
responded in very moving ways. "Be wary of who you call your
friend," one young man urged, adding that "there are manipulative
people today who will do anything to get ahead." This statement
allies Iago with people who are determined to "get ahead," a stock
response which would, one hopes, later be probed and revised in
class discussion.

   The student who sees Iago as someone who will do anything to
get ahead is bringing the patterns and preoccupations of his own
culture to bear upon his reading of the play. Eleanor Rowe's fas-

cinating study of the reception of *Hamlet* in Russia reveals that Shakespeare's plays have long had this effect on readers and audiences, especially when they come to the plays with very little of the historical preparation Sinfield spoke of. Rowe ends her book with the following observation: "Perhaps partially because of the trauma of her history and the collective and individual pain of her people, Russia has tended to react to *Hamlet* by reaching for immediate applicability, by assigning to the play and its hero an immediate moral and social value."[17] As each new generation of Russians invented its own *Hamlet,* so each generation of student-readers will read Shakespeare's plays somewhat differently. Only a few of these students will proceed from first to second and third and fourth readings. When they do, they may discover, as one of my most thoughtful students did, that "I now realized that I could never act as rationally as I had originally wanted Othello to act. I am now much less critical of his character . . . and have a better feeling for the entire play. . . . each time I read the play I reevaluate my feelings and that's what keeps me going back."[18]

NOTES

1. William G. Perry, *Forms of Intellectual and Ethical Development in the College Years: A Scheme* (New York: Holt, Rinehart and Winston, 1968), pp. 51–52.

2. David Bartholomae and Anthony Petrosky, *Facts, Artifacts and Counterfacts: Theory and Method for a Reading and Writing Course* (Portsmouth, N.H.: Boynton/Cook, 1986), pp. 21, 26–27.

3. It is only a fairly mature student-reader, returning to the text for the second or third time, who can say, as does a student interviewed in *Women's Ways of Knowing: The Development of Self, Voice, and Mind,* by Mary F. Belenky et al. (New York: Basic Books, 1986), that "a good interpretation of a poem is firmly grounded in the poem itself, while a bad interpretation contains too much of the reader and too little of the poem." The authors commented that "it takes time to learn to attend truly to the object, to wait for meanings to emerge from a poem, rather than imposing the contents of your own head or your own gut" (p. 98). What constitutes "the reader" and what constitutes "the poem" is hotly debated by reader-response critics, and many would dispute this distinction.

4. I. A. Richards, *Practical Criticism* (1929; repr., New York: Harcourt, Brace & World, 1956), pp. 227, 228, 230.

5. This is Jonathan Culler's argument in *Structuralist Poetics,* as paraphrased by Elizabeth Freund in *The Return of the Reader: Reader-Response Criticism* (London: Methuen, 1987), p. 82.

6. Jonathan Culler, *The Pursuit of Signs: Semiotics, Literature, Deconstruction* (Ithaca: Cornell University Press, 1981), p. 63.

7. I noticed the same interpretive convention being applied by my eleven-year-old son, who said, after reading *Wuthering Heights,* that Cathy and Heathcliff "went too far" and should not have been so cruel to others.

8. Alan Sinfield, "Give an account of Shakespeare and Education, showing why you think they are effective and what you have appreciated about them. Support your comments with precise references," in *Political Shakespeare: New Essays in Cultural Materialsim,* ed. Jonathan Dollimore and Alan Sinfield (Ithaca: Cornell University Press, 1985), pp. 140–41.

9. Published work on teaching Shakespeare generally focuses on how the plays are taught rather than how they are received. Two recent British books are *Teaching Shakespeare: Essays on Approaches to Shakespeare in Schools and Colleges,* ed. Richard Adams (London: Robert Royce, 1985) and Veronica O'Brien, *Teaching Shakespeare* (London: Edward Arnold, 1982). For American approaches, see *Teaching Shakespeare,* ed. W. Edens et al. (Princeton: Princeton University Press, 1977). A great deal has been written on the subject, as the seventeen-page annotated bibliography in Edens and the fifteen-page one in Adams indicate.

10. Maurice Charney, *How to Read Shakespeare* (New York: McGraw Hill, 1971), pp. 84–85.

11. I encountered a very similar response to *The Winter's Tale* in another class. Speaking of Leontes' jealousy, a first reader remarked: "Everything [would have] worked out if they took the time out to trust in each other. They need to discuss their problems and everything would have worked out."

12. James L. Calderwood, "Speech and Self in *Othello,*" *Shakespeare Quarterly* 38 (1987): 301.

13. Calderwood, "Speech and Self in *Othello,*" 301–2.

14. A high school teacher reported to me that in her class a recurring response to *Othello* was "I felt angry." As one sixteen-year-old first reader put it, "I was mad at Othello for believing Iago so much and murdering Desdemona. I'm glad he died too." Although more naively expressed, this response is similar to that of some of my first readers.

15. Susan Suleiman, in her introduction to *The Reader in the Text: Essays on Audience and Interpretation* (Princeton: Princeton University Press, 1980), discusses Wayne Booth's concept of the "implied reader," or "participant" vs. the "later reader" or "observer" (pp. 22, 26). The teaching of Shakespeare requires particular attention, I would suggest, to the differences between these two kinds of readers: if, as Iser says, the text has the function of recreating the original social and cultural context for the later reader, what happens if that reader disregards or reinterprets this context in ways that produce what Iser calls "idiosyncratic realizations" of the text? How, as teachers, not only of individual students (which we are when we read papers) but of students in groups (which we are when we preside over class discussions) do we respond to such readings?

16. In *The Act of Reading: A Theory of Aesthetic Response* (Baltimore: Johns Hopkins University Press, 1978) Wolfgang Iser observes that readers attempt to reduce the complexity of the text, by creating a "black-white" structure in a process he calls "consistency building." The reader selects (and thus omits) based on what seems familiar; but while doing so, he/she is "bombarded" by "alien associations" that modify the formulated *gestalt,* or "consistent interpretation" (pp. 125–26, 132).

17. Eleanor Rowe, *Hamlet: A Window on Russia* (New York: New York University Press, 1976), p. 179.

18. I am grateful to my colleague Elizabeth Wilson and to Kathleen Thornton for allowing me to use their students' answers to my questions for the purposes of this study.

APPENDIX A

Fall 1987   English 144

The following questions are intended to help you shape your thinking about *Othello* and should serve as the basis for your essay. Your essay need not address each question directly, but should try to respond to most of them in some way. Throughout the essay, try to distinguish between your reactions or interpretations before and after seeing the film. There are no "right" or "wrong" answers to these questions: we are looking for intelligent and thoughtful essays on the play Shakespeare wrote and the way the film interprets or revises it. Don't repeat yourself, and please type if possible; otherwise, use black ink and leave margins for comments.

1. Give some thought to the way Shakespeare directs your sympathy to one or more characters. How and when does it shift from one character to another?

2. Did you find yourself wondering what you would do in the characters' situations? If so, how did this affect your feelings about them and about the play?

3. How did the film affect your assessments of the characters? Did it cause you to change your interpretation of the play, and if so, how?

4. What, for you, is the most disturbing aspect of *Othello*?

APPENDIX B

Othello Questions

Answer each question with one or two sentences. Please do not repeat the question in your answer; just identify it by number. Do as many as you can and if you get stuck, move on.

1. What was your first reaction to (or feelings about) the major characters?

2. What was your second, or revised reaction to these characters after you completed the play and thought about it?

3. Try to describe how you felt in general after reading the play.

4. Give an example of the way a character's language or choice of words reveals his/her personality or character.

5. Why did you pick that character for #4 and that particular example? Now do the same with another character, looking for the very best and most characteristic example of his/her language.

6. Do you think Shakespeare wants you to sympathize with some characters more than others? Which ones and why?

7. How do your sympathies change at different points in the play?

8. What parts of the play did you find most probable, or believable?

9. What parts did you find least probable or believable?

10. Does the question of probability or believability affect your enjoyment of the play?

11. In your opinion do plays and other works of literature have "messages" or "themes"? If these two words have different meanings for you, explain.

12. Does *Othello* have one or more messages or themes, and if so, what are they?

13. How are these themes or messages important or relevant to your own life and the society you live in? (If they are not relevant, explain).

14. When you use the word "tragic" what do you mean?

15. What is tragic about this play?

16. If you were leading a discussion of this play what aspects of it would you emphasize or draw attention to?

17. If you were directing the play, what staging or visual considerations would you be especially aware of?

18. Has reading the play changed your thinking on any subject or aspect of life?

19. Are you male or female?
How old are you?
What class/grade in school or college?
Have you ever read/studied Shakespeare before? Which plays?
Have you ever seen a film or a production of a Shakespeare play?

Index